Environmental Policy in Japan

Edited by

Hidefumi Imura

Professor, Department of Urban Environment, Graduate School of Environmental Studies, Nagoya University, Japan

Miranda A. Schreurs

Associate Professor, Department of Government and Politics, University of Maryland, College Park, USA

A CO-PUBLICATION OF THE WORLD BANK AND EDWARD ELGAR PUBLISHING

 **THE WORLD BANK**

Edward Elgar
Cheltenham, UK • Northampton, MA, USA

© Hidefumi Imura and Miranda A. Schreurs 2005

Published by
Edward Elgar Publishing Limited
The Lypiatts
15 Lansdown Road
Cheltenham
Glos GL50 2JA
UK

Edward Elgar Publishing, Inc.
William Pratt House
9 Dewey Court
Northampton
Massachusetts 01060
USA

This book has been printed on demand to keep the title in print.

A catalogue record for this book
is available from the British Library

ISBN 978 1 84542 370 4

Contents

Figures

Tables

Boxes

Acronyms

a.	acre
APEC	Asian-Pacific Economic Cooperation
ASEAN	Association of Southeast Asian Nations
CAC	command and control
CAT	Construction and Transfer Program
CDM	Clean Development Mechanism
CEC	Central Environmental Council
CEC	Communitarian Elite Corporatism
CERCLA	Comprehensive Environmental Response, Compensation and Liability Act
CFC	chlorofluorocarbon
CIESIN	Center for International Earth Science Information Network
CITES	Convention on International Trade in Endangered Species
CL	compensation levy
CO	carbon monoxide
CO_2	carbon dioxide
COP	Conference of the Parties
CP	cleaner production
DBJ	Development Bank of Japan
DCI	Discretionary Cooperative Implementation
DDT	dichlorodiphenyltrichloroethane
DENR	Department of Environment and Natural Resources, Philippines
DSD	Dual System Deutschland
EA	Environment Agency
EANET	East Asia Acid Deposition Monitoring Network
ECO ASIA	Environmental Congress for Asia and the Pacific
EIA	environmental impact assessment
EIS	Environmental Impact Statement
EP	end-of-pipe
EPR	extended producer responsibility
ERCA	Environmental Recovery and Conservation Agency
ESCAP	Economic and Social Commission for Asia and the Pacific
ESI	Environmental Sustainability Index

EU	European Union
FBR	fast breeder reactor
FDI	foreign direct investment
FILP	Fiscal Investment and Loan Program
g	gram
GDP	gross domestic product
GEC	Global Environment Center
GNP	gross national product
ha	hectare
IDEA	Initiative for Development in East Asia
IEA	International Energy Agency
IETC	International Environment Technology Center
IGES	Institute for Global Environmental Strategies
IPCC	Intergovernmental Panel on Climate Change
ISA	Industrial Sector Association
ISD	Initiatives for Sustainable Development
ISO	International Standard Organization
IUCN	World Conservation Union
JBIC	Japan Bank for International Cooperation
JCO	Japan Nuclear Fuel Conversion Company
JDB	Japan Development Bank
JEC	Japan Environment Corporation
JEXIM	Japan Export-Import Bank
JICA	Japan International Cooperation Agency
JSP	Japan Socialist Party
kcal	kilocalorie
KEPCO	Kansai Electric Power Company
kg	kilogram
kl	kiloliter
km	kilometer
km^2	square kilometer
LDP	Liberal Democratic Party
LNG	liquid natural gas
LPG	liquid petroleum gas
m	meter
m^3	meter cubed
METI	Ministry of Economy, Trade and Industry
MHA	Ministry of Home Affairs
MHW	Ministry of Health and Welfare
MITI	Ministry of International Trade and Industry
MLIT	Ministry of Land, Infrastructure and Transport
MOC	Ministry of Construction
MoE	Ministry of Environment, Korea

MOE	Ministry of the Environment
MOF	Ministry of Finance
MOFA	Ministry of Foreign Affairs
NEDO	New Energy Development Organization
NEPA	National Environmental Policy Act
ng	nano gram
ngTEQ/Nm^3	nano gram toxicity equivalency quantity/Normal m^3
NIES	National Institute for Environmental Studies
NIMBY	not in my backyard
Nm	normal meter
NGO	non-governmental organization
NO$_x$	nitrogen oxides
NO$_2$	nitrogen dioxide
NPO	non-profit organization
O$_3$	oxygen
ODA	official development assistance
OECD	Organization for Economic Cooperation and Development
OECF	Organization for Economic Cooperation Fund
Pb	lead
PCA	pollution control agreement
PCBs	polychlorinated biphenyls
PCDDs	polychlorinated dibenzo-*p*-dioxins
PCDFs	polychlorinated dibenzo-furans
PCSC	Pollution Control Service Corporation
PET	polyethylene terephthalate
pg	pico gram
pgTEQ/m^3	pico gram toxicity equivalency quantity/m^3
ppb	parts per billion
ppm	parts per million
PPP	polluter pays principle
R&D	research and development
SBFC	Small Business Finance Corporation
SEPA	State Environmental Protection Administration, China
SMEA	Small and Medium Enterprise Agency
SMEs	small and medium-sized enterprises
SMO	social movement organization
SO$_2$	sulfur dioxide
SO$_x$	sulfur oxides
SPM	suspended particulate matter
t	time
TEMM	Tripartite Environmental Ministers Meeting
TEPCO	Tokyo Electric Power Company
TEQ	Toxicity Equivalency Quantity

TSL	two-step loans
TSP	total suspended particulates
UK	United Kingdom
UNCED	United Nations Conference on Environment and Development
UNEP	United Nations Environment Program
UNFCC	United Nations Framework Convention on Climate Change
US	United States
USA	United States of America
WBCSD	World Business Council for Sustainable Development
WSSD	World Summit on Sustainable Development

Contributors

Jeffrey Broadbent, Department of Sociology, University of Minnesota, USA.

Koji Himi, Former Director-General, Pollution Control Center of Kanagawa Prefecture, Japan.

Hidefumi Imura, Department of Urban Environment, Graduate School of Environmental Studies, Nagoya University, Japan.

Tomohiko Inui, College of Economics, Nihon University, Japan.

Yu Matsuno, School of Business Administration, Meiji University, Japan.

Akira Morishima, Faculty of Human Environmental Studies, Hiroshima Shudo University, Japan.

Yong Ren, State Environmental Protection Administration, China.

Miranda A. Schreurs, Department of Government and Politics, University of Maryland College Park, USA.

Ryota Shinohara, Department of Environmental and Symbiotic Sciences, Kumamoto Prefectural University, Japan.

Kazuhiro Ueta, Department of Economics, Kyoto University, Japan.

Fumikazu Yoshida, Graduate School of Economics, Hokkaido University, Sapporo, Japan.

Preface

This book was made possible by the generous support of the Program for The Study of Japan's Development Management Experience, also known as the Brain Trust Program, entrusted to the World Bank Institute by the Japanese government. Farrukh Iqbal, Tsutomu Shibata and Migara De Silva of the World Bank deserve special recognition and thanks for the great deal of work they put into this project. This project benefited tremendously from their intellectual insights, editorial advice, and organizational skills. They must also be thanked for prodding the authors and editors along to complete their revisions in a timely fashion. Dr Iqbal and Dr De Silva played a critical role in helping to organize two author workshops, the first of which was in Kyushu University in Fukuoka, Japan from 9-10 December 1999 and the second at Hokkaido University in Sapporo, Japan, from 13-14 June 2000. Mr Shibata and Dr De Silva further organized two highly successful dissemination seminars, which provided the project's authors with an opportunity to make public their findings and obtain valuable critique from discussants. The first dissemination seminar was held at the World Bank Headquarters in Washington, D.C. on 7 May 2002. The second was held at Chulalongkorn University in Bangkok, Thailand, from 23-4 June 2003. The World Bank Office in Thailand and the Thailand Environment Institute cooperated in bringing a group of Thai and Laotian environmental specialists to participate in the seminar.

Numerous individuals contributed their insights on draft papers and made helpful suggestions on how to improve the project as a whole. Others participated as presenters in the workshops and dissemination seminars adding their intellectual viewpoints to the discussion. We wish to acknowledge and express our gratitude to: Sarunphong Articharte, Daniel Biller, Raweewan Bhuridej, Anna Brettell, Susmita Dasgupta, Michele De Nevers, Viengsavanh Douangsavanh, Toshio Fujinuma, Kristalina I. Georgieva, Yuzo Harada, Patchamuthu Illangovan, Hiroyuki Kato, Nalin Kishor, Morio Kuninori, Atsuhito Kurozumi, Frannie Léautier, Mohan Munasinghe, Bundit Pattaweekongka, Youwalak Petcharuttana, Noritada Terasawa, and Hirofumi Uzawa.

Editing a book with authors from multiple countries and linguistic backgrounds is always a challenge. Myonnie Bada, Rachel Penrod, Evelyn Chia, Marcus Schaper and Justin M. Franks deserve special recognition for their invaluable assistance in helping to transform workshop papers into book chapters. They worked on English editing, the reference and acronym lists, checking the chapters for consistency, and copy-editing. We also wish to thank Edward Elgar, Dymphna Evans, David Vince, and the staff of Edward Elgar for their support during the publication process and an anonymous reviewer for comments and suggestions made on an earlier version of this manuscript.

Acknowledgements

The findings, interpretations, and conclusions expressed herein are those of the authors and do not necessarily reflect the views of the Board of Executive Directors of the World Bank or the governments they represent.

The World Bank does not guarantee the accuracy of the data included in this work. The boundaries, colors, denominations, and other information shown on any map in this work do not imply any judgment on the part of the World Bank concerning the legal status of any territory or the endorsement or acceptance of such boundaries.

Rights and Permissions

1. Learning from Japanese Environmental Management Experiences

Hidefumi Imura and Miranda A. Schreurs

INTRODUCTION

Japan's environmental history has two outstanding features that are of particular significance to industrializing countries: the tragic environmental damages incurred in the process of rapid economic growth in the 1950s and 1960s and the country's subsequent success in controlling industrial pollution while continuing to grow economically.

Japan was a late industrializer that faced severe industrial pollution problems. Many developing countries, especially the rapidly developing economies in Asia and Latin America, are pursuing economic development paths that are scarred by pollution much like Japan faced in the past. Japan's pollution problems were compounded because of the country's high population density and the proximity of industrial areas to residential ones. This is a situation also faced by many developing countries in Asia and Latin America where there has been rapid urbanization. There may, therefore, be some lessons that can be learned in other countries both from Japan's mistakes and from how Japan has approached its air, water, solid waste and toxic pollution problems and improved its energy efficiency levels.

There are some success stories in industrial pollution control elsewhere in Asia (Singapore is perhaps the best example) and there is evidence of growing environmental awareness in many developing countries (Rock 2002). Nevertheless, governments still tend to give economic development precedence over environmental protection and see pollution control as too costly. The Japanese experience suggests that waiting to address pollution problems until economic growth has been achieved may not only be harmful to the natural environment and human health, it can actually cost a country more. Countries following an industrialization-first, clean-up later approach to development, risk replicating the environmental failures of earlier industrializers, including Japan, and weakening their long-term economic growth potential.

There are three main components to this book. The first part introduces Japan's environmental history, its key environmental regulations and the forces that have driven Japan to introduce environmental regulations and programs. The second part examines the various formal and informal institutional mechanisms and policy instruments that have been introduced over the past several decades to implement pollution control and energy conservation. The concluding chapters put Japan's experiences into a comparative perspective with other industrializing countries as well as with China, arguably one of the countries that will most impact the global environment in the coming decades.

Japan's attitude and approach towards pollution control and environmental protection have changed considerably over the course of the past several decades. Pictures of Japan in the 1960s are replete with images of individuals suffering from horrible pollution diseases. The quality of life in Japan's crowded urban areas as well as in many smaller communities that became the homes to heavy industry complexes was seriously eroded by pollution problems. Relations between enterprises and citizens became increasingly antagonistic because of the government's and industries' failure to address the pollution that was harming human health and basic environmental conditions. Eventually this resulted in wide-scale media campaigns and citizens' protests against polluting industries and the government for its weak national environmental policy.

So serious were the problems that the government and industry were forced to respond to citizens' demands for change, and by the mid-1970s Japan had an extensive regulatory program for environmental protection in place. Economic, social and cultural factors unique to Japan influenced both the emergence of serious environmental problems and the later adoption of quite effective countermeasures. Japan has done much to improve its own air and water quality, to promote recycling and reduce energy intensity. Changes have been made to environmental laws, programs and management styles that put Japan among the ranks of the nations with the most advanced environmental programs.

At the end of the 1960s, Japan was considered among the most polluted countries in the world. A decade later, it was beginning to achieve recognition for its environmental clean-up efforts. Today, in many areas, although certainly not all, Japan is an environmental technology and policy leader.

Yohei Harashima and Tsuneyuki Morita (1998) found that Korea and China have in recent years introduced similar laws to those found in Japan, but what is noteworthy is that they adopted these laws at relatively earlier periods in their economic development. That is, when China introduced framework air pollution legislation, for example, its per capita gross national product was considerably less than when Japan introduced its framework air pollution legislation. This suggests the possibility of avoiding the Kuznet curve predictions that a society will only focus on environmental protection when it has obtained a relatively high level of per capita income (Harashima and Morita 1998). Research on diffusion of environmental ideas and policy instruments suggests that similar learning can occur in relation to implementation of policy instruments and governance mechanisms (Jänicke and Jörgens 1998; Kern 2000; Lafferty and Meadowcroft 2000; Lafferty and Coenen 2000).

Much of this volume focuses on issues of policy implementation. Many developing countries have substantial environmental regulations, but implementation of those regulations is often problematic. China is a good example of a country that has introduced considerable environmental policies but has not been equally aggressive about implementation (Economy 2004). Thus, the question arises why, once pollution control measures began to be implemented, did Japan succeed in a relatively short period of time in successfully implementing most of those regulations? How was it able in the space of a few years to reduce emissions and improve dramatically its energy efficiency?

The relative speed with which the Japanese environmental situation improved is really quite remarkable even if not all of Japan's pollution problems were solved. For developing countries that are suffering from air and water pollution, toxic emissions and energy inefficiencies and struggling with finding ways to ameliorate these problems, Japan is an important case to examine (Organization for Economic Cooperation and Development 1977a, 1994a and 2002).

Several lessons can be learned from the Japanese case. The single most important one is that the approach to economic development of industrialization first, pollution control later can come at an unacceptably high price to human health and the environment. The most egregious examples of this are the victims of the horrific pollution diseases, such as Minamata mercury poisoning and *itai-itai* (literally, 'pain, pain') disease from cadmium poisoning. Victims suffered from both terrible physical and neurological damage. Pregnant women had to fear the birth of deformed and stillborn infants (George 2001; Broadbent 1998; Huddle and Reich 1975; Ui 1989 and 2002; Kawana 1988).

Pollution was also costly in economic terms. As just one measure of this, according to the Committee on Japan's Experience in the Battle against Air Pollution, in 1988 there were 100,000 individuals who were certified by the government as sufferers of air pollution. The country had to pay out 100 billion yen annually in pollution victim compensation (1997, p. 45).

Another critical lesson is that it is possible for government and industry to address pollution while continuing to grow economically. In Japan's case this was done through large investments in pollution control equipment, the development of new environmental governance institutions, governmental assistance to industry for pollution control and the development of more economically and environmentally efficient production processes. As a result of these improvements, Japan has been labeled one of a small group of states that has ecologically modernized; this has been done through technological and policy innovations that have improved energy efficiency and controlled many classic pollutants (Jänicke and Weidner 1997; Dryzek 1997; Moore and Miller 1994; Tsuru and Weidner 1989; Organization for Economic Cooperation and Development 1994a and 2002; Barrett 2005).

Japan is still learning lessons as well. In recent years, Japan has discovered the importance of greening official development assistance (ODA) and playing a more active role in global environmental protection. After years of being criticized for supporting environmentally destructive development projects in developing countries that impoverished indigenous communities or caused destruction to natural areas (Bevis 1995; Dauvergne 1997 and 2001) and paying only limited attention to global environmental degradation, Japanese approaches to environmental protection overseas and internationally have started to change. The shift is no doubt in part an indication of a growing awareness that in the future Japan too will be impacted by the severe environmental problems facing many parts of Asia. There is, however, also genuine concern about the long-term implications of global environmental destruction.

The Japanese government in recent years has become actively involved in institutional capacity building and environmental technology and infrastructure development in East and Southeast Asia. Over the course of the 1990s and into the 2000s, there has been growing emphasis placed on the greening of Japanese ODA and providing financial assistance to non-governmental organizations (NGOs) involved in environmental protection activities in developing countries.

Related to this emphasis on greening of ODA is the growing recognition that environmental protection will require regional responses. There is limited capacity in much of Asia for dealing with the scale of pollution affecting the region. Japan as a pollution control front-runner must take on the role of helping to spurn the growth of environmental research and monitoring networks and the development of cooperation projects in East and Southeast Asia (Schreurs and Pirages 1997).

There is also growing recognition of the need to adapt environmental governance structures to meet the demands of new environmental challenges. Numerous innovations in Japan's governance structures have altered significantly how environmental decision making and policy implementation occur (Schreurs 2002).

Japan has learned from past successes and failures and the examples of other countries about environmental governance. Over time there has been an empowerment of environmental administration at the national and local levels. This began with the creation of an environmental office within the Ministry of Health and Welfare and a pollution control office in the Ministry of International Trade and Industry in the 1960s, followed by the establishment of an Environment Agency (EA) in 1971 (Hashimoto 1988). The EA was elevated to Ministry of the Environment in 2001. In the past decade or two, the issues dealt with by the government have expanded as new global environmental issues have emerged. There is now a Minister for Global Environmental Affairs and global environmental departments in several ministries.

Other institutional lessons have been learned as well. Japan has been less oriented towards open and participatory policy making than many European countries. In fact, Japan has been criticized for not doing more to promote a role for civil society in environmental decision making. There are signs of change here as well. Compared with the situation of three and four decades ago, there is increased collaboration among government agencies, business interests and citizens' groups. Enterprises are starting to take voluntary initiatives for environmental protection, and there is increased citizens' participation in environmental policy making and implementation. There is greater emphasis on environmental education and research and both government and industry are more accepting of NGOs. The Japanese government and industry have set up organizations to provide financial assistance to non-profit groups doing environmental activities in developing countries. As Japan is forced to consider how to move society in a more sustainable direction, the government is starting to appreciate the need to open up the policy-making process to greater citizen participation.

There are still many environmental challenges confronting Japan; among them are how to approach sustainable development, mitigate climate change and reduce the risks posed by the expanding use of chemicals. Since the 1990s, Japanese policy makers and society have struggled to address persistent and new environmental challenges while also dealing with economic stagnation. Some progress has been made, but much remains to be done.

This book does not suggest that Japan is a model of sustainable development or that it does not still have some substantial environmental issues to address. Yet, considerable progress in pollution control has been achieved in Japan and the question to be addressed is why?

It is the objective of this book to consider what factors may have contributed to Japan's relatively successful efforts at dealing with severe industrial pollution and problems associated with rapid urbanization. While there are now numerous studies of Japanese environmental politics and policy, surprisingly little systematic attention has been paid to the institutions, management systems and   financial mechanisms that were established in order to implement environmental laws and programs.

Japan's environmental policies have been influenced by other countries and by international developments, and thus, in many respects, resemble the environmental policies found in other industrialized states (Jänicke and Weidner 1997). Yet, Japanese environmental management style is in many ways distinct from that found in Europe or the USA. There is less emphasis on litigation, more emphasis on administrative guidance and considerable use of voluntary mechanisms for policy implementation. This book examines many of these environmental policy instruments and how they are used in Japan.

INDUSTRIAL POLLUTION CONTROL AND ENVIRONMENTAL PROTECTION IN JAPAN

As we will see in subsequent chapters, there are many factors which contributed to Japan's pollution control efforts. Some are political or social innovations, others are more technological. The authors contributing to this project examine these efforts from different disciplinary backgrounds, including economics, political science, sociology and engineering. As a whole, the book examines the changing roles and attitudes of government, industry and citizens towards pollution control and the roles each has played in more recent years in promoting environmental protection and technological innovations that have reduced environmental stresses. It examines the formal and informal institutions that formed between government and industry to facilitate investment in pollution control technology development and adoption. It considers the importance of environment-related laws and regulations in stimulating behavioral changes and the government's financial assistance to industry for pollution control investment. The leading role in advancing pollution control played by many local governments is also a focus of attention. Some prefectures and municipalities enforced stricter environmental regulations than were required by the national government and pioneered the establishment of sophisticated environmental monitoring and inspection systems to achieve their goals. Also considered is the role played by media campaigns and citizens in helping to raise awareness of environmental matters. They placed pressure on government and industry to introduce pollution control measures in the 1970s and open the policy-making process to environmental groups in the 1990s. Japan is developing a more participatory form of environmental governance.

Over time there have been substantial changes in Japan's pollution control strategies. Pollution control and energy-saving initiatives progressed rapidly, beginning in the 1970s, mainly because aggressive investment was made in new plants and equipment. Tightened anti-pollution regulations and increased energy prices also acted as incentives. Initially, end-of-pipe technology (the retrofitting of pollution control equipment to existing production facilities) was frequently employed. Over time, industries have determined that it is often more efficient both in terms of environmental benefits and cost-effectiveness to replace entire manufacturing processes with cleaner production technology. Thus, polluting facilities and equipment have been largely replaced and environmental control measures promoted. Many firms now employ experts and engineers specializing in environmental management.

Since the 1990s, Japan's environmental policy has begun to focus more on coping with global issues and responding to changing national conditions. Despite Japan's economic problems (the 1990s were dubbed 'Japan's lost decade'), a number of new environmental laws were enacted, reorienting the direction of national environmental policies. The most important among them were the enactment of the Basic Environmental Law in 1993 and the subsequent Basic Environment Plan. Long-term targets and national action plans are spelled out in the Basic Environment Plan. Under this new framework legislation, the scope of environmental policies was expanded to not only control pollution but also deal with broader issues related to 'sustainable development.' The law calls for a more holistic or comprehensive approach to addressing environmental management rather than addressing pollution problems separately. It also encourages broader stakeholder participation in policy making and implementation. These developments suggest that policy makers have come to recognize that there are limitations to earlier pollution control models and new approaches to environmental protection need to be considered.

INTERNATIONAL ENVIRONMENTAL PROTECTION

In reaction to demands that Japan contribute more to international society and the growing severity of pollution problems around the globe, Japan has become an increasingly important player in international environmental protection. Many of Japan's international efforts draw upon its own history of environmental degradation and development of anti-pollution control measures. One example of this can be found in relation to the environmental initiatives of local communities, NGOs and local governments. Local initiatives played a very important role in Japan's environmental quality improvements. Especially interesting are the many local voluntary pollution control agreements that were established. These local experiences are starting to be shared with other communities in Asia. There have been many initiatives by local governments in recent years to promote international environmental cooperation in the Asian region and elsewhere. It is also increasingly the case that both national and local governments in Japan are trying to export Japanese methods of local environmental management to developing countries. This book, thus, also considers such local government initiatives and considers their applicability for other countries.

There is growing appreciation of the need to move society in a more sustainable direction. There is no doubt that the Japanese economy benefited greatly from market globalization after World War II. Japan's economic growth was achieved in part by importing energy and natural resources and exporting industrial products. As a result Japan has a relatively large ecological footprint that impacts the environment domestically as well as in developing countries.

If Japan is to truly move in the direction of more sustainable development, then attention must be turned not only to pollution problems within Japan, but finding ways to reduce resource utilization in Japan that causes environmental damage in developing countries. This can and must be done both through behavioral and regulatory changes in Japan as well as by assisting developing countries in improving their environmental protection capacities.

As noted above, beginning in the 1990s, Japan began to place greater priority on environmental projects within its ODA programs. The role of private enterprises and their direct investment in environmental measures overseas is also becoming increasingly important. There has been a significant movement among Japanese enterprises to relocate their production facilities to other countries, where wage and other production costs are relatively cheaper. Major destinies for relocation since the 1980s have been China and Southeast Asian countries. There are considerable gaps between the environmental regulations of Japan and developing countries. While some Japanese-affiliated companies undoubtably try to benefit from weaker environmental enforcement overseas, many Japanese enterprises are being encouraged to observe Japanese standards in their overseas operations. This should have a favorable impact on the dissemination of environmental technologies and practices in East and Southeast Asia.

Japan is well positioned to strengthen international cooperation for environmental protection. Japan's domestic experiences with severe pollution and extensive pollution control initiatives can provide many possible lessons (both positive and negative) for developing countries. Japan's experiences, know-how and financial resources also place a responsibility on Japan to act as an international leader in the promotion of sustainable development.

AN OVERVIEW OF THE BOOK

This book presents a study of Japan's environmental policies in order that policy-relevant analysis and results may be made available to policy makers, academicians, students, businesses and NGOs. Japan's failures and successes in environmental policy are broadly examined. The project reviews how the integration of development and environmental policies was carried out, what legislative and institutional systems were introduced, what policy instruments were adopted and proved to be efficient, what common and different features are observed between the environmental policies of Japan and other industrialized nations and what lessons useful for developing nations can be drawn from Japanese experiences.

The book introduces the formal and informal institutions that influence how Japan's political and economic systems work. There is discussion of government industry relations, Japanese-style business management, the business culture deriving from Eastern thought (Confucianism), the expectations of social responsibility of business firms and the middle-class consciousness of Japanese society. The volume identifies major characteristics of Japan's environmental policies and discusses the conditions that have enabled or inhibited effective policy development and enforcement.

While the authors involved in this project recognize the importance of the social, political, economic and environmental contexts in which development occurs, and do not suggest that lessons are easily transferable from one society to the next, we nevertheless feel that it is a worthwhile exercise to consider how Japan addressed pollution control in the past and how its approach to environmental policy is changing in response to new environmental challenges.

The book does not attempt to cover all environmental issues. Rather it addresses predominantly issues associated with industrial pollution control as opposed to nature conservation or wildlife preservation and attempts to examine how economic development and environmental protection have been increasingly integrated over time. Readers will discover that there have been major changes in Japan's approach to environmental protection. The differences are very apparent if one compares the period of the 1960s, the time around the passage of the Basic Law for Pollution Control of 1967, and the period when the Basic Environmental Law of 1993 was enacted. As will be described later in this book, there have been changes in terms of the environmental policies being addressed, the policy instruments employed, the environmental awareness of citizens and industrial and governmental attitudes and behaviors.

The first group of chapters examines Japanese environmental policy from historical, institutional and developmental perspectives. In Chapter 2, 'Japan's Environmental Policy: Past and Future', Hidefumi Imura suggests that much can be learned from Japanese experiences with severe pollution, especially with respect to the costs to society of failing to prevent environmental damages and delaying the adoption of countermeasures. Imura begins with an overview of the geographical situation and population of Japan showing that because of its high population density and the intensity with which land is used, Japan is a hard test case for environmental protection. His chapter sketches the broad changes that have occurred in environmental policy from the Meiji era through the era of high growth and beyond. The chapter surveys factors that contributed to Japan's pollution problems and briefly surveys some of the responses to environmental degradation of the government, industry and society. Imura argues that Japan's experience with environmental problems during its own industrialization, and its responses to those problems, provide useful material for consideration by the rapidly developing economies in Asia and Latin America as well as the economies in transition in central and eastern Europe.

In Chapter 3, 'Japanese Environmental Policy: Institutions and the Interplay of Actors', Hidefumi Imura provides an overview of Japanese environmental actors and institutions, that is the formal and informal rules governing the actions of individuals and organizations. The chapter begins with a broad overview of political and financial institutions at the national and local levels and then discusses several key environmental actors, laws and policy making practices. The chapter examines the development of the Environment Ministry and its relations to other governmental ministries, the role of business interests, political parties, local governments and NGOs. It provides an overview of important legislation, including the Environmental Impact Assessment Law, the Environment Basic Law, the Environment Basic Plan and the Non-Profit Organization Law. It also focuses attention on several unique aspects of Japanese environmental policy making, including such institutions as '*shingikai*' ('advisory councils') and '*gyousei shido*' 'administrative guidance.' Importantly, the chapter also places these environmental institutions in the societal and political contexts in which they operate.

Chapter 4 is entitled the 'Economic Implications of Pollution Control Policy in Japan.' In this chapter, Kazuhiro Ueta argues that the costs of pollution in terms of human lives, environmental degradation and costs to industry and society can be large. Japan's painful experience with Minamata mercury poisoning and other pollution-related diseases shows that the costs of polluting can be extremely high. In response to these problems, Japan developed a unique form of the polluter pays principle (PPP) and introduced a pollution-related health damage compensation system. As a result, there were major improvements in environmental quality in Japan. There has, however, been some problem shifting to other countries through the relocation of firms to developing countries.

Chapter 5, 'Japan's Environmental Politics: Recognition and Response Processes', by Jeffrey Broadbent, explores how cultural, social and political patterns have transformed over time in Japan and influenced environmental policy development and outcome. Broadbent considers four stages involved in addressing environmental matters: problem recognition, policy making, implementation and durability. He then examines each of these stages across four historical periods in environmental policy: from 1955-1967 when citizens mobilized in response to their pollution-related grievances; 1967-1975 when political elites responded to those complaints; 1975-1987, a period that Broadbent labels as transitional; and since 1987, a period of globalization of environmental protection.

In Chapter 6, 'Japan's Environmental Policy: International Cooperation', Hidefumi Imura discusses how Japan's role in environmental protection internationally has expanded substantially. In the past, Japan was heavily influenced by foreign pressure or *gaiatsu*. Today, it is playing a larger role internationally in environmental protection, especially in Asia. This chapter traces the development of environmental ODA programs and the philosophies behind them. The chapter describes how Japanese ODA has become more environmentally focused as a result of changing policy priorities.

The second group of chapters focuses attention on policy instruments. In Chapter 7, 'Environmental Policy Instruments', Hidefumi Imura discusses the policy instruments employed in Japanese environmental management. Policy instruments are the tools used to enforce behavioral change. This chapter begins with an overview of different types of environmental policy instruments, including regulations, economic measures and voluntary approaches. This latter category includes pollution control agreements, environmental management systems for industry, environmental plans at the national and local levels, environmental impact assessments, education and information. The chapter surveys the changing use of environmental policy instruments in Japan and the reasons behind those changes, including the emergence of global issues. The chapter also sheds light on the high costs in terms of human lives, environmental degradation and financial layouts of ignoring pollution problems.

In Chapter 8, 'Case Studies of Environmental Politics in Japan', Fumikazu Yoshida examines Japan's development and environmental policies and their relationship to freedom in society. His chapter reviews national level development goals and policies, the tools used to implement those goals and case studies of local outcomes linked to those goals, highlighting the implications for democracy at the local level. The relationships between national development goals, policy tools and local outcomes can be illustrated by using several specific policy cases. This chapter does this by examining four policy areas, national/regional land development, energy, waste management and environmental impact assessments.

In Chapter 9, 'Local Government, Industry and Pollution Control Agreements', Yu Matsuno explores the history of pollution control agreements in Japan. His chapter begins with an overview of the structure of local governments and the power relationship that exists between the central and local governments in pollution control and prevention. Matsuno explores the fascinating history and diffusion of pollution control agreements. Pollution control agreements are now widely used by local governments as an extra-legal means of encouraging industry to reduce pollution.

In Chapter 10, 'Japan's Environmental Policy: Financial Mechanisms', Tomohiko Inui, Akira Morishima and Hidefumi Imura introduce the environmental finance mechanisms that have been critical to the success of implementation efforts. They suggest that very important to Japan's efforts at pollution clean up has been the power the central government obtained under the law to identify local areas that are seriously polluted and require them to develop Pollution Control Programs. Localities that are designated as heavily polluted are eligible to receive special financial assistance from the government. The central government has also provided financial assistance to localities to aid in the development of sewage systems and municipal solid waste incineration. Numerous arrangements exist to promote environmental protection in the private sector. The Japan Development Bank, for example, provides loans to companies to promote energy saving. The Japan Environment Corporation provides technical and financial assistance to private companies, including small and medium-sized enterprises.

In Chapter 11, 'Environmental Industries and Technologies in Japan', Hidefumi Imura, Ryota Shinohara and Koji Himi discuss the crucial role played by environmental technology in pollution control. The cases of air pollution, energy saving, waste disposal and the development of clean car technology are looked at in detail. The chapter discusses the roles played by both government and industry in researching and developing pollution control technologies. They note that while environmental technologies are expensive, there are often many win-win situations in which long-term costs to industries are reduced as a result of their introduction. The authors argue that sustainable development will require the development of cleaner production technologies and discuss the special situation of developing countries.

The next two chapters put Japan's environmental policy style into a comparative context. Yong Ren assesses Japan's environmental management experiences from the perspective of a Chinese environmental policy expert in Chapter 12, 'Japan's Environmental Management Experiences: Strategic Implications for Asia's Developing Countries.' He argues that several factors have been key to Japan's environmental management success. First has been the development of various mechanisms for enhancing cooperation among different policy actors, such as inter-ministerial consensus building, national local government burden sharing in pollution control activities and industry's quasi-voluntary compliance with government guidance. Second is the relatively successful linking of economic development and environmental protection in the period beginning in the 1970s. Third has been the creation of an effective environmental policy system at the national level and fourth is the existence of a strong environmental financing system.

In Chapter 13, 'Environmental Policy-making in the Advanced Industrialized Countries: Japan, the European Union and the United States of America Compared', Miranda A. Schreurs surveys broad trends in environmental protection in Japan, the European Union and the USA. Schreurs explores how ideas have diffused among and between these regions, but also how differences in their political, economic and social structures have led to their rather distinct approaches to environmental governance. The chapter focuses in particular on the different role that environmental groups have been able to play in Japan compared with those in the West. The chapter suggests that Japan has been most effective in areas of environmental protection that can be addressed with environmental technologies. A weakness of the Japanese system has been the limited role accorded to environmental NGOs although this is beginning to change.

The concluding chapter, 'Evaluating Japan's Environmental Policy Performance', argues that one of the more outstanding achievements of Japan's environmental policy was its relatively effective enforcement of environmental legislation and control measures introduced to address the terrible pollution problems that faced the country as a result of its rapid industrialization. There are possible lessons in this experience for other countries that need to tackle environmental issues, especially industrial pollution problems. A strength of the Japanese approach has been the high degree of government-industry cooperation in implementing policy goals. This was achieved making use of both local and national policy instruments, including strategies for development of pollution control technologies, financial mechanisms for promoting pollution control technology research and development and voluntary pollution control agreements. Also important were the environmental institutions that emerged. In the twenty-first century, however, Japan will have to rely more on market forces and the initiatives of businesses and citizens and move away from its interventionist government policy style. The role of the government in environmental policy is shifting from that of a regulator to a planner that encourages voluntary environmental efforts by different stakeholders. Japan is now experimenting with the creation of a society based on resource recycling ('sound material-cycle society' or *junkan-gata shakai*). This may promote new environmental industry, and thereby facilitate an industrial transformation towards sustainable development. Throughout the 1990s, Japan was the largest donor country of ODA and put special emphasis on environmental cooperation. Even so, Japan's international leadership for environmental actions needs to be strengthened.

2. Japan's Environmental Policy: Past and Future

Hidefumi Imura

LAND USE AND GEOGRAPHICAL CONDITIONS

Japan's environmental constraints are heavily influenced by its special geographic conditions. The country's land area is equivalent to only 1/25 of the United States of America (USA) and 1/26 of China. Compared with many countries, however, Japan is relatively large. It is about 1.5 times the size of the United Kingdom (UK). Still, Japan's habitable area is extremely limited; steep mountains, volcanic land, and hills cover about 70 per cent of the land (Statistics Bureau 2002).

As much as 70 per cent of Japan's total population is concentrated in a region called the Pacific Belt, which extends from Tokyo to the northern part of Kyushu Island, along the coasts of the Pacific Ocean and the Inland Sea (Figure 2.1). The climate in this corridor is mild and the transportation network is highly developed. Arable land is used intensively. Coastal regions, especially around the three large metropolitan areas of Tokyo, Nagoya, and Osaka, are especially congested. Many industrial complexes and energy facilities, including power plants and oil refineries have been constructed in the coastal plains (*The Asahi Shimbun* 2002). Despite its limited land space, the country has pursued economic development aggressively. The nation's gross domestic product (GDP) when considered in relation to land size is impressively large as illustrated in Table 2.1. If the intensity of habitable land use in Japan is set at 100, in comparison the USA only measures at 5.8. Other densely populated nations like the Netherlands and Germany have considerably lower land intensity ratios than Japan as well, respectively, 69.1 and 48.1. Energy consumption per habitable area in Japan is quite large. Assuming Japan to be 100, the USA is 17.0 and Germany 72.5. Compared with several other densely populated countries, however, Japan does reasonably well. The Netherlands comes in at 145.2 and Korea at 113.3.

The heavy concentration of the population and industry in a few regions places major constraints on economic, energy and environmental policies.

Burdened by crowded land and limited resources, Japan has been forced to move in the direction of more sustainable development. Geographic and resource constraints have contributed to Japan's adoption of regulations controlling the emission of pollutants and the use of fossil fuels that are among the most stringent in the world. The challenges have been made even more serious by the lack of suitable land for the siting of energy and industrial facilities and the difficulties of obtaining local consent for development projects.[1]

Table 2.1   Land Use Intensity in Industrialized Countries

	GDP	Primary Energy Consumption	Crude Steel Production
Japan	100.0	100.0	100.0
The Netherlands	69.1	145.2	58.3
Germany	48.1	72.5	43.8
South Korea	33.4	113.3	137.7
UK	34.1	70.1	26.9
France	20.0	33.2	12.1
USA	5.8	17.0	3.8

Notes: Arable land area data are used as a proxy of habitable land area. Figures for Japan are set at 100. Based on 1995 data.
Source: Estimated from data in Yano Tsuneta Kinenkai 1998.

JAPAN'S DEVELOPMENT INTO A MODERN NATION

At the beginning of the Edo period (in the early 1600s) Japan entered an era of self-imposed isolation that shut the country off from almost all contact with the rest of the world. For the next two hundred years, Japan enjoyed peace and stability. During this era, the Japanese established a societal, cultural and educational foundation that ensured the nation's later development into a modern state. The population was predominantly engaged in subsistence agriculture. The entire country was divided into small provinces ruled by feudal landlords. Efforts were made to increase primary production within these provinces, but population growth remained constrained by the carrying capacity of nature. The extent of arable land and the agricultural productivity of that land remained limited. In this society, a harmonious relationship was maintained between man and nature and this assured natural capital productivity. Many studies refer to Japan in this period as a model of sustainable development (Ishikawa 1994; Makino, Oishi and Yoshida 1991). The inaugural issue of the government's annual report on a 'sound material-cycle society' takes up the Edo period as an example of an efficient society that reused and recycled resources (Ministry of the Environment 2001).

Figure 2.1 Map of Japan and the Pacific Belt

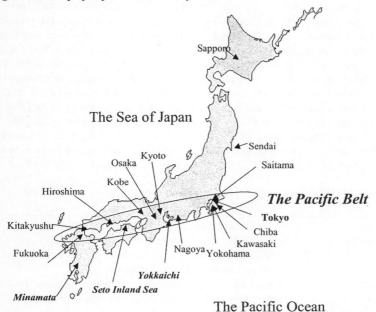

Notes: The map does not include Okinawa or other small islands located in the south-east. Japan and Russia have territorial disputes over several of the Kuril Islands, which lie to the east of Hokkaido.

In the mid-nineteenth century, Western powers confronted Japan with militarily-backed demands that it open its market. Western countries had already colonized a large part of Asia, and Japan risked losing its independence. Under these uncomfortable circumstances, Japan's leaders abandoned their policy of isolation in 1853. Turmoil ensued and the country fell into civil war until in 1867 the Shogun turned over power to the Meiji Emperor, and a new government was formed. The Meiji Restoration of 1868 is widely recognized as the start of Japan's modernization. It can also be viewed as a typical example of decision making in response to 'external pressures' (*gaiatsu*) (Ikuta 1995, p. 21; Sakaiya 1993, pp. 20-2).

In the transition period following the Meiji Restoration, the new government implemented a wide range of measures modelled on European examples. By the end of the nineteenth century, Japan's industrial revolution was well under way. The groundwork for capitalism had been laid. But problems emerged. A number of the new factories that were built in cities caused serious air and water pollution. Pollution problems were also bad around mines and smelting factories located in mountainous areas. A well-known example is the Ashio Copper Mine, situated along the upper stream of the Watarase River, in Tochigi Prefecture, one hundred kilometers north of Tokyo. After the Meiji restoration, the copper mine was made into a modern copper-refining center. The modernization of the mine, however, led to the discharge of large quantities of waste water into the river. The polluted water harmed fish and damaged rice that was irrigated by the river's waters. The Ashio Copper Mine case is particularly well known because the farmers of the region received the backing of Shozo Tanaka (1841-1913), a Diet member, who took up their cause. By 1901 the situation was so bad that he took the dramatic step of directly appealing to the emperor to address the problem. In response, in 1911 the government did enact the Factory Law, the first law to control polluting industrial activities, but it was a weak measure that had little real impact. Shozo Tanaka died dissatisfied (Tsuru 1989).

Table 2.2   Japanese Environmental Policy (1868-1945)

1868	Meiji Restoration.
1877-87	Serious pollution problems arise from the Ashio Copper Mine in Tochigi Prefecture and from smoke emissions in the Besshi Mine in Ehime Prefecture.
1897	Forest Law and a forest reserve system are introduced.
1911	Factory Law enacted, requiring large factories to obtain approval before construction and factory inspectors to conduct pollution control.
1918	Hunting Law amended to ban hunting except as a designated sport.
1919	Law for the Protection of Historical Sites, Scenic Beauty and Natural Monuments enacted.
1931	National Park Law amended and national park system introduced.

The nation's priority was industrial production; effective pollution control technology was rarely adopted. In a pattern that was to repeat itself many times in Japan's race to develop, in most cases victims of pollution received little more than a small amount of monetary compensation if they were lucky enough to receive anything at all (Environment Agency 1991, pp. 1-2).

It should be noted, however, that although little was being done to prevent pollution, several laws related to nature conservation were enacted. These included the Forest Law of 1897 and the Law for the Protection of Historical

Sites, Scenic Beauty and Natural Monuments of 1919. In 1931, the National Park Law was amended and a national park system was introduced (Table 2.2).

This budding interest in conservation was rudely abrupted by the Great Depression in 1929 and the subsequent rise to power of the Japanese military. Once the military gained control over national policy, environmental concerns were basically totally neglected. This was especially true during the Pacific War from 1937-45 (Hashimoto 1999, pp. 25-6).

INDUSTRIALIZATION: MIRACLE AND TRAGEDY

Catching Up with the West

The nations of Europe and North America have over two centuries of experience with industrialization since the Industrial Revolution began in England. Japan's history with industrialization goes back only a century. Japan sprinted down the long road of industrialization that was slowly walked by the West. Japan had a latecomer's advantage; it could learn from the experiences of the Western forerunners. Half a century after the Meiji Restoration, Japan had succeeded in joining the ranks of the world's modern industrial powers even though it was still considerably less developed than the industrialized states of Europe and North America. As a result of the Pacific War, however, the nation's industrial facilities and urban infrastructure were decisively damaged.

Defeat in the war meant the country was subjected to an Allied Occupation from 1945-52. The Occupation forces instituted a series of reforms of Japan's political, economic, educational and social systems. These reforms had far-reaching implications for Japan's subsequent course of development (Reischauer 1977, pp. 103-9; Gibney 1998, pp. 9-10). They included democratization, the introduction of public electoral and local autonomy systems and land reform. These reforms provided the subsequent basis for the rise of an environmental civil society, local environmental initiatives and citizens' anti-pollution movements. This is another instance of national policy reform under foreign pressure or *gaiatsu*.

Government-guided Industrial Policy

Immediately after the end of World War II, production in the mining and manufacturing industries fell to one-seventh of their pre-war levels. There were severe food shortages and high inflation. Strong and effective government industrial policy was necessary to restore the economy and put Japan on track towards becoming an advanced industrialized country (Ikuta

1995, pp. 6-8). The Japanese government presented a series of industrial and land development policies to achieve economic growth. The Ministry of International Trade and Industry (MITI) played a particularly important role as a kind of national headquarters for making plans and implementing programs to enhance the industrial infrastructure, promote exports and strengthen the international competitiveness of industries. It did this by providing guidance and financial assistance to private enterprises. Japan's government-guided industrial policy began in the Meiji era when the government set out to make Japan a wealthy and militarily strong nation. Government involvement in the economy was particularly pervasive when resources were mobilized for the wartime economy beginning in the 1930s. In the post-war period, the government continued to intervene, directly and indirectly, in industrial activities. The industrial policies of MITI worked effectively in helping the country reconstruct its destroyed economy (Sakaiya 2000).

Favorable international conditions helped Japan's post-war economic growth. Japan benefited from market globalization and the movement towards a free trade regime. Japan, moreover, was able to enjoy an abundant oil supply from the Middle East and other parts of the world at prices that were cheaper than for domestic coal. Due to the loss of old industrial facilities in the war, Japanese industry had to start again from scratch, but this also meant that they were able to build state-of-the-art production systems that were highly efficient for the time. New factories and plants were built with the newest technologies available.

There was little doubt among Japanese political leaders or the people about the need to catch up with the USA and other industrialized nations. After the immediate period of post-war turmoil and confronted with the political strains caused by the Cold War, the Japanese government concentrated its policy attentions on high economic growth. An Income Doubling Plan was presented to the people in 1960. With an annual growth rate of over 10 per cent through the latter half of the 1960s, the Japanese economy continued to expand until the oil crisis of 1973. Indeed, the national income doubled in less than ten years. By the early 1970s, Japan was the world's largest producer of ships, radios and televisions.[2]

The rapid push towards industrialization, however, occurred with little appreciation of the risks involved. There was especially little understanding of the ecological constraints to growth and the negative environmental consequences of some industrial activities. Japan's development process began to show the strains of 'compressed industrialization' (Teranishi and Oshima 1997).[3] Japan was quite successful as a latecomer in terms of the rate of expansion of its industrial production, but this expansion came at a heavy price in the form of pollution. The growth rate in energy consumption exceeded that of GDP as shown in Tables 2.3 and 2.4.

Table 2.3   *Japan's Economic Growth, Energy Supply and Consumption*

Year	1965	1970	1980	1990	2000
GDP in real terms (trillion yen in constant 1995 prices)	123.00	204.10	312.70	469.80	535.70
Population (million)	98.30	104.70	117.10	123.60	126.90
Primary energy supply (million tons of oil equivalent)	168.90	319.70	397.20	486.30	558.70
Final energy consumption (million tons of oil equivalent)	108.50	211.20	264.50	322.90	375.10
Primary energy supply per unit of GDP (tons/million yen)	1.37	1.57	1.27	1.04	1.04
Primary energy supply per capita (tons/person)	1.72	3.05	3.39	3.93	4.40
CO_2 emissions (million tons of carbon)	106.00	207.20	251.30	287.10	316.90
CO_2 emissions per unit primary energy supply (tons of carbon/tons of oil equivalent)	0.63	0.70	0.63	0.59	0.57
CO_2 emissions per person (tons of carbon/person)	1.08	1.98	2.15	2.32	2.50

Source: Energy Data and Modeling Center 2002, p. 3.

Japan was caught up in the 'myth of growth', the idea that economic growth and expansion of material consumption will increase social welfare and solve all social conflicts. The Japanese believed that there could be no limit to growth as long as resources were made available for production.

Economic Growth and Energy

Energy is fundamental to most production and consumption activities and as a result energy consumption is typically viewed as an indicator of economic activities and living standards. The use of fossil fuels, however, generates air pollutants, such as sulfur oxides (SO_x), nitrogen oxides (NO_x) and carbon dioxide (CO_2). Energy consumption, therefore, should be viewed not only as an indicator of a nation's wealth, but also of its potential environmental problems.

Until the post-war economic reconstruction of the 1950s, Japan's major energy sources were hydropower and domestic coal.[4] Black smoke from coal-fired chimneys was initially seen as a symbol of economic prosperity. In the 1950s, amazingly high values of dust, exceeding 100 tons/km^2 per month, were recorded in industrial cities. This figure is more than ten times the level of today. In the 1960s, coal was replaced by oil, but oil use too contributed to SO_x pollution.

Table 2.4   Annual Growth Rates in Energy Supply and Demand

Period	1965-70	1970-80	1980-90	1990-2000
Real GDP	11.3	4.4	4.1	1.3
Population	1.3	1.1	0.5	0.3
Primary energy supply	13.6	2.2	2.0	1.4
Final energy demand	14.2	2.3	2.0	0.0
Primary energy supply/unit GDP	2.1	(2.1)	(1.9)	0.0
Primary energy supply/capita	12.2	1.1	1.5	1.1
CO_2 emissions	14.3	2.0	1.3	1.0
CO_2 emissions/ unit primary energy supply	0.6	(0.2)	(0.7)	(0.3)
CO_2 emissions/ person	12.9	0.8	0.8	0.8

Notes: Percentage change. Figures in parentheses represent negative growth.
Source: Estimated using the data from the Energy Data and Modeling Center 2002, p. 3.

Japan's GDP achieved more than a fourfold increase in real terms from 1955-70. Energy demand increased twofold from 1965-74, and approximately sevenfold from 1955-74. Air pollution levels in Japanese cities in the 1950s and 1960s were comparable to levels in many developing countries today (Committee on Japan's Experience in the Battle against Air Pollution 1997, pp. 33-4; World Health Organization and United Nations Environment Program 1992).

Japan's economic growth was the product of an industrialization that promoted the expansion of heavy industries such as iron and steel, shipbuilding and petrochemicals. In 1955, heavy industries accounted for 44.7 per cent of total industrial production while the share of total industrial exports was 37.8 per cent. In 1970 these figures rose to 62.6 per cent and 73.0 per cent, respectively. The 'investment calls for investment' mechanism was put into force, further propelling the trend in rapid growth. Private capital investment for production facilities was promoted by increasing exports and by the improvement of public infrastructure through the building of roads, railways and harbors.

Table 2.5   Energy Sources in Japan *

Year	1955	1965	1980	1990	2000
Coal	47.2	27.0	17.0	16.6	17.9
Oil	17.6	59.6	66.1	58.3	51.8
Gas	0.4	1.2	6.1	10.1	13.1
Hydropower	27.2	10.6	5.2	4.2	3.4
Nuclear	0.0	0.0	4.7	9.4	12.4
Renewable	7.0	1.5	1.1	1.4	1.3

Notes: *Per cent of total supply.
Source: Energy Data and Modeling Center 2002, p.30.

Specialization in heavy industries was made possible by the availability of oil imported from the Middle East and other regions at a relatively cheap price. This resulted in an increased rate of energy consumption that remained greater than the economic growth rate throughout the rapid growth period. The relationship between economic growth and primary energy requirement in Japan is demonstrated in Table 2.4, and the change in energy sources is shown in Table 2.5. The demand for primary energy registered a five fold increase, and the total oil supply increased to 245 million kiloliter (kl) in 1970, roughly twenty times greater than the 12 million kl oil supply of 1955. With this expansion of economic activities, it was quite natural that a rapid increase of fossil fuel consumption caused air pollution in industrial areas.

Japan's dependence on imported energy sources became extremely large. In 1990, Japan imported 92.9 per cent of its coal, 99.7 per cent of its oil, and 94.6 per cent of its natural gas (Yano Tsuneta Kinenkai 2003).

The 1960s and 1970s: Human Tragedy from Environmental Pollution

It was in cities and areas designated for development by the government, plus the country's four major industrial areas where the most serious industrial pollution problems took place. Air pollution from the petrochemical complexes was the most devastating (Yoshida 2000; Saruta 2000; Committee on Japan's Experience in the Battle against Air Pollution 1997, pp. 40-3). There was severe water pollution in semi-enclosed water bodies such as Tokyo Bay, Ise Bay, Osaka Bay and Seto Inland Sea because of industrial and household wastewater coming from coastal regions. The water pollution in Dokai Bay in Kitakyushu, one of the four major industrial areas specializing in iron and steel industries, became notorious because of the accumulation of contaminated sludge and malodors (Kitakyushu City 1999; Metropolitan Environmental Improvement Program 1990). Dokai Bay had the undesirable distinction of being nicknamed the 'Sea of Death'. In

Toyama, where a mining company's activities polluted the water basin of the Jinzu River, residents came down with what is known as '*itai-itai* disease' (literally, 'it hurts, its hurts'), a form of cadmium poisoning.

There was also degradation of nature, diminishment of greenery in and around cities and loss of wildlife. Coastal industrial development that relied on land reclamation from the sea caused loss of natural seashores. It became hard to find places, such as the 'white beaches with green pine trees' that were made famous in *ukiyoe* paintings like those by Utakawa Hiroshige. High-speed Shinkansen or 'bullet trains', which began operations between Tokyo and Osaka in 1964, caused noise and vibration pollution when passing through densely urbanized areas (Funabashi 1986; Funabashi, Hasegawa, Hatanaka and Katsuta 1985).

Yokkaichi asthma

The Japanese were among the first to experience the true terror that can accompany environmental degradation. In the late 1960s, Japanese cities such as Tokyo, Kawasaki, Yokohama, Yokkaichi, Osaka, Kobe and Kitakyushu recorded annual average concentrations of sulphur dioxide (SO_2) ranging from 0.06 to 0.11 parts per million (ppm). Hourly observed values were frequently much higher than these averaged values, reaching levels three to five times higher than current national ambient air quality standards allow (Committee on Japan's Experience in the Battle against Air Pollution 1997, pp. 40-3).

Health risks posed by industrial neglect were of particular concern. The formation of petrochemical complexes and the construction of power stations in industrial areas caused extensive air pollution from SO_x and other pollutants. In 1955 construction of the first 'industrial complex' ('*kombinat*') in the country began in the Yokkaichi area. Three petrochemical complexes were constructed. When the construction of the third complex was completed in 1973, the city had an oil refinery capacity of 505 thousand barrels, and an ethylene production capacity of 701,000 tons per year. It was one of the largest petrochemical complexes in Japan (Chikyu Kankyou Keizai Kenkyukai 1991, p. 28). In the late 1950s, soon after the start of plant operations, inhabitants began to suffer from asthma and other ailments. In the early 1960s junior high schools located on the seashore near the plants were forced to keep their windows closed, even in summer, due to the offensive odor from the factories (Hashimoto 1988, pp. 60-1).

In 1960 the municipal government formed a special investigation committee to conduct a health survey of the inhabitants. The total emissions of SO_x in the city amounted to 130,000-140,000 tons per year, thirty times greater than current emissions. According to measurements carried out in 1963-64, the average concentration of SO_x in the most polluted district was eight times higher than the values of unaffected districts. An epidemiological survey conducted in that district (1962-63) found that about 20 per cent of the inhabitants were suffering from asthma (hence, the term 'Yokkaichi asthma'), and this rate was several times higher than that in non-polluted districts. Automatic monitoring of SO_x, which started in December 1962, revealed extremely high concentrations, often exceeding 1.0 ppm, a level harmful to human health (Yoshida 2000).

Despite these condemning data, companies neglected the growing protests of inhabitants. They avoided effective control actions for years. Instead, they focused their attention on continued plant construction, which made the pollution problems for the region worse. Conditions became so bad that in 1967 inhabitants of the most polluted district filed a damage suit against six companies of the industrial complex. The case was concluded in 1972 when the court handed down a decision that the defendant companies were guilty of illegal actions (Metropolitan Environmental Improvement Program 1990, Annex 10). This event facilitated the creation of the health damage compensation scheme formally started in 1974. This compensation system is discussed further below.

Minamata mercury poisoning
Internationally, the best known of Japan's pollution diseases is Minamata mercury poisoning. Mercury poisoning incidents occurred not only in Minamata on the island of Kyushu, but also in Niigata, on the main island of Honshu. Inhabitants were inflicted by organic mercury poisoning because chemical companies dumped mercury wastes directly into water streams. These cases were adjudicated in courts of law.

Mercury contamination can cause horrific health damage (Metropolitan Environmental Improvement Programme 1990, Annex 10). [5] Mercury becomes increasingly concentrated as it goes up the food chain. The poisoning in Minamata began because of a defective production process for acetaldehyde. Mercury waste was dumped into waterways that eventually made its way to the open bay where fish absorbed the mercury through their skins. Humans who consumed the contaminated fish were exposed to high levels of mercury.

One reason the problem became so bad was that there was no authorized scientific data to explain the mechanisms of organic mercury poisoning or its relationship to human disease. Another reason, however, was that the company that was responsible for the mercury dumping in the first place did not publicize internal experimental data that showed there was indeed a problem. The factory hid its responsibility for causing the disease and continued to use the same defective production process, thus tragically increasing the number of victims.

Table 2.6 Citizens' Response: Development or Environment

Question: Do you think that with the development of industry the occurrence of environmental pollution is unavoidable? Or, do you think pollution must not be allowed even though it is necessary for the development of industry?
Responses*:

Year	Aug. 1966	Dec. 1971	Oct. 1975
Environmental pollution must absolutely not be allowed	27.4	48.3	51
No idea	5.6	10.1	7
The answer depends on the degree of damages	37.7	28.3	26
Environmental pollution is unavoidable	29.3	13.2	16

Question: Which of the following ideas is closer to your own view? (A) We must endeavor to conserve resources and the environment even if it might lower the rate of economic growth. (B) Conservation of resources and environment must be sought within the limit of not undermining economic and income growth (year of questionnaire, 1990).

Responses:

Close to (A)	21.1
Rather closer to (A)	37.6
Rather closer to (B)	29.2
Close to (B).	16.7

Notes: *Per cent.
Sources: Environment Agency (1976), *Annual Report on the Quality of Environment 1976*, Tokyo: Okurasho Insatsukyoku, chapter 2, section 3 and Environment Agency (1992), *Annual Report on the Quality of Environment, 1992*, Tokyo: Okurasho Insatsukyoku, chapter 2, section 2.

Public reaction to pollution
While the public were satisfied with their standard of living, demands began to grow for improvements in 'quality of life'. Public concern over the country's deteriorating environmental conditions resulted in strong political pressures for the central and local government to take measures to control polluting industrial activities and to preserve and restore the natural environment. Following the rapid diffusion of televisions in the 1960s, Japan entered the mass information age. Environmental protection campaigns run

by the media helped increase public awareness of the deteriorating environmental conditions across the country.

In 1968, the government officially recognized that damage to health was being caused by industrial pollution. The specific cases that triggered this recognition were the Yokkaichi, Minamata and *itai-itai* diseases described above. Slowly public opinion shifted to the idea that pollution must not be allowed in the name of industrial development. People began to look at factories and plants as sources of pollution; by the early 1970s, there were widespread citizens' movements criticizing industries and opposing the construction and operation of factories and plants. The results of public opinion polls carried out by the government and a number of research institutions demonstrate remarkable changes in public opinion concerning development and environment. The results of surveys conducted by the Prime Minister's Office in August 1966, December 1971 and October 1975 are shown in Table 2.6.

The surveys asked whether people thought environmental pollution was avoidable. In 1966, 29.3 per cent of respondents answered that environmental pollution was unavoidable, while 27.4 per cent replied that environmental pollution must not be allowed. In 1975, 51 per cent replied that environmental pollution must not be allowed and a mere 16 per cent had the view that environmental pollution was unavoidable. A survey conducted by the Economic Planning Agency in 1990 found that 58.7 per cent of respondents felt environmental protection was necessary even if doing so might slow the pace of economic growth.

By the second half of the 1960s, the pressure of industrial activities on the environment had passed the breaking point (Table 2.7). This resulted in a relatively sudden and drastic change in overall societal attitudes towards growth and the environment. In the political atmosphere of the 1960s, anti-pollution activities were viewed as being synonymous with being 'anti-industry' and 'anti-government' and the movement was largely ignored. Over time, however, this changed as the anti-pollution movement gained strength and joined with other protest movements (such as the anti-Vietnam War movement) in criticizing the government and the ruling Liberal Democratic Party (LDP) for failing to take effective control measures.

A limited political response

Despite the shift in public attitudes, the dominant opinion of industry leaders was that environmental measures would sacrifice the competitiveness of Japanese industries, hamper economic growth and reduce social welfare. In this period of conflicting normative pressures, the government enacted the Basic Law for Pollution Control in 1967. The law established some controls on pollution, but also included a special clause that reflected industrial concerns that environmental regulations would slow economic growth.   The so-called 'harmonization clause' sought to keep a strong place for economic development in environmental policy by calling on environmental protection measures to be 'in harmony with sound economic development' (Hashimoto 1987b; Yamamoto 1987).

Table 2.7   Responses to Environmental Hazards (1945-70)

1949	Tokyo Metropolitan Government introduces an ordinance to control pollution from factories, the first pollution control ordinance in the country.
1955-65	With the start of Japan's rapid industrial growth, pollution problems become increasingly serious throughout the country, especially in the four large industrial areas and other newly industrialized areas.
1957	Natural Parks Law enacted and systematic natural park system established, with classification of national parks, quasi-national parks and prefectural natural parks.
1958	Water Quality Conservation Law and Factory Effluent Law enacted to prevent water pollution from factories and other facilities.
1962	The Law Concerning Controls on the Emission of Smoke and Dust, the first national law to prevent air pollution, enacted.
1963	The Hunting Law amended and renamed as the Wildlife Protection and Hunting Law, introducing wildlife protection area and 'hunting-free' reserves.
1965	Pollution Control Service Corporation established to specialize in pollution prevention measures through its construction and transfer program and loan program.
1967	Basic Law for Environmental Pollution Control enacted, establishing environmental quality standards and developing regional environmental pollution control programs.
1968	Air Pollution Control Law enacted, expanding areas of regulation and introducing the first regulations on automobile exhaust gases.
1969	The first annual report (or White Paper) on environmental pollution submitted to the Diet, in accordance with the request by Basic Law for Environmental Pollution Control; Law for Special Measures for the Relief of the Pollution-related Patients enacted to introduce a system for supplying medical treatment for pollution victims.

The principal aim of the Basic Law was to protect human health and conserve the living environment from what are known as the 'seven typical public nuisances (*kogai*)': air, water and soil pollution, noise, vibration, ground subsidence and offensive odors. The Basic Law's measures included regulations on emissions, land use and facility location; development of pollution control facilities; monitoring; research and study, and; subsidies. The law also provided for planning and measures in areas with serious pollution problems through Regional Pollution Control Programs (see Chapter 10).

The 1970s: Introduction and Enforcement of Systematic Pollution Control Measures

Eventually leading politicians of the LDP came to realize that if the protest movements continued and grew, they would threaten the party's ability to govern or even to remain in power. Thus, they decided to take drastic measures to control environmental pollution (Ui 2002; Vogel 2000, pp. 88-9). The so-called 'Pollution Control Diet' of 1970 enacted or amended fourteen pollution control laws and other environmental measures. The Environment Agency was also established during this extraordinary Diet session.

Based on the new and amended laws, a regulatory system was rapidly developed. Industries had no choice but to respond to these movements. Categories of facilities to which emission standards were applied were extended. This occurred, for example, with the control of NO_x. New innovative pollution control systems were adopted, such as area-wide control of SO_x. New legislation was enacted, an important example being the Law Concerning Compensation for Pollution-related Health Damage (1973) aimed at obliging the polluter to compensate pollution sufferers. The Kanemi-Oil polychlorinated biphenyls (PCB) food poisoning incident (1968) and PCB pollution resulted in further legislation, requiring examination of new chemicals prior to production and import (1973). Regulation on the disposal of hazardous waste was strengthened although the Environment Agency at that time had relatively little to do with control of this problem. These environmental protection measures, combined with structural economic changes as well as major adjustments in energy supply and efficiency, led to major progress in the 1970s concerning a number of pollutants including the control of toxic substances in the environment (Environment Agency, 1980).

International influences on policy developments in Japan
There were several important international events that influenced environmental policy developments as well. The first was the United Nations Conference on the Human Environment held in Stockholm in 1972. The subsequent Organization for Economic Cooperation and Development

(OECD) Council Recommendation on the Polluter Pays Principle (1972) influenced domestic discussions regarding the responsibilities of polluters and the government's role in providing financial assistance to private firms to adopt environmental measures. Movements towards tighter regulation of automobile exhaust gas in the USA and Europe, especially in California, provided strong incentives to strengthen government regulation and promote the development of exhaust gas control technologies by automobile manufacturers. The Environmental Policy Review made by the OECD Environment Committee in 1976-77 provided good policy guidance to Japanese environmental authorities and citizens. The review pointed out the poor quality of urban amenities in Japanese cities while it presented a number of positive evaluations of achievements in pollution control (Organization for Economic Cooperation and Development 1977a, pp. 88-9). The report had a long-lasting impact on the government and people.

Figure 2.2 Changes in International and Domestic Oil Prices

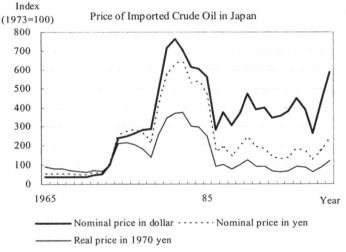

Source: Energy Data and Modeling Center 2000, p. 43.

Implementation of environmental regulations

After the regulatory changes of the early 1970s, steps were taken by central and local governments as well as by business enterprises to control air and water pollution. Under the new measures and guidelines and the watchful eyes of a critical citizenry and media, the iron and steel industries, petrochemical plants and power generation companies were obliged to devote great efforts towards pollution control. Pollution control technologies such as flue-gas desulfurization and denitrification were developed and rapidly disseminated (Himi 2000a; Nakajima 2000).

Due to the relatively effective enforcement of the pollution control measures, the country very quickly dealt with its critical environmental state. Thus, by the time when the OECD Environment Committee conducted its environmental policy review of Japan in 1976-77, conditions had improved substantially. The OECD report presented a number of important observations and conclusions concerning the special features of Japan's new environmental policies. The report concluded that Japan had been able to maintain economic growth while decreasing pollution, and there had been marked environmental improvement before the recession that followed the 1973 oil crisis (Organization for Economic Cooperation and Development 1977a). Japan had shown that it is possible to increase production while decreasing pollution provided that appropriate control mechanisms are developed.

The report observed that Japan's approach to pollution control relied heavily on the setting of ambient standards by the national government, coupled with the setting of emission standards by local governments. Japan relied to a large extent on planning rather than market mechanisms to reduce pollution. This was done by using *gyousei shido* (administrative guidance) in the spirit of a planned economy. It also pointed out the special moral forces that compelled companies to take measures: polluting industries were looked on as villains that should be castigated. Pollution abatement became a must for industry.

The report further suggested that pollution abatement was achieved by sophisticated control technologies. Costs were high, but the impact of such additional costs on the Japanese economy and the competitiveness of industry was not great. These conclusions may provide useful lessons and suggestions to other countries, especially the rapidly industrializing economies in Asia and other regions.

Table 2.8   Energy Consumption in Manufacturing Industries

Year	Energy Consumption per unit GDP (kcal/yen)
1965	5.10
1973	6.24
1981	3.92
1993	2.91
2000	3.06

Notes: GDP given in 1995 prices. Peak energy consumption per unit GDP was in 1973.
Source: Energy Data and Modeling Center 2002, p. 231.

Structural change, the oil shocks and new approaches to energy

It is important to realize that it was not just the introduction of environmental regulations, but also shifts in energy policy that contributed to the improvement in environmental conditions. After the first oil crisis, greater attention was given to national energy security measures. Increased oil prices hit hard the heavy and chemical industries, the major sources of industrial pollution. The Japanese economy shifted from 'rapid economic growth' to 'steady economic growth.' In response to the oil shock and the need for energy conversion, the use of imported coal was encouraged. The potential environmental risks from the expanded use of coal were largely avoided thanks to the availability of advanced environmental technologies, which had been developed to control pollution caused by oil use.

The use of natural gas was also promoted primarily because it does not emit SO_2. To conform to the tightened regional air pollution controls, many power stations in urbanized areas switched their fuel source from oil to liquid natural gas (LNG), by constructing special harbors for LNG tankers. The use of LNG proved to be advantageous not only because it controlled conventional air pollutants but also because it reduced the production of CO_2 from fossil fuels. Emissions of CO_2 from LNG and oil are about 58 per cent and 81 per cent that of coal, respectively, per production of the same caloric value of energy (Global Environmental Department 1992b). Recognizing that the world production of natural gas is limited and that demand for natural gas could increase internationally disrupting supplies and causing radical price increases, large-scale users such as power companies, concluded long-term (e.g., 20-year) contracts with natural gas producing countries in an effort to ensure stable supplies.

Table 2.9   International Comparison of Energy Consumption*

	1971	1999
Japan	123	96.2
Germany	214	130
France	177	150
UK	314	184
USA	443	265
South Korea	220	320
China	2,274	908

Notes: *Per Unit GDP. Tons of oil equivalent/million US $ in 1995 constant prices.
Source: Energy Data and Modeling Center 2002, p. 231.

Table 2.10 Environmental Policy (1970-85)

1970	Pollution Countermeasures Headquarter set up with the Prime Minister at its head in order to take quick and effective measures to control environmental pollution; Diet Session on environmental pollution held, and enactment and amendment of fourteen environment-related laws made including revisions to the Basic Law for Environmental Pollution Control, enactment of the Law Relating to the Prevention of Marine Pollution and Maritime Disaster, Waste Disposal and Public Cleansing Law and Water Pollution Control Law.
1971	Offensive Odor Control Law enacted; Environment Agency established as a government organization for comprehensive environmental administration including environmental pollution control and nature conservation.
1972	United Nations Conference on the Human Environment held in Stockholm and the Declaration on Human Environment adopted; Nature Conservation Law enacted, prescribing policy for nature conservation and defining systems of nature conservation areas.
1973	Pollution-related Health Damage Compensation Law enacted, introducing the compensation system for health damages caused by environmental pollution; Law Concerning Examination and Regulation of Manufacturing, etc. of Chemical Substances enacted requiring examination of chemicals prior to production and import.
1974	Air Pollution Control Law amended to introduce area-wide total pollutant load for sulfur dioxide.
1976	Vibration Regulation Law enacted.
1978	Law Concerning Special Measures for Environmental Conservation of the Seto Inland Sea enacted; Water Pollution Control Law revised with measures to reduce phosphorus pollution and a system of area-wide total pollutant load control introduced.
1980	Convention on Wetlands of International Importance Especially as Waterfowl Habitat (Ramsar Convention), Convention on International Trade in Endangered Species (CITES) of Wild Fauna and Flora, Convention on the Prevention of Marine Pollution by Dumping of Wastes and Other Matter (London Convention) put into effect for Japan.
1984	Law Concerning Special Measures for Conservation of Lake Water Quality enacted; Cabinet Decision made on the implementation of Environmental Impact Assessment (EIA) for public work projects.

Figure 2.2 shows the change in international and domestic oil prices. Increased oil prices from 1975-85 accelerated energy saving efforts in

energy-intensive industries. The total energy demand of manufacturing industries remained fairly steady or even showed a slight decline. The oil shocks also produced an overall industrial restructuring that favored industries that were less dependent on energy, such as electronics, computers and communications. Energy consumption per unit of GDP decreased rapidly as shown in Table 2.8, and it is now one of the lowest among industrialized nations (Table 2.9). In sum, the poverty of Japan's domestic energy resources has been an advantage rather than a disadvantage for economic development and environmental control. It has pushed the nation towards cheaper and cleaner energy sources.

The 1980s: A Period of Limited Policy Change

Following the establishment of a basic environmental legal framework in the 1970s, there was a movement towards reducing government intervention and promoting private economic initiatives. Few new pieces of environmental legislation were introduced (Table 2.10).

Problems such as air pollution from NO_x in urban areas and water pollution by organic materials from households became central issues of concern. In 1982 the area-wide total pollutant load control system was applied to reduce NO_x in designated areas. The Water Pollution Control Law was amended in 1983 and the area-wide pollution control system for organic materials was introduced for Tokyo Bay, Ise Bay and the Seto Inland Sea. The Special Law for Water Quality Control in Lakes was enacted in 1984. It prescribed the designation of the lakes and reservoirs for important water use and the adoption of measures according to comprehensive plans for lake restoration. To prevent groundwater pollution by hazardous substances such as trichloroethylene and tetrachloroethylene, a guideline was adopted in 1984 and the Water Pollution Control Law was amended in 1989. Environmental impact assessment procedures for public works were also developed following their introduction by Cabinet decision. In the absence of a comprehensive law on EIA, however, EIAs could only be carried out by Cabinet Decision or specific laws and as a result, there were many weaknesses in the system. An EIA Law was eventually adopted in 1997 (Kawana 1996; Harashina 1996; Asano 1994).

As living standards improved and acute pollution was abated, public interest shifted towards leisure activities and the creation of a pleasant living environment. Following the 1976 OECD policy review, amenity issues such as neighborhood greenery, pleasant waterside areas and harmonious landscapes became matters of central interest to the environmental administration and were gradually embodied in environmental and urban planning and public works policy. Today, the word 'amenity' is often used in official documents of central and local governments (Nishimura 2002), and the National Comprehensive Development Plan (1998) has a section regarding the 'creation of local communities which are beautiful and full of amenities' (National Land Agency 1999).

Bubble Economy and Environmental Disruption

Speculative investment in land development
In 1972, Kakuei Tanaka, who at the time was Minister for International Trade and Industry, authored a book entitled, *Building a New Japan: A Plan for Remodeling the Japanese Archipelago*. Tanaka was born in a poor town in Niigata Prefecture, and had a strong desire to diminish the income gap between local areas and Tokyo. His idea was to create a number of development projects across the country and diminish the time distance between local cities and Tokyo by constructing high-speed transportation networks based on Shinkansen (bullet train) railways and highways. Tanaka became the President of the LDP and then was elected to be Prime Minister (1972-4).

Prime Minister Tanaka's popularity was initially very high. At the time that his policies were being introduced, Japan's rapid industrial growth and the export of Japanese industrial products to the USA triggered trade frictions. In response, domestic capital began looking for domestic projects to invest in and Tanaka's development policies became an outlet for investment. There was a land development boom across the country.

The land development boom was halted by the oil crisis and Tanaka was forced to resign due to the ensuing economic turmoil, political conflicts and his involvement in the Lockheed bribery scandal. Nevertheless, stimulated by Prime Minister Tanaka's ideas, many prefectures and municipalities undertook projects to develop large-scale industrial bases. Some of these large-scale land development projects received financial support from the national government. Examples include the consolidated development plan of Isahaya Bay (Nagasaki Prefecture) and that of Nakaumi (Shimane Prefecture). Many projects, however, ended in failure, leaving vast tracts of land ineffectively utilized and shouldering central and local governments with large deficits and financial burdens (Suwa 1997, pp. 203-28).

Diminishing regional gaps with high-speed transportation networks
Consolidated National Development Plans are now published every 7-10 years; they have all retained the same general principles and grand design of the original Tanaka idea. Their principal aim has been to diminish the regional gaps between Tokyo and local areas through the construction of a high-speed transportation infrastructure, and they have had some success. The average income of the inhabitants in Tokyo was more than seven times higher than the national average in 1955, but the gap had decreased to a

factor of 1.5 by 1995. Large-scale national expenditures were put towards the construction of local area infrastructure, and this contributed to income redistribution among regions.

After the oil crisis, Japan's industrial structure changed drastically, and the industrial development model based on heavy and chemical industries became outdated. In 1982, the government presented a new industrial development model named 'technopolis', in order to promote high-technology industries that would be located close to airports for the convenience of transporting lightweight but high value-added products such as integrated circuits. The government designated 26 technopolis areas (Motani 1999). Technopolis development has had favorable economic impacts for local economies with relatively small environmental impacts, although it caused some new types of environmental pollution, such as ground water pollution from chemicals (trichloroethylene, tetrachloroethylene, etc.) used in integrated circuit factories (Ochiai 1986).

The bubble economy and its aftermath

From 1980-85, the US dollar appreciated 60 per cent. The strong dollar hurt US exporters and strengthened protectionist pressures against foreign goods. This led to the Plaza Accord in September 1985 among finance ministers from the USA, Japan, the UK, France and West Germany and the subsequent strengthening of the yen (Uekusa 2000). The Japanese government pursued an easy monetary policy, keeping interest rates low in an effort to help firms that were having trouble exporting under the much higher-valued yen. The easy money policy led to a 'surplus money phenomenon'; financial institutions began to invest their huge surpluses in enterprises which, in turn, began to look for ways to invest this money. In 1988 the government presented a new idea for local development: promoting land development for resorts and recreational areas, the idea being to direct investment towards land and real estate rather than in industrial development in order to suppress industrial production capacity increases which would worsen the export pressure to the USA and feed the already serious trade frictions (Shimada 2000; Vogel 2000, pp. 67-71). Unfortunately, as a result of this program, large forested areas, agricultural lands, and regions of environmental importance and scenic beauty were transformed into golf courses and hotels (Suwa 1997, pp. 178-9; Taniyama 1990). Lands in suburban areas were developed as real estate. There was a huge boom in speculative investment by Japanese capital domestically and abroad. Lack of strict land use control, weak physical planning, very high land prices and speculative investment in land caused great environmental disruption. This was especially the case in large cities and local areas where large-scale development projects occurred.

The bubble eventually burst and the investment boom slowed. By the early 1990s, investments that once looked rosy ended in bankruptcy and institutions tottered under their debts. The Japanese economy has suffered very seriously from the after effects of these bad investment decisions. This has made it more difficult for the country to allocate resources to environmental protection.

Globalization and the Environment

Japan's high reliance on overseas resources

Japan heavily depends on imports of natural resources from abroad. According to 1997 data, Japan imported 99.7 per cent of its oil, 59 per cent of food (in terms of total caloric values) and 54 per cent of its timber (Table 2.11). Japan was able to achieve its economic growth and industrial development thanks to the market globalization and free trade regime realized after World War II. Japan imported natural resources, and manufactured industrial products for domestic and foreign markets. With the growth of industrial production, there was a labor shift from agriculture to industry in the 1950s and 1960s and a population migration from rural areas to cities. Japanese people also rapidly changed their dietary habits. They began to consume more meat and wheat, while rice consumption decreased.

Table 2.11 Dependency on Imports for Natural Resources*

Year	1970	1980	2000
Coal	57.1	80.1	98.1
Crude oil	99.5	99.8	99.7
Petroleum production	11.7	6.5	15.0
Natural gas	33.5	91.2	96.8
Iron ore	97.0	99.6	100
Bauxite	100	100	100
Timber	48.3	56.3	52.0
Food (total calorie supply)	40	47	60
Wheat	81	90	89
Meat	11	19	48

Notes: *Per cent.
Source: Yano Tsuneta Kinenkai 2003, pp. 110 and 141.

Impacts on agriculture and forestry

In the Edo period (1600-1867) and until the Meiji Restoration, Japan had a completely self-supporting economy.[6] Population increase was constrained to a level which agricultural production could support. There were about 27 to 30 million people in Japan during this period and almost 90 per cent were involved in rural agriculture. Agriculture was based on paddy rice production, and paddy fields played important roles in preserving ecosystems. They also contributed to the scenic beauty of the traditional rural landscapes (Yoneyama 1998; Ootsuka 1998; Sasaki 1999).

Rural ecosystems and natural scenery remained relatively well preserved until the 1950s. After this time there was a rapid loss of natural areas as the country entered the period of high economic growth. Agricultural lands were transformed for industrial and urban use, and varieties of birds and insects became extinct due to the heavy use of agricultural chemicals. The size of agricultural land owned by a typical Japanese farmer is 1.2 hectares, much smaller than the farms in Europe and, especially, the USA. As a result, Japanese agriculture is often not internationally price competitive.

The situation of forest industries was similar. Japan's mountainous natural conditions protected large tracts of forest: 68 per cent of the archipelago is covered by forest. But forests on flat lands have rapidly disappeared and the suburbs of large cities are losing their greenery as well.

Domestic forest industries could not compete with imported timber because of high labor costs and steep mountainous conditions, which are unsuitable for commercial timber production. Japan is now the largest timber importer in the world and is often criticized for cutting trees abroad. Perhaps as a result of this criticism, Japan's import of timbers has sharply declined from 42.4 million cubic meters in 1980 to 26.2 million cubic meters in 2000 (Yano Tsuneta Kinenkai 2003, p. 179).

The increasing productivity gap between the manufacturing industry and primary industry sectors has been a result of market globalization. Market globalization helped Japan achieve economic growth, but at the price of a decline of agriculture and forestry and the loss of many beautiful areas.

Japanese enterprises and the hollowing out of industry

Another ramification of market globalization after the mid-1970s has been the hollowing out of Japanese industry. Increased domestic labor costs and the appreciation of the yen pushed a number of manufacturing industries to shift their production bases abroad. Japan's foreign direct investment in Southeast Asia and China increased at the beginning of the 1980s.

Japanese foreign investment has at times been criticized for being a form of pollution export. Japanese industries have been criticized for moving polluting factories abroad. Although the criticism may not be completely justified, in 1991, Keidanren (the Federation of Economic Organizations), which is the most influential horizontal business association in Japan, issued guidelines for the overseas operations of Japanese business firms (Keidanren 1991b). The guidelines ask Japanese firms to abide by the environmental standards of the host country as a minimum requirement, and apply Japanese standards to the management of harmful substances.

With increasing concerns over climatic change, depletion of the ozone layer, diminishing tropical forests and desertification, Japan's environmental policy has become increasingly concerned with global and international issues. Japanese enterprises have had to change their business practices as well. Japanese firms have been pushed to narrow the gaps in business culture between Japan and the USA and Europe in order to obtain 'the global standard', a Japanese-made English term.[7] Integration of environmental considerations into business practices is one element of the global standard companies have been urged to follow. Indeed, the spread of international environmental management standards in Japan that were proposed by the International Standard Organization (ISO) in 1992 has been remarkable. As of July 2003, 12,392 Japanese sites had acquired ISO 14000 accreditation, a remarkably large figure compared to many other countries: Spain (3,960), Germany (3,820) and the USA (3032) (Global Environmental Forum 2003).

The 1990s: Global Environmental Issues and Revitalization of Environmental Policy-making

Growing worldwide concern over global environmental problems stimulated a second wave of interest in the environment in Japan. Many specific events helped activate this concern, including the formation of the Montreal Protocol on Substances that Deplete the Ozone Layer (1986), the publication of the United Nations report 'Our Common Futures' (United Nations Environment Program 1987), the establishment of an Intergovernmental Panel on Climate Change (IPCC) in 1989, the holding of the United Nations Conference on Environment and Development (UNCED) in Rio de Janeiro in 1992, the formation of the United Nations Framework Convention on Climate Change (UNFCC) in 1992, the establishment of environmental working groups in the ISO in 1992, and the hosting of the Third Conference of the Parties to the UNFCC in Kyoto in 1997, among many others. Stimulated by these international events, the economic boom that worsened environmental pressures, and Japan's growing role in international affairs, the public became aware of the importance of global environmental problems. Government and industry are giving renewed attention to environmental issues and have become involved in international cooperation for environment and development.

To revamp the legislative framework provided by the Basic Law for Pollution Control and the Nature Conservation Law established close to a quarter of a century earlier, the Basic Environmental Law was enacted in November 1993. The law embraces the entire environmental regulatory administration, and declares that Japan should pursue economic development through 'activities that will reduce loads to the environment as much as possible' and 'help maintain sound economic development while enhancing the blessings of the environment' (Article 3 of the Basic Environmental Law). It also spells out the nation's responsibilities for promoting international efforts to cope with global environmental issues such as global warming, ozone layer depletion, marine pollution and decreasing biological diversity (Articles 5 and 32) (Asano 1994; Ishizaka 2000; Kurasaka 2004).

New environmental legislation was enacted to promote comprehensive measures to reduce NO_x emissions from motor vehicles in metropolitan areas, promote appropriate disposal of industrial and hazardous waste, and to encourage recycling and waste reduction.

Legislation was also enacted to address global environmental issues. The Council of Ministers for Global Environment Conservation established the Action Program to Arrest Global Warming in 1990, and various pieces of legislation were adopted concerning the protection of the ozone layer, imports and exports of hazardous waste and conservation of endangered wildlife. The Law for Promoting Measures to Cope with Global Warming was enacted in 1999 (Table 2.12) (Minowa 2004).

Table 2.12 An Age of Global Environmentalism (1985-2003)

1987	World Commission on Environment and Development (the Bruntland Commission) announced its report 'Our Common Future' in Tokyo, proposing the concept of 'sustainable development'; Law Concerning Compensation and Prevention of Pollution-related Health Damage amended, and Category of Class I Area for compensation of air pollution-related diseases repealed.
1988	Law Concerning the Protection of the Ozone Layer through the Regulation of Special Substances and Other Measures enacted; Vienna Convention for the Protection of the Ozone Layer put into effect for Japan.
1989	Montreal Protocol on Substances that Deplete the Ozone Layer put into effect for Japan; Council of Ministers for Global Environment Conservation set up; Director-General of the Environment Agency appointed as the Minister of State in charge of global environmental problems.
1990	Action Program to Arrest Global Warming decided at the Council of Ministers for Global Environment Conservation.
1991	Law for Promoting the Use of Recyclable Resources enacted.
1992	Law Concerning Special Measures for Total Emission Reduction of NO_x from Automobiles in Special Areas enacted, introducing special measures in Tokyo and Osaka areas; Law for the Conservation of Endangered Species of Wild Fauna and Flora enacted; UNCED (Earth Summit) held in Rio de Janeiro, and Rio Declaration on Environment and Development and Agenda 21

adopted; Convention for the Protection of the World Cultural and Natural Heritage put into force for Japan; Law for the Control of Export, Import and Others of Specified Hazardous Wastes and Other Wastes enacted in order to meet the requirements of the Basel Convention on the Control of Transboundary Movements of Hazardous Wastes and Their Disposal.

1993　The Japan Fund for Global Environment created within the Japan Environmental Corporation to support the activities of environmental non-governmental organizations (NGOs); Basic Environment Law enacted; Convention on Biological Diversity put into effect for Japan.

1994　Basic Environment Plan decided by the Cabinet.

1995　National Strategy of Japan on Biological Diversity formulated by the Council of Ministers for Global Environment; National measures for a final and complete solution to the Minamata disease issue approved by the Cabinet.

1996　Air Pollution Control Law amended to deal with the problem of specific air pollutants other than the conventional pollutants.

1997　EIA Law enacted; the Third Session of the Conference of Parties to the UNFCC held in Kyoto and Kyoto Protocol adopted.

1998　The Energy Conservation Law of 1979 amended to introduce 'top-runner' method of energy efficiency standards, reparation and implementation of energy conservation plans by private enterprises, etc.; Law for the Promotion of Measures to Cope with Global Warming enacted to promote measures to reduce greenhouse gas emissions.

1999　Law Concerning Special Measures for the Control of Dioxins enacted; Law Concerning the Registration of Transfer and Release of Hazardous Chemical Substances enacted.

2000　Basic Law for Building a Sound Material-cycle Society enacted.

2001　Creation of Ministry of the Environment as a result of entire governmental organization reform.

2003　Law for the Encouragement of Environmental Preservation Activities and the Promotion of Environmental Education enacted.

Industry and the global environment

In the 1990s, Japanese firms began to take the view that they were in a position to take on a leading environmental role within the world business community (Mitsuhashi 2000). In the past, the business world had taken environmental actions reluctantly compelled by laws and media campaigns. More recently, their actions have been more vigorous and often have involved voluntary initiatives. The range of involved industries has also increased. Earlier, manufacturing industries were the major actors compelled to take environmental measures. Now service industries, including retail and wholesale, distribution, banks and insurance companies have become important environmental actors. The environmental awareness of business was particularly high just before the UNCED in 1992. Enthusiasm for environmental protection diminished somewhat as a result of the collapse of the 'bubble economy', but the basic tendency towards greater environmental awareness has not changed.

Administrative change

The Japanese national government administration was entirely restructured effective 6 January 2001. The former system of Cabinet Office and 22 ministries and agencies was reorganized cutting the number of ministries to 12. Importantly, the reform resulted in the creation of a Ministry of the Environment. The new ministry has a status equivalent to other large ministries such as the Ministry of Economy, Trade and Industry, and Ministry of Land, Infrastructure and Transport (MLIT).

New Challenges for Japan's Environmental Policy

New political directions

Environmental priorities have changed due to the transformation of industrial structures, the change in production and consumption systems, and scientific information. In the 1960s and 1970s, the country was focused on solving acute industrial pollution problems. In the 1980s and the 1990s, the country turned its attention to urban air pollution from automobile traffic, eutrophication of lakes, dioxin and other endocrine disrupters in the environment, and global issues such as climatic change. As a result, there is a good chance that the antagonisms that characterized relations between polluting industries and pollution victims will be replaced over time by environmental partnerships between businesses and citizens (Ministry of the Environment 2003a). There is also now more use of economic incentives and voluntary approaches rather than simply policy instruments based on command and control.

New environmental objectives include promotion of 'eco-efficiency' and the creation of a resource recycling society or 'sound material-cycle society'. 'Environmental industries' producing not only 'end-of-pipe' control technologies but also involved in 'cleaner production' technologies and resource recovery and recycling are becoming more common. Since the enactment of the Recycling Law (the Law for Promoting the Use of Recovered Resources) in 1991, a number of laws have been enacted to promote the effective utilization of resources by resource recovery and recycling of wastes.

At the beginning of the twenty-first century, Japan is still confronting problems that arose during the bubble economy. A common feature underlying many of Japan's economic and political problems has been the system of administrative guidance that protects producers. A 'political, administrative and business complex' has dominated the country, and 'consumers have had little freedom of choice and find it difficult to satisfy their own desires' (Sakaiya 1993, p. 269). Reflecting these trends, Japan's domestic environmental legal structure has not emphasized the role of citizens and public review.

The reform of economic structures and the governmental system have become central policy issues. Government planning and interventions were accepted when Japanese industries were in their infancy, but today's Japan needs to minimize the government's role, rely more on market mechanisms, and broaden partnerships among citizens, NGOs and businesses. Deregulation, the adoption of more consumer-oriented policies, privatization and decentralization all have been advocated, even if they have not yet been successfully put into effect. This is likely to result in further developments in environmental policy, including more voluntarism and use of market mechanisms.

Reform of high-consumption lifestyles
Another key issue is the reform of Japan's high-consumption lifestyle. In the past, environmental degradation was largely attributed to industrial production activities. However, in the rich industrialized countries, it has become more and more widely acknowledged that materialistic cultures have resulted in the overuse of natural resources and environmental degradation. Recent opinion polls in Japan clearly indicate that consumer behavior and values have changed (Global Environmental Forum 2001, pp. 191-5). A greater proportion of people prefer environmental protection to convenience. There also have been a number of consumer movements seeking new, more benign lifestyles in harmony with such objectives as energy saving, reduction of waste from households, and recycling of materials.

Environmental measures related to public works and EIA
Large investment in public works has improved Japan's environmental infrastructure in terms of municipal wastewater and solid waste treatment systems and provision of urban amenities. In many cases, however, public work projects have been a source of environmental degradation. The building of roads, new towns, railways, harbors and airports have been the responsibility of the Construction and Transportation Ministries (now combined in the form of the MLIT). The political, administrative and business triangle formed around public works projects created a strong pro-development and anti-environment power bloc that dominated both national

and local politics. It was the primary cause of the bubble economy and has been a stumbling block to environmental policy making. In recent years, the public has grown critical of the corruption this cosy triangle has bred and began calling for more public review and public participation procedures in decision making related to public works. This led to the enactment of the EIA Law in 1997 (see Chapters 3 and 8).

Local actions and NGO initiatives

Japan is a centralized country; the center has strong control over local governments and the public has not been given a large role in policy making. Lessons from the past, however, suggest that local governments can be effective at promoting environmental protection. In the 1960s, it was local governments that took the initiative in environmental policy making when the central government failed to establish an effective legal framework. Although local initiatives were discouraged throughout much of the 1970s and 1980s, more recently decentralization policies have been pursued. This should have a favorable impact on local environmental policy-making initiatives and facilitate public participation.

In addition, international cooperation on a non-governmental basis and the importance of initiatives by NGOs, citizens and local governments have been increasingly emphasized as necessary for the protection of the global environment. Following the Rio Declaration and Agenda 21, a number of prefectural and municipal governments started to examine their roles in the protection of the global environment and several prepared a Local Agenda 21 or other local action plans for the prevention of global climatic change (Jichiro 1993; Yoshida 2001).

Resource recycling society or 'Sound Material Cycle Society'

Various research institutions have presented new ideas about technologies to support sustainable development. Two, named 'Factor 4' and 'Factor 10', were conceived in Germany (von Weizsaecker and Lovins 1997; Schmidt-Bleek 1994) and another, 'Zero-Emissions', by the United Nations University (Suzuki 2000). They advocate the need to develop modern recycling technologies, new industrial production methods, and distribution and consumption systems that will minimize the generation of wastes. Changes in today's affluent lifestyles are also imperative if a 'sound material cycle society' (*junkan-gata shakai*) is to be realized.

A Basic Law for the Establishment of a Sound Material Cycle Society was enacted in June 2000 (Table 2.13). This has led to various legislative initiatives to promote the recycling of container and packaging waste, electric home appliances, construction material (demolition waste), food waste and so forth. In 2001, the Law on the Promotion of Green Purchasing was enacted mandating that the national government take initiatives in promoting the procurement of recycled products (Table 2.13) (Yanagi 2004). In a similar vein, the Ministry of Environment (MOE) prepared the Law for the Encouragement of Environmental Preservation Activities and the Promotion of Environmental Education (2003).

Table 2.13 Recycling Policy (1995-2001)

1970	Waste Disposal Law enacted.
1991	Waste Recycling Law enacted.
1995	Container and Packaging Recycling Law enacted, prescribing obligatory duties of business parties for recycling containers and packaging.
1998	Electric Home Appliances Recycling Law enacted, prescribing producers' and retailers' responsibility to recover and recycle TV sets, washing machines, refrigerators, air conditioners, etc.
1999	Special Law for Controlling Dioxin and Similar Substances enacted.
2000	The Construction Materials Recycling Law; Green Procurement Law, Basic Law for Building a Recycling-oriented Society and Food Recycling Law enacted; Waste Disposal Law amended.
2001	MOE created as a result of the reform of national governmental system, and the administration of waste management and recycling of the former Ministry of Health and Welfare transferred to MOE; Full Enforcement of the related laws: Basic Law for Building a Recycling-oriented Society, The Construction Materials Recycling Law, Amended Waste Disposal Law, The Home Electric Appliances Recycling Law, Green Procurement Law, The Food Recycling Law.
2002	Law Concerning Resource Recovery from Used Cars enacted.

Global environmental issues

Japan's environmental policies are placing more stress on global environmental issues and international environmental cooperation. One particular area where this can be seen is in relation to climate change. The UNFCC entered into force in 1992 and led to the establishment of a Conference of the Parties (COP). The COP holds annual meetings to discuss and coordinate international actions for climate change mitigation. Notably, the third COP (COP3) was hosted by the Japanese government. Held in Kyoto in December 1997, COP 3 resulted in the formulation of the Kyoto Protocol, an international agreement addressing climate change. The Kyoto Protocol establishes legally binding commitments for developed countries to reduce a basket of six greenhouse gases (GHG): CO_2, methane (CH_4), nitrous oxide (N_2O), hydrofluorocarbons (HFCs), perfluorocarbons (PFCs) and sulfur hexafluoride (SF_6) by at least 5 per cent by the target years of 2008-

12. In the conference negotiations, separate targets were established for the developed states. Japan's target was set at a 6 per cent reduction of 1990 greenhouse gas levels by the end of the 2008-12 period.

Even though the USA withdrew from the Kyoto process in March 2001, Japan ratified the agreement in May 2002. With Russia's ratification of the agreement, the Kyoto Protocol came into force in February 2005. Japan is now developing a variety of policy and voluntary instruments to implement the agreement (Minowa 2004).

In its climate change mitigation strategies as well as in relation to other environmental problems, Japan is placing more emphasis on international cooperation with countries in Asia and the Pacific region. Reflecting this change in policy direction, the amount of development assistance for environmental projects has increased significantly since the early 1990s.

CONCLUSION

Environmental pollution posed a severe trial for the Japanese post-war economy. The scars left by the environmental pollution of the past can still be seen today, but the measures that were subsequently enforced by the central and local governments did help Japan to overcome the most serious of its pollution problems. Visitors to Japan's industrial cities, once notorious for their air and water pollution, now find that the serious environmental problems that plagued these places in the past have largely been solved.

Continued rapid economic growth, which was made possible in part by the use of innovative technologies, had multiple affects. On the one hand, the surge in the economy caused environmental disruption. Yet on the other, it made it possible for the Japanese economy to bear the costs necessary to institute measures to sustain the environment. These measures included the development and dissemination of sophisticated technologies, such as flue gas desulfurization and denitrification equipment, computerized air and water pollution monitoring systems, advanced waste water treatment technologies and simulation methods to predict the diffusion of pollutants.

There was large-scale public investment in the construction of an improved urban environmental infrastructure. This included municipal sewerage systems and garbage incineration plants. The cost of these environmental measures was significant, 70 trillion yen went for sewerage systems alone during 1965-2002 (Nihon Gesuido Kyokai 2002; see also Chapter 10), but the cost was certainly much smaller than what would have been incurred to society had no control measures been taken. Public environmental investment has been good for the environment; it has also helped sustain the country's economic growth, create jobs and energize local economies.

In October 1993 the Group on Environmental Performance of the OECD completed its second environmental performance review of Japan (Organization for Economic Cooperation and Development 1994). The report confirmed that environmental conditions had improved in Japan. It suggested that there were several reasons for this. First, the Japanese economy went through major structural changes in the 1970s and 1980s, and this was accompanied by major investments to reduce the pollution burden and increase energy efficiency. Moreover, the report found that the public had become more concerned about improving the quality of life, and in particular access to natural areas and pleasant urban surroundings. The 1993 OECD report criticized the lack of cooperation among government agencies and ministries and noted the need for improved integration of environmental concerns into economic and sectoral policies.

In October 2001, the OECD conducted its third environmental performance review of Japan (Organization for Economic Cooperation and Development 2002). It found that the most important pressures on Japan's environment today originate from transport, agriculture, industry, and particularly, the growth of energy demand and private final consumption. It also listed priority issues for Japan, such as urban air pollution, waste management, water eutrophication, nature conservation, climate change, chemical management and international cooperation for environmental conservation. A central theme of the review was the evaluation of the effectiveness and efficiency of Japan's environmental policy. The report concluded that, overall, the mix of instruments used to implement environmental policy is highly effective, but important gains in cost-effectiveness could be achieved through wider use of economic instruments. The report recommended that Japan strengthen and extend the use of economic instruments and ensure that voluntary agreements become more transparent, effective and efficient, while appropriate enforcement of regulatory measures be continued.

A downside to the improvements is that people are now paying less attention to pollution issues, even though problems like acid deposition caused by SO_x and other air pollutants and contamination of water quality in rivers and lakes have attracted growing international concern.

In the coming years, Japan will have to struggle to develop means for dealing with new environmental challenges. One of the biggest challenges in the twenty-first century will be to stabilize CO_2 and other greenhouse gas emissions, and to create a sound material-cycle society.

NOTES

[1] In the 1960s and 1970s, there were a number of resident protests against the construction of polluting factories. At the time, there was no legal procedure to ensure environmental consultation of the public related to development projects. Because there was no national EIA law until 1997, many local governments introduced their own EIA schemes based on local ordinances or guidelines. The most disputed projects in the 1990s were power and municipal waste incineration plants.

[2] The city of Kitakyushu, which was located in one of the four major industrial areas of the country, presents a local example of the transitions that Japan went through during this period. For a time, the 'seven-color smoke' that enveloped the city was regarded as a symbol of industrial development and economic prosperity, but eventually the pollution came to be seen for what it was. Kitakyushu later devoted great efforts to controlling pollution and became a successful model of environmental improvement in an industrial city. It also began programs to transfer its experiences and lessons to other Asian cities. The city received the United Nations Environment Program (UNEP) Global 500 award in 1990 and the Local Government Honors at the Earth Summit in 1992 for its achievements (Kitakyushu City 1998).

[3] 'Compressed industrialization' is a direct translation of a Japanese word *Ashuku-Kogyouka*, which means very rapid industrialization in a short period of time. Compressed industrialization is common to East Asian economies.

[4] Japan had a rather large domestic coal mining industry until coal was replaced by imported oil in the early 1960s. After the oil crisis, new power plants began to use coal again, but the share of domestic coal used was very small because it was comparatively expensive relative to imported coal.

[5] Minamata disease destroys nerves, thereby affecting senses and actions. Many patients suffered convulsions and died. Minamata babies were born with mental or physical disorders. As of May 2003, there were 2,265 designated patients of Minamata disease.

[6] Foreign trade was conducted only with Dutch and Chinese ships, a limited number of which were allowed to come to Nagasaki, a port city in the western part of Japan, for trade.

[7] For most Japanese, the words 'global standards' are synonymous to the values and business rules that the USA government and businesses are forcing others to follow.

3. Japan's Environmental Policy: Institutions and the Interplay of Actors

Hidefumi Imura

JAPANESE SOCIETY: INFORMAL RULES

The Japanese People

Edwin O. Reischauer's *The Japanese Today* is an excellent study of Japanese society and Japan's political system, business organization and relations with the rest of the world. Reischauer states: The Japanese 'have been extremely responsible to changing external conditions.' Of course, 'there are cultural continuities and the persistence of some traits more than others, but no more so than elsewhere in the world' (Reischauer 1977, p. 125). '(S)till when all is said and done, the Japanese do remain a very distinctive people. This is true even though modern technologies which Japan shares with the West tend to produce a certain convergence of traits.... (I)n some traits, the Japanese turn out on average to have quite different norms from those common in Western countries. And significantly, some of these differing norms have behind them long historical antecedents and therefore may be all the more likely to persist to some extent into the future' (Reischauer 1977, p. 126). The book also discusses how the Japanese adapted themselves to Western civilization: 'When the Japanese first confronted the superior technology of the Occident, they comforted themselves with the idea that they would adopt "Western science" but stick to "Eastern ethics." The Chinese and other Asian peoples had much the same concept. But the Japanese soon learned that there was no clear dividing line between techniques, institutions and values. They tended to be all of a piece' (Reischauer 1977, p. 129).

The book, especially its chapters on 'Society' and 'Government and Politics', makes a number of observations that are very useful for understanding the background of decision making in Japan. The book's analysis of groups, mass culture and political heritage, in particular, will help readers understand how negotiations between different actors are made and how decisions are reached in Japan.

Taichi Sakaiya's *What is Japan? Contradictions and Transformation* (1993) is another book which provides rich ideas for understanding the natural, cultural and historical background of Japanese society. If contact with knowledge, technology and systems was sufficient, every country would today be a modern industrial state. However, this is not the case because it takes certain sets of values, attitudes and social systems to digest and internalize these inputs and spread them throughout society. Sakaiya suggests that Japanese culture began in the rice field. He suggests that the very labor-intensive rice cultivation helped shape what are now considered to be characteristic features of Japanese people and society and formed the basis for Japan to absorb Western technology so easily.

The group

Societies differ greatly in the relative emphasis placed on the individual and the group. The Japanese are much more likely than Westerners to operate in groups (Reischauer 1977, pp. 127-37). The group emphasis has affected the style of interpersonal relations. A group player is appreciated more than a solo star. Cooperativeness, reasonableness and understanding of others are the virtues most admired. A key Japanese value is harmony. Achieving harmony often requires a subtle process of building mutual understanding, almost by intuition, and avoiding clear-cut decisions. Decisions should not be left up to any one person but should be arrived at by consultation and committee work. Consensus is the goal.

To operate their group system successfully, the Japanese have found it advisable to avoid open confrontations. Any sharp conflict of views is avoided before it comes out into the open. To avoid confrontations and maintain group solidarity, the Japanese make extensive use of go-betweens. In delicate transactions a neutral person listens to the views of the two sides and finds ways around obstacles, or else terminates the negotiations without the danger of an open confrontation or loss of face on either side.

Mass culture

Like other countries, Japan has its divisions by local community, school, business enterprise, and so on, but these are surface divides that do not reach deeply down into society in the way that ethnic differences, class or cast divisions, or religions do elsewhere (Reischauer 1977, pp. 213-24). The homogeneity of Japan's mass culture can be attributed to many sources, but two factors stand out in particular. These are the extraordinary uniformity the society already had when the Japanese entered the nineteenth century and the determination of the government in modern times to develop a unified citizenry through political centralization and uniform education.

Education has been the chief tool in shaping national uniformity. The mass media together with education are the major shapers of mass society.

The role of television is similar to that in other countries. Nation wide networks breed a great deal of uniformity. Moreover, with less than a tenth of the number of American newspapers, the Japanese have the largest newspaper circulation per capita among the larger countries of the world. Japanese newspapers are surprisingly uniform in format and content. The great weakness of Japanese newspapers is their distressing uniformity in coverage and treatment.

A standardized educational system and the mass media may be basic in relation to giving the Japanese their uniformity as a mass culture, but these are underlain by a well-ordered, smoothly functioning society as a whole. New stories, fads and ideas sweep the whole land more or less uniformly, inspiring similar reactions throughout. The Japanese are particularly subject to nationwide moods.

Political heritage

Japan achieved rapid industrialization, but there is another aspect of modern Japan that has also attracted much attention. This is Japan's transformation in less than a century and a half from a fully-fledged feudal land into a firmly based, exemplary democracy (Reischauer 1977, pp. 237-43). The single most important aspect of the Japanese political heritage was the strong sense of unity. This contrasted greatly with the situation today in many developing countries, which often had little sense of political unity until after undergoing colonialism. Another political asset the Japanese derived from their past was a strong sense of the ethical basis for government, drawn from their Confucian heritage. Closely associated with this were their relatively high standards of honesty and efficiency in political administration. Within the limits of the system, almost all administrators were absolutely loyal to their superiors, scrupulously honest, meticulous in the performance of their duties, and efficient, at least by premodern standards. These high standards of administrative efficiency continued without break into the modern period, accounting for the relative smoothness of the transfer of power and change of systems following the Meiji Restoration.

Social networks and political organization in Japan

The characteristics of the Japanese people influence the form that social networks take among actors and political organizations. Group consensus and decision making ensures the need for informal negotiations, which involve the trading of information, trust and support.

Businesses and other organizations operate under conditions strongly influenced by politics and the state. Jeffrey Broadbent and Yoshito Ishio (1998) studied state-society, and especially state-business relationships in Japan. They describe Japan as an 'embedded broker' state: 'In East Asia including Japan, the state exercises much weaker formal regulatory control

over business, but it engages and "guides" business in more subtle ways'....
Through such networks and mutual trust, the Japanese government has
provided 'business with guidance that allowed coordinating collective efforts
toward producing a stronger national economy. Business trusts the state to
absorb business' concerns and give good collective guidance based on it'....
The state "guidance" is shorthand for formulation of policies that rationalize
the collective best interests of the business community as a whole. 'The
guidance takes place, not so much through heavy-handed bureaucratic
regulatory commandism nor macroeconomic fiscal manipulation, but in the
form seen among businesses themselves...[,i.e.,] networks of communication,
trust and resource exchanges' (p. 79).

State guidance includes helping 'sunrise' or targeted industries to grow
rapidly with protection and 'sunset' industries to decline gracefully with a
minimum of disruption to business productivity and the workforce. The
system worked well for manufacturing industries when Japan was achieving
economic growth, but it failed to work effectively in relation to the financial
sector when decisive actions were necessary to address the financial crisis
caused by the burst of the bubble economy. An advantage to group decision
making and consensus building is that it does not produce absolute winners
or losers, thereby lowering the costs that might otherwise be incurred by
social disruption. On the other hand, there is the disadvantage that the state
and society tend to avoid firm decisions, and thus reaction time is delayed.

THE ROLE OF INSTITUTIONS IN ENVIRONMENTAL POLICY DEVELOPMENT

The World Development Report 1999-2000 refers to 'institutions' as sets of
formal and informal rules governing the actions of individuals and
organizations and the interactions of participants in environmental actions
(World Bank 2000). Institutions can be formal, taking the shape of
constitutions, laws, regulations and contracts, or they can be informal (e.g.
values and social norms). The institutional framework for the environment
rests on two pillars. There are formal legal rules, which ensure that
environmental regulation and standards to protect human health and
ecosystems are enforced, that citizens' rights to live in a clean and healthy
environment are respected, and market forces to guide environmentally
sound business activities are maintained. There are also social capital and
norms, which are the unwritten rules of behavior that allow cooperation and
dispute resolution, with low transaction costs.

The formal institutional aspects of environmental policy are shaped by
environmental legislation and environmental organizations of central and
local governments, corporations and non-governmental organizations

(NGOs) (Figure 3.1). However, the efficacy of environmental policy is largely dependent upon informal rules that have been long upheld in society. Such informal rules may include various social norms such as the relationships between government and private firms, the business culture of private firms, the environmental awareness of citizens and businesses and environmental morals and ethics (Lall 2002).

THE JAPANESE SYSTEM OF GOVERNMENT

Japan's present constitution, promulgated in 1946, adopted a parliamentary cabinet system, which was similar to, although not identical to that of the United Kingdom. The government is composed of a legislative branch, an administrative branch and a judiciary branch, each of which is independent of the others (Nippon Steel Human Resources Development Co. Ltd. 1999, pp. 69-72; Foreign Press Center 2000). Legislative powers are vested in the Diet, which is the highest organ of state power and its sole law-making body. The Diet is made up of a House of Representatives and a House of Councilors, both of which consist of elected members. The Diet has committees to discuss environmental issues: The Environmental Committee of the House of Representatives and the Special Committee on Pollution and Environmental Issues in the House of Councilors. Environment-related bills are to be discussed at the meetings of each committee and committees must approve them before they are passed to House sessions.

Administrative power is vested in the Cabinet, which consists of the Prime Minister and ministers of state. The Prime Minister is elected by the Diet, and the Cabinet is collectively responsible to the Diet in the exercise of its administrative power.

The judiciary branch of government is made up of the Supreme Court and inferior courts including the high courts, the district courts, the family courts and the summary courts. Judicial decisions played an important role in establishing new legal principles to deal with environmental issues and instituting new environmental measures by government (Awaji 1989; Metropolitan Environment Improvement Program 1990).

Local affairs are conducted at two levels of government: prefectural and municipal. The country has 47 prefectures and 3230 municipalities as of 1 April 2000 (Yano Tsuneta Kinenkai 2000, p. 61). Prefectural governors, mayors and local assembly men and women are all chosen by direct election. All prefectures and municipalities have autonomous powers in conformity with national laws. Municipalities that satisfy certain population criteria are eligible for designation as 'cabinet-order designated cities,' which have administrative and fiscal powers on a par with prefectures. In 2003, 13 municipalities had this designation: Yokohama, Osaka, Nagoya, Sapporo,

Kyoto, Kobe, Fukuoka, Kawasaki, Hiroshima, Saitama, Chiba, Kitakyushu and Sendai.

Figure 3.1 Elements of Policy Evaluation

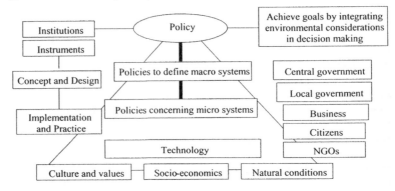

Government Finance

The national budget consists of a general account, special accounts and a budget for government-affiliated organizations (Statistics Bureau 2002, pp. 120-41). The general account includes core national expenditures for government activities and public services. The primary sources of governmental income are taxes, but government bonds have been used to fill the growing income deficit due to increasing public work expenditures in the 1980s and economic slowdown in the 1990s: the FY 2000 general account totalled 85 trillion yen, of which 32.6 trillion yen was financed by government bonds (Yano Tsuneta Kinenkai 2001). This reliance on the issuing of government bonds is increasing their redemption cost, and diminishing the level of expenditures available for implementing national policies, especially for public works projects.

The special accounts comprise funding for a number of specific objectives such as medical insurance, government bond adjustments and pension insurance. These include a special account for road improvement, built from revenue obtained from the taxes on gasoline and diesel oil for vehicles. The reform of this special account has been discussed in the context of 'green taxation' (Yokoyama 1994), and was spotlighted in Prime Minister Junichiro Koizumi's reform policies focusing on the privatization of the Japan Highway Public Corporation (*Nihon Doro Kodan*) (Inose 2003; Tanaka 2004).

The local budget as a whole is classified into an ordinary account and a public service account. The latter comprises accounts for water utilities, traffic management, hospital operations and other public services. The ordinary account incorporates the general account and all special accounts not covered by the public service account. For FY 2000, the total local revenue was 88.9 trillion yen, but only 39.4 per cent of the total or 35.12 trillion yen was financed by local taxes, while the remaining was financed by the local allocation taxes, subsidies from national government and local government bonds. The local allocation taxes are collected by the national government and allocated to prefectures and municipalities according to their financial conditions. This system is often criticized as it can be used by the national government to exert control over local governments (The Council for Decentralization Reform 1996; Abe 2001).[1]

Development of Formal Institutions for Environment

Enactment of environmental laws and the creation of government organizations to implement environmental laws are good illustrations of formal institutions. As discussed in Chapter 2, national environmental policy was very weak in Japan in the early 1960s. This began to change slowly after this time as new laws and organizations were established.

The Law for Controlling Dust and Soot from Factories was enacted in 1962 by the co-initiative of the Ministry of Health and Welfare (MHW) and the Ministry of International, Trade and Industry (MITI). But the Law was deficient in many respects: 1) it was able to control air pollution in the designated areas where pollution was already serious, but unable to prevent pollution in new industrial areas which were under development, 2) only MITI was authorized to regulate factories and no such power was delegated to local governments, and 3) it stated that a balance should be sought between environmental protection and the sound development of industry. At that time, the MHW had only a small pollution control unit within the Environmental Sanitation Division. This unit initiated studies on the health damages caused by air and water pollution. Then, with the increasing number of damage cases, special divisions to deal with pollution-related matters were created: an Industrial Pollution Division in the MITI in 1963 and a Pollution Division in the MHW in 1964 (Hashimoto 1988, pp. 41-91). An inter-ministerial coordination committee for pollution control was also created at the vice-ministerial level in 1964. These efforts marked the beginning of the creation of environmental laws at the national level. The Basic Law for Pollution Control was enacted in 1967 (Prime Minister's Office 1969).

As described in the previous chapter, throughout the 1960s, the Japanese economy continued to grow rapidly, the deterioration of environmental quality became more and more visible, and there was exploding public concern about health damages. Eventually, the national government was forced to take firm and systematic measures. The milestone event was the

Special Diet Session on Environment Pollution Control held in 1970, which enacted a large number of new environmental laws that became the framework upon which environmental regulation has been based in Japan for much of the past three decades.

Creation of the Environment Agency

The Environment Agency (EA) was created in 1971. It had as its mandate to promote policies for pollution control and nature conservation. It was under the jurisdiction of the Prime Minister's Office, but its Director-General was a Minister of State and a member of the Cabinet. One of the EA's major activities was the planning of basic environmental policies and overall coordination of environmental measures implemented by other ministries and agencies. It was empowered to set nationwide environmental quality standards for air and water as well as atmospheric emission and water effluent standards for factories and plants based on individual laws such as the Air Pollution Control Law and Water Pollution Control Law. The Agency also was put in charge of implementing environmental laws, including the Nature Preservation Law, the Natural Parks Law and Pollution Victims Compensation Law. It promoted environmental research and study, through the National Institute for Environmental Studies (NIES) and its subordinate institutions, the Center for Global Environment Research and the National Environment Training Institute (Kondo 2001).

Positions within the newly created EA were filled by various ministries and agencies, and especially, the MHW, MITI and the Ministry of Finance (MOF). The EA was like a colony of the strong ministries. Ministry of Health and Welfare and MOF officials alternately took the post of Administrative Vice-Minister, the top career official post in the EA. The presence of MITI officials, however, was carefully limited in order to avoid the influence of its pro-business policy. Environment Agency decisions were indirectly influenced by other ministries, because it was not easy for officials sent from other ministries to present policies which were at odds with the policies of their home ministries to which they would eventually return.[2]

Creation of the Ministry of the Environment

In January 2001, the government of Japan entirely reorganized its administrative system (Table 3.1). The objectives of this reform were fourfold: creating a more streamlined and efficient administrative framework; restructuring administrative operations to harness the leadership of private citizens; developing an administration that has the public's trust; and creating an administration that is capable of providing the public with quality service. The reform also was intended to reinforce the prime minister's political leadership. The Cabinet Office and 22 ministries and agencies were consolidated into a Cabinet Office and 12 ministries (Shima 2000, pp. 178-86). In this process, the EA was reformed as the Ministry of the Environment (MOE). It is the smallest ministry in terms of personnel and budget size. Various politicians and citizens proposed creating a larger and more powerful ministry by merging the environmental sections dispersed across various ministries and agencies. However, there was resistance from the relevant ministries and agencies, and it was finally decided that the municipal waste management division of the MHW would be shifted to the new Environment Ministry but not other divisions in other ministries (Suwa 2001). The structure and roles of the Environmental Ministry are shown in Figure 3.2.

The MOE has the Central Council for Environment and several other committees as its advisory bodies (*shingikai*). The Central Council is established on the basis of the Basic Environmental Law. Members of the Council are renowned scholars, academicians, representatives of different interest groups and other influential opinion leaders. The Minister for Environment asks the Council to study and discuss important policy issues and prepare reports that can be the basis for formulating new policies. The Ministry also sets up an expert committee when it plans to formulate new policies or enforce new measures. The committee investigates technical questions and offers advice to directors of relevant administrative sections.

Table 3.1   Ministries in Japan as of January 2001

Cabinet Office
National Defence Agency
National Safety Committee
Financial Agency
Ministry of Public Management, Home Affairs, Posts and Telecommunications
Ministry of Justice
Ministry of Foreign Affairs
Ministry of Finance
Ministry of Education, Culture, Sports, Science and Technology
Ministry of Land, Infrastructure and Transport
Ministry of Agriculture, Forestry and Fisheries
Ministry of Economy, Trade and Industry
Ministry of the Environment
Ministry of Health, Labor and Welfare

Source: Shima 2000.

It is still premature to conclude what impact this restructuring has had on environmental policy. Some people say that the new ministries, which were created by the merging of ministries and agencies, have gained more independence because they are larger and, thus, presumed to be more powerful. To give an example, the Ministry of Construction (MOC), the Ministry of Transport and the National Land Agency were merged into the Ministry of Land, Infrastructure and Transportation (MLIT). This new ministry handles more than 90 per cent of Japan's huge public works expenditures. Many people feared that new intra-ministerial conflicts would occur between sections with different ministerial histories and organizational cultures.

Most of the roles and responsibilities of the EA were transferred to the MOE. There is little reason to expect drastic changes in environmental policy as a result of the reorganization although some people fear that the MOE might simply become another vertical ministry and lose its unique role as a horizontal coordinator. As an agency under the Prime Minister's Office, the EA had the important role of providing horizontal coordination across vertically divided ministries. What is promising is that the MOE will no more be a colony of other ministries since it has groomed a number of its own officials for leadership positions.

Relationship between the Environment Agency/MOE and Other Ministries

All ministries and agencies have some responsibilities related to environmental issues leading to a system of vertical fragmentation. Prior to the administrative reforms of 2001, the MOC was responsible for environmental protection regarding public works and infrastructure construction; the MITI provided guidance to private businesses for industrial pollution control, energy conservation and industrial waste management, and the MHW had a budget to subsidize municipal construction projects of waste incineration plants.

The EA was to take a leadership role in promoting environmental policy as well as provide coordination and advice to other ministries and agencies. The Director-General of the EA was authorized to issue recommendations to other Ministers when he or she felt it necessary and appropriate. It was, however, often difficult for the EA to do this due to the independence of other ministries and agencies. The 1994 Organization for Eocnomic Cooperation and Development (OECD) Environmental Performance Review of Japan pointed out that Japan's agencies and ministries seem to act independently in a spirit of competition rather than cooperating fully (p. 113; Sakaiya 1993, pp. 43-4).

The MOE is authorized to coordinate policies among ministries. This is difficult to realize in practice. When the EA was established, it had the strong support of public opinion and the media, both of which demanded the EA play a more active role in controlling polluting industrial activities. By the 1980s, however, environmental conditions had improved and public support for the EA's activities faded. The EA began dealing with broader quality of life issues such as the improvement of urban amenities, but its ability to be effective was limited by other ministries and agencies with greater resources that had their own large-scale environmental projects. This was good to the extent that environmental policy was being integrated into other policy areas, but it is in fact questionable whether other ministries were really giving top priority to environmental projects and measures (Suwa 2001).

The Weakness of the EA: Environmental Impact Assessment (EIA)

By the late 1970s, people were increasingly aware of the need for a shift from curative to preventive measures in environmental policy. Attention was focused on the need for environmental impact assessment schemes. The EA sought to gain a legal basis to intervene when projects of other ministries might have negative impacts on the environment. Its attempt to have an Environmental Impact Assessment Law enacted, however, resulted in severe confrontations with other ministries, especially the MITI and the MOC. From 1978-84, the EA failed in the face of opposition from these ministries to get a draft EIA law submitted to the Diet. The MITI did not want the EIA to apply to electric power plants because it might provide fodder to the anti-nuclear movement. The MOC feared that public participation in the EIA might deter the implementation of public work projects. These ministries wanted to have any EIA law under their control, limiting public participation and minimizing the role of the EA. After hard negotiations, a draft law was submitted to the Diet, but the bill failed to become law when the House of Representatives was dissolved in 1984 before acting on the bill (Kawana 1996; Kurasaka 2004, pp. 40-1).

Public opinion and the opposition parties strongly backed the establishment of EIA schemes. As a compromise, the EIA was formalized by a Cabinet Decision in 1984: the Decision on the Procedures of EIA for Public Work Projects. Cabinet Decisions serve almost as guidelines but failure to comply is not punishable under the law. Under this Cabinet Decision, EIAs were conducted according to the administrative guidelines of relevant ministries and agencies until the enactment of the 1997 EIA Law (Comprehensive Research Committee on the EIA System 1996).

New Wind in the 1990s and a Revitalized Environment Agency

In the 1990s, the EA's situation improved due to the emergence of global environmental issues and related international developments and growing domestic concerns about how environmental constraints might affect economic activities. Many influential politicians formed a non-partisan policy group to promote global environmental actions. Their activities together with changing business attitudes and the increasing environmental consciousness of the public resulted in the enactment of the Basic Environmental Law in 1993. Subsequently other laws were enacted: the EIA Law in 1997, the Law Concerning the Promotion of Measures to Cope with Global Warming in 1999 (Ministry of the Environment 2001a, pp. 109-10), and the Basic Law for Building a Sound Material Cycle Society in 2000 (Ministry of the Environment 2001b, pp. 27-8).

In the past, the EA's responsibilities were limited to pollution control and nature conservation in national parks. The passage of the Basic Environmental Law allowed the EA to expand its scope to deal with broader environmental issues including the facilitation of voluntary actions of citizens and business and international environmental cooperation   (Suwa 2001; Fujii 2001).

Causes of the Transformation in Environmental Policy

What led to the environmental policy advances made in the 1990s? First, the global tide is rising in favor of environmental policy. There is growing recognition that human society has to establish a new paradigm of sustainable development that balances economic development and environmental protection. The Japanese people have shown sympathy towards this idea (Global Environmental Forum 1992). Second, external rather than internal movements largely motivated the change in attitude in Japan. Participation in international society and catching up with the new political and social movements of Europe and America have been important motivating factors. Also important were the series of international conferences on global environmental issues, such as the Earth Summit and the Conferences of the Parties to the United Nations Framework Convention on Climate Change (UNFCC). The environmentalism and environmental actions of citizens, NGOs and green parties in European nations, and especially material recycling in Germany, influenced very much public opinion and attitudes in Japan (Imaizumi 2001).

Since the Meiji Restoration, Japan has learned many things from the West. In his best-selling book, Ezra F. Vogel discussed the virtues and the talents that turned Japan's economy into a powerhouse. He wrote that one of the reasons for Japan's success was the capacity and willingness of the

Figure 3.2 Organization of Ministry of the Environment

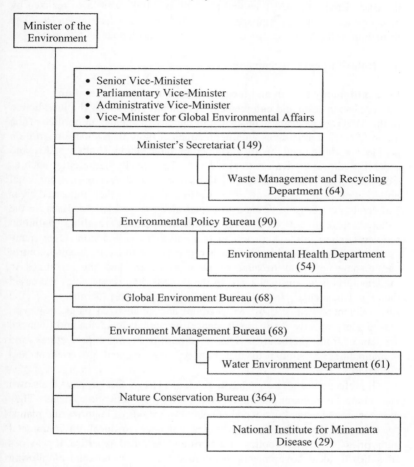

Notes: Figures in parentheses are the number of staff as of March 2002.

Japanese to learn from the West (Vogel 1979, 2000, pp. 31-2). A similar observation may apply to Japan's environmental effort and achievements. In the late 1960s and early 1970s, Japanese leaders decided to implement measures to reduce pollution, and environmental clean up was rapidly accomplished borrowing ideas from developments primarily in America. Vogel attributes this achievement to the fact that Japanese leaders had a highly educated public that recognized the need for environmental clean up and were willing to implement measures toward that end (Vogel 2000, pp.

88-9). Advances in institutional setups in the 1990s, such as the enactment of the Basic Environmental Law and the birth of MOE, were also realized by bold political decisions supported by the public and industrial leaders. The formation of the MOE was premised on similar developments in Europe.

The Role of Local Government

Local autonomy system and local environmental administration
The implementation and enforcement of national laws under the jurisdiction of the MOE are principally delegated to the environmental authorities of the 47 prefectures. Large cities with populations of more than about one million people are designated by the Cabinet to have administrative status and capability almost equivalent to prefectures. Historically, large cities such as Yokohama, Kawasaki, Osaka and Kitakyushu faced severe environmental pollution problems as a result of their efforts to expand their industrial areas and create new large-scale industrial sites along the coastlines. Because the national government took little action to address resulting pollution problems, these cities were left to themselves to take action. Over many years, they accumulated know-how and experience in environmental control and management and because of their large size had the resources to implement policies on their own. In the process these large cities increased their independence from prefectural governments (Ministry of the Environment 2001a, pp. 281-8). Medium and small-sized cities, however, lacked such capacity. They are dependent on guidance, advice and financial assistance from prefectures. This relationship between prefectures and municipalities is similar to that between the national government and prefectures.

All prefectures and designated large cities (Tokyo, Osaka) have their own environmental research institutes and monitoring network systems. They monitor air and water quality and conduct inspections of factories and plants. As with the EA, the MOE provides guidance to local environmental authorities as to general policy directions and technical expertise. It provides subsidies to local governments to improve their environmental monitoring systems, promotes measures related to the Basic Environmental Plan, and drafts local action plans for reducing carbon dioxide (CO_2) emissions, among other activities.

National environmental policy is implemented through a decentralized environmental administration system. MOE has about 1000 personnel. The environmental departments of the 47 Prefectures and 11 large cities have 6441 personnel engaged in pollution control and 2105 engaged in nature conservation (as of October 1998). In addition, 23 per cent of municipalities (cities, towns and villages) have special divisions dealing with environmental affairs (Ministry of the Environment 2001a, pp. 283-4).

The relationship between the national and local governments largely depends upon local financing capability. National ministries exert various controls over local governments using legal and financial tools, and each prefecture is vertically linked to the national government. Horizontal relations between prefectures are very weak. Prefectures typically decide issues without input from neighbors. Although many environmental problems cross prefectural borders, prefectures tend not to cooperate very much. In some cases, the national government must coordinate trans-border issues. For example, the 'Law on Special Measures for the Conservation of Seto Inland Sea', which was enacted in 1973 for water quality control and nature conservation in the Seto Inland Sea, places responsibility on the national government to coordinate actions among the ten relevant prefectures. The law stipulated that these prefectures can establish pollution control measures more stringent than those of other prefectures. Area-wide total water pollutant load controls were also institutionalized for overall reduction in the pollutant loads entering waters. This system was created to achieve the reduction of pollutants originating from different prefectures, by allocating permissible pollutant loads for each prefecture (Ministry of the Environment 2001a, pp. 170-4).

Vertical relationships between central and local governments
The central government has strong control over local governments. Control is exerted through official notices (*tsutatsu*) that are sent from the national ministry to local governments regarding the implementation of national laws, and various forms of unofficial guidance. In some cases, local governments have to receive permission or licenses from national ministries when they undertake projects. Their finances are also controlled by the national government. The national government allots the 'local allocation tax' to prefectures and municipalities according to their fiscal conditions, and it is usually hard for local governments to undertake large projects without receiving subsidies from national ministries. The MLIT, for example, provides subsidies for construction of municipal sewerage systems (up to one-half of the investment cost), subways and harbors, and the MOE provides subsidies for municipal waste incineration plants.

Local governments are largely dependent upon national financial assistance. They operate under what has come to be known as '30 per cent local autonomy', because only 30-40 per cent of total local revenues is derived from local taxes, with the remainder being financed by the local allocation taxes and subsidies provided by the national government. The local allocation taxes are collected by the center and allocated to local governments. The actual financial situation, however, differs greatly between rich and poor prefectures or municipalities (Statistics Bureau 2002, pp. 131-2).

Local legislation: ordinances and guidelines

As many environmental problems take place at the local level and have their
roots in local activities, prefectures and municipalities can enact their own
environmental ordinances (Tanakura 1994). Local ordinances must be in
conformity with national legislation, unless otherwise stated in national laws.
Local governments are authorized to set standards more stringent than the
national level. They are allowed to do so under the Basic Environment Law
out of respect for the efforts and achievements which local governments
made in protecting the environment prior to the enactment of national
environmental laws.

An example of the role of local legislation can be demonstrated in relation
to environmental impact assessments. As noted above, the central
government adopted a Cabinet Decision on the EIA in 1984. Meanwhile, a
number of local governments established their own EIA schemes, which
generally were more comprehensive and advanced with respect to public
participation than the prevailing national scheme. As a result of this, when
the national EIA law was enacted in 1997, there were discrepancies between
national and local EIA schemes in terms of selection criteria for projects,
study items and rules of public involvement. Many local governments, for
example, exercised fairly comprehensive EIA rules that have applied even to
small projects. Local ordinances on the EIA were enacted applying the EIA
to smaller-scale projects than covered by the national EIA Law. The national
law applies only to large-scale projects. The EIA Law has some provisions
that allow flexible application of national and local schemes. Still, when
conflicts between the two systems cannot be resolved, local governments are
expected to amend their ordinances and make them compatible with the
national scheme (Katagiri 1996; Kitamura 1998).

When a new national law is enacted, prefectures and municipalities may
enact similar local ordinances. The Basic Environmental Law, for example,
encourages local governments to enact similar local ordinances, and
therefore many local governments enacted a 'basic environmental
ordinance', stipulating their basic environmental policy directions. They
have also established environmental councils (*shingikai*) which have similar
membership composition and responsibilities to the national councils
described below.

Local decision making

Local decision making is similar to decision making at the national level, but
is often more flexible. This is especially the case in smaller municipalities.
Mayors and prefectural governors are directly elected by public vote. They
therefore must stay abreast of public opinion and enforce even the most
ambitious of policies when there is strong public support for such action.
Furthermore, they can make important decisions themselves, in contrast with

national decision makers who must deal with a system that divides responsibilities among various ministers in charge of a specific policy area. Therefore, local governments can experiment with new policies that have not been adopted by the national government. Historically, the environmental leadership of mayors and prefectural governors has been very important.

Two faces of local government
Local governments have two faces: they promote local area development and at the same time they promote environmental protection policies (Yagishita 1986). On the one hand, mayors, prefectural governors and local government officials have passionately promoted land development plans that convert forestry and agricultural lands into golf courses. They have invited large-scale industrial development projects and polluting factories to their areas. They have undertaken ecologically disastrous public works projects although many development projects were implemented according to national plans with financial subsidies from the national government. Local governments were responsible for the environmental degradation caused by their development plans and the huge deficit left as a result of investment in unnecessary development projects.

At the same time, it was local governments that were faced with pollution problems and the demands of pollution victims that they enforce strict control measures against polluting industrial activities (Imura 1989). When national environmental legislation was not established, local governments instituted their own environmental legislation and regulatory systems. Their pioneering initiatives were later followed by the central government. Thus they often played a 'precursor' role in national environmental policy formulation and institutional arrangements.

Local initiative: a case study of the Tokyo Metropolitan Government
In December 2000, the Tokyo Metropolitan Government under Governor Shintaro Ishihara amended its Pollution Control Ordinance to enable stricter regulation of exhaust gas emissions from diesel-fueled trucks and buses.

The Tokyo metropolitan area has been suffering from air pollution caused by its large number of automobiles and heavy-duty, diesel-fueled vehicles. The Tokyo Metropolitan Government had requested that the national government strengthen the nationwide exhaust gas standards, but the response was very slow (Hirota 1994). Under the strong political leadership of Governor Ishihara, the Tokyo Metropolitan Government set its own standards for particulate matters contained in diesel vehicle exhaust gas. Trucks and buses that cannot meet the standards will not be allowed to run in Tokyo Prefecture after October 2003.

Until Governor Ishihara made this move, it had generally been taken for granted that it was not possible for a single prefecture to set and implement air pollution standards for automobiles because vehicles travel across prefectural borders. Different regulatory standards among prefectures would therefore cause confusion. Moreover, there was fierce resistance from transportation industries against tighter regulations. Nevertheless, the Tokyo Metropolitan Government acted. Their initiative forced MOE to hasten its time schedule for enforcing new national regulatory standards. Eventually, in 2001, the national Law on the Control of NO_x from Automobiles was amended (Ministry of the Environment 2001a, pp. 128-9).[3]

The bold attempt of Governor Ishihara stimulated other prefectural governors and mayors who in the past hesitated to implement policies differing from those at the national level to take their own initiatives. Some prefectures such as Mie and Fukuoka prefectures introduced local environmental taxes, an example being their imposition of an industrial waste tax.

The changing role of local governments
In the 1950s and 1960s, local governments played a major role in initiating the use of environmental controls. After national uniform schemes were established in the 1970s, and local environmental authorities were given certain responsibilities under national law, for a time local governments stopped playing the role of pioneers in the formulation of environmental policies. It became easier for local governments to simply implement national laws, and follow what was decided by the central government rather than try to initiate their own new policy ideas. In national and local politics, the political power of 'progressive groups' declined. Moreover, because local governments needed financial assistance from the central government to install more sophisticated monitoring systems and undertake advanced scientific studies, they found it difficult to implement policies without the support of the central government.

Many local governments also were eager to promote public works to improve transportation and other infrastructures. They were often the source of plans for environmentally disruptive development projects. Environmental departments in many local governments fell upon hard times. Some were restructured because there was a strong feeling among local development powers that the role of environmental policy must be decreased as many critical environmental problems had been solved (Kondo 1983).

The situation changed somewhat in the 1990s, as revisions to national environmental policies affected the local level as well (Tanakura 1994). Local governments gained a new coordinating role in integrating environmental considerations into development policies, plans and programs; playing catalytic roles encouraging voluntary actions by business and citizens; and disseminating information (Takagi 1994; Oku 1994). The traditional method of command and control is being replaced by softer forms of guidance of various stakeholders to encourage voluntary actions. These changes are related to the emergence of global environmental issues and the idea of 'think globally, act locally'. Increasingly it is being recognized that decentralized efforts are imperative to encourage the participation and collaboration of a greater number of citizens and businesses. Integration of development and environmental policies is much easier at the local level as a single mayor or prefectural governor can make all decisions. At the same time, the financial difficulties of the central government have also been a factor pushing greater self-reliance at the local level even though the financial situation of most local governments makes it difficult for them to be more autonomous. Strengthening the financial basis of local governments will be imperative for future environmental protection efforts.

ENVIRONMENTAL POLICY FORMATION

The Shingikai Method

As pointed out by Reischauer, Japanese decision making places importance on 'harmony' and 'consensus', and the avoidance of open confrontation. The *shingikai* method is a typical Japanese way of group decision making and building consensus among various interest groups. Many important policy decisions of government ministries are made based on discussions and reports of *shingikai* and expert committees (*kentokai*). Each ministry has advisory councils, which are established according to special provisions of relevant laws. The Ministry of Economy, Trade, and Industry (METI), for example, has a Council for Industrial Structure, which deals with environmental issues in relation to industrial policy. The Basic Environmental Law has a special clause on the establishment of the Central Council for Environment. Expert committees are organized by decisions of the directors of relevant administrative departments (usually by the *kyokucho*, the director general of a bureau). *Shingikai* of different ministries may reach different conclusions, reflecting their memberships and objectives.

A *shingikai* is a good way to collect various views of experts representing different business fields, interest groups and academic areas, and build consensus among key interest groups and leading opinion leaders. However, there has been criticism of this 'closed' method, because the selection and nominations of committee members are up to the discretion of government ministries and agencies (Suda and Nakamura 1995). *Shingikai,* therefore, may not always represent the opinion of diverse interest groups.

Public Policy Review

Local governments were the first to enact local freedom of information ordinances. Following their lead and in response to the increasing demand by the public for the right to demand the disclosure of government information, the national government enacted a freedom of information law in 1999 (the Law Concerning the Disclosure of Information Owned by Administrative Organizations). In response to this law and development of information technology, government ministries started an effort to publicize the records of their committees by creating Internet homepages. Thus, the accessibility to government information was drastically improved in the 1990s. However, direct contact of national government administration with broader stakeholders, especially citizens and NGOs, is very weak. Being aware of this weakness, the MOE held a number of public meetings in local cities to hear public opinions concerning the implementation of the Basic Environment Plan (Environment Agency of Japan 1997, pp. 609-66)

A law for national policy performance review (the Law Concerning the Review of Policies Implemented by Administrative Organizations) also was enacted in 2001 and went into effect the following year. This law requires each ministry to conduct reviews of its policies. For this work to be done, each ministry is required to prepare a basic plan describing the objectives and methods to be used for policy reviews. Information disclosure and public relations are very important to these review processes (Ministry of the Environment 2002b). As a result, environmental information concerning governmental policies and projects has become much more readily accessible.

Environment and Industrial Policies

Historically, the METI (and its predecessor, the MITI) has had strong links to businesses. It used various forms of administrative guidance to influence industrial behavior and typically consulted with industries prior to formally enforcing policies. The MOE (and its predecessor, the EA) has always been at a disadvantage in this regard because it has not been able to establish similar networks to industry, making it difficult for the ministry to consult or negotiate with industry before enacting new environmental laws or enforcing tighter regulations. This has meant that the MOE has had to win the support and consent of the METI in order to introduce new environmental laws. This was often difficult, however, since the alliance between METI and industries made for a politically strong bloc. The MOE, and the EA before it, had no powerful constituencies supporting it making its position weaker in relation to the METI. In the past, the MITI overrode many attempts by the EA to alter programs or laws. In some cases, however, public support or campaigns by the mass media did lend support to the EA. In cases where there was strong public support, the ruling Liberal Democratic Party (LDP) at times opted to support the creation of environmental policy over the objections of industry.

Negotiations for Consensus Building

When the government enacts new environmental laws, officials of the MOE first prepare a draft. In this process, they hear the views of the Central Council for Environment and special committees established under the Council. Members of the Central Council are supposed to represent the interests of Japanese society as a whole although this may not always occur in practice. Officials of the MOE must also consult and negotiate with officials from other ministries in what are usually very tough negotiations (Suwa 2001). Officers of each ministry are very keen to protect the power basis of their organization. In cases where there is conflict among ministries, it is the leadership of politicians, public opinion and media campaigns that often exerts influence upon the final government decision.

Political Parties

In the 1960s, special national and local political conditions made it possible for local governments to take the initiative in environmental policy making. There were serious political conflicts between the LDP and the opposition parties, and especially the Japan Socialist Party and the Japan Communist Party, on basic policy issues, including the US – Japan Security Treaty. In the 1960s and 1970s, the opposition parties put their energy into winning local elections; they won elections for governors and mayors of influential cities and prefectures, including Tokyo, Kanagawa, Kyoto, Osaka and Yokohama. These opposition prefectural governors and mayors were eager to present unique policies that would distinguish them from the LDP. They criticized the LDP for promoting economic growth policies that resulted in severe pollution and impinged on basic human health. Because of this criticism, the LDP decided to hold the Special Diet Session on Environmental Pollution in 1970. The LDP and economic leaders noticed that they might lose power if anti-pollution and anti-industry movements continued (Hashimoto 1988, pp. 156-8).

Since the 1960s, environmental protection has received broad public support, but it was not taken up as a critical national policy issue until 1970 because it was felt that the environment would not win votes. Some political parties similar to the Green parties in Europe were created, but they were not successful at winning seats in national elections. Instead, it has been necessary to get the ruling LDP to support environmental policy change. While this has not always been easy, once the LDP does choose to support new environmental legislation, it has been relatively easy to gain the support of opposition parties for policy change. This in turn has meant that when environmental policies have been introduced in Japan, they have usually been passed with broad political support.

Getting the LDP, which had as its primary concern national economic development and the protection of industries, to move to protect the environment, however, was not easy. In the 1960s, the LDP was concerned that environmental regulations might adversely impact the national economy and industrial activities. Eventually though pressures built up to a point where the LDP leadership realized it had little choice but to act to protect the environment. Since the opposition parties were eagerly taking up environmental issues as a political theme, public support for action was high, and international pressures were strong, the LDP was pushed to take action. Thus, eventually, the LDP chose to strike a balance between its strong industrial interests and the interests of the broad public, and opted to introduce environmental controls (Environment Agency 1983a; Imamura 1989).

The LDP was in control of Japanese politics for close to four decades. Following the end of the Cold War, however, Japanese national party politics fell into turmoil. Indeed, the LDP Prime Minister Kiichi Miyazawa was not able to attend the United Nations Conference on Environment and Development (UNCED) in 1992 because of the political confusion. He was one of the only heads of state not present at this major environmental summit. He lost his position soon after the Conference. The LDP also lost its firm grip on politics. A coalition of parties, which excluded the LDP, won a majority in the Lower House in 1993. Political scientists often dub this the end of the 1955 system since it was in this year that the LDP formed and from this time that the party held a monopoly on the position of prime minister (Foreign Press Center 1999; Hayashi 2000; Sakaiya 2000).

Several prime ministers have acted in one form or another to further Japan's environmental standing. The Coalition Cabinet led by Morihiro Hosokawa passed the Basic Environmental Law in November 1993. After a new coalition among the LDP, the Social Democratic Party (formerly, the Japan Socialist Party) and Sakigake Party formed in 1994; Prime Minister Tomiichi Murayama from the Social Democratic Party was elected Prime Minister. As a socialist, Murayama tried to solve environmental issues that the LDP had not handled well, such as the certification of Minamata disease patients. There had been considerable conflict between the government, which feared increasing further the number of patients as it would require further payments to them, and residents who felt they deserved certification as Minamata victims (Ministry of the Environment 2001a, p. 342).[4] Prime Minister Ryutaro Hashimoto was a famous pro-environment politician, and many important environmental decisions were made under his regime

(Hashimoto 1994). He decided to host the Third Conference of the Parties to the UNFCC meeting in Kyoto in 1997 and promote international environmental cooperation. He initiated the Environmental Model Cities Project in China, and created the new MOE (Suwa 2001). Unfortunately, he had to resign as Prime Minister because of the bad national economic situation.

A notable political development in the 1990s was the formation of a rather strong group of politicians from different political parties who were interested in Japan taking on a leadership role in international environmental policy. In 1991, the former Prime Minister Noboru Takeshita formed a committee composed of persons of key standing in government, industry and academia to take international actions for global environmental protection; this group was later reorganized as 'Global Environmental Action' (GEA), an NGO. Also, in 1998, the Institute for Global Environmental Strategies (IGES) was created by the initiatives of former Prime Ministers Murayama and Hashimoto.

Environmental Policy Reforms

Toward more effective and efficient environmental policy
A number of important regulatory reforms have been made in order to achieve more stringent control targets and improve effectiveness and efficiency. In the 1970s and 1980s, air and water pollution controls were gradually tightened, and new control systems, including area-wide total emission controls for air and water pollutants were introduced. In the 1990s, the Japanese environmental policy under went large-scale restructuring, and the environmental administration was consolidated so that environmental considerations could be more effectively integrated in sectoral policies (Asano 1994).

In the 1960s, Japan began using regulatory standards, technical guidelines, and monitoring and inspection systems to deal with environmental problems. During the 1970s, a 'command and control' system was widely used to curb pollution. Environmental policy in this period focused on pollution control and energy efficiency. Most environmental achievements were local in nature, and they were made possible by the efforts of industry sectors and the availability of end-of-pipe control technologies, such as flue gas desulfurization and denitrification equipment and automobile exhaust gas controls (Organization for Economic Cooperation and Development 1977a).

Beginning in the 1980s, the major targets of Japan's environmental policies shifted from local pollution problems to global problems such as climatic change, urban air pollution caused by automobiles, the increasing volume of household wastes, increasing energy consumption and the CO_2

emissions of the transport and household sectors. No longer were industrial production activities seen as the main source of pollution. People's daily activities, consumption, and global environmental problems such as climatic change and ozone layer depletion became central policy issues. Traditional pollution control approaches based on standards and regulation proved ineffective to solve these new types of problems (Amano 1994).

During this period, there also has been a shift away from Japanese-style 'command and control' to 'voluntary actions' that are premised on the spirit of participation and partnership. In Japan, 'command and control' has been exercised in combination with various forms of administrative guidance. The growing reliance on a voluntary approach is in part a reflection of the desire of business to minimize government intervention in their activities. The use of economic instruments is also increasingly being discussed, especially in relation to the reduction of CO_2 emissions. Greater emphasis is being placed on the enhancement of partnerships and collaboration among government, business and citizens.

Basic Environmental Law and Basic Environmental Plan

The Basic Environmental Law was passed by the Diet in November 1993 with the unanimous support of all parties. The law provides a new basis and framework for national environmental policy and administration and can be seen as a response to the globalization of environmental concerns (Imura 1994; Ishino 1994).

For more than two decades, Japanese environmental policy and administration were governed by the Basic Law for Pollution Control and the Natural Environment Preservation Law, enacted in 1967 and 1972, respectively. One reason for the formation of the Basic Environmental Law was that the Pollution Control Law was considered outdated and not well suited for coping with emerging global environmental problems, such as climatic change.

The Basic Environmental Law was based on the October 1992 proposal of two advisory councils to the EA, the Central Council for Pollution Control and the Central Council for Natural Environmental Preservation. The proposal concluded that the existing laws were insufficient in helping to resolve modern problems and called for reviewing the economic systems of mass production and consumption. It advocated the need to move toward a society in which economic development placed small loads on environment while changing people's behavioral patterns and lifestyles. The proposal stated that regulatory measures would no longer be sufficient for a new environmental policy and that 'voluntary, economic measures' should be considered instead. This statement was made with a view to encouraging voluntary action by businesses and citizens and promoting economic measures such as environmental charges and taxes that would help bring about reduced CO_2 emissions (Masuhara 1994, pp. 8-11).

The law was an important step toward reform of Japan's environmental policy and administration. The basic law was intended to coordinate the enforcement of various environment-related laws that up until this time had been enforced separately by various ministries and agencies. The law requires the national government to lay out a 'basic environmental plan' articulating its long-term environmental policy and direction. The law requires the promotion of life cycle impact analysis of products and the use of recycled resources. It emphasizes the importance of environmental education, learning and information. It has a special clause on international cooperation for global environmental protection, and stipulates that Japan should take international initiatives. The law states that the national government should conduct research and monitoring, offer support to developing countries, and support international environmental activities of local governments and NGOs. Local governments are also encouraged to take similar actions for environmental management in their jurisdictions.

The three basic principles stipulated by the Basic Environment Law are that: 1) the blessings of the environment should be there for present and future generations to enjoy; 2) a sustainable society should be created where environmental burdens created by human activities are minimized, and; 3) Japan should contribute actively to global environmental conservation through international cooperation (Masuhara 1994, pp. 28-33).

In accordance with the new law, the Cabinet decided upon the Basic Environmental Plan in December 1994. The Basic Environment Plan sets long-term objectives for environmental policy to the beginning of the twenty-first century. It also provides the basis for governmental policies to be adopted in the early 2000s, and sets out activities to be carried out by local governments, private corporations, NGOs and citizens. The Basic Environment Law also encourages local governments to prepare their own environmental basic plans; a number of prefectures, cities and towns have done so. They have prepared local action plans or programs for arresting global warming, traffic pollution control plans, and Local Agenda 21 in accordance with the Agenda 21 approved at the 1992 Rio Conference. The EA provided technical guidelines for helping local governments work on these plans or programs. In preparing such plans or programs, local authorities consult with citizens and businesses to build a consensus on measures to be put into the program (Jichiro 1993).

The Role of Business

Industrial efforts
It was heavy and chemical industries, such as the iron and steel, oil refinery, chemicals, paper and pulp and cement industries that played a locomotive role in Japan's post-war economic growth. At the same time, these were the industries that caused pollution problems and subsequently had to make large investments in the development and installation of pollution control technologies. They had to spend large sums for environmental control, damage recovery and compensation to victims (Ministry of the Environment 2001a, pp. 336-44).[4] Those industries that caused damage to human health were later seriously criticized, and some company managers were found guilty of illegal actions.

Industries learned very severe lessons from their polluting activities. In the late 1960s and 1970s, when the pollution problems were most serious, they generally were reluctant to accept environmental regulations. They maintained the view that environmental protection would undermine the economic development of the country. They frequently opposed initiatives of the EA, such as the 1984 Draft Law on EIA.

In spite of their concerns about the economic impacts of environmental regulations, we now know that environmental regulation did not have a significant adverse impact on the Japanese economy. On the contrary, it provided Japan with various benefits. Combined with the tightened international oil market, energy conservation efforts were stimulated which greatly contributed to the overall increase in productivity of Japanese industry. Energy and environmental constraints facilitated a fundamental change in Japan's industrial structure. Industries capable of producing high added value but less energy and resources were promoted.

Business associations and changing business attitudes
In the 1990s, there has been a shift in the environmental policy paradigm. Very rapid and remarkable changes have been observed in the attitude of Japanese industry with regard to the environment. A good illustration is the formation of Keidanren (Japan Federation of Economic Organizations) 'Global Environment Charter' in May 1991, which issued guidelines for ensuring business activities that work in harmony with the environment.

Keidanren (now, Nippon Keidanren) is the most influential business association in Japan. Its 'Global Environment Charter' states that: 'In carrying on its activities, each company must maintain respect for human dignity, and strive toward a future society where the global environment is protected. We must aim to construct a society whose members cooperate together on environmental problems, a society where sustainable development on a global scale is possible, where companies enjoy a relationship of mutual trust with local citizens and consumers, and where they vigorously and freely develop their operations while preserving the environment. Each company must aim at being a good global corporate citizen, recognizing that grappling with environmental problems is essential to its own existence and its activities' (Keidanren 1991; Tachibana 1994). The Charter provides suggestions about the positive roles and responsibilities of private companies in establishing a new model of industrialization.

In 1997, Keidanren published a Voluntary Action Plan, a compilation of industry-wide action plans of 37 industrial associations, that addresses four action areas: 1) global warming 2) waste disposal 3) environmental management systems (International Standard Organization (ISO) 14000 series), and 4) overseas business activities (Organization for Economic Cooperation and Development 1999; Keidanren 2003).

There are also several other business associations which have a strong influence on national environmental policy making, such as Keizai-Doyukai, a society of influential business leaders, and the Japan Chamber of Commerce. Like Keidanren, they have standing committees to discuss the implications of environmental issues. Following Keidanren's publication of its 'Global Environment Charter', Keizai-Doyukai issued its 'Recommendations on Measures to Apprehend Global Warming: Tasks to Undertake Now for the Sake of Future Generations' in October 1991, as well as its declaration, 'Our Resolution toward the Prevention of Global Warming' (Keizai-Doyukai 1999). These documents included not only recommendations addressed to private corporations but also messages to the government and to the general public. These associations have also kept close ties to international business initiatives such as the eco-audit program of the International Chamber of Commerce and the 'Changing Course' report of the World Business Council for Sustainable Development (WBCSD).

In the early 1990s, many top leaders of the business world expressed the opinion that Japanese firms should be aware of the global environmental implications of their expanded economic activities and that they should utilize their financial power and technologies to protect the global environment. Many firms in manufacturing, services and the commercial sectors created new divisions to examine the linkage between their activities and the global environment and to direct their actions toward the protection of the global environment. 'Corporate citizenship', or the idea that business firms should be good citizens who live in harmony with society, became popular. The word 'eco-business' was created and the use of goods benign to the earth has been advocated (Expert Panel on Eco-Business 1990).

What was the reason for this change in business attitude? First, Japanese enterprises have grown up to be leading companies internationally; they learned a lot about environmental issues from European and American companies through various business assemblies such as the WBCSD and the

ISO. Second, the influence of heavy and chemical industries decreased due to changes in the industrial structure: companies from broader sectors including wholesale and retail, distribution, banking, insurance and trade were involved with starting various environmental actions. Admittedly, the changes took place with capitalist interests in mind.

Companies discovered that it was imperative for them to exhibit concern for the protection of the earth in order to compete with other companies in the domestic market as well as to survive in the European and American markets, where consumers were quite concerned about the environment. Growing environmental concerns in developing countries also demanded Japanese enterprises investing overseas to improve their environmental record. Finally, it should be kept in mind that the Japanese economy was at the peak of the bubble economy at the beginning of the 1990s, when industries' environmental awareness was aroused. Once the bubble burst, their interest in the environment dropped somewhat, but it is still high in business sectors that wish to find chances in eco-business.

Industry Decision Making and the Relationship of Government to Industry

Industry decision making takes place at two levels: at the individual enterprise level and the industrial group level. Industrial group decisions are made at meetings of industrial associations, such as the Japan Iron and Steel Federation, Japan Chemical Industry Association, Federation of Electric Power Companies and Japan Automobile Manufacturers Association. Such Japanese-style group decision making sometimes promotes collusion (*dango*) and at times has been criticized for violating the anti-trust law (Ikuta 1995, pp. 110-11; Muto 2003).

The Japanese administration consists of vertical ministries that deal with the affairs of special industry sectors and horizontal agencies that coordinate the policies of different ministries. MITI, in particular, had strong powers to control most manufacturing industries and the energy sector. The Ministry of Construction had the largest public works budget. It was distributed to local governments and the construction and housing industries. The control is exerted by direct regulation by law, financial assistance and various forms of informal communications or administrative guidance. Administrative guidance is often addressed to an industrial association. Enterprises belonging to an association discuss how to respond to the guidance.

Through such connections, government ministries and industrial sectors develop common interests. The closeness of the government industry relationship is illustrated by the fact that retired high-level government officials are received by private companies as top management members. This practice is known as 'parachuting' or 'descent from heaven' (*amakudari*) (Ikuta 1995, pp. 11-12). Some say this is an example of central government control and a legacy of the wartime economic system (Sakaiya 1993, pp. 250-2). It is at times viewed as a form of excessive government intervention in industry and has been criticized by America and Europe (Ikuta 1995, pp. 23-5). Japan is now an economic superpower, and its industry has developed the ability to finance, develop and gain access to international markets by itself. Therefore, the role of government industrial policy is undergoing major changes.

New business norms
New ways of thinking about the relationship between the environment and economy are taking root in Japan. Although still somewhat superficial, enhanced public awareness of the environment and changing business attitudes suggest possibilities for new forms of economic development. Various economic instruments are being considered as a means of integrating ecological value into markets. The economic implications of environmental measures have traditionally been judged using short-term criteria such as the effect of measures on gross national product (GNP) growth. Slowly efforts are being made to consider their implications from the criteria of long-term sustainability. Japan's past experiences provide some practical lessons about the economic implications of environmental measures, especially the positive impacts pollution control can have on technological innovation and public health, and suggestions about how to improve compatibility between environmental and economic policies (Yamaguchi 2000; Mitsuhashi 1999).

Public works and the environment
Since the 1980s, large-scale public works projects have been major causes of environmental degradation and disputes. Japan's national and local economies are excessively reliant upon the construction industry and public works, and the special political structure makes it difficult to change this structure. The construction industry accounts for 10.2 per cent of all employed persons and construction investment amounts to nearly 20 per cent of the national gross domestic product (Yano Tsuneta Kinenkai 2001, p. 292). Fiscal spending policy for public works has been adopted in order to maintain economic growth; it has been used as a kind of 'opium'. Subsidies from central to local governments are the easiest way to create jobs in local provinces. Thus, public work projects have been used to reallocate the national budget to local provinces, which do not have good industrial facilities to provide jobs for local people.

Construction companies tend to support the LDP. The construction industry in Japan has been free from international competition, and depends upon public works. Politicians can allocate public works projects to local provinces and construction companies, sometimes legally, sometimes illegally. Construction companies are among the strongest supporters of LDP candidates in local constituencies. Public participation in the decision-making processes of public works has been carefully prevented by coalitions of politicians and construction companies. They opposed the enactment of the EIA Law, as they feared that it might strengthen citizens' involvement in decisions and deter the implementation of projects (Suwa 1997, pp. 124-41).

Existing political structures create barriers to public participation in decisions regarding public works projects and the allocation of budgets to different projects. Some development plans that were decided upon decades ago are still not yet complete, but despite opposition remain alive and are scheduled to be implemented without any modifications to plans that were drawn up decades ago before environmental awareness was very high. Examples include the Large-scale Dam Construction Project of Nagara River, the Reclamation Project of Shinji Lake and the Reclamation Project of the Ariake Sea. Despite citizen protests, construction moves forward. There has also been little change in the share of public works accorded to various sectors. Emphasis has been given to transportation infrastructure enhancement, including highways, Shinkansen railways, harbors and airports. Lower priority projects are urban environmental infrastructure improvements, such as sewerage systems, municipal waste treatment plants and parks, although the allocation of budgets to these projects has increased gradually (Cabinet Office 2002).

Regional allocation of public works projects also raises equity questions between dwellers in large cities and those in local provinces, as more budget typically goes to local infrastructure construction than to urban environmental infrastructure improvement. One can find very nicely paved roads in remote agricultural areas where there is little traffic. Projects have been created and undertaken in local provinces as a means for these areas to receive subsidies. This has resulted in a number of environmental disputes.

The Role of Citizens

Protest against pollution and development projects

'People power' ultimately decides national policy. People power has manifested itself in two ways. First, citizens' movements have arisen against polluting industrial activities and large-scale public projects that might have disruptive environmental impacts. Second, major environmental issues have changed. These two forces have been the primary impetus for the advancement of environmental policy in Japan.

Until the occurrence of pollution problems during the period of rapid economic growth, the word 'environment' (*kankyo*) was a relatively new concept. After air and water pollution problems resulted in many pollution victims, Japanese came to realize that large-scale industrial activities could have devastating impacts on human health and the environment. A number of neighborhood pollution protest movements arose in cities. Citizens' movements were the driving force behind the pollution control efforts of the local and central governments and industry. More recently, citizen involvement in environmental protection has taken on new forms.

Increasing public awareness and consumer initiatives
Another driving force of environmental policy based on people power is the consumer movement. In order to achieve 'sustainable consumption,' the role of consumers rather than producers has come to be emphasized. Recent opinion polls in Japan clearly indicate that consumer behavior and values have changed. A greater proportion of people prefer environmental protection to simple convenience. According to an opinion poll, a significant proportion (about 20-35 per cent depending upon items) was willing to pay more for environmental protection through increased commodity prices (Global Environmental Forum 2001, p. 195). There also have been a number of consumer movements seeking new, more benign lifestyles in harmony with such objectives as energy saving, reduction of waste from households, and recycling of materials. There are gaps, however, between awareness and behaviors: increased environmental awareness does not necessarily mean environmentally sound behaviors.

With their increasing standard of living, citizens have started to identify themselves as polluters. They are beginning to recognize the environmental consequences of their affluent lifestyles, mass consumption and one-way use of resources. In the 1990s, the top item of environmental concern was the recycling of resources. Many municipalities adopted a separate collection system for household wastes, including paper, cans, bottles and plastics.

Cooperation between consumers and producers
After the oil crises in the 1970s, Japan's industrial structure rapidly shifted toward service industries. These industries are closer to end users and do not require factories or plants, which need much energy and other resources. Instead, they are 'indirect' rather than 'direct' users of energy and other natural resources. Consumers are final users of such 'indirect' energy and resources. It is slowly being recognized that consumers can contribute to energy saving by reducing their material consumption, changing their lifestyles and using recycled products. There is a growing possibility of collaboration between consumers and producers (Imura, 1997).

The Role of Non-profit Organizations (NPOs)[5]

Non-profit Organization (NPO) Law

Japan has a long history of organizations made up of ordinary citizens working for the public benefit. However, such activities have developed within an institutional framework that provided only a very weak legal status for the private non-profit sector. For legal reasons, Japan's NPOs (another term commonly used for NGOs in Japan) have therefore assumed many different roles. They include public service corporations (*koeki hojin*) that are covered under civil law and special laws and voluntary organizations (*nin'i dantai*) that do not have corporate status. Thus, NPOs have been typically weak in Japan in terms of their social recognition, number of members and their financial base. This has made it quite difficult to realize cooperative relationships among all stakeholders in society. After the Kobe earthquake of 1995, however, the activities of NPOs and voluntary organizations were spotlighted. The government enacted the 'Law to Promote Specific Non-profit Activities' (NPO Law) and it went into effect in December 1998. The Law allows for much easier incorporation of NPOs, giving them legal status as NPO corporations (Economic Planning Agency, 2000). Now, NPO corporations can enjoy financial benefits. The law was amended in 2001 in order to provide tax incentives to business firms and citizens to donate to NPOs. The amended Law also establishes controls over NPOs in terms of the areas and types of activities that they may be involved in to ensure that they are limited to non-profit missions.

The status of Japanese NPOs

Two main problems were typically sited as reasons for the weakness of environmental NPO activities in Japan. One was the problematic legal status of NPOs and the other was their insufficient financial situation. To a certain extent, these difficulties were solved by the enactment of the NPO Law, but fundamental problems remain unsolved.

Environmental NPOs can be classified into three types: public service corporations (*koeki-hojin*) that have a strong 'public service element'; organizations that have a very high level of specialization in one particular field, enabling them to support themselves by undertaking work under contract (these usually are 'corporations' in the legal sense or limited liability companies), and; organizations that act on behalf of the environment at the community level and are typically voluntary. This third category accounts for the overwhelming majority of environmental NPOs (Japan Environmental Association 2001). Most of the public service corporations are established by the initiative of central or local government, and their budget size is usually much larger than the others, having some support from the government.

There are times when the interests of different types of environmental NPOs clash, and so it is difficult to consider environmental NPOs as making up one united sector. It is more or less impossible to avoid situations arising where the activities of public service corporations and profit corporations run counter to the principles of organizations that operate under the status of voluntary organizations. A large proportion of voluntary organizations value their independence so much that links between separate organizations are often weak. Most organizations operate totally separately from one another. This can be considered another factor contributing to the tendency for the environmental NPO sector to be fragmented (Seko 1999).

Table 3.2   Financial Status of Environmental Non-Profit Organizations

Name of organization	Wild Bird Society of Japan	WWF Japan	Nature Conservation Society of Japan
Year of foundation	1934	1971	1949
Number of paid staff	80	34	15
Number of members	53,500	58,000	15,771
Annual budget (million Yen)	1,166	495	247
Breakdown of income sources (%)			
Membership fees	19.2	43.5	43.9
Donations	1.7	32.4	15.0
Income from business undertakings	55.3	6.7	27.3
Others	23.8	17.4	13.8

Source: Economic Planning Agency, 'Shimin Dantai tou Kihon Chosa' ('Report on Basic Survey of Citizens Action Groups'), April 1997, Economic Planning Agency, Tokyo.

NPO's lack of a financial basis

According to a questionnaire survey targeting NPO corporations and voluntary organizations (*nin'i dantai*) conducted by the Cabinet Office in 2000, there are a total of 87,928 'citizens action groups' which are non-profit groups that do not have the status of public service corporation (Cabinet Office, 2001). If one classifies these according to field of activity, about 10 per cent work in the environmental field. That means there are around 8500 NPOs (excluding public service corporations (*koeki-hojin*)) working in environmental fields. On the other hand, the 2001 edition of 'Environmental NGO List' targeted 14,390 organizations by questionnaire (Japan Environmental Association 2001). The criterion for inclusion in that survey was that the main activities and goals of the organizations had to be related to environmental conservation; the legal status of the organization was not considered.

These surveys show that the environmental NPO activities in Japan are comparable to those of Germany as far as the numbers of organizations are concerned. However, the financial basis of Japanese environmental NGOs is very weak: according to the 'Environmental NGO List', about 45 per cent of environmental NGOs have an annual budget of less than 1 million yen. If we exclude public service corporations in the definition of NPOs, this rate is much higher.

Table 3.2 shows the financial status of three large environmental NGOs in Japan. Even very large NPOs, like the Wild Bird Society of Japan and WWF Japan, only have memberships of around 50,000. Assuming as a rough estimate an annual membership fee of 5000 yen per person, the revenue from membership fees would be 250 million yen per year. Even if we add in revenue from donations (which vary greatly from year to year), it must be very difficult for NPOs to cover their fixed costs (e.g. the wages of full-time staff). Therefore, many NPOs must supplement their weak financial base by securing business undertakings. As a result, income from business undertakings accounts for a considerable portion of the revenue of very large environmental NPOs. NPOs must specialize if they are to act as effective information brokers and producers of policy proposals. This, however, requires funding to pay staff, strengthen networks and outsource. The main issue for environmental NPOs in Japan thus comes down to the question of how to strengthen their financial bases.

The NPO Law and the Changing Structure of the Environmental NPO Sector

The aim of the NPO Law is to grant corporate status to voluntary organizations conducting activities in any of 12 areas, including environmental conservation. Either a prefectural governor or the Director-General of the Economic Planning Agency (now a Cabinet Office) approves the granting of corporate status, as long as the organization's main objectives are not political or religious in nature. The NPO Law will resolve many problems that organizations face. For example, voluntary organizations previously had to register contracts under the name of a private individual serving as a proxy as they did not have corporate status. This was a risky proposition for the proxy, but it was the only means for many groups to operate (Seko, 1999). The law was amended in 2002. A major point of this amendment was the introduction of preferential tax treatment for NPOs. However, this scheme is applied only to the NPOs which have received a special certificate by the Director-General of the National Tax Agency, and it is not easy for many small NPOs to get this status (Suwa 1997, p. 352).

While there is high overall acclaim for the NPO Law because it recognizes citizens' activities in the legal system, the mere gaining of corporate status will not lead to an increase in the level of social recognition of NPOs. Discrepancies could also arise between those organizations that qualify for corporate status and those that do not. Small-scale organizations working at the community level may be disadvantaged. This could mean a weakening of those organizations that are best versed in community level matters and local ecosystems and that can act as go-betweens when problems arise.

Some efforts are emerging to enhance cooperation among NPOs in an effort to strengthen the entire sector. The Wild Bird Society of Japan has worked with many regional branches and aims for a structure with a total membership of 300,000 in the long term. It can use this structure to collect and centralize information from the regional branches. In the future, several of the regional branches are likely to apply for corporate status as independent organizations under the provisions of the NPO Law and the Wild Bird Society group will thus become a loose alliance of these organizations (Suwa 1997, pp. 353-4).

The Nature Conservation Society of Japan is assisting the National Federation of Workers and Consumers Insurance Cooperatives by carrying out recruitment and screening work as part of the Federation's environmental conservation program, which provides subsidies for activities and research related to environmental issues. Even though the Nature Conservation Society does not itself give subsidies, it can make available its nationwide network and contribute to work that aims to optimize the allocation of funds within the environmental NPO sector. This experiment by the Nature Conservation Society is highly significant for strengthening and enhancing the allocation of funds (Suwa 1997, pp. 354-60).

Many other organizations also are working to strengthen the NPO sector in other ways. For example, some voluntary organizations are working to expand their membership. Other organizations are making use of the power of information networks to become 'virtual large-scale organizations'. Following the enactment of the NPO Law, the Japan Environment Corporation created the Japan Fund for Global Environment, using both government funding and private sector funds. It subsidizes activities such as tree planting and wildlife protection which are carried out by Japanese and overseas citizens group in developing countries.

Ways for environmental NPOs to strengthen their financial basis
The main sources of revenue for environmental NPOs are membership fees, donations, subsidies from the private sector, fees received for work undertaken under contract and income from business enterprises. Because the level of social recognition of NPOs is still not high, NPOs cannot count

on an increase in the number of members to solve the problem of covering fixed costs. The provision of an appropriate tax system for donations is very important. NPOs are typically granted some kind of preferential tax treatment in many other countries. The Law was amended to introduce preferential tax treatment, but only a small number of certified NPOs can enjoy this scheme as mentioned above.

Subsidies from the private sector are not likely to become an important means of strengthening the financial basis of NPOs. The programs provided by the subsidy-giving groups in the Japanese private sector mostly target the fields of science, technology and education. There are few that target environmental activities. In addition, most subsidies are for research or individual projects. Virtually no money is given towards the general running and upkeep of organizations. From the point of view of the subsidy-giving groups, it is troublesome to give subsidies for the general running of organizations because the subsidies must be given in small lots, meaning that many hours of office work are required, and also because once one starts to give this kind of subsidy it is very hard to stop. Large-scale environmental NPOs, especially those having the status of *shadan hojin*, are highly dependent on income from business enterprises. It will become important for some environmental NPOs to enter 'green marketing', such as environmental auditing and certification work or development of eco-friendly products (Economic Planning Agency 1999).

Traditionally Japanese have not felt NPOs to be necessary because it was believed that the government would take care of all problems. This way of thinking has totally changed. Today's environmental problems are complicated and diverse, ranging from global issues to neighborhood problems and it is understood that the government cannot take up all these topics. Agenda 21 highlighted the importance of NPOs. So did the Basic Environmental Law and the Basic Environmental Plan (Ministry of the Environment 2001c, p. 279). Realizing partnerships between government and NPOs and developing the capacity of NPOs not only in terms of their financial basis but also their professional know-how are challenges for the future.

Role of the media
The role of newspapers and TV is especially vital in environmental education. In the late 1960s and early 1970s, the media played an essential role in encouraging citizens' anti-pollution movements and calling for stronger government actions. Since the late 1980s, they also have played a vigorous role in raising awareness of global environmental issues and encouraging the government to take action to control chlorofluorocarbons and stabilize the emission of greenhouse gases. Their role in disseminating environmental information to the public has become quite important.

Increasingly the internet and other advanced communication tools also play a vital role in disseminating environmental information.

CONCLUSION

This chapter has discussed the roles of central and local governments, businesses, citizens and NPOs in environmental policy making. It has discussed the cultural and societal background of Japan and formal and informal institutions that rule the actions of individuals and organizations. Japan has developed modern legal, governmental and educational institutions that are very similar to their Western counterparts. Still, informal institutional rules result in unique outcomes.

National environmental programs have been subject to major reforms. Japan's environmental policies rely increasingly upon participatory approaches based on voluntary actions of business, citizens and NPOs. Historically Japan has had a strong government, one of the reasons why the activities of NPOs have been weak. In the future, however, the role of NPOs most certainly will be strengthened.

NOTES

[1] In addition to financial control, officials sent from the national government to local governments often assume high posts such as vice-prefectural governors and directors in charge of fiscal affairs.

[2] Most government officials in Japan are selected by national examination when they are in their early 20s. They are assigned to their home ministry and 'registered' in their personnel record. They gradually identify themselves with their home ministry. Positions are almost as good as guaranteed to these officials even upon their retirement from their ministry, which for most occurs in their 40s or 50s. It is often criticized that they work more with the interest of their ministry and the expansion of their administrative power base in mind rather than in the best interests of the state. This is a manifestation of Japan's 'group society.'

[3] Law Concerning Special Measures for Total Emission Reduction of Nitrogen Oxides and Particulate Matters from Automobiles in Specified Areas.

[4] The number of residents who wanted to be certified was so great that many of them did not receive compensation payments. More than 2200 patients were certified as of April 2000. Total compensation for Minamata disease was 152.7 billion yen (as of the end of December 2000), while the total amount of payment to air pollution health victims was close to 1 trillion yen for the period 1974-87.

[5] The author would like to acknowledge Mr Keisuke Takegahara for his help with information on the role of NPOs.

4. Economic Implications of Pollution Control Policy in Japan

Kazuhiro Ueta

INTRODUCTION

Pollution control policy should not be evaluated only from the perspective of environmental effectiveness; efficiency and equity must be considered as well. Among the various social problems that have afflicted Japan, environmental problems most gravely reveal the complexities of politics, economics and society. What are the lessons to be learned from the Japanese experiences with environmental disruption and environmental policy?

Environmental disruption was already serious during the Meiji Era (1868-1912) due to industrialization and urbanization, especially in metropolitan areas such as Osaka and in mining areas such as Ashio (Iijima 1979; Tsuru 1989). In reviewing the history of pollution control policy in pre-war Japan, pioneering legislative initiatives such as the 1877 Regulations Concerning the Establishment of Manufacturing Plants in Osaka Prefecture stand out. This piece of legislation was quite progressive even by today's standards. In addition, effective pollution countermeasures and policies were executed in some areas. World War II, however, put an end to these developments.

Due to geographical conditions, there is an extremely high intensity of land utilization for industrial activity. Gross national product (GNP) per square kilometer of inhabitable area in Japan in 1978 was 12 times that of France and 30 times that of the USA. The around Tokyo was about 18 times the national average, indicating extremely high land use intensity in the nation's capital (Environment Agency 1983a, p. 52). In spite of the great potential for environmental and health damage from the high concentration of industrial activities near residential areas, pollution control policy was not considered necessary by government and industry during the 1950s. The government and industry were concerned with narrow growth-oriented economic policies (Chikyu Kankyo Keizai Kenkyukai 1991, pp. 28-48). As a result, *kogai* (pollution) problems became serious and eventually started to attract public attention.[1] Nowhere was the suffering from pollution diseases, such as Minamata, *itai-itai*, and Yokkaichi asthma, so acute as in Japan

(Chikyu Kankyo Keizai Kenkyukai 1991, pp. 28-48). The number of certified victims of pollution-related diseases totalled more than 100,000 in the Class I category, where multiple substances may contribute to a disease, and approximately 2,000 in the Class II category, where a single substance is linked to a disease, by the end of 1987 alone. The true number of pollution victims is certainly much higher (Tsuru 1999, p. 150).

One of the most infamous pollution incidents was Minamata mercury poisoning. The Chisso Corporation, located in Minamata, Kyushu, had an acetaldehyde plant, which generated methyl mercury during production. In May 1956 physicians at the factory's hospital reported to local health officials that 'an incident of inexplicable disease' had been discovered. Although this was reported in the local media and there was subsequently a decade of protest activities by afflicted fishermen, it was only in September 1968 that the Ministry of Health and Welfare announced officially that Minamata disease was 'caused by the methyl-mercury compound contained in the factory effluents of the Chisso Minamata factory,' (Ministry of Health and Welfare 1968). During this protracted period when the suffering of the victims was largely ignored, critical occasions to mitigate the damage were missed. The serious health damages (and even fatalities) caused by the contaminated wastewater from the Chisso company can be attributed not only to the company's negligence but also to the government's failure to respond to citizens' complaints.

Tragically, the government did not require pollution controls for industrial activities until environmental degradation was widespread and pollution-related diseases began affecting large numbers of people. Why was there such delay in the introduction of policy for the prevention of such serious environmental damage and illness? The answer is simple. The government was preoccupied with economic rehabilitation; damage to human health was a secondary concern.

Damage to health is irreversible; money cannot compensate for loss of health. While recognizing this fact, the Committee on Japan's Experience in the Battle against Air Pollution attempted to determine the cost in monetary terms of the government's delayed response. A simulation was conducted using the damage function:

health-related damage = health-related damage per victim x number of victims per ton of SO_2 emission volume x SO_2 emission volume

where health-related damage per victim and number of victims per ton of sulphur dioxide (SO_2) emission volume were estimated based on actual compensation data. Using this economic model, the committee estimated the optimal time when Japan should have introduced SO_2 reduction measures. The committee found that 'the economically rational timing for investment would have been approximately 8 years earlier. Japan should have executed air pollution response measures more quickly' (Committee on Japan's Experience in the Battle against Air Pollution 1997, pp. 88-90). For polluting companies, which by court order had to compensate pollution victims and restore environmentally damaged areas in the cases of Yokkaichi, Minamata, and *itai-itai* disease, a preventive approach based on government mandated pollution control would have proved much cheaper. This shows that allowing industries to pollute can not only adversely affect health, it is economically inefficient even in the narrowest sense of the term.

These are typical examples of government failure in the field of pollution control policy. The history of post-war Japan shows that in the pursuit of growth we have incurred absolute loss of human life and environment.[2] A paradigm shift is necessary: instead of thinking in terms of 'catastrophe and cure,' it would be more economical and healthful to incorporate environmental considerations into economic planning from the start.

SUCCESSFUL POLLUTION CONTROL EXAMPLES

During the economic miracle from 1946-76, the Japanese economy grew 55 times in size. This was the world's most rapid pace of industrial growth; the Japanese economy grew at a much faster pace than did the economies of other developed countries. This growth, however, resulted in severe *kogai*. Japan may well have had the world's worst industrial pollution problems.

Japanese pollution control policy changed drastically in the late 1960s and 1970s. Whereas there was virtually no policy intervention in the 1960s, in the 1970s Japan adopted relatively advanced environmental policies compared with other industrialized countries. Japan's pollution control policy in the 1970s is often considered quite successful and pioneering. There was a rapid reduction of SO_2 emissions, auto-gas regulation, and the application of the polluter pays principle (PPP) to stock pollutants. Below the limitations and economic implications of these policies are considered.

Reductions in SO_2 emissions from stationary sources[3]
Atmospheric concentrations of SO_2 rose from .015 parts per million (ppm) in 1960 to .060 ppm in 1965, as a result of rapid economic growth and a pollution-intensive industrial structure (Broadbent 1998, Figure 1.3; Environment Agency of Japan 1982). Intensive pollution caused asthma and other respiratory diseases at that time. Emissions of SO_2, for example, became the focus of the famous Yokkaichi asthma pollution case. This was one of the four major pollution cases that went to trial. In all four cases, the courts eventually ruled in favor of the plaintiffs (the pollution victims). Partly in response to these cases, the '*kogai* Parliament' of December 1970

mandated 14 strict regulatory pollution laws that helped Japan take important steps in the direction of strengthening environmental policies.

An SO_2 ambient standard was established in 1969 and strengthened in 1973. During this time the ambient standard in Japan was more stringent than the standard in any other country. In order to attain Japan's national ambient standard, emissions standards were introduced (which specified the quantity of pollutants discharged by given sources per unit of time). The response of Japanese firms to the SO_2 regulations was remarkable. Total national SO_2 emissions decreased from almost 5 million tons in 1970 to half this amount within only 5 years, falling to 1.143 million tons in the 1980s. This brought about the best ratio of SO_2 emissions per capita and per unit of gross domestic product (GDP) among industrialized countries (Broadbent 1998, pp. 14-15).

Consequently, after the mid-1960s, the concentration of SO_2 began a long decline, until it reached .015 ppm in 1980. Although many environmental problems, including nitrogen oxide (NO_x) air pollution, waste management, overcrowding and depopulation of some regions remained, this rapid reduction of SO_2 levels is remarkable, especially in international comparison. One of the main contributing factors to the reduction of SO_2 emissions per capita and per unit of GDP among industrialized countries from 1974-86 was fuel gas desulfurization. The adoption of desulfurization equipment was promoted through pollution control investment by private enterprises.

The introduction of the emissions standards at the beginning of the 1970s caused a rapid increase of investment in anti-pollution equipment and measures. The percentage of GNP invested by private enterprises in anti-pollution equipment was three times higher in Japan than in other industrialized countries. Another reason for such rapid growth in the adoption of desulfurization equipment was that the government assisted pollution control investment by private enterprises through various financing mechanisms. Although there has been no comprehensive and systematic study of the efficiency and the macroeconomic effect of pollution control policy on the Japanese economy, some studies suggest that air pollution control measures for SO_2 and nitrogen dioxide (NO_2) at stationary sources have had little or no negative impact on Japan's economic growth, employment, currency stability and export rates (Organization for Economic Cooperation and Development 1977a, p. 84).

Favorable interest loans for research and development (R&D) and investment in pollution control equipment are granted by specialized institutions such as the Japan Development Bank (JDB), Small Business Finance Corporation (SBFC), People's Finance Corporation, and Environmental Pollution Control Service Corporation. These organizations, which are supervised and regulated by the Ministry of International Trade and Industry (MITI, now the Ministry of Economy, Trade, and Industry

(METI)), allocate public funds to private firms to cover pollution control costs (Organization for Economic Cooperation and Development 1977a, p. 74). Japanese environmental policy also gives assistance to private enterprises investing in anti-pollution equipment through a virtual subsidization policy. This takes the form of tax benefits and favorable interest loans. For example, there is a 59 per cent special depreciation in the first year for pollution abatement equipment, a reduction in the commodity tax for low pollution automobiles, a subsidy for the promotion of desulfurization in the form of a reduction in customs duty on imported crude oil that is desulfurized, and lending programs that offer favorable interest loans for anti-pollution control.

R&D subsidies were composed of direct subsidies at the stage of research and experiment and favorable interest loans and special depreciations for firms putting new technology to practical use. R&D funds were supplied with a 66-75 per cent subsidization rate in the 1970s, far better than the normal rate of 50 per cent. Similarly, through the R&D subsidy system managed by the Small and Medium Enterprise Agency (SMEA), R&D funds for pollution abatement were granted at a rate of 75 per cent (the normal rate was 50 per cent). The JDB and SBFC gave favorable interest loans to firms attempting to use new technologies. The JDB advanced funds mainly to large corporations that had R&D programs for the development of rotary or Compound Vortex Controlled Combustion engines and equipment for desulfurization and denitrification.

Tax incentives were also used to promote environmental protection. Special depreciation permitted firms to delay payment of taxes on corporate profits. This had the effect of allowing firms to borrow funds without interest. The reduction of, or exemption from, fixed property taxes played an important role in encouraging investment in pollution control equipment, because such equipment often needs large plant and stock yards.

Favorable interest loans and tax incentives have been used by MITI, the Agency of Industrial Science and Technology and the SMEA, all of which are semi-independent organizations under MITI (now METI) and share the aim of developing Japanese industry. These government ministries and agencies shared a similar policy style. They set policy targets and then mobilized resources using public finance instruments in order to obtain them. In the case of economic development policy, the shared target was to realize a targeted economic growth rate in order to catch up with Western countries. In the case of pollution control policy, the policy target was to attain a stipulated ambient standard in order to resolve societal conflict. Both were done through a combination of regulation and financial investments and loans. Both are inherent parts of Japan's industrial policy that was premised on the notion of 'get dirty, then clean-up' (Poole 1988, p. 78).

Both the rapid growth in the economy and the subsequent rapid introduction of pollution control technologies attest to the effectiveness with which this policy style, of setting targets and mobilizing national resources to attain them, worked in Japan. It is important to realize that there were some special resources that ministries could turn to for revenue when implementing policies. One rather unique source is known as the 'second budget,' an annual source of revenue derived from postal savings (Lee 1999, pp. 30-48).

Government ministries are able to draw on this budget, providing them with some flexibility and making them somewhat less accountable to the public when using these funds. This policy style was responsible for both the increase in pollution due to rapid economic growth and Japan's subsequent quick success in responding to and controlling pollution.

Economic effects of auto-gas regulation[4]

The story of how regulations placed on automotive exhaust affected the Japanese and American auto industries is particularly interesting. Automakers and the industries associated with them accounted for about 10 per cent of Japan's GDP in the mid-1970s and together form a framework that supports the Japanese economy. By the late 1960s though, the production and widespread sale of autos was causing an escalation in social costs in such forms as polluted air, excessive noise, traffic jams, and accidents, all of which had to be endured by the public. Gradually it became apparent that environmental countermeasures were needed, especially to curb the release of air pollutants.

In 1972 the Environment Agency of Japan announced a policy limiting the volume of automobile exhaust gases based on the amended United States Clean Air Act. The so-called Muskie Law aimed at reducing carbon monoxide (CO) and hydrocarbon concentrations in automobile exhaust to one-tenth of contemporary levels by 1975, and NO_x levels to one-tenth by 1976. The 1975 standards were to be fully enforced. The 1976 standards, however, encountered resistance from automobile companies that asked for substantial easing of the standards on the grounds that they would be difficult to implement for technical reasons. The research department of the Japan Industrial Bank applied a cost benefit analysis performed by the National Academy of Sciences to this issue and reached the following conclusion: 'If automobile emissions standards are implemented, it will unavoidably: 1) push up automobile prices, 2) increase fuel consumption and 3) lower vehicle performance. Therefore, the demand for automobiles will decrease, many related businesses will suffer adverse effects, and annual production will decline by 82,700 million yen; this will cause a total loss of 94,000 jobs, which, in addition to adverse effects on the international account balance, will have major adverse effects on the national economy. It is important that we have cautious, scientific discussion on the matter, and not be dominated by emotions,' (Hanayama 1978, pp. 95-9). As a result, the central government instructed the Central Council for Environmental Pollution Control to re-examine the policy.

Public opinion, however, reacted strongly against any re-examination of the policy. The seven major cities of Tokyo, Kawasaki, Yokohama, Nagoya, Kyoto, Osaka and Kobe organized research groups on automobile exhaust control to inquire into the matter.[5] Automobile companies were asked to present their prospective compliance dates and to explain their cases regarding the technical feasibility of meeting the 1976 standard. As a result of the hearings it became apparent that only two major automobile companies were insisting that meeting the deadline was difficult on technical grounds and that the other companies had already developed technologies to satisfy the 1976 standard. A research group organized by seven major cities published a report that concluded the proposed 1976 standard was technically achievable. The report also set forth the social responsibility of automobile companies to develop new approaches to raise fuel efficiency and obtain needed pollution abatement technology (Hanayama 1978, pp. 95-9). In the end, the pressure from the environmental policy standards supported by social pressure encouraged technological development.

The outcome of this regulatory battle was a leap forward in technological expertise. Though the automakers eventually received a two-year reprieve, by the time the regulations went into effect in 1978, they had effectively reduced the levels of poisonous auto emissions to clear the stringent policy standards. Moreover, this was done in such a way as to not burn fuel wastefully. Japanese compact cars became the world leaders in fuel economy. Seen in a broader perspective, the pressure toward technological innovation to meet the government's requirements became a catalyst for the auto industry to move forward in international competition as seen by the advance of Japanese cars into the USA and other overseas markets (Miyamoto 1989, pp. 155-6).

Events unfolded in a very different direction in the USA. When the Clean Air Act Amendments were unveiled they were hailed as revolutionary. The amendments had a provision permitting the postponement of an enforcement date however, and the National Academy of Sciences was charged with the duty of conducting studies to determine whether the necessary technologies could be developed on schedule. When the opinion was set forth that the standards would in fact damage the US auto industry, the postponement clause was promptly employed. In addition, the US government received a report from the Academy indicating that attaining the target would involve technological difficulties. The government then postponed the final stage of tightening regulations for a period that extended to five years. Ironically, this attempt to provide protection had a reverse effect. The postponement allowed

US automakers to continue producing dirty vehicles that consumed great quantities of gas. This contributed to a relative decline in the overall competitiveness of US cars and boosted the popularity of Japanese cars in the USA market (Miyamoto 1989, p155-6). In other Japanese industries as well, the 1970s were a time when efforts to meet tough standards gave birth to numerous pollution control technologies. Until then it had been taken as an article of faith that the imposition of environmental regulations would sap the vitality of industry and retard the economic growth rate. But as the contrast between the Japanese and US auto industries makes clear, there are at least some cases where a compelling need for stricter controls will generate demand for new technologies, accelerate the speed of innovation, and ultimately make an industry more dynamic. As with production technologies, necessity is the mother of invention; social needs for environmental protection can drive anti-pollution expertise forward.

The Organization for Economic Cooperation and Development (OECD) Environment Committee issued the following statement: 'The possibilities of science and technology are such that they extend the frontiers of rationality. A rational decision is a decision that takes into consideration costs and benefits; the trouble is that it is not only very difficult to determine benefits (i.e. damages avoided), it is often impossible to estimate costs. Costs of processes that have not yet been invented cannot be estimated. They are often said to be very high or even infinite ('it can't be done'), but may well turn out to be reasonable. They are, moreover, often based on overestimated costs. The Japanese experience in the field of pollution abatement lends support to the idea that to a large extent it is not technology that should constrain policy choices, but policy choices that should constrain technology' (Organization for Economic Cooperation and Development 1977a, pp. 85-6).

The experience of Japan's auto industry was of precisely this sort and can be offered to the world as a lesson on the benefits of enforcing rigid standards. For that matter, other industries had much the same experience: as stricter regulations came into force, they came up with one innovation after another in the field of pollution control technology, eventually becoming forerunners in 'ecobusiness.' Thanks to these developments in the 1970s, Japan's anti-pollution devices rank among the world's best. Japan's experience with environmental regulation and competitiveness provide an example of the Porter hypothesis – that environmental regulations increase firms' competitiveness (Porter and Linde 1995, 119-32).

To sum up this period as one in which regulations always led to technological innovations and enhanced competitive power would be overstating the case. After all, regulations affected some companies and industries far more than others and promoted changes in the industrial structure of the entire economy (Jänicke and Weidner 1995, p. 18). No doubt there were also various cases in which companies shifted plants overseas in a bid to escape anti-pollution initiatives and moves to strengthen pollution regulations at home. In some cases, Japanese companies sought new sites for factories in developing countries that had not yet experienced much damage from pollution, placed their highest priority on development, and had only uncoordinated and ineffectual pollution control policies and standards.

If Japan's experience is to be effectively communicated to the developing world, quantitative analysis must be conducted on the overall response by industries and companies to environmental controls. The studies should strive to ascertain domestic circumstances and international surroundings. Factors that will affect individual businesses facing the need to comply with new standards should also be considered. In certain scenarios, businesses must make a choice between developing pollution control technologies and shifting production offshore. It is imperative that researchers clarify how conditions like these differ from one industry to the next. It is also important to study how industries are being altered over the long term by the globalization of business, the advent of the information age, and other major shifts in the configuration of the economy.

PAYING FOR POLLUTION CONTROL AND VICTIM COMPENSATION

One method to make enterprises more responsible for damages caused to the environment by their activities is to include a monetary assessment of environmental losses in the costs of production. This procedure is known as internalization of externalities and/or social cost. Calculating the costs of environmental disruptions and including them in the production costs of an enterprise serves as the foundation of an economic approach to external diseconomies such as environmental pollution.

Extending the scope of the costs of an enterprise to include externalities is essential to address the failure of the market mechanism to deal adequately with the environment. The regulated internalization of costs by private corporations due to environmental losses is known as the PPP. Generally, this principle has been adopted by all developed economies. Its aim is to hold the producer as the first entity responsible for covering the cost of environmental damage it creates. It does not mean that the producer ought to be the sole party responsible for the costs, but that the business ought to be aware of the negative effects of its production. Environmental expenses can be shifted to consumer prices and reduced as a result of improvements in technology. It is important that these calculations be taken into consideration when major economic decisions are made by corporations.

The PPP was originally introduced in 1972 by the OECD as an economic principle in order to prevent distortions in international trade and improve the allocation of resources (Organization for Economic Cooperation and Development 1977a, p. 20). Its aim was not originally to condemn or to punish the producer for losses incurred to the environment. The PPP can be suspended when it leads to disturbances in international trade. The form and scope of its implementation is left solely to governments to determine.

The OECD report pointed to the PPP as one of the salient features of Japanese environmental policy (Organization for Economic Cooperation and Development 1977a, p. 20). In Japan, the principle is not understood as a 'polluter pays principle' but rather as a 'punish polluters principle,' which suggests that polluters are guilty, and must be punished. In this sense, the report asserted that Japanese environmental policy was largely non-economic and not based on economic theory. However, as we have already pointed out, the Japanese government also encouraged producers (polluters) to adhere to environmental protection policies through tax incentives, subsidies, and low-interest loans. Comparing government subsidies to outlays by private enterprises in response to the PPP, it is evident that financial aid to polluting enterprises from the public sector was far greater than the money offered by individual enterprises for pollution control (Miyamoto 1981, p. 252). This shows that the PPP has not been applied strictly to pollution control policies. Another unique experience in pollution control policy in Japan is the pioneering application of the PPP to the health damage compensation system and the restoration of polluted areas. Who is to be compensated and how, and who is the one to compensate and how, were questions that had to be answered by administratively determined rules.

Pollution-related Health Damage Compensation

The pollution-related Health Damage Compensation System is essentially a levy (and, thus, will be referred to hereafter as compensation levy (CL)). Its main purpose is to secure the level of funding dictated by compensation requirements; levy receipts are decided first, and then a levy rate is set. Emitters of SO_2 do not know at the time of emission exactly what the levy rate will be. Although the original recommendation by the Central Council for Environmental Pollution Control was to consider NO_2, particulates and SO_2 as pollutants under the compensation scheme, levies were not imposed on NO_x and other presumably health-deteriorative pollutants. The health damages covered by the CL framework are stipulated as cumulative and irreversible. Yet the entire burden of compensation disbursements is imposed on emitters in the (time (t)-1) year even though health damages in any fiscal year will be partly the result of emissions in the (t-2) year and earlier. In the process of collecting levies, the identity of polluters is kept secret. While SO_2

emitting firms outside the designated areas are also called upon to pay the levy, pollution victims outside of designated areas are not eligible to receive compensation under this system.

Viewed in light of the PPP, the CL framework is unique in several ways. The PPP was the first method in the world institutionalized as a way of compensating pollution victims. However where polluters share a collective responsibility, the PPP is not as effective as the CL framework, especially in cases where the responsible polluters are not identified (Tsuru 1999, p. 148). Admittedly, the CL system places an unfair burden on current emitters of SO_2. At the same time, the amount of compensation (levies) may be virtually unresponsive to even major decreases in SO_2 emissions. This is accentuated by the fact that compensation is driven by total requests made by applicants; as the program becomes better known requests will likely expand. The amount of stipulated compensation is both independent of current SO_2 emissions and, as suggested before, tends to induce expansion of the levy rate.

The converse is that excessive burdens placed on current emitters of SO_2 may serve as a deterrent to polluters. In general, if the amount of compensation for damage is averaged over polluting emissions, the levy rate becomes lower than the marginal damage cost of such emissions (the rate of a Pigouvian tax), thereby inviting a greater-than-optimal level of pollution (Hamada 1977, pp. 97-9). But in cases where damage is cumulative and irreversible, past pollution problems were serious, and total compensation is covered by a levy on current emissions, the levy rate could exceed the Pigouvian tax rate. Levy rates were designed in accordance with the need for funds, with adjustments made to allocate the burden between stationary and mobile sources of emissions and among various areas. It is theoretically possible for levy rates to be higher than the corresponding Pigouvian tax, but whether the implemented levy rates provide an anti-pollution incentive to enterprises requires independent empirical analysis.[6]

A Japanese-oriented Approach to the PPP

Independent of OECD discussions on the PPP, a Japanese oriented PPP was created in the early 1970s. The Japanese PPP was developed in response to Japan's unique experiences and policies: the PPP was interpreted in Japan not simply as an economic principle but as a principle of justice and fairness. The scope of the principle's application widened to include restoration of contaminated land in addition to the original framework idea of relief for victims. The main reason the widened interpretation of the PPP was accepted was that the actual pollution problems confronting Japan were beyond the scope of the OECD's framing of responsibility.

The kind of 'stock pollution' that affected Japan in the 1960s and 1970s and the cost of that pollution were not easily dealt with under the OECD's formulation of the PPP. Examples of stock pollution include the pollution of rice fields because of cadmium that contaminated irrigation waters (Yoshida, Hata and Tonegawa 1999, pp. 215-29) and the hazardous waste pollution that contaminated soils in the Love Canal in the USA in the late 1970s. This type of stock pollution can be found everywhere in the world. Determining who should be held financially accountable for the restoration of contaminated land has become a very critical issue in many countries. In the case of Japan, the Pollution Control Public Works Cost Allocation Law was enacted in 1975 and was applied to cases where there was a need for restoration of contaminated land. It was pioneering in the sense that this was the first application of the PPP to stock pollution. This idea was followed by the Superfund Law which was enacted in the USA in 1978.

Under the framework used by the Pollution Control Public Works Cost Allocation Law to determine the cost allocation for the restoration of contaminated lands, restoration projects were conducted by the public sector. These projects became government public works projects run by the central or local governments. The costs for the projects were shared among polluting enterprises according to their particular pollution contribution rates. In cases of contaminated lands, it is often not easy to locate all polluting enterprises that should be held responsible. In some cases, polluting enterprises have even gone bankrupt by the time the pollution is discovered. In those cases, the public sector has to pay the cost of restoring contaminated land.

This is quite different from the Superfund Law where polluters and/or responsible parties such as landowners are liable for pollution damages. The USA does not turn these into public works projects because it is less inclined to spend public funds than is Japan. Potentially responsible parties including not only polluters but also owners of contaminated land have to pay the clean- up cost. While the pioneering application of PPP to stock pollution in Japan has been admirable, it is clearly necessary at times to modify it to incorporate the use of public funds to pay restoration costs (Ueta 1992, pp. 179-97).

A similarly widened application of the PPP has been necessary for the design of mandatory waste recycling systems. The OECD proposed the concept of extended producer responsibility (EPR), which means that the producer has to take at least some responsibility for collecting and recycling wastes associated with their products. While the relationship between the EPR and the PPP concepts remains controversial, the EPR is clearly a version of the PPP (Organization for Economic Cooperation and Development 2001, p. 21). The PPP has been applied to an increasingly wide array of environmental issues and in the process it has become necessary to redefine what is meant by 'the polluter pays.'

Environmental Problem Shifting

The response of polluters to pollution control policies has varied. There were considerable positive and even proactive responses to environmental regulations in Japan, including substantive technological innovation. However, there was also environmental problem shifting. Environmental problem shifting can take various forms. It can involve changing a medium, such as the passing of waste from water to sludge. It can involve shifting the time factor by, for example, diluting waste. It can also entail substitute shifting, such as altering the public's energy preferences from fossil fuel to nuclear power. Finally, another serious yet common shift involves moving an environmental problem from one region or country to another.

This discussion is pertinent for the environmental and resource issues facing Asian countries such as Thailand, Malaysia, Taiwan, and Japan (Ueta 1992, pp. 198-9). The relationship between environmental disruption in these areas and the economy, companies, and the lifestyles of the Japanese people is deeply rooted. Foreign investment among Thailand, Malaysia, Taiwan, and Japan greatly affects the accountability of polluters and the ability of victims or governments to require damage compensation. Pollution exports in the form of environmental disruption through direct foreign investment are often tied to the advance of multinational corporations into regions where there are weak environmental controls. This form of pollution export is hardly on the decline. Economic globalization has added to the complexity of Asia's environmental problems. Since the mid-1980s, governments have encouraged foreign direct investment in domestic industries and in the process have become dependent on multinational corporations for a significant portion of their economic output.

An infamous example of pollution export occurred when the Japanese Joint Corporation ARE, which set up operations in Malaysia, was charged with releasing radioactive waste and ordered by a regional high court in 1992 to stop factory operation (Ueta 1996, p. 173). The unfortunate reality is that the amount of investment in pollution control equipment overseas is generally less than the domestic figure, and many overseas production facilities operate with absolutely no air pollution control equipment. It is clear that the environmental double standard that exists between developed and developing countries is firmly entrenched. Another example of pollution export occurred in Taiwan in a region that takes in exported Japanese 'waste products.' These 'waste products' consist of old batteries and personal computers, which are disassembled for the recovery of valuable materials such as lead, platinum, and palladium.

Reprocessing operations were originally carried out in Japan until rising labor costs and increasingly tough environmental standards made these businesses less and less profitable. Thus given that Japan took advantage (and is still taking advantage) of gaps in labor costs and pollution control, export of 'waste products' is a more accurate term to apply than simply 'products.' Indeed, factories that reprocess Japanese batteries are now a major source of lead pollution. According to one study carried out by a group of professors at the National Taiwan University (Zhang 1989), mental aptitude indices for children at kindergartens in the vicinity of such reprocessing facilities are significantly lower than average and blood level contamination by lead is significantly higher. The only possible source of this contamination is the reprocessing facilities. This situation has rapidly become a salient social and political issue, receiving wide coverage in the Taiwanese press.[7]

To help combat this problem, the Taiwanese government established regulations in 1990 prohibiting the import of used sulfuric acid batteries. As a result, the composition of lead scrap exports from Japan (the official category in trade statistics, although used batteries comprise the bulk of such scrap) shifted dramatically. In 1989, a total of 67.1 per cent of such exports were bound for Taiwan, with a mere 4.1 per cent going to Indonesia. By contrast, in 1990 the Taiwanese component fell to 37.5 per cent, with Indonesia's portion rising sharply to 34.6 per cent (Ueta 1992, p. 199).

The change in destination countries was instigated by Taiwanese regulations, and serves as proof that hazardous waste tends to flow across borders from countries with tough environmental regulations to countries with weak regulations, or, stated differently, from high-cost locations to low-cost ones. This is an example of an international, hierarchical 'billiard ball effect.' Effective solutions will require for starters the construction of a pan-Asian international environmental protection framework consisting of a common Asian body of environmental regulations and the establishment of a corresponding environmental management organization.

The changes brought about by Taiwan's decision are indicative of an international 'pollution hierarchy.' Addressing the root causes of environmental disruption in Asia will necessitate employing at least a pan-Asian, if not a global, cooperative approach. The Japanese government, individual companies, and non-governmental organizations will be required to play a major role in this process. This relationship extends beyond secondary industry to primary and tertiary industries. Japan is the world's largest consumer of tropical lumber, accounting for almost 40 per cent of worldwide trade. In 1989 it imported approximately 20 million cubic meters, primarily in log form (Ueta, Ochiai, Kitabatake and Teranishi 1991, p. 240). Japan is being pushed to take responsibility for tropical forest protection. This is not merely because of its economic status and power, but because the cutting of tropical forests has a direct connection with the Japanese economy, companies, and lifestyle.

The issues of tropical lumber and forests is almost prototypical of North – South problems centering on primary industrial products, clearly illustrating the relation between importing, consuming, developed countries, and exporting, producing, developing countries. Tropical lumber is an object of trade despite the fact that the costs of forest regeneration are not being included in prices. Consequently, the problems that require consideration are neither the theory of free trade as propounded by developed countries nor sovereignty over resources as stressed by developing countries, but rather that the sustainability of tropical lumber cannot be guaranteed under the current free trade system and a system of national sovereignty over resources.

Japan's way of life with regard to food is also broadly connected to Asia. About one-third of Japan's total food imports are of fishery products, half of which come from Asia. For example, air freight imports of tuna, which stood at 15,000 tons in 1985, had nearly tripled to 43,000 tons just six years later in 1991. Taiwan and Indonesia alone shipped 68 per cent of this figure. There may be a short-term economic gain for Asian economies inspired by Japan's massive imports of fishery products in support of its rich eating habits. On the other hand, it cannot be denied that the situation has changed Asian food production patterns and destroyed traditional food-related ways of life. The people of the Association of Southeast Asian Nations (ASEAN) countries will soon begin to face a seafood shortage as a result of wanton overfishing. This can be seen as nothing other than the sacrifice of future social benefits for the sake of short-term private profits.

The Tokyo fish market controls an overwhelming proportion of the international trade in shrimp and prawns, such that 40 per cent of exports worldwide arrive there. All over Asia, mangroves, important in the preservation of coastal land, are being destroyed so that shrimp farms can be constructed. To allow the water temperature management required for more efficient cultivation, water is pumped from underground, often leading to land subsidence. This kind of environmental disruption is not hard to address from a technological standpoint, but the monopolistic element introduced into the international market by the power of Japanese buyers means that countermeasures are difficult to initiate. Countermeasures require the costs of pollution prevention be included in the individual asking price for shrimp.

Primary industries should practice environmentally sound resource use. Unfortunately, primary industries all too often engage in wasteful resource use and environmentally destructive practices. This makes it difficult to implement environmental policy (Walden and Rosenfield 1990, p. 14). It is clear that the Japanese economy, companies, and lifestyle are intimately connected with environmental disruption and resource depletion in Asia. Doubtless, this trend will become stronger as rapid economic growth in Asia continues to be fueled by the internationalization of the Japanese economy. The question remains as to how Japan ought to confront these problems.

CONCLUSION

In many respects the Japanese pollution experience is rather unique. Cases of health damage have led to the development of a precautionary principle. In general one can say that Japan has responded positively to pollution control involving technological innovation and the application of a uniquely Japanese version of the PPP. In addition, environmental regulations have been used as a catalyst to increase firms' competitiveness, as the automobile industry clearly demonstrated. At the same time, there have been more negative reactions, such as environmental problem shifting. An effective critique must take into account both positive and negative responses to environmental issues and seek to integrate and understand them. The task for the future must be addressing and understanding the barriers to successful pollution control policy.

NOTES

[1] The word *kogai* first appears in the 'Rivers Act' of 1896 and the ordinance of Osaka Prefecture and is rendered in English as 'disamenities inflicted on the public' (Tsuru 1999, p. 23).

[2] On the terminology and concept of 'absolute loss', see Miyamoto (1989, p. 111).

[3] This section depends heavily on Hamamoto and Ueta (1996, pp. 73-89).

[4] This section draws upon Ueta (1993, pp. 30-49) and Ueta (1995, pp. 55-67).

[5] Local initiatives in the field of environmental policy in Japan in the 1960s and early 1970s were quite unique in form and powerful in terms of effect (Ueta 1993, pp. 30-49).

[6] The empirical analysis was done by Matsuno and Ueta (2000, pp. 194-214).

[7] See, for example, *Zhonggou Shibao*, 26 February 1990.

5. Japan's Environmental Politics: Recognition and Response Processes

Jeffrey Broadbent

INTRODUCTION

The chapters in this book amply demonstrate Japan's success in addressing some severe environmental problems, but they also show it has ignored others. Japan has surprising capacity for coordinated action. Between the end of World War II and 1965, Japan produced the world's most rapid economic growth rates. But during that time, its growing and unregulated industries also produced the world's fastest growing rates of pollution, for example sulfur dioxide (SO_2) air pollution. Yet, from 1965-80, Japan adroitly changed direction and reduced SO_2 air pollution far more rapidly and thoroughly than the USA, England, France or West Germany (Broadbent 1998, p. 15). Moreover, the air stayed better for decades. However, in a further contrast, Japan did not respond to all its industrial pollution with the same alacrity. Japan did relatively little, for instance, to control the dumping of toxic waste. Why did Japan respond to some pollution problems, such as air and water pollution, so quickly and effectively yet ignore other environmental problems, like toxic waste and landscape degradation? The answer lies in the social and political processes that channeled the response to environmental problems, from recognition to policy implementation. Not only government by itself, but also many organizations and the general public played contributing, though often conflictual, roles in these processes. This chapter will examine the social and political processes that produced Japan's array of environmental successes and failures, and from that examination, draw some lessons for those who would protect the environment in other, especially developing countries.

The examination of process requires a close look at the shifting balance of support for different environmental issues and policies, the power held by the various 'stakeholders', the understandings and institutions that informed and channeled their efforts, and the mechanisms and instruments that implemented the resulting policies. The organizations, interest groups and institutions typical of capitalist industrial democracies – parties, parliaments, ministries, the media, business, labor, the public, non-governmental organizations (NGOs) and protest movements – all existed in Japan. They interacted not only in pursuit of their own often divergent interests, but also through the media of existing understandings and loyalties, institutional channels and informal relationships of power. To understand the environmental outcomes, we need to examine the patterns in the processes that shaped them.

Formal institutions such as the existing bureaucratic divisions, the voting and parliamentary systems and the legal system allocated formal authority over political decisions. But, informal institutions, such as accustomed networks of collaboration, also provided levers of power. At the same time, these organizations and interest groups understood and evaluated the world according to their usual attitudes, beliefs and values, so that the political process also depended upon these cultural aspects. These various social and cultural conditions interacted with the mounting environmental effects wrought by rapid industrial growth and urbanization to produce a distinct set of policy outcomes.

Any process of political decision-making has both relatively widespread or generic and relatively local or particular aspects. Many nations have dealt with generic environmental problems such as air pollution, for instance, but they have often responded in their own ways. Japan has been no different.[1] Japan's environmental response processes reflected its particular sets of interested groups – not only government, but business, labor and civil society – and also its patterns of interests (ideal and material) and institutions. Together, these formed a particular distribution of power. Interested groups had to work through existing institutional and cultural contexts. In any nation, these principles indicate that good environmental management involves the whole society.

At the time when Japan developed its first environmental policies, power was, for a democracy, highly concentrated within the three dominant elites – top government officials, ruling political party leaders and business peak associations. These three formed a closely tied (though internally competitive) 'elite community'. Which of the three 'really' dominated the others has long been debated. But most scholars agree that, in contrast to the powerful, elite triad, the ordinary people of Japan, at least in terms of formal political participation, have been relatively weak. The typical participatory vehicles of the Euro-American democracies, such as autonomous civic associations formed around issues and citizen referenda, only started to achieve much presence in the mid-1990s. In their place, the muffled demands, if not adroitly coopted by the ruling triad, have found expression in sporadic movement outbursts. Over the decades since World War II, though, ordinary citizens, when pressed by community health and well-being problems, such as pollution, have increasingly pushed back against unresponsive governments, parties and businesses. In so doing, they gradually expanded their awareness and use of the democratic potentials inherent in their post-War democratic constitution.

As this political sketch already indicates, a given policy response is not just a 'reflection' of what a physical, environmental problem may require for its solution (such as a reduction in a certain pollutant). It also depends upon the possibilities allowed by the existing social and political system, defined broadly as above. Accordingly, to understand how Japan came to have certain environmental policies and instruments, we have to assess not only the 'objective' environmental situation, but also the complex political process that reacted to (and indeed before that, produced) the environmental situations. Clearly, in thinking about transferring a given policy to another nation, we have to consider the possibilities in that light. If that nation lacks certain crucial background political conditions that made the policy work in Japan, the chances for success would diminish. Even if successful in Japan, the same environmental policies might not garner the needed political support to operate well in another country. Alternatively, though, our understanding of these necessary political conditions could help us modify the policy so that it would stand a better chance of success in the new setting. Such is the hope and potential utility of this study.

Environmental management may sound like a bureaucratic job. During the implementation stage of formal policies, bureaucracies often do much of the work. But before implementation, policy-making proceeds through recognition (of a problem) to response (political processes leading to policies). After initial implementation, to make a permanent change, the policy must be steadfast and not fade into neglect. Problem recognition, policy-making response, policy implementation and policy durability make up the four general stages of the political process. This total process extends far beyond the apparatus of formal policy-making. It involves interested groups throughout society, and often from abroad. Understanding the processes that led to Japan's environmental policies requires tracing their emergence through all four stages of the political process.

FOUR STAGES OF THE POLITICAL PROCESS

The success of an environmental policy and instrument (mechanism) depends upon its fit with the situation, not only the environmental situation but also the social and political one. To discover the relation between policy and process, this chapter analyzes a number of Japan's environmental response processes. The chapter follows a more general set of four stages that societies typically undergo in response to environmental (and societal) problems: problem recognition, policy-making response, policy implementation and the durability or 'sticking power' of the policy. Not all environmental solutions come about through formal government policy, of course. Within these four general stages, autonomous business and public responses must be considered as well.

Stage 1: Problem Recognition

Problem recognition is the process by which individuals and groups define and attach meaning to, or frame, a situation (Gamson 1992; Snow and Benford 1992). Concerning environmental problems, recognition involves labeling an ecological change as an environmental issue having a good or bad meaning.[2] In attaching meaning, people 'frame' or 'construct' the problem (Keck and Sikkink 1998, p. 4; Hannigan 1995). People soak the issue with belief and meaning, imbuing it with weight and legitimacy. This meaning touches on moral and material interests, and either impels or repels action. Framing factory smoke as 'progress,' for instance, generates popular support, while framing it as 'pollution' generates resistance. Given their power, frames easily become political tools. They usually start with a few people and then spread until they threaten existing frames and engender frame conflict (such as is found in contrasting political speeches). Stage 1 alerts us that the meaning of any given ecological situation is not given; it is not a 'fact' obvious to all. Its meaning is given by people; an environmental problem is a social construction (Hannigan 1995).

Stage 2: Policy-making Response

Policy-making response is the process by which a group (movement, organization, business, or nation) 'makes up its mind' about how to respond to a given problem and its frames. Formal institutions partly define the course of policy-making: democracies are more open to citizen opinion than dictatorships. However, even democracies exhibit cross-national variations in openness (Kriesi, et al. 1995) and in the location of dominant decision-making power (such as in ministries, legislatures or courts). The location of the core of power in Japan remains a much debated issue. Many scholars argue that core power lies with the relatively autonomous government ministries, purveyed by their persuasive ties to business and other sectors of society (Evans 1995; Broadbent and Ishio 1998; Broadbent 2001). Other scholars give greater weight to the ruling political party. In either situation, with long-lasting dominance by a powerful elite, popular policies can become largely symbolic – intended to quiet down the outsiders while keeping benefits flowing to the insiders. However, under sufficient outside pressure, policies can become serious, redistributing actual benefits including environmental quality (Edelman 1977). In any case, the move from recognition to policy-making in the environmental field often becomes a highly contested process.

Stage 3: Policy Implementation

Policy implementation is the process by which a decision-making body attempts to get the target population to follow the new policy. States (and other organizations) vary in their capacity to implement policy (Kitschelt 1986). Success in implementation depends upon the delivery vehicle as well as the design of the 'instrument'. Policy often fails to reach its target intact due to incompetence or corruption (Pressman and Wildavsky 1973). Even if implemented properly, the instrument has to motivate the target actors to change their ways. To work, the instrument has to fit the societal context. Market-based emissions trading, for instance, may reduce air pollution in the USA, but not in China. Ministerial guidance may work in Japan, but not in the USA.

Stage 4: Policy Durability

Policy durability refers to the stability of the new policy and its effects. If setting up a new and effective environmental regime is a national 'learning process' (Social Learning Group 2001), how well do the lessons stick? Once put in place, do the new environmental rules and practices become firmly institutionalized, taken-for-granted habits and expectations, as the theory of ecological modernization would hope (Mol and Sonnenfeld 2000)? Or, if not, are they at least continually enforced? Or, do they fade away, gradually eroded by resistance from the regulated who 'capture' and neutralize the responsible government agency (Sabatier 1975)? In the latter case, each new environmental problem may be equally contested, frames and practices shifting in a perpetual see-saw battle between pro and con interest groups (Schnaiberg and Gould 1994).[3] In general terms, these four stages apply to any problem in any country, society, organization, or group. Yet, they take on specific qualities for each country and situation, depending upon cultural and social patterns, interested groups including movements, as well as institutions and historical timing.

HISTORICAL PERIODS OF JAPAN'S DEVELOPMENT

Japan's response to environmental problems went through four historical periods, with both stable and changing aspects. Chapter 2 divides the history of Japanese environmental policy formation into three periods: I. Classic Age (1955-73), II. Transition (1974-87) and III. New Age (1988-). In turn, the

Classic Age can be divided into two parts: A. 'Unrestrained Pollution' (1955-67) and B. 'Environmental Reform' (1967-75). This further division cuts Japan's (post-World War II) environmental politics into four major historical periods: I. A, I. B, II and III. Each of these historical periods exhibited a different typical content for each stage of its environmental reaction process (Table 5.1). This chapter will focus on the first three periods, when most of the policies discussed in this book were made and implemented.

Table 5.1 Japan's Environmental Response by Historical Period

Period	Classic A	Classic B	Transition	New Age
Stage	(1955-67)	(1967-75)	(1975-88)	(1988-)
Recognition	Movements	Elites	Bureaucratic	Various
Policy-making	Little	Reform	Pragmatic	Global
Implementation	Little	Demand	Cooperation	Diffuse
Durability	N.A.	High	Mixed	Unclear

During the first three periods (until 1988):

• The political and social dynamics of environmental response evolved around a fairly stable axis of political institutions, as described in the next section.
• As a general rule, the initial recognition of environmental problems tended to come from the victims, not from experts or government agencies.
• Japan's environmental policy-making typically occurred through inter-elite negotiation under external pressure.
• The implementation of the policies was usually discretionary cooperative implementation.
• The durability of reforms, while relatively high, depended upon the political orientation of the government (local or national) charged with administering the law.

In the fourth period, from 1988 onwards, a number of important shifts, especially due to globalization, changed the process and content of Japan's environmental response. Since most of the policies discussed in this book were made during the first three periods, space considerations prevent a full treatment of the fourth period.[4]

To understand Japan's response qualities requires first a sketch of the general distribution of power in Japan. Then we can turn to a more detailed look at the key response processes in historical periods I. A, I. B and II.

POLITICS, SOCIETY AND IDEOLOGY IN JAPAN

In Japan as in many countries, the formal political institutions do not adequately describe the real channels of power. The exact nature of those channels remains a hotly debated topic. Most scholars agree, though, that real decisions are at most *modified, but not really made*, by public debate in the legislature (the Diet). Rather, real decisions are made in direct negotiation between the members of the dominant triad – government officials, party politicians and the representatives of powerful interest groups, in particular, the business associations (Masumi 1995). These elites, as a whole and in segments, go through complicated phases of cooperation and conflict. They all feel a relatively strong sense of nationalism and ethnic solidarity though, and are tied up in social obligations to each other, which moderates their conflicts (Broadbent 1998, pp. 348-50).

In formal terms, Japan's political institutions consist of a bicameral elected legislature (the Diet) with a Prime Minister (selected by the ruling party in the Diet) and Cabinet, a set of administrative Ministries and Agencies and a judicial system culminating in a Supreme Court. In practice, these three institutions achieve a different balance of power than in the USA. In the Japanese bicameral national legislature, the majority political party in the House of Representatives appoints the Prime Minister and Cabinet. The national ministries, while officially implementing policy, actually play a major role in crafting it as well. The national judiciary usually plays a relatively passive role, rarely challenging government or business activity.

Local governments consist of similar institutions on a smaller scale; the governor is elected, but the vice-governor (and usual successor) is appointed by the national government. Most of local governments' budget is doled out by the national government, limiting local fiscal autonomy, but not discouraging all initiative (Muramatsu 1997). Local governments have some degree of policy-making autonomy. Hence, they are sometimes the source of innovative policies that work their way up to the national level.

The major interest groupings of business and labor take the form of pyramidal national hierarchies. In a form of government called corporatism, business and union leaders consult directly with government ministries to make relevant policy. While labor organizations have some 'voice' in matters of labor policy, business organizations exercise great influence over all areas of public policy.

In Japan, the three top elites – ministries, ruling political party and peak business associations – tend to work out policy preferences among themselves. Until the 1990s, other political parties have had ancillary effects, as have other interest groups such as labor. However, this 'Ruling Triad' is not monolithic; it contains tribes, camps and clusters. Within the ruling party (the Liberal Democratic Party (LDP)), *policy tribes* of politicians form within distinct policy domains concerning labor, economic growth, construction, the environment and so forth (Inoguchi and Iwai 1987).

In contrast, *policy camps*, the soul of corporatism, take shape in advisory councils (*shingikai*) for specific policy areas, where government officials present policy drafts for commentary by selected interest groups and academics. The relevant ministry plays the role of a 'mediator' between different interest groups as well as with the LDP policy tribe (Broadbent 2000). In the course of guiding and negotiating mutually acceptable policy, the ministries develop long-standing social relationships with their interest groups consisting of expectations of reciprocal support and dependency. These social relationships produce 'social capital' (relational credit) that the camp members use to get help from each other (mediated by the bureau or agency) (Broadbent 2001).

These tribes and camps carry various ideologies and interests. From the end of World War II, one central Japanese ideology was to catch up to the USA in economic terms. This goal had the impulse behind it of rebuilding not only the ruined infrastructure, but also, after military defeat, the national pride. Concerning political institutions, extremists of the right and left wanted to move toward more authoritarian ideals – imperial or socialist – respectively. However, the main political leaders accepted the new democratic institutions, sometimes grudgingly, and decided to work within them. The crashing down of wartime imperial ideologies left the populace largely disillusioned with nationalism and open to alternatives. They coupled democracy, the capitalist market economy and the attainment of personal and national material prosperity with proving the global respectability of Japanese civilization. Still, the state and businesses used the traditional habits of loyal social organization to further these goals, leaving little public opportunity for critique and the development of alternative goals. Into this pervasive 'developmentalism', environmental problems emerged like an uninvited and unwelcome guest, without legitimacy or welcome.

Party-centered policy tribes and bureaucrat-centered policy camps sometimes form joint policy *clusters*, cooperating to further a mutual agenda. However, as political parties often strike deals based on expediency, they are not so reliable for any individual interest group. The ruling party, at least, did not develop such deep trusting ties with most interest groups (Broadbent 2000). The 'pro-growth cluster' – composed of LDP leadership, business peak associations and economic ministries (Ministry of International Trade and Industry (MITI), Ministry of Finance, Ministry of Construction, Ministry of Transportation – usually dominated Japanese politics during periods I and II. MITI tried to guide business to follow national economic policies that it believed would best help national prosperity (Johnson 1982; Okimoto 1989).

However, other factors often foiled MITI's national-economic-interest rationality. LDP politicians of the 'construction tribe' (*kensetsu zoku*), for instance, arranged high-paying government contracts for collusive general contractors (*dango*), getting huge kickbacks in return. This money fed the national LDP political 'machine', feeding patronage and bribery to local voters. The construction contracts, in turn, created a 'construction state' (*doken kokka*) which, while creating local jobs, built endless public works (dams, harbors, tunnels, railway stations, roads, etc.), sometimes of dubious utility, often with destructive environmental effects (Broadbent 1998; Masumi 1995; Woodall 1996). When in the late 1980s the USA pushed Japan to increase domestic consumption (in hopes of increasing imports), the Japanese government put even more money into public works. This strategy drove Japanese public debt to world record levels in the 1990s.

Against the pro-growth clusters stood a shifting environmental cluster. Its members included pro-environment government agencies (sometimes), (rising and falling) victims' groups, protest movements and citizens' organizations, (perpetually out of power) opposition political parties (notably the Japan Socialist Party (JSP)), (sporadic) court decisions and (occasionally) innovative local governments. The mass media, often sympathetic with citizen environmental concerns, played a crucial role in spreading public awareness of these issues (Broadbent 1998).

Unions affiliated with the JSP, especially those representing government workers such as teachers, post office workers, government clericals and railroad employees (before privatization), often took pro-environmental stances. Until the 1990s, the JSP, as a party-out-of-power in the Diet, often criticized government growth and environmental policies. On a smaller scale, the Japan Communist Party played a similar role, though rarely cooperating with their long-time rival, the JSP.

Often, even the different pro-growth clusters (tribes and camps) such as the construction cluster and the national growth cluster (around MITI), clashed over national policy and budget priorities. Growth clusters clashed all the more with advocates of environmental protection.

Still, Japanese elites shared a strong common sense of nation, ethnicity and social hierarchy, and were embedded within networks of reciprocal mutual aid (Broadbent 1998). This commonality meant that under high levels of pressure from outside (from citizens or foreign countries) the three elites (LDP, ministries and business) could cooperate in rapid policy making and effective implementation. When outside pressure was weak, though, the policy clusters could fall into divisive conflict, and the tribes and camps into internal cronyism or corruption. Under favorable pressures, the Japanese elites' style of networked policy making allowed for information exchange and consensus building during the policy formation period.

In contrast, in the USA, isolated interest groups develop fixed positions and then lobby politicians, making compromise more difficult. The losing minority will often resist the new policy through lawsuit and non-compliance.

Japan's networked, mostly pro-growth elites tended to exclude outsiders and non-members, such as the general public. Elite government and business assumed a vertical, paternalistic stance toward society, producing an 'administered society' or 'nationalist-paternalist capitalist state' (Bellah 1985; Fukui 1992). Ordinary members of society faced the shaping force of a bureaucratic state at every turn in their lives. Until recently, for instance, voluntary associations could not incorporate (become a 'legal person' with all the legal benefits of that status), and philanthropic or government grants were scarce.

In ordinary towns and villages, traditional residents' associations such as the Young Peoples' Club (*seinendan*) usually complied with the ruling political hierarchy. The lack of more independent associations hampered and slowed the initial resistance of local residents to pollution in their communities. By the mid-1960s, though, courageous and ethical local leaders throughout Japan converted their traditional associations into vehicles of protest. This was the mobilization process of the first wave of protest (see below).

Even today, almost no associations enjoy tax-exempt status as non-profit organizations. As a result, ordinary people have had little chance to exercise an independent, responsible voice in politics or to develop an ethic of citizenship. Civil society, ideally the birthplace of activism and voluntary citizen associations, did not start maturing in Japan until the mid-1990s (Pekkanen 2000). From then on, Japan experienced a rapid rise in the number of citizens' voluntary associations. These associations have a weak but slowly growing influence on politics and policy.

As a consequence of a weak civil society, when elites took little initiative, it was very hard for ordinary citizens to get environmental problems on the political agenda. As they worked to do so, they also had to contend with the paternalistic elites, who disparaged their efforts as selfish. Elites felt that protest movements suffered from too much 'egotism'; they violated the proper Japanese ethics of social harmony (*wa*) and abiding by collective goals (set by the elites) (Broadbent 1998, p. 169). Thus, especially in the early decades, achieving environmental recognition and response meant morally contending with traditional paternalism and hierarchy.

PROCESS STAGES BY DEVELOPMENT PERIOD

Period I. A: Unbridled Pollution 1955-67

During this period, Japanese elites pursued industrial growth with a single-minded determination and ignored environmental problems. After World War II, rapid economic growth soon gave Japan the highest density per square kilometer of industry, energy use and population of any industrial nation. By 1980, with only 0.3 per cent of the world's surface area and 3 per cent of the world's population, Japan accounted for about 10 per cent of the world's economic product and about 10 per cent of total world exports. Japan imported the world's resources, made, consumed and exported products, and kept the leftover waste. This waste accumulated on Japan's crowded islands, polluting air, water, soil, ocean and population. Ecological damage, most noticeably human illness from industrial pollution, became the worst in the world.

The Japanese government did very little environmental management. For the first two decades, until the mid-1960s, the government, the ruling political party (LDP) and private business largely denied the existence of serious pollution. As a result, the authorities did not make or implement effective pollution-control policies. In the only noteworthy government accomplishment, MITI persuaded power plants and some industries to reduce local air pollution. Otherwise, pollution victims and their supporters received very little government attention. Official denial, by giving pollution victims no legitimate way to seek help, created severe social tensions.

The victims of pollution illness not only had to figure out the causes of their illnesses themselves, they also had to do so against the fearsome weight of the state and elite disparagement. Given official denial, local authorities and village leaders also rejected and castigated the victims. Their neighbors stigmatized and ostracized them as sick due to their own faults.

From the mid-1960s, finding no response from government, victims of pollution increasingly took matters into their own hands. Local activists, often high school teachers affiliated with the Japan Federation of Teachers (*Nikkyōso*), ethical scientists and others helped demonstrate the link between mercury pollution and the illnesses. The first protest movements targeted the sources of pollution, such as the Chisso plant in Minamata. The movements complained, fielded protest movements, filed suits in court and voted for opposition-party politicians. With mass media dissemination, images of the crippled hands and deformed babies of mercury-poisoned fishermen in Minamata became a powerful cultural 'icon'. In many other Japanese towns, the news and pictures inspired shock and then recognition of local environmental problems. The spread of these images changed the public framing of industrialization from 'progress and civilization' to 'pollution of health and nature'. Japan's agrarian, Shinto-Buddhist culture had always sought unity with nature; these complaints forced it to see nature as a distinct object with limited capacity.

Minamata-type movements sought recognition, apology and compensation. By the mid-1960s, however, a new type of movement emerged aimed at prevention. In 1964, the government announced plans to build an oil refinery complex in the cities of Mishima and Numazu. Local residents feared the pollution from the complex, and organized a strong grassroots movement that successfully forced the government to abandon the plan. Resisting a government-sanctioned project was a daring step for ordinary people – taking it made them realize the new rights guaranteed by their post-war democratic constitution (McKean 1977; Broadbent 1998). The success of the Mishima Numazu protest movement also shocked government bureaucrats and industrial leaders, forcing them to recognize and deal with a new 'people power' in democratic Japan. Movement opposition stalled industrial projects around the country. Local protest movements also elected local governments, mayors and governors from opposition parties. On their own, these local governments tried to reduce local pollution: by 1970, 44 prefectures had pollution prevention ordinances (Masumi 1995, pp. 98-9). Industrial Yokohama, under a JSP mayor, concluded Japan's first Pollution Control Agreement (PCA), with considerable effect in reducing local pollution. From 1965, under guidance from the Ministry of Health and Welfare (MHW), some prefectures began taking surveys of pollution and entering into informal PCAs with local polluting factories. After that, PCAs quickly spread as a non-confrontational way to reduce pollution.

Alone within the Japanese state, the MHW sympathized with the pollution victims. To spur public concern, the MHW installed pollution-monitoring stations at busy points in major cities that continually displayed the local concentration of air pollutants for all passersby to read (Kawana 1988).

At first, facing mounting pressure, the 'growth cluster' of the MITI, business and the LDP growth tribe agreed to a limited compromise; the government passed the 1967 Basic Law Against Pollution. This law, however, did not have any practical effect on pollution. As a result, environmental protest continued to escalate through the 1960s and reached a peak in 1970 (Figure 5.1).[5] The protestors held public discussion forums, picketed government offices, stopped industrial projects and filed lawsuits. Under the democratic constitution, the government rarely used force or intimidation to suppress the movements. With movement electoral support, opposition party mayors and governors rose to a peak in 1970 (then governing about one-third of the Japanese population). Progressive governors initiated the practice of local PCAs which later spread. In the early 1970s, the Japan Supreme Court awarded victories to the 'big four' pollution cases: Minamata and Niigata mercury poisoning, Yokkaichi asthma and *itai-*

itai cadmium poisoning. 'People's power' ushered in an era of pollution reform.

In sum, during Period I. A, protest movements were the major carriers of environmental change. They and their supporters recognized ecological disturbance from factory waste as an environmental problem, and forcibly brought this problem into the public agenda. Supported by the democratic freedoms guaranteed in their society and by increasingly intense media coverage, these first movements spread their recognition to communities throughout Japan, setting off ripples, and then a wave, of environmental protest. This wave sensitized Japanese culture to environmental problems, as well as their new democratic rights, and put insistent pressure for solutions on recalcitrant elites. In Phase I. B, following this impulse, the response process moved into the stages of policy-making and implementation.

Period I. B: Pollution Reform 1967-75

The most dramatic political event during this time was the Pollution Diet that produced 14 new anti-pollution laws and set up the Environment Agency. Like a sudden judo throw, these laws changed many environmental practices throughout Japan's economy. Such dramatic reforms are rare in any nation's history. How did Japan make it happen?

First of all, the wave of environmental protests peaked during a propitious political moment. During the late 1960s, popular support for the LDP was on the decline. By 1970, fewer than 50 per cent of voters voted for the LDP; the party held only a narrow majority of legislative seats in the national Diet (see Figure 5.1). The weakness of the ruling party provided a political opportunity for the protest movements. The LDP feared further erosion of electoral support, leading to its loss of the Diet. Business leaders and economic officials feared that local protests would make it hard to build any new factories (Broadbent 1998; Masumi 1995, pp. 98-9). Their fears made the elites more willing to compromise (Masumi 1995, p. 100).

After a flurry of consultation between the three ruling elites, the historic 1970 'Pollution Diet' passed 14 major anti-pollution laws. These laws, plus the implementation mechanisms worked out between 1970 and 1973, formed the basis of Japan's great environmental successes. All told, 149 new pollution-related national laws and local regulations were passed during the 1970s. The new laws gave priority to reducing pollution over industrial growth, rapidly lowered air and water pollution, compensated many pollution victims, and led to other beneficial changes (Masumi 1995, pp. 98-100).

The new laws established an array of rules and institutions designed to reduce industrial pollution in particular. The laws made polluters financially responsible to their victims under civil law, determined cost allocation for pollution control, and provided for mediated dispute resolution. They allowed prefectural governments to set environmental laws that were more stringent than national ones. They amended existing laws concerning air and water pollution, traffic pollution and noise, hazardous material transport, waste disposal and sewage, toxic waste and Natural Parks. These laws set up the Environment Agency.

Figure 5.1 Environmental Protest and Political Changes (1958-1993)

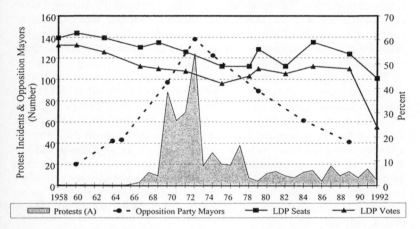

On paper, these new laws constituted the strictest anti-pollution regime in the world (Huddle, Reich and Stiskin 1975; Pempel 1982, p. 231). However, the new laws did not immediately reduce existing pollution. As a result, the wave of protest rolled on, peaking again in 1973 (see Figure 5.1). Additional pressures also peaked. In the early 1970s, the Japan Supreme Court granted victories to the four big pollution lawsuits. Foreign pressures multiplied: the USA passed its National Environmental Protection Act in 1969. The 1972 United Nations Stockholm Conference on the World Environment strongly criticized Japan for its pollution problems. The director of the new Environment Agency (set up in 1971) attended the conference and returned home, determined to control air pollution.

In 1971, ministerial bureaus followed 'standard practices' in seeking to implement the new laws. For each targeted industry, such as steel making, bureau officials set up an advisory council with industry representatives (from the many industrial sector associations (ISA) or *gyokai*) and experts from academia. Working cooperatively but under ministerial guidance, and with a general sense of urgency, the council members developed emission standards for each industry, closely tailored to its needs and capacities. They then implemented the new standards through the ISAs. ISA members (individual firms) obeyed because they felt well-represented and respected bureaucratic judgment. Within the ISA, firms negotiated their shares of the economic burden and the government subsidies for the costly pollution control investments. The ISAs also trained technicians and helped firms exchange related technical expertise and experience.

The resultant measures represented very innovative regulatory instruments, such as area-wide pollution emissions standards, pollution control managers in factories, and the polluter pays principle (PPP) fund to compensate victims. The success of each of these instruments depended upon Japanese culture and social relational patterns. Without Japan's ethic of collective responsibility reinforced by the system of communication and negotiation through advisory councils led by government ministries, these instruments would not have worked as well, if at all.

The new laws set pollution emissions standards according to area-wide levels of pollution, rather than by individual factory emissions. MITI and other government agencies worked closely with businesses, first getting their collective agreement on the need to reduce air pollution, then asking their advice on how best to set and meet the new pollution standards. Government agencies subsidized the costs of the changeover, easing the burden of industry at enormous financial cost to the public treasury. Such policies would have raised objections in the USA, where culture stresses individual responsibility. In Japan, however, where collective responsibility seems natural, public responsibility for such collective problems can be more easily (value) rationalized.

One of the additional 1971 laws required that certain factories have their own pollution control managers and supervisors. In 2000, employed pollution control managers and supervisors numbered 40,000 and 23,000, respectively, and 470,000 had passed the national certification program for pollution-control managers. This program passed through a birth process similar to that of emissions standards.

A 1973 law created a 'PPP' fund to compensate pollution victims. The fund was based on the European idea of the PPP (Weidner 1989c, p. 489).[6] The fund made compensation automatically available to victims suffering from any of four air pollution-related and three water pollution-related symptoms. Compensation included free medical care, and rehabilitation and physical handicap compensation. By 1991, the compensation fund held about 24.4 billion yen ($190 million) and provided considerable support to victims of severe pollution-induced illnesses.

The operation of the PPP fund may also illustrate the effect of Japanese culture on environmental management. The European countries, following a command and control approach, designed the PPP system to penalize polluting companies, forcing them to pay the entire cost of compensation without government subsidy. In its official rhetoric, the Japanese PPP system also followed this strategy. The Japanese fund was supposed to be comprised thus: 80 per cent from factories emitting smoke and soot, assessed according to their pollution emissions, and 20 per cent from car owners as a tonnage tax. Some Japanese scholars, jokingly calling the PPP a 'punish polluters principle', say the fund worked as advertised – its onerous fees convinced air polluters to reduce pollution. Other scholars, however, say the Japanese government heavily subsidized the funds so as not to excessively burden industry.

The 1970 laws permitted local governments to demand stricter environmental standards than those set by the national government. This law spurred the use of PCAs. This law added legitimacy to the local ordinance and PCA movement that had started in the 1960s. As voluntary agreements, the PCAs left enforcement up to the local government bureaucracy and business. Citizens sometimes stimulated or participated in setting up the PCAs, but they could not enforce them (through lawsuits, etc.). The government retained wide discretionary powers to implement them. As a result, the strictness of the PCA depended upon the political will of the local government. Opposition-party affiliated local governments made stronger use of the PPP law, concluded more aggressive PCAs, passed many pollution regulations, and set up pollution complaint bureaus (Broadbent 1998, Ch. 8; Wallace 1995, pp. 243-4; Weidner 1989b, p. 473; Weidner 1989c, p. 490). Around Tokyo (then run by Socialist governor Minobe), PCAs set the strictest standards on power plants, often demanding zero emissions (a switch to natural gas). The more conservative local governments, however, especially those dominated by the LDP, tended not to take a proactive stance toward pollution or negotiate tougher PCAs (Broadbent 1998, p. 284; Ui 1989, pp. 563-5).

In the final analysis, two-thirds of PCAs had no effect on local pollution, but some, especially those targeting large central pollution sources, were effective. Some of the stricter prefectural regulations embarrassed the central government into strengthening the national laws. Such feedback from the periphery to the center is typical in the USA, but at the time was new in Japan. Of course, PCAs deal only with local, single-firm problems, so they cannot provide a comprehensive national solution.

The Japanese policy-making style – inter-elite cooperation under external pressure – produced the benefits of sporadic rapid response, but left holes in coverage. Since the new environmental policies were compromises to public pressure, they only addressed issues targeted by public protest. Consequently, the policies ignored issues not targeted by the public, including the less obvious, long-term effects of pollution, such as toxic waste. Toxic waste thus became an ecological 'time bomb', invisibly accumulating until harmful enough to 'blow up' and cause panic.

In their implementation, the new laws of this period relied upon considerable bureaucratic discretion and close cooperation between the regulators and regulated. Government officials had great latitude in defining the specific emission standards and means of solution in any given case. The formal laws and regulations defined no specific standards, required no impact assessment and provided no funding for enforcement (Imamura 1989, p. 44; Matsubara 1971, p. 167; Upham 1987).

These policy-writing tactics, typical of Japan, gave little legal leverage to ordinary citizens, minimizing the danger that ordinary citizens would file lawsuits or raise other official barriers (class action lawsuits, environmental impact assessments) to industrial projects in the future. Japanese citizens are not permitted to file class-action suits, and cannot sue the government for non-enforcement of standards (Feinerman and Fujikura 1998, pp. 260-2; Shibata 1989, p. 37). Instead, regulation and enforcement remained at the discretion of, and divided among, national and prefectural bureaus.

PCAs also proceeded through government discretion and cooperation with business. They indicate the importance of local government 'autonomy' (*jichi*) in Japan. While quite dependent for their discretionary budgets upon allocations from central governments, a degree of decentralization allowed prefectures to engage in policy innovation. As a result, local governments sometimes produced new regulatory instruments or standards that met popular approval and eventually spread to the national level. This example illustrates the importance of decentralization of government, and of multiple sources of policy initiation, for the solution of environmental problems.

The preceding examples indicate that Japan's typical style of implementation can well be labeled discretionary cooperative implementation (DCI): bureaucratic discretion in setting standards and close cooperation with industry in implementing the standards. This style could only operate effectively under certain necessary societal conditions: a powerful demand from society, a ministry quite determined to accomplish its mandate, a cooperative business community and ruling political party, a thick web of social capital networks among the elite actors, a relatively acquiescent citizenry and a shared sense of collective responsibility – all features of Japanese culture. In Japan, bureaucrats have traditionally held much higher status and authority than politicians, business leaders or the ordinary people.[7]

In contrast, the US style of 'command and control' implementation assumes quite opposite societal conditions: individualized units that bear isolated responsibility for their actions, authorities that are supposed to impersonally apply sanctions stipulated by formal law, and ordinary citizens who can often initiate legal suits for violation of standards. As is obvious, the two styles of implementation assume and depend upon two very different social and cultural contexts.

In particular, Japan's implementation style depended upon MITI's close ties to the business community. The Environment Agency could not have done the same. While often chafing at the 'interference', Japanese business leaders tend to trust the expertise and dedication of MITI officials to the best interests of business and the nation. Therefore, if after sufficient discussion, MITI urges new environmental protection measures, business tends to follow suit. This kind of relationship between economic ministries and the business community has been noted as 'embedded autonomy', the key ingredient of East Asian economic success.[8]

MITI business negotiations were not dictatorial; they were reciprocal (Samuels 1987). Environmental reform laws, for example, appeared 'reluctantly', in a series of gradually more effective (and expensive) compromises with movement pressure: the 1967 Basic Law, the Pollution Diet with 14 Laws, implementation laws and then actual pollution reduction and compensation. This reluctance indicates MITI's basic priority: business welfare for national economic success.

Period II: Transition Era 1975-88

Improvement in the most obvious environmental problems, coupled with the recession-inducing 'Oil Shock' (sudden oil price rise) of 1973, turned the nation's attention back to the economy during Period II. The environmental reforms of the prior period continued in force or suffered gradual decline. But Japan rejected new environmental responsibilities, both domestic and international, and disregarded its effects on foreign and global environments (through logging, fishing, smelting and dumping, for instance).

Most of Japan's new environmental improvements during this period came as a by-product of energy conservation measures. Through active coordination between MITI and business, Japan attained lower use of energy per unit of gross national product (GNP) than other Organization for Economic Cooperation and Development (OECD) countries. At the same time, seeing a new global demand, Japanese car manufacturers invented the world's most energy-efficient and low-emissions automobiles, increasing their sales in the US market.

Partly as a result of these measures, Japan's economy overcame the high oil prices and rose to unprecedented heights of wealth and prosperity. An intense building boom of urban development, public works (dams, roads and railways), plus resorts and golf courses transformed the landscape. Coupled with land speculation, these projects sometimes had dubious public value and needlessly destroyed the natural ecology.

As noticeable pollution declined and the economy changed, the wave of environmental protest fell to a low ebb. Unlike their counterparts in the USA and Germany, Japanese environmental movements had been very locally based, so did not draw in many outside participants, did not have a strong basis in a universal ethic of 'environmentalism', and did not leave behind strong national environmental NGOs or parties.[9] The movements did spin off a few small NGOs that were seeds for the future however, and deeply imprinted the idea of environmental rights and health in the minds of ordinary people.

Inspired by these ideas, ordinary people began to transform the household-oriented economy and daily culture in environmentally friendly ways. Japan's farmers were using huge amounts of pesticides and chemical fertilizers per hectare. Housewives, however, began to seek healthier organic foods and environment-friendly products, and idealistic youth set up organic farms and communes to supply this need; responsive Co-op (*Seikyo*) stores spread throughout Japan.[10] Citizens complained to their local governments more freely about environmental problems (Broadbent 1998, p. 325). Local governments set up complaint windows and allowed citizens greater participation in making town development plans (Broadbent 1989a).

Despite growing 'grassroots' interest in lifestyle change, the few fledgling environmental NGOs of the time faced very harsh conditions. They encountered bureaucratic and business opposition, lacked the right to incorporate or attain non-profit, tax-exempt status, and got little financial support from foundations and the government (unlike in the USA). Moreover, they lacked widespread popular support – ordinary people were not used to giving money to an organization in Tokyo (usually) to fight for an abstract cause (national or global 'environmental problems') as opposed to a problem in their own neighborhood. Without dues-paying members, fledgling national environmental NGOs could not support themselves (Broadbent 1998, pp. 286-92; Dunlap, Gallup and Gallup 1992; Miller and Moore 1990; Schreurs 1997). In addition, to 'fill' the social space, government and businesses set up 'tame', quasi-governmental environmental NGOs. In this harsh social environment, citizen NGOs and civil society in general did not prosper.

During the late 1970s, without the hammer of popular pressure, environmental policy stood still and/or retreated. Under industry pressure, the Japanese government ended its required business fund to compensate pollution victims and stopped certifying any new victims (Environment Agency (Kankyocho) 1987, p. 193; Shibata 1989; Weidner 1989a). Even some existing laws were inadequately implemented – some victims of the Minamata and Niigata mercury poisoning had not received government aid for more than 20 years after their court victory. New environmental measures faced similar resistance. The Environment Agency repeatedly tried to pass a law requiring a public environmental impact assessment for large projects, but was always quashed by MITI, the LDP and business leaders (Barrett and Therivel 1991, p. 98; Broadbent 1998, p. 294; Hashimoto 1987a, p. 77; Tsuru 1989, p. 39).

Positive environmental policy came about as an unintended benefit of other pursuits. Spurred by the 1973 and 1978 'oil shocks', MITI and the auto industry worked toward a more efficient use of energy. In 1974, MITI started its 'Sunshine Project' promoting alternative sources of energy; in 1978, it initiated its 'Moonlight Project' promoting energy efficiency and nuclear power. As policy instruments, MITI organized joint research consortia, provided subsidies and set up a certification program for energy conservation specialists (required at plants above a certain size). The joint consortia developed ways to reuse waste heat and monitor fuel usage, even finding the technology a commercial success (Choy 1989, pp. 5-6; Flavin and Young 1993, p. 193; Hashimoto 1987a, pp. 76-7; Matsuoka 1989, p. 447; Ministry of International Trade and Industry 1988). The Japanese government subsidized the costs of the activities; it also subsidized the business costs of new energy conservation operations with grants and low-interest loans (taken, ultimately, from tax revenues and public savings).

The policies and implementation strategies worked. Japan rapidly conserved energy. Between 1973 and 1988, Japan's gross domestic product (GDP) grew 81 per cent, but its energy use grew only 16 per cent, putting its efficiency ahead of other OECD nations. In other words, Japan burned less oil per unit of GDP -- thus emitting less air pollution than without the energy conservation measures.

As with pollution control measures, energy conservation measures illustrate certain key qualities of Japanese social organization and culture. Both measures emerged from and were implemented through collective negotiation and persuasion between government bureaucracies and the business community, with the LDP as a vehicle and political bellwether. Both measures 'socialized' the costs of change in ways consistent with accepted habits of collective responsibility in Japanese culture. MITI's energy conservation programs illustrate once again Japan's style of cooperative (inter-elite) policy-making and negotiated implementation.

Efficiency reforms also occurred in the Japanese auto industry, but by a different path. The stringent 'Muskie Law' in the USA proposed higher fuel economy standards for all US cars. The USA, and Japan in its wake, ultimately abandoned the strict Muskie standards. However, the Honda and Toyota motor companies, against the advice of MITI but under strong demand from some local governments, developed high efficiency cars that met the Muskie standards anyway. Their new cars proved to be wildly successful in the US market.

These two paths to energy efficiency show that Japan is not monolithic; despite bureaucratic centrality, it also has free market qualities. The two pathways also illustrate a common point, that environmental protection can sometimes take place by accident (or 'serendipity'). Environmental reformers at any level can seek out and support these kind of 'win-win' solutions to environmental problems.[11]

In 1976, the government passed a new waste handling law requiring local governments to supervise recycling, incineration and the safe disposal of toxic waste (Ishino 1989). However, as usual, implementing these regulations depended upon bureaucratic discretion. With little citizen complaint on this issue many local governments neglected their duty, and firms continued to dump toxics illegally (Weidner 1989c, p. 494). By the 1980s, the accumulated effects of toxic waste from various sources started to manifest. Some municipal well water became contaminated with carcinogenic organochloride compounds, making it necessary for them to close down (Hashimoto 1987, p. 80; Ishino 1989). Newspapers began to report rising rates of unusual human fetal deformities.

Along with industrial waste, the wealthy consumer economy generated a huge amount of paper and other household waste, overcoming limited landfill capacities. The government decided to incinerate most of it, causing a proliferation of giant trash incinerators (over 1000). As realized only belatedly, the smoke from these incinerators spread the carcinogen dioxin over the surrounding neighborhoods, adding to the level of toxic pollution.

Abroad, Japan's harvesting of world resources (timber, minerals, fisheries) produced a massive global ecological 'footprint'. Japanese companies systematically stripped Southeast Asia's rain forests of their exotic hardwoods, and the ocean of its fish. In 1986, Japan consumed two-thirds of world imports of timber and half of world tropical hardwood imports, often for throw-away uses such as concrete forms (Dauvergne 1997; Nihon Bengoshi Rengokai 1995; Pearce and Warford 1993, pp. 291-3). Japanese companies deployed 60 huge mechanized fishing ships using gigantic drift nets. Along with vast quantities of usable fish, these nets also killed an enormous number of unwanted fish, turtles, dolphins and other animals.

To escape domestic laws, Japanese companies began to 'export' their most polluting plants (Ui 1989; Watanuki 1979, p. 112). Japanese oil, aluminum, and other refineries set up shop in Indonesia, Venezuela and Brazil. Japanese chemical companies exported dichlorodiphenyl-trichloroethane (DDT) and other toxic pesticides to Third World countries in great quantities (Iijima 1998; Watanuki 1979, p. 122). Their resource extraction often destroyed the habitats of indigenous peoples, such as the Australian aborigines and Malaysian Panang (Iijima 1998).

Despite this growing ecological impact, Japanese government, business and the public (except for a few small NGOs) displayed little recognition of the problem until the 1990s. To the contrary, the Japanese government rejected most international environmental agreements (Feinerman and Fujikura 1998, p. 253; Weidner 1989c, pp. 519-21). This behavior led some observers to label Japan the world's 'eco-outlaw' (Begley and Takayama 1989, p. 70; Miyaoka 1998, p. 167).

In sum, this period saw accidental, but little intentional environmental improvement. Public pressure had induced the government to clean up air and water pollution. A different sort of external pressure enabled MITI to persuade big industries to conserve energy. Without public recognition and uproar, however, potential 'problems' like invisible toxic pollution, poor quality of urban life and foreign ecological degradation went untended. While new forms of pollution and environmental abuse developed apace ordinary people were becoming more aware and concerned about environmental issues – with portent for the future.

Period III: New Era

During Period III, the twisting conflux of economic bust, globalization, political transition and an aging society further transformed Japan and its response to ecological change. Japan's growing entanglement with the global economy, coupled with its own sudden economic decline after 1990, made it increasingly sensitive to foreign demands. Japanese leaders wanted to move away from dependence on the USA and strengthen economic ties to Europe and China. Foreign pressures pushed Japan into accession to numerous international environmental pacts, such as the Montreal Protocol on stratospheric ozone depletion, and the Convention on International Trade in Endangered Species (CITES). The impending problem of global warming stimulated Japan's citizens and NGOs, generating broad participation in the United Nations Rio Conference in 1992. The 1993 loss of power by the long-ruling LDP led to a coalition government ruled by opposition parties more favorable to civil society and environmental concerns. This government initiated the 1993 New Environmental Basic Law containing strong support for a sustainable society and for stopping global warming. Governmental and popular enthusiasm for global environmental issues continued to grow, culminating in Japan's hosting of the 1997 Kyoto Conference and later support for the Kyoto Protocol on greenhouse gas reduction (despite US withdrawal). Helped by new government grants and a small but increasing amount of corporate philanthropy, various environmental NGOs took root in Japan – a new, delayed phenomenon (compared to similar OECD countries). At the same time, a new wave of traditional-style local protest movements arose against the insidious health effects of toxic waste and nuclear power plants.

DISCUSSION OF THE FOUR STAGES

Problem Recognition

As seen in Period I. A, public recognition of environmental problems was usually initiated by the victims and their supporters. By the 1960s, local high school teachers backed by the JSP-oriented Japan Federation of Teachers (*Nikkyoso*) helped, started and even led local environmental movements. Once informed of the connection between their illness and factory outputs, ordinary Japanese people had little cultural barrier against understanding that. Moreover, ordinary people led the way in recognizing not only environmental problems, but also the political potential of their new democratic rights and freedoms (of assembly, speech, the press, etc.) guaranteed by the post-World War II constitution.

From the mid-1960s onward, the mass media played a crucial role in spreading the recognition of pollution problems to other communities throughout Japan. More and more movements noticed local environmental problems, and joined the wave of protest. The new movements not only held meetings, protest marches and sit-ins – they also elected politicians who promised to defend their interests in a clean environment. Through this process, the major opposition parties abandoned their unqualified support for industrial growth and recognized the importance of environmental problems. Science also played an increasing role in identifying environmental problems over the course of the four periods.

On the other hand, up until the mid-1960s, most ministries and the ruling party (LDP) practiced 'official denial' of pollution. Enterprise unions usually joined with their companies to deny and reject pollution complaints. However, after the mid-1960s, help from certain sectors of government emerged, first from the Ministry of Health and Welfare and from opposition party local governments, and after its formation from the Environment Agency. After 1988, government and business also began to recognize environmental problems in a more proactive way.

The necessary first step toward solving environmental problems lies in the public recognition of their existence. Next, people have to be able to discuss the problem, complain to the government and if they do not get a solution, exercise other forms of pressure. Public pressure leads to the creation of policy and to the serious implementation of policy 'instruments'.

The presence or absence of public recognition and pressure influences the next three stages of solving environmental problems (policy-making, implementation and durability). In Japan during the 1960s, the public noticed and successfully pushed for the reduction of air and water pollution. However, the public did not notice or push for the reduction of most forms of toxic waste (except mercury and other chemicals that caused obvious disease), so despite laws against toxic waste dumping it continued. Nor was the public very concerned about Japan's foreign or global environmental impact. Only in the 1990s did polychlorinated biphenyls (PCBs), dioxin and other toxins that produce disease, get publicly recognized and mobilize protest pressure. Likewise, public recognition of Japan's foreign, if not global, creation of environmental problems increased in the 1990s.

Public recognition and pressure require democracy and democratic rights. Therefore, the existence of democracy is a necessary condition for the solution of environmental problems (at least in large, complex societies). A comparison of Japan's successes in controlling air pollution with failures in the Soviet Union and Eastern Bloc further supports this conclusion. However, the USA's failure to control power plant emissions shows that democracy alone is not enough. There must also be strong public demand (to use the democratic institutions) and a state with the capacity to implement the law.

Policy-making Response

Japan's form of inter-elite cooperation under external pressure can also be called 'communitarian elite corporatism' (CEC) (Broadbent 1998). The three dominant elites – ministries, party and business – have a joint structure. Ministries have sufficient autonomy to develop their own national policies, and they have sufficient connectedness to temper the policies with joint consultation and then persuade other elites into a coordinated response. Without ministerial guidance, parties and the business community would fall into factional fighting as in the USA. If, on the other hand, the ministries became the puppet of either the ruling party or a particular set of business interests, they would lose their guidance capacities. Economic pro-growth ministries enjoyed dominance, but under high external pressure, they expanded their circle to include even environmental agencies.

Business, party and ministerial elites shared many social ties and a strong common ethnic identity, from pre-World War II times to the present. Thus, they formed a kind of elite community. Each elite sat at the top of a pyramid of loyal affiliated subordinate organizations that reached out into their respective social sectors. This neo-corporatist formation gave Japan high potential social control and relatively low social voluntarism in ordinary society. Except in times of crisis, most people felt fairly comfortable being members of paternalistic organizations. As crisis drove people to exercise the rights inherent in their constitution, however, they increasingly questioned the traditional hierarchies.

Different external pressures impinged on the triadic core: the 1960s-70's wave of environmental protest (using increasingly forceful tactics), the oil shocks, global market opportunities and foreign criticism. Riding this wave, responsive local governments initiated stricter local pollution controls, and courts supported the claims of victims against polluting companies.

Pressures from Japanese citizens shifted the balance within the triadic core, adding legitimacy to environmental voices. Members of the pro-growth cluster, used to getting their way, had to concede initiative to the Ministry of Health and Welfare and the Environment Agency. These concessions did not change the pro-growth elites into environmentalists, however. The elites responded expediently – at first with symbolic policies (the 1967 Basic Law) gauged to puncture the expanding balloon of protest. When this did not work, they made real compromises (the 1970 Pollution Diet and its aftermath). Under MITI's guidance, businesses followed the intent of the law to real effect – for instance, the amazingly quick reductions in air pollution in the late 1960s and the 1970s.

In strictly economic terms, domestic environmental protests forced the reallocation of capital and investment in Japan toward public health and social welfare. Given the strong sense of society-wide ethnic solidarity in Japan, even business elites may not have seen this as a zero-sum game.

Pressures from outside Japan were different, however; they threatened the prosperity and welfare of the entire society, and so generated a different elite reaction and response pattern. The sudden quadrupling of oil prices in 1973 did not bring extra profits to Japan's oil companies (who did not own the supply chain). Rather, it affected the viability of the entire Japanese economy, dependent as it was and still is upon a favorable balance of trade (upon selling lots of good, cheap manufactured products to foreign countries).

In this case, MITI, spreading out the investment costs and cushioning them with subsidies, readily persuaded the business community to conserve energy. This kind of rational response would not be possible in a highly individualized, disparate, uncoordinated business array (as energy inefficiency in the USA testifies). At the same time, individual businesses, seeing a market, were not unable to break away from MITI guidance, as Honda and Toyota's development of energy-efficient cars exemplifies. The contrasting styles of energy conservation and auto development illustrate the flexibility of the Japanese state business relationship.

Japan's CEC style of policy-making depended upon a number of factors. At heart was a long tradition of ministerial dominance over society. The long political dominance (1955-93; revival after 1994) by a single, pro-business political party (the LDP) solidified the post-war triadic core. During this period, business gradually gained in wealth and independence from the ministries. The triadic core stayed in power despite pluralistic tendencies injected by democratic institutions by periodically compromising with intense public demand (Calder 1988). But without intense demand, the pro-growth core tended to ignore environmental issues.

The importance of the LDP in setting the conservative, pro-business tone of the entire dominant triad became very evident when the LDP lost power in 1993. From the 1960s, when opposition parties took control of local governments, they often passed much more effective local pollution ordinances and PCAs (Broadbent 1989b). But when the LDP lost control of the Lower House of the Diet in 1993, the new governing coalition rapidly passed more effective environmental laws, including the revised Basic Environmental Law (containing strong recognition of global warming and the idea of sustainable development).

The LDP achieved its long political dominance by providing rural patronage benefits, bribes and jobs. The jobs came from public works projects supported by the well-oiled construction state (*doken kokka*) and collusive bidding (*dango*) 'machine' (Broadbent 1988). In the 1990s, citizens' increasing recognition of their own right to a high quality of life led to movements against the rampant public works program of the LDP – electing anti-dam Governor Tanaka in Nagano Prefecture, for instance.

In the 1990s, business, in its own voluntary responses to environmental problems, began a voluntary program of environmental reform. This program included widespread adoption of the International Standard Organization (ISO) 14000 series that was quite effective in reducing pollution. Government also became more proactive in environmental issues, such as in hosting the 1997 Kyoto Conference and supporting the resulting greenhouse gas reduction protocol.

Implementation

As detailed in the preceding sections, the instruments used to implement both Japan's environmental laws and its local PCAs drew on Japan's social and cultural context. Area-wide pollution emissions standards, pollution control managers in factories, and the PPP fund to compensate victims all required extensive consensus building under ministerial guidance, support and assurance. These instruments relied on Japan's traditional ethic of collective responsibility, but also required the social organization and relational habits to express those values.

Japanese bureaucrats had considerable discretionary latitude in how strictly to interpret and administer the law in each case. They reached their decisions after lengthy collective negotiations in advisory councils with the leaders of the targeted industrial sector. The implementation then occurred down the ranks of the pyramidal (corporatist) and hierarchical industrial sector association (ISA). This style of discretionary cooperative implementation allowed for considerable communication and coordination.

The pattern of legal sanctions also reinforced this style. Japanese law is not administered through 'blind justice' (impersonal universalism) as is the ideal in the USA. Nor is Japanese law intended to give power to ordinary citizens. Law administrators, using their wide discretionary powers, see and treat each case on a 'case-by-case' basis. To support their discretion, they write formal laws and regulations in vague terms without specific standards or funding for enforcement. This kind of law also minimizes the ability of ordinary people to challenge that discretion – to make claims and sue on a legal basis.

Durability

To judge from performance, once put in place, the environmental reforms of the 1970s tended to keep operating. There were attempts at rollback, especially when a conservative minister was put in charge of the Environment Agency.

Citizen protests had forcefully put environmental considerations on every policy table. These struggles made the environment part of everyday discourse, and caused environmental institutions to be set up at every level of government. Once initiated, every new environmental concern and scientific finding reinforced this new environmental paradigm (Dunlap and Catton 1994), sinking it deeper into common-sense assumptions.

These changes set the stage for dramatic changes during the 1990s. The widespread and effective adoption of ISO 14000 series standards by Japanese businesses in that period flowed from their acceptance of environmentalist common sense. A similar underlying ideological change supported the government's decision to host the 1997 Kyoto Conference.[12] These new ideals did not extend to all domestic environmental issues however, or to Japan's effect on foreign environments.

CONCLUSION

Our analytical review has yielded some insights into the political processes that produced Japan's environmental successes and failures during the periods under study. Concerning problem recognition, the first stage of the process, the labeling of a new environmental condition as a problem, usually came not from the 'experts' or the 'officials', but from the ordinary people – those hurt by the change and others who sympathized with them. That the labeling of an environmental change as a 'problem' should come from ordinary 'grassroots' people indicates the need to respect such 'humble' sources of knowledge. One social scientist has referred to this source of environmental recognition as 'popular epidemiology', and accords it an important role in the environmental policy-making process (Brown 2000).

This term, popular epidemiology, serves well to indicate the typical sources of Japan's initial recognition of environmental changes as problems. Once awakened to the possibility in the 1960s by the images of Minamata, ordinary people in local communities accurately identified environmental problems and their sources, such as polluting factories, and demanded improvement. The continuing pressure in many communities for improvement – though usually only concerned about local improvement – collectively added up to a general political pressure that brought about the celebrated national environmental policies of the 1970s. That such popular epidemiology could occur testifies to the respect of basic political freedoms by the Japanese political system.

The Japanese case illustrates what probably is a very generalizable principle – that fixing environmental problems depends upon the activism of ordinary citizens. Accordingly, political systems without basic political freedoms, if they want to solve their environmental problems, may have to grant some degree of political freedom at least to citizen environmental groups and to the media. Japan's initial rebuff of citizen environmental complaints meant a considerable lag time in policy response. This delay significantly raised the costs of solving pollution problems later on. If the Japanese government had listened to the voice welling up from the polluted grass roots and caught the problems earlier, the long-run costs of remediation would have been far less.

For the second stage of the process, the policy-making response, Japan's typical response pattern is one of inter-elite cooperation under external pressure. This style, as we have seen above, had its good points – under sufficient external pressure, the networked elites could coalesce to produce a rapid and effective response. Their capacity to do so depended upon a relatively ethical and disciplined core bureaucracy, and a hierarchical organization of industry willing, under crisis at least, to follow bureaucratic orders (Desai 2002). This style of response, however, given its political intent to quiet citizen demand, tended to address only the exact demands made by the vociferous public, not other problems lurking unseen beyond public awareness. Therefore, fairly bereft of 'policy-steering' by science, the Japanese government did not cover other emerging environmental issues that experts, not the ordinary public, could have seen. Accordingly, Japan's response left holes in its coverage of environmental problems. It responded effectively to air and water pollution, but not, for instance, to the more invisible and slow-acting ground water pollution by toxic waste.

This bureaucratically centralized system had another positive environmental side-effect. In its pursuit of national energy security, MITI enforced a range of energy conservation measures, coupled with sufficient subsidies for the costs. Industry also responded efficiently to this key issue – giving Japan an extremely low energy to GDP ratio.

In contrast, more pluralistic political systems such as the USA open to the demands of many interested groups developed policies with more comprehensive coverage of all environmental problems. They were also more open to autonomous innovation in problem-solving by citizens, businesses and other organizations. However, on the negative side, such systems were more subject to 'gridlock', to immobilization by the very diversity of competing demands. Furthermore, the actual implementation of the resultant policies tended to vary according to the party in power, Republican or Democratic. Accordingly, they were sometimes less able to implement effective policy. A good comparison is regarding fossil fuel burning power plants – in the 1970s, Japan quickly put advanced pollution control equipment on its dirty power plants, while the US, 30 years later, had yet to accomplish this goal. Laxity in the USA in this regard intensified its problems of health damage from soot in the air, for example, and from acid rain damage to forests and lakes. Successive US administrations and Congresses succumbed to the influence of the power industry, financial and otherwise, in varying degrees weakening their public health commitments in this regard.

What lessons might the Japanese response stage, in comparison with more pluralistic systems, have for environmentally concerned politicians, officials or ordinary citizens in developing countries? Such countries may have very weak party systems or be outright authoritarian states. Even democratic systems may be very fragile, often just emerging from authoritarian conditions. The population may lack basic freedoms or, if present, the habits of using them. Accordingly, the ordinary people may put forth at best only the tiniest buds of popular epidemiology, nothing able to exert great pressure upon the political elites for improvements. Under such conditions, a pluralistic approach depending upon very active citizen input would not produce effective policy response to environmental problems. Nor would the centralized bureaucracy alone, without disciplined local agencies, be able to produce effective policy.

In addition, the growth of the capitalist economy produces strong business interests that want to avoid environmental regulation. These business interests fight against environmental regulation, often with more political access and effect than citizens who want to support such regulation. Furthermore, the specific array of interests within the domestic business community can have a powerful effect upon a nation's environmental problems and policies. In this regard, Japan's array of powerful economic interest groups differed from those in the USA, Australia and Canada to distinct effect. Japan's domestic energy companies do not make major profits from increasing domestic oil and gas consumption. Accordingly, they do not have a strong economic interest driving them to resist energy conservation. In the USA, however, the oil industry controls much of the world's oil and gas trade and production, and profits greatly from its use. Under the current Bush Cheney administration, those companies virtually control national energy policy. That is a major reason why this administration has resisted attempts to conserve energy and reduce carbon dioxide emissions. In addition, the major US automobile companies make more money by selling big 'gas guzzling' cars, so have only developed fuel-efficient cars under pressure from the popularity of Japanese auto models.

Applying these insights to the typical situation of developing nations, concerned officials' and activists' best strategies may be to work for incremental improvement in basic political support for effective environmental policy. They can try to produce increasing political recognition and approval of the important role of citizens' environmental groups and activities. At the same time, they should try to sponsor environmental citizen groups, activities and participation in policy-making however they can. They should also make a realistic assessment of the array of business interests and their orientations toward various types of environmental protection. It may be that they can construct 'win-win' coalitions that inspire business support, or at least do not stimulate their antagonism. Hopefully, this strategy would induce a growth toward the political conditions needed for successful environmental policy.

At the third stage of the process, implementation, Japan typically used DCI. DCI involves bureaucratic discretion in setting standards and close cooperation with industry in implementing the standards. In order for this procedure to produce any outcome beneficial to the environment, the bureaucratic officials have to be very ethical; they must adhere to the spirit or intent of the law. Whereas the Western bureaucratic ideals remain the inflexible imposition of the law, the DCI approach stresses more bureaucratic autonomous creativity by local officials to make the most effective fit between the intent of the law and the local conditions. At its best, in a relationship known as 'embedded autonomy' (Evans 1995), this procedure allows officials to negotiate with businesses and other actors to adjust regulations to maximize environmental benefits in a given situation. If the officials 'sell out' to business interests, however, the system would degenerate into ineffective 'cronyism'. Such bureaucratic sell-out, although hard to research, no doubt occurred at times in Japan. However, Japan generally has a fairly 'clean', if autocratic, reputation for its bureaucracy. It also has a sufficiently active local citizenry community so that such sell-outs are likely to be noticed, criticized and protested, sometimes to political effect.

For most developing (as well as developed) countries, bureaucracies wield a great deal of power, but they may also be quite 'corrupt' – officials may seek 'rent' from their status, rather than the impersonal making and implementation of policy. Such tendencies mean that bureaucracies cease to be reliable autonomous agents of policy implementation, environmental or otherwise. Under such circumstances, the main option for those publicly minded officials, or other persons who would protect the environment, is to work to activate the victims of pollution to seek their own environmental rights. These new interested groups will then, by their demands, somewhat redress the imbalance of power and push other authorities toward properly implementing environmental policies. Indeed, opening up the political 'space' and freedom for such groups to demand redress of their own grievances, factious and 'selfish' though they may be, is an essential part of the democratic process.

The fourth stage of the process refers to policy durability. In Japan, once facilities for reducing a certain type of pollution were installed in large companies, they became accepted and retained as part of normal operating routine (institutionalized). The MITI and other agencies helped install not only the requisite pollution-removal and energy-conserving equipment, but also the monitoring personnel needed to keep it functioning well. National certification programs kept these personnel up-to-date in their skills. Also, agencies and offices to receive and process pollution complaints were established at all levels of government. These kinds of measures did not always extend to small and medium-sized enterprises, which remained more environmentally problematic.

Japan's emphasis on the centrality of bureaucratic mediation of policy implementation, and on the ethical duty of business and the public to cooperate therewith, helped the durability of policies once implemented. These traits helped Japan avoid the tendency so often found in more pluralistic societies of policy regress. In pluralistic societies, once the interest group(s) pushing for a given policy lose interest, the policy tends to 'lose steam'. Alternately, the groups supposedly under regulation 'capture' the responsible agency, rendering it ineffective (Sabatier 1975). In either case, bureaucracies effectively let it lapse, making it into a 'paper policy' decorating the law books, but without effect in practice.

Most societies, developed or developing, do not have Japan's rather high levels of popular obedience to the bureaucracies (nor Japan's levels of bureaucratic ethicality). What then is the environmentally concerned official, politician or activist to do to promote the durability of good environmental policies and practices? The rightness of policy can become a potent weapon. Once a good policy is passed on paper, even if not implemented or allowed to lapse, the policy becomes a legitimate moral standard. To the degree that the new policy accords with global standards, it gains more moral strength. Against this standard, actual enforcement and behavior can be judged and criticized. Domestic environmental officials and politicians can bring the actual, now 'deviant' behavior to the attention of international organizations, both governmental ones such as the United Nations and the World Bank, and civil ones such as the World Wildlife Fund or Greenpeace. In turn, in a 'boomerang' effect, such international organizations may put pressure on the domestic governments to live up to their laws (Keck and Sikkink 1998). In these ways, local people can work to improve the effectiveness and durability of environmental policies.

In conclusion, the broad social and political contexts behind Japan's environmental successes and failures can be summed up as: a functioning democracy respectful of formal rights and freedoms, a legal and court system respectful of formal law, an ethical, autonomous core bureaucracy embedded in networks of reciprocity with other elites, a relatively obedient, neo-corporatist social structure within the business and labor sectors respectively, a strong and widespread dedication to national improvement, sufficient market competitive freedom to allow entrepreneurship by large corporations, sufficient autonomy to local government to allow them policy innovation and stricter standards, a culture stressing collective responsibility, and a citizenry increasingly awakening to the rights and duties of democratic citizenship. The formal institutions of democracy were a necessary but not sufficient condition of Japan's successful air pollution control (as a comparison with the USA's dirty power plants will quickly indicate). Success also required an engaged citizenry using the tools of democracy, and a dominant elite willing to allow popular demands.

NOTES

[1] In this chapter, I use the nation as the relevant unit of analysis. By nation I mean a geographical area with a state controlling the legitimate use of force. The term 'society', as used here, refers to patterns of social relationships among the people within a nation; 'culture' refers to commonly held beliefs, preferences, moral standards and technologies within any group of people. Social and cultural patterns, as well as economic and political factors, may well overflow national boundaries, come from outside, as with globalization, or subdivide within the nation.

[2] In this chapter, the term 'ecology' refers to the bio geo chemical systems of the planet. In the current geological age until the development of human civilization, these systems exhibited a punctuated equilibrium. Industrial civilization, with its massive use of 'resources' and output of 'waste', is in the process of changing the current ecological equilibrium, with unknown effects. Human-induced ecological changes destroy the life conditions of many species; mobile species flee to safety if they can. Only culture-using species such as human beings can recognize and label the ecological changes as collective 'problems'. By so recognizing and labeling them, people make ecological changes into environmental problems. An 'environment' is the ecology as it bears upon a certain site or subject, in this case human beings. Hence, an 'environmental problem' means something recognized as such by people (even if it is only deleterious to another species).

[3] The learning curve would differ by society, some learning fast and thoroughly, and others not, depending upon societal conditions. Learning would presumably make the solution of successive environmental problems easier. In that case, an environmental problem cropping up early on the learning curve would have a harder time than one arising later.

[4] For a full analysis of the four periods, see Broadbent (2002).

[5] This data comes from: (1) a count of environmental protest events in the Asahi newspaper (Broadbent 1998); (2) a count of protest events reported in a year-by-year compendium of

Japanese environmental incidents that ends in 1975 (Iijima 1979).

[6] The Pollution-related Health Damage Compensation Law of 1973.

[7] Traditional popular adages (*kotowaza*) express this status hierarchy: 'revere the bureaucrats and despise the people' (*kanson minpi*).

[8] Peter Evans calls this relationship 'embedded autonomy' (Evans 1995). The term 'embedded' refers to the ministry being situated within dense social relationships with the business community. The term 'autonomy' refers to the ministry not being 'seduced' by those close ties into being a puppet of the business community, but rather retaining its own independent capacity to make and advocate policies for the benefit of the whole business community, or perhaps the whole society.

[9] A social movement consists of a set of people in sustained opposition to the policies or institutions of the established government, elites and society; often using 'unruly' means to generate political pressure. The movement can give rise to different kinds of social movement organizations (SMOs), ranging from diffuse aggregations to tight hierarchical bureaucracies, but usually encompassing most of the activists. An NGO is usually an established, registered formal organization employing full-time staff, collecting dues from many members who are not activists, and using accepted political means of working toward its policy goals (della Porta and Diani 1999, pp. 13-19).

[10] Literally 'Life Cooperative Union' (*Seikatsu Kyodo Kumiai*).

[11] In the USA, Environmental Defense has had great success with this approach.

[12] Why this change spread to the pro-growth cluster in Japan but not in the USA is an intriguing question.

[13] James Scott (1998) analyzes this phenomenon in his book, *Seeing Like a State*. This logic encompasses both socialist and capitalist societies, so is broader than the logic of 'capital accumulation' often used to explain this kind of polarity (O'Connor 1996).

6. Japan's Environmental Policy: International Cooperation

Hidefumi Imura

INTRODUCTION

External forces and foreign pressures (*gaiatsu*) have been very powerful factors contributing to changes in Japan. *Gaiatsu* has been utilized by actors within Japan as a political tool to help push through changes to society which could not be easily achieved by other means (Ikuta 1995, pp. 21, 27, and 31).

Japan's environmental policy decisions have been influenced strongly by international factors and relationships. Environmental policy changes in the 1960s and 1970s were shaped to a large extent by the new policies adopted in the USA and Europe and discussions in international conferences. Likewise, the reform of Japan's environmental policy in the 1990s was made under the influence of Japan's participation in international conferences and agreements and the initiatives of international scientific communities, such as the Intergovernmental Panel on Climate Change (IPCC).

After World War II, Japan placed priority on its relationships with the USA and other Western nations. Japan's relations with its Asian neighbors were often strained. China, for example, protested when Prime Minister Koizumi paid a visit to Yasukuni Shrine, which commemorates Japan's war dead. There are also still territorial disputes, as exists between China and Japan over the Senkaku Islands. With the economic development in Asia in the last few decades, Japan has shifted its priorities, especially in trade and economic relations, towards greater contact with developing countries in Asia, including China and the countries of the Association of Southeast Asian Nations (ASEAN). The shift is reflected in the increasing Japanese trade in the region. The share of ASEAN, China and other Asian newly industrialized economies in total Japanese exports increased from 28.7 per cent in 1970 to 44.6 per cent in 2000, while the share of the US and European Union (EU) member states also increased from 37.0 per cent to 48.6 per cent (Yano Tsuneta Kinenkai 2003, pp. 343-45). Japan's international cooperation for environmental protection also has been focused on countries in Asia even though economic disparities in the region complicate the search for cooperative solutions.

As a result of economic growth, per capita consumption of energy and other resources in Asia is increasing; however, per capita consumption levels remain considerably smaller in the developing countries of Asia than in Japan and other industrialized countries.

Japan has taken several important initiatives for the advancement of international environmental policy. The government has expanded its development assistance programs for environmental protection in developing countries. It chose to host the international conference where the Kyoto Protocol was established in December 1997. It has also been actively engaged in technology transfer and other assistance to mitigate environmental problems in developing countries. An important question for Japan is what it can and should do in the realm of international environmental policy and bilateral cooperation. Can Japanese experiences, especially in relation to environmental policies, governance structures, and environmental technologies, be effectively transferred and utilized in developing countries?

Environmental Protection Needs in Asia and the Pacific Region

Asia will become economically more influential in the world during the twenty-first century as its industrial production increases. At the same time, Asia will have the largest environmental impact of any region in the world due to the natural resources that will be required for industrial production and consumption by a population that makes up 50 per cent of the global population.

Asia is rich in biological diversity because of its varied climatic systems. It has monsoon, oceanic, as well as inland dry climate conditions; this variety has produced diverse ecological systems. This valuable natural environment is rapidly vanishing due to industrialization and development. It is imperative for Asia to realize a pattern of production and consumption that will minimize environmental impacts and protect natural ecosystems from expanding areas of human activity.

Although industrialization has occurred at various times in countries throughout Asia, they share common experiences with rapid development. As a result, the economic gap among countries in the region is quickly narrowing. A look back on Japan's environmental history during the twentieth century sheds some light on how nations in Asia might go about solving environmental issues that they face as a result of rapid industrialization (Imura and Katsuhara 1999).

The problems Asian countries face can be categorized into three groups. The first category includes problems arising from increasing industrial production such as pollutants and industrial waste being released into the air and water near factories and power plants. The second category is urbanization. Economic functions tend to be heavily concentrated in cities. Asia has experienced rapid urbanization as a result of recent economic growth. As a consequence, many Asian countries are suffering from air pollution due to increasing automobile traffic, waste water from increasing urban populations, and solid waste generated by citizens with higher standards of living.

If industrialization and urbanization represent one side of economic development, then the resulting environmental problems found in the underdeveloped regions represent the other side. The issues facing underdeveloped regions in Asia include the need for preservation of ecological systems that are being pressured by large populations and poverty. The income gap between urban and rural areas and developed and underdeveloped areas is widening in many parts of Asia.

Asia and Globalization

The world is undergoing globalization. In Japan it has become common to use the English phrase, 'global standard.' The ideals and values of Western society such as capitalism, the liberalization of trade, capital and investment, democracy, scientific rationalism, and industrialized production are spreading. For many Japanese people the goal is to obtain US values and a US-style economic system; inherent Japanese cultural values are being denied. Yet the question still remains whether or not economic, industrial and consumption systems and life styles initiated by the West and now being disseminated on a global basis are environmentally sound. Such systems are certainly superior in terms of material affluence, but what will be their impact on the global environment if spread throughout Asia and other parts of the world? If globalization of the economy means to implement US-style systems on a global basis, the effects on the global environment could be drastic (Imura 2002).

Production and consumption systems must shift to a new type of system that can minimize impact on the environment. While Asian countries inevitably desire to follow much the same industrializing process Western countries went through, they should seek different development patterns. Taking motorization issues as an example, establishing transportation systems that have little environmental impact should be one of the top priorities for Asian cities.

Japan is in a position to play a special role in Asia in terms of promoting pollution control and environmental protection. Since the early 1990s, Japan has begun to play a more active role in disseminating environmental technology, information, and know-how in Asia. Learning from its successes and failures, Japan's own policy priorities have shifted as has its approach to the provision of environmental assistance.

JAPAN'S FOREIGN ENVIRONMENTAL POLICIES

Organizations involved in International Environmental Cooperation

The environment has become an increasingly important issue in Japan's diplomacy. There are now numerous ministries and agencies in Japan playing a role in environmental development assistance and international environmental negotiations. The Ministry of Foreign Affairs (MOFA) is responsible for the formulation of common official development assistance (ODA) guidelines, implementation of ODA loans and promotion of technical cooperation. In the early 1990s, the Ministry of Foreign Affairs created the post of Ambassador for Global Environmental Issues and placed more emphasis on greening ODA.

The Japan International Cooperation Agency (JICA) and the Japan Bank for International Cooperation (JBIC) are responsible for financing and implementing most ODA projects. The JBIC is a relatively new institution. In October 1999, the Japan Export Import Bank (JEXIM) and the Overseas Economic Cooperation Fund (OECF) were merged to form the JBIC. In April 2004, the administrative status of JICA, which had been a special corporation, a kind of semi-governmental agency under the control of the MOFA, was changed to an independent administrative organization. Although its English name remained unchanged, its Japanese name was changed from *kokusai kyoryoku jigyoudan* to *kokusai kyoryoku kiko*. For a long time, the president of JICA was held as an *amakudari* post for the MOFA. As a result of the reform, JICA will have more freedom to decide its own policy. JICA is mainly responsible for technical cooperation projects including project identification studies, dispatch of experts and acceptance of trainees, while the JBIC is in charge of ODA loans.

The Ministry of Economy, Trade and Industry (METI) also has its own form of environmental assistance for developing countries known as the Green Aid Plan. The Green Aid Plan aims to help developing countries in taking measures against pollution caused by industrial activities by transferring Japanese technologies. The first projects, started in 1992, were for the transfer of flue-gas desulfurization technology to China and Thailand.

The Ministry of the Environment (MOE) also has accumulated expertise and technical know-how in international environmental cooperation. In the early 1990s, the Environment Agency (EA) established a Global Environmental Department by elevating its former division for international cooperation to departmental status. This was done so that the EA could take a leadership role in international environmental policy discussions and cope with important international negotiations. When the EA was reformed and became the MOE, a more powerful Global Environmental Bureau was formed.

At the same time that the government has implemented a number of international environmental programs and projects, private firms have strengthened their roles in technology transfer through commercial channels. Japan's foreign direct investment (FDI) recorded a peak in 1998: 7.4 trillion yen (or US $600 billion) of which 33.4 per cent was directed to the USA, 38.7 per cent to Europe, and 16.0 per cent to Asia. FDI to Asia recorded a peak in 1997: 1.5 trillion yen or 22.6 per cent of the total FDI for that year (Ministry of Finance 2003). Many Japanese enterprises in the manufacturing sector moved their production bases to other parts of the world, although investment in Asia shrank somewhat after the Asian economic crisis in 1997. The movement of companies overseas has contributed to the dissemination of Japan's relatively more efficient production technologies to developing countries. It also has meant a reduction in domestic emissions of pollutants.

Environmental non-governmental organizations (NGOs) are also playing a greater cooperative role overseas, especially at the grass roots level. Some municipalities and prefectures are promoting environmental cooperation based on sister city relations with foreign cities (Yoshida 2001, pp. 47-55).

Internal Bureaucratic Rivalry

While environmental issues have become an important component of Japan's foreign policy, it is not unusual for there to be competition between or among ministries in determining environmental positions. Opinions are sometimes divided over how to respond when the international community moves towards the formation of an agreement that will require Japan to enforce new regulations or change existing policies. In deciding on a Japanese policy position on climate change during the 1997 Kyoto Conference, for example, the EA and the Ministry of International Trade and Industry (MITI, now METI) differed substantially in their perspectives. The EA favored the proposal put forth by the EU that called upon industrialized countries to achieve ambitious reductions of their greenhouse gases, while the position of MITI was closer to that of the USA; MITI was reluctant to require action without the participation of developing countries.

These kinds of internal conflicts between and among ministries are not normally publicized, but can be discerned because of the different tones that can be found in their reports. MITI's basic policy on global climatic change, which differed somewhat from that of other ministries, was outlined in a report published by the Global Environment Committee of the Council of Industrial Structure, an advisory body to MITI, on 12 March 1997 (Global

Environmental Committee of the Council of Industrial Structure 1997). The report expressed concerns about the conflicts between economic growth and environmental objectives and the difficulty of achieving targets without the participation of developing countries. It concluded with the need to develop innovative technology, a typical Japanese approach to pollution control.

The different positions of ministries on the climate change issue reflect differences in their mandates. An important role of MOE is the formulation of national environmental policies that are in harmony with international decisions. The MOE can take relatively flexible positions in response to requests to join international agreements. Other ministries such as METI may find this more difficult because they are more closely connected to business interests that may be affected by new regulatory requirements. Generally, this business support puts METI in a strong position in inter-ministerial negotiations, but international environmental trends and changing environmental norms have helped to strengthen the MOE's position in the policy formulation process.

Changes in International Environmental Policy Priorities

Achieving harmonization with US and European environmental policy was a main concern of Japan's international environmental policy until the mid-1980s. Priorities were placed on bilateral cooperation with the USA and participation in discussions among industrialized countries, such as in the Organization for Economic Cooperation and Development (OECD). Since the mid-1980s, priorities have shifted to international negotiations about environmental agreements in which the role of developing countries is increasingly important. In this period, Japan expanded substantially its cooperation programs with developing countries, especially in Asia.

China initiated reform and economic opening policies in 1978 and has become more integrated into the global economy since the Cold War ended. Japan's international environmental policies have had to adapt rapidly to the changing regional conditions in Asia. Japan increased significantly its ODA to China as a result of its reforms and the seriousness of its pollution problems although from 1990-95 aid was cut off in response to the Tian'anmen incident. In 1996, Japan restarted its aid disbursements to China, placing priority on environmental projects (Ministry of Foreign Affairs 1999).

Changes in Korean Japanese relations are also noteworthy. Rapid economic development in Korea and the policy of former President Kim Dae-Jung in favor of establishing an amicable relation with Japan encouraged new regional environmental cooperation in Northeast Asia. The First Tripartite Environmental Ministers Meeting (TEMM) of Japan, China, and Korea was held in Seoul in 1999. Subsequently annual meetings have been held in Beijing, Tokyo, and Seoul on a rotating basis. The environment ministers agreed in these meetings that the three countries should cooperate in the promotion of environmental industries and in systematic studies of the sand dust problems facing the region that are exacerbated by soil degradation in Northwest China (National Institute of Environmental Research, Korea 2004).

The EA set up a forum for informal dialogues among Environmental Ministers and high-level government officials of the countries in Asia and the Pacific Region. This forum was named the Environmental Congress for Asia and the Pacific, or ECO ASIA. The Environment Agency has hosted ECO ASIA's yearly meetings since 1991. In September 2000, Japan hosted the Fourth Ministerial Conference on Environment and Development of the United Nations Economic and Social Commission for Asia and the Pacific (ESCAP) (2000, pp. 1-101). The meeting was held in Kitakyushu City back-to-back with the 2000 meeting of ECO ASIA.

Increasing Environmental Technology Markets in Asia

There is increasing competition between Western countries and Japan in the expanding Asian market. Competition in environmental technology transfer is also likely to intensify. Japan, with its advanced environmental technologies, including air pollution control devices and monitoring instruments, has been enthusiastic about providing environmental ODA to developing countries in Asia. However, US and European companies also want to export environmental technologies for urban waste disposal, sewage systems, industrial effluent waste management, and air pollution control (International Trade Administration 1993, pp. 1-38). The technologies that are lowest in cost and easiest to maintain are most in demand in Asian countries. Technological development that can meet this demand is essential. Countries such as China are making an effort to nurture environmental industry, encouraging the development of their own environmental technologies (People's Republic of China 2002, pp. 19-21; Overseas Environmental Cooperation Center 2004, pp. 1-25).

ENVIRONMENTAL COOPERATION WITH ASIA

Regional Cooperation

Issues related to the future of the environment are on the common agenda for Japan and other Asian countries. Countries of the region must work cooperatively to deal with the problems they face. Recent opportunities for international discussions among these countries have been increasing.

Examples include environmental discussions within the Asia Pacific Economic Cooperation (APEC) forum; meetings of international bodies, like the United Nations' ESCAP conferences; and ECO ASIA, a forum set up by the EA where high-level government officials (including ministers), experts from international organizations, and private organizations and environment researchers in the region can freely exchange viewpoints. ECO ASIA aims at promoting long-term activities for environmental protection by governments and relevant organizations in Asia and the Pacific Region (Environment Agency 2000, pp. 1-17).

One of the major objectives of these conferences is to coordinate each country's policy on solving common problems such as climatic change. The Third Tripartite Environmental Ministers Meeting of Japan, China and Korea, in particular, exchanged views on national responses to the implementation of the Kyoto Protocol. Other important objectives are raising awareness of various regional problems and exchanging information on effective measures. It is expected that these discussions will provide a basis for further development of environmental technology transfer and financial cooperation.

Environmental ODA

ODA philosophy and ODA reform
Japan's ODA philosophy has changed with time to include a greater role for environmental protection. In June 1992, the Cabinet approved Japan's Official Development Assistance Charter, which established the broad philosophies underpinning Japanese aid policy (Overseas Environmental Cooperation Center 2001, pp. 157-9).

The Charter states that environmental conservation is a task for all humankind. It confirms Japan's commitment to assist developing countries in tackling environmental problems, using its technology and know-how. It also identifies countries in East Asia, including members of ASEAN and China, as priority recipients for Japan's ODA. The Charter states that Japan will help people suffering from famine and poverty, aid refugees, and provide assistance for the basic human needs sector and emergency humanitarian aid. Priorities are placed on assistance for human resources and capacity development to encourage self-help efforts towards socioeconomic development.

The Charter was reviewed in 2002 to address new development challenges such as peace building and the enhancement of the transparency and efficacy of ODA. An important background factor of this review was Japan's financial situation. As a result of a large government deficit, the government has had to cut Japan's total public expenditures, including its ODA budget, which had been growing for years. Politicians and citizens, moreover, have become more concerned about the effectiveness and impact of Japanese ODA. Economic and fiscal strains in the late 1990s have led to debate on ODA reform issues. ODA has been closely examined within the government. In 1998, the Ministerial Council on External Economic Cooperation, comprising government ministries and agencies involved in ODA activities, decided that measures to improve transparency should be taken, by formulating a medium-term policy and establishing country-specific assistance programs. Country programs, which are prepared for three to four countries every year, define priority issues and sectors in each recipient country (Ministry of Foreign Affairs 2002b, pp. 125-30).

Japan's environmental ODA policy
During the decade between the 1992 United Nations Conference on Environment and Development (UNCED) and the 2002 Johannesburg World Summit on Sustainable Development many major environmental aid programs were initiated by Japan. At the UNCED the Japanese government announced that it would increase Japan's ODA for the environment. Japan pledged to expend approximately 900 billion to 1 trillion yen in bilateral and multilateral aid to support environmental protection over five years from 1992 to 1996; contribute to the preservation of the world's forests, water, and air, as well as help improve the ability of developing countries to deal with environmental problems. As partnership between donors and recipients is particularly important in environmental cooperation, various assistance schemes suited to the development stages of recipient countries are used to enhance their efforts to identify, formulate, and implement effective projects through policy dialogue. The first goal was reached in FY 1995. By 1996 a total of 1.5 trillion yen had been spent (Ministry of Foreign Affairs 2002b).

The government's priority on environmental assistance was reaffirmed with its 1997 announcement of the program, Initiatives for Sustainable Development (ISD) toward the Twenty-first Century at the United Nations Assembly for the Overall Review and Appraisal of the Implementation of Agenda 21. The ISD included action plans for air and water pollution, waste disposal, climate change, nature conservation, afforestation, fresh water problems, and public awareness building. In the same year, the Kyoto Initiative on aid for global warming programs in developing countries was announced. The Kyoto Initiative stated that Japan would provide support for global warming programs in addition to traditional environmental programs, providing ODA loans at the most concessional rates available.

At the Johannesburg World Summit, the government announced its Environmental Conservation Initiative for Sustainable Development (Ministry of Foreign Affairs 2002b). In contrast with earlier plans, the Environmental Conservation Initiative makes mention of Japan's difficult economic and financial conditions and emphasizes the responsibility and role of developing countries in resolving their own environmental problems. As a top principle for Japan's environmental cooperation, it lists capacity building and human resources development in developing countries. This means that Japan, confronted with financial difficulties, is determined to use its ODA budget more efficiently. For environmental projects, this means a combination of 'hard' cooperation (infrastructure building and equipment provision) and 'soft' cooperation (human capacity building) (Ministry of Foreign Affairs 2002a).

In March 2003, Japan's ODA Charter was amended. The new Charter continues to give priority to environmental projects and Japan's relations with Asian countries, but has a somewhat new thrust. It states that the objectives of Japan's ODA are to contribute to the peace and development of the international community, thereby helping to ensure Japan's own security and prosperity. Its priorities are poverty reduction; sustainable growth; addressing global issues, such as global warming and other environmental problems; infectious diseases; population; food; energy; natural disasters, and; peace building (Ministry of Foreign Affairs 2003).

Environmental ODA and capacity building
Though developing countries may have much need for assistance in environmental areas, they tend to put priority on development projects. Environmental programs are often neglected. It is important to help developing countries improve their own skills and capacities for dealing with environmental problems. Japanese assistance focuses on training people in developing countries and the dispatch of experts. Japan's establishment of environmental centers in developing countries is one example of an effort to help to strengthen and improve the environmental management capacity of developing countries. Japan has provided such cooperation to Thailand, Indonesia, China, Mexico, Chile, and Egypt (Japan Society for International Development 2003, pp. 1-112). In 2004, new center projects also started in Vietnam and the Philippines. The Environmental Research and Training Center in Thailand, moreover, started a program for South-South cooperation, serving as a training center for people from neighboring countries.

While improving capacity in developing countries is an underlying principle of Japan's environmental ODA, implementation of this goal can be problematic due to a lack of human resources, not just in the developing country, but on Japan's end as well. Unfortunately, there are not many Japanese experts who have high levels of expertise relevant to developing countries and are willing to work in the environmental aid field.

NGOs are also starting to play a role in human capacity building overseas. NGOs are particularly suited to activities geared towards specific local communities, where they can contribute to environmental plan making as well as environmental education of local people. The Japanese government has started to support the environmental cooperation programs of NGOs through grant assistance for grass-roots projects and the NGO subsidy framework (Ministry of Foreign Affairs 2002c, pp. 36-7 and 53-54).

Japan's ODA budget and environmental cooperation

Japan was the world's top donor of ODA among the 21 Development Assistance Committee members of the OECD for 1991-2000. Environmental projects rapidly expanded their share of Japan's ODA during this time.

ODA expenditures for the environment peaked at 536 billion yen in 1999, an amount equivalent to 33.5 per cent of the total budget as shown in Table 6.1. The majority was loan assistance, which is used mostly for bilateral aid. The share of grant aid and technical cooperation was small. The breakdown of the bilateral aid by field is shown in Table 6.2. In the early 1990s, the largest portion (66.9 per cent in 1994) was spent for projects to improve the living environment. Examples include improvements to basic infrastructure to provide safe drinking water and urban sewage systems. In the late 1990s, priority shifted somewhat to pollution control (40 per cent in 1999). Most of the aid is used for so-called 'brown issues' (e.g. industrial pollution control and sewerage treatment plants). Spending for so-called 'green issues,' such as forest conservation, remains small.

Table 6.1   Japan's Environmental ODA by Aid Type*

	1990	1995	1999	2000
Grant aid	22.8	42.8	29.4	24.4
Loan assistance	124.4	170.8	464.5	380.1
Technical cooperation	13.2	22.3	28.3	25.3
Multilateral assistance	4.9	40.0	13.6	15.4
Total	165.4	276.0	535.7	463.2

Notes: *Billion yen.
Source: Ministry of Foreign Affairs, Japan's ODA Annual Report 2002.

Special interest rates on ODA loans for environmental projects

Since 1995, Japan has been granting ODA loans for environmental projects at interest rates 0.2 per cent lower than loans for ordinary projects. Since 1989, even upper-middle-income countries whose gross national product (GNP) exceeds a certain level have been eligible for environmental ODA projects. The border between upper-middle and lower-middle income class countries was a 1995 per capita GNP rate of $3,035 in 1997 (Ministry of Foreign Affairs 1998, p. 386). Thanks to these changes, the percentage of ODA loans granted for environmental programs grew from an average of less than 10 per cent of all bilateral loans during 1986-90 to an average of about 20 per cent during 1992-96.

Table 6.2   Japan's Bilateral Environmental ODA by Aid Field

Bilateral Aid*	1990	1995	1999	2000
Living environment	43.2	129.6	130.3	102.5
Forest conservation	12.7	25.2	8.9	16.8
Pollution control	74.1	18.3	209.0	60.8
Disaster prevention	15.6	45.3	65.6	42.1
Other projects	79.6	17.6	108.3	216.7
Total	165.2	236.0	522.1	438.9

Notes: *Billion yen. All projects other than multilateral projects are counted. Other projects include environmental impact assessment, environmental administration and marine pollution.
Source: Ministry of Foreign Affairs, Japan's ODA Annual Report, 2002.

Japan's environmental ODA projects have covered four major fields: living environment improvement, protection of forests, combating pollution, and disaster prevention. The majority of projects receiving environmental soft loans were in the areas of living environment improvement (e.g. drinking water and sanitation) and disaster prevention. Only about 20 per cent of all environmental soft loans, or 4 per cent of all bilateral loans, funded projects for the promotion of anti-pollution measures and global environmental issues, such as climatic change (Japan International Cooperation Agency, 2001, pp. 136-9; Overseas Environmental Cooperation Center 2001, pp. 6-22). In order to encourage developing countries to tackle environmental issues, in 1997 Prime Minister Ryutaro Hashimoto during a visit to China announced that Japan would further relax loan terms (International Development Center 1998). It lowered interest rates to 0.75 per cent and extended the repayment period to 40 years with a grace period of 10 years.

The new soft terms are applied to environmental loans that fund projects designed to improve the global environment, such as forestry, energy conservation, new energy sources, as well as anti-pollution technology for reducing air and water pollution and promoting better treatment of wastes. These conditions are the same as those of the World Bank Group's International Development Association and are the most favorable conditions available in the world. This substantial lowering of interest rates on environmental ODA loans is a demonstration of the Japanese government's interest in promoting measures for global and regional environmental protection, especially in Asia, where rapid industrialization is causing increasingly serious pollution problems.

Technical cooperation: JICA

Another important form of Japanese aid is technical cooperation, that is, the transfer of technology and knowledge for socioeconomic development. JICA is responsible for the technical cooperation aspect of Japan's ODA programs; as of December 2003 it had more than 1,300 staff members working both in Japan and in its approximately 50 overseas offices (Japan International Cooperation Agency 2003, p. 13).

JICA implements a number of environment-related projects. In FY 1989 JICA allotted 10 billion yen (10.1 per cent of JICA's entire budget for project implementation) to projects in the environmental field; by FY 1998 this figure had grown dramatically to 30.4 billion yen (19.6 per cent of the total budget). JICA hosts a number of environmental training courses covering various issues in addition to sending experts abroad. In 2000, it brought in 2,227 trainees from developing countries and sent 505 experts overseas to work on environment-related projects. JICA has started work on state of the environment country studies and an assessment of various countries' needs for environmental cooperation. It has introduced environmental centers in key developing countries in order to strengthen their institutional capacity for environmental management. These can be categorized as 'project-type technical cooperation', in which grant aid for facilities, dispatch of Japanese experts and acceptance of trainees from recipient countries are combined (Japan International Cooperation Agency 2001).

While JICA is implementing a number of technical cooperation projects in the environmental field, JICA itself has few experts in relevant fields. Thus, it must recruit experts from private companies, central and local governments, and NGOs on a case-by-case basis. Moreover, it is the MOFA, not JICA that decides the basic direction of international cooperation policy. In reality, JICA has had little freedom or power to establish international environmental cooperation policies or programs independently. In October 2003, as a part of the reform of the national government system, JICA was transformed into an independent administrative organization. This reform has given JICA greater independence from central government control.

Bilateral loans: the Japan Bank for International Cooperation

The JBIC is in charge of implementing the bilateral loan programs that formerly were dealt with by the OECF in addition to commercial base loans which JEXIM was handling until the two organizations were merged in 1999.

Loans in the environmental field increased sharply in the 1990s even though the JBIC's total loans began to decrease in 1995. There were various reasons for the decrease in total loan disbursements. One factor was Japan's growing government deficit. Another was that traditional economic infrastructure project needs were lowered because of the economic growth achieved by many of Japan's ODA recipients in Asia. These countries began to utilize multiple channels for the financing of infrastructure projects, including commercial loans and FDI. Third, Japanese politicians and businesses began expressing concern about the use of ODA that may improve productivity in recipient countries. The rapid industrial expansion in China and other countries in Asia is perceived as a threat to Japanese industries. Thus, there are growing demands that ODA should be limited to purposes such as environmental protection and poverty alleviation. This is a major reason behind the increasing budget for environmental projects. In the case of China, the share held by environmental projects was 65 per cent of total loans in 1999. In the future, however, Japan's weak economic condition in the early 2000s and the rapid economic growth of China are likely to cause a decline of the total ODA budget for environmental projects.

Concerns have been expressed about the environmental consequences of development projects financed by the JBIC. Responding to this, the JBIC published a new environmental guideline in April 2002, a revision of its former guidelines (Japan Bank for International Cooperation 2002b). The JBIC also began publishing an annual environmental report to further green Japan's ODA (Japan Bank for International Cooperation 2002a). A weakness of both JICA and the JBIC is their relatively small number of employees who are specialists in the field of environmental protection. The JBIC is also institutionally constrained because it must operate under the guidance of MOFA and the Ministry of Finance.

A limitation of Japan's bilateral loans is that a recipient must be a government organization or a government-affiliated institution. In an effort to find a way to work with private enterprises, the JBIC created a system called 'two-step loans' (TSL): the recipient country sets up a special environmental fund using the low interest loan of JBIC, and private enterprises can borrow from the fund through handling banks. A system for providing loans to environmental projects of small local enterprises is being experimented with in Indonesia, Thailand and the Philippines. In designing the environmental TSL system, it was assumed that there would be many enterprises willing to borrow from the fund and the money would circulate as a 'revolving fund.' Initial responses suggest, however, that the system needs to be improved so that enterprises will be more willing to invest in pollution control (Mori 2002).

Environmental Cooperation with China

Japan's environmental cooperation with China has special significance for both countries from the viewpoint of not only the environmental but also the political and economic security of East Asia. Diplomatic relations between the two countries were normalized in September 1972. The Japan China Peace and Friendship Treaty was concluded in August 1978, the same year that China's reform and open-door policy started. In 1979, China requested Japan to provide 'yen loans' to assist China's new economic policy. In the late 1980s, China became the largest recipient of Japan's bilateral ODA. Although Japan's aid to China was cut after the Tian'anmen incident, China was once again the largest recipient of Japan's bilateral ODA by 1997.

With its rapid economic development, China's emissions of sulfur oxides, nitrogen oxides, and carbon dioxide have increased greatly, consequently increasing the damage from acid rain and aggravating environmental pollution. For this reason, when a Japanese high-level mission on economic cooperation visited China in March 1992, the two governments agreed that they would make the environment one of their future ODA priorities. In April 1996, the Japan China Comprehensive Forum on Environmental Cooperation met for the first time and exchanged views on environmental cooperation between the two countries. This Forum consists of high-level government officials and environmental experts from Japan and China, and holds meetings in China and Japan alternately (Ministry of Foreign Affairs 1998, pp. 56-60).

Japan's bilateral aid to China for the period from 1979-99 amounted to a total of US $14.5 billion: $3.8 billion of grant aid and technical cooperation and $10.7 billion of loan aid including untied loans. This amount was almost equivalent to a half of the total bilateral aid China received. In parallel with ODA, direct investment of Japanese private enterprises in China also increased: a total of US $38.8 billion was invested for 20,383 projects from 1979-2000 according to a Chinese source (Mitsubishi Research Institute 2002, p. 526). Economic interdependence between the two countries has become stronger with the trend towards market globalization and China's rapid industrial growth. In 2001, China was the second largest trade partner for Japan next to the USA, while Japan was the largest trade partner for China. In fact, the export of Japanese products such as iron and steel to China largely contributed to the economic recovery of some Japanese industries in the 2003-4 fiscal year (Japan Iron and Steel Federation 2004).

At the implementation level, cooperation is already taking place in water and sewer improvement, waste treatment, antipollution technology, and forest preservation. The Japan China Friendship Environmental Protection Center, built with Japanese grant aid, opened in May 1996, and since then, it has been gradually reinforcing its ability to serve as a national research center for environmental policy and administration as well as a center for environmental cooperation between China and Japan.

The Future of Japan – China Environmental Cooperation

At the September 1997 Japan China summit meeting, Prime Minister Hashimoto proposed the idea of 'Japan China Environmental Cooperation Toward the 21st Century,' and China agreed to it in principle. The concept had two main thrusts: establishment of a nationwide environmental information network with the Japan China Friendship Environmental Protection Center at its core and promotion of an environmental model cities' program. Computer systems were to be installed and training programs established in 100 major cities in China.

Chonqing, Gui Yang and Dalien were designated as environmental model cities. In these cities environmental regulations have been intensified, ODA loans with special interest rates for environmental projects have been provided, and technical cooperation has been promoted. Their focus has been on technical measures against urban air pollution and acid rain.

Environmental cooperation between Japan and China expanded substantially in the 1990s supported by the increased ODA budget. Japanese businesses welcomed the environmental ODA to China as they were interested in exploring the environmental technology market there. China has accepted the cooperation in order to modernize its retrofit technologies using Japanese funds. In the 2000s, however, the bilateral relation between Japan and China will be subject to drastic changes. China has achieved astounding growth and is strengthening its economic power. As a result, it will be a growing competitor to Japan in many industrial sectors. In the environmental field, China is trying to nurture its own environmental industry by developing local technologies. The transfer of advanced pollution control technology, such as flue-gas desulfurization, has at times been unsuccessful due to its high cost of operation and the lack of local expertise in maintenance.

The MOFA published a report entitled, 'Economic Cooperation Program for China' in October 2001. Starting with a review of the recent political, economic, and social developments in China, the report identifies China's priority issues in development and presented Japanese economic cooperation policies for China. The report explicitly states that because China has already achieved high economic growth, there is growing skepticism in Japan about the need for providing assistance to China. In summary, it concludes that China should implement economic infrastructure development in the developed coastal areas based on its own funds, while Japan should provide complementary support for less developed regions of the country. In western China, there is still strong local demand for Japanese ODA for environmental projects such as water and sanitation. In the future, environmental cooperation should come increasingly through business initiatives and FDI.

LOOKING TO THE FUTURE

In order to enhance Japan's international cooperation for environmental protection into the next decades several issues will need to be addressed. One is a question of leadership. Japan is an island nation geographically separated from Europe and the USA, and there have been geographical and linguistic barriers making active participation in international dialogue for environmental protection difficult. The situation, however, has improved remarkably in the last two decades or so. Japan is increasing its presence in various international meetings. Nevertheless, some people still suggest that Japan's leadership is weak relative to its economic power.

Japan has relatively good experiences with environmental policy implementation, but such information has not yet been systematically analyzed or made available to other nations. The largest obstacle here is a language problem.

Japan must strengthen its environmental initiatives as a member of Asia. It has already created regional forums such as ECO ASIA; joined the Meetings of the Three Environmental Ministers of Japan, China, and Korea; and expanded its environmental aid to Asia, especially to China and Southeast Asian countries. It has to make further efforts to consolidate these cooperation programs.

Many Japanese local governments have instituted 'inter-local' or 'inter-city' environmental cooperation, in which they investigate the applicability of their experiences to developing countries. A unique example is the cooperation between Kitakyushu, Japan and Dalien, China. Municipal level cooperation between the two cities attracted the attention of the central governments. These cities provided suggestions which led to the creation of the Japan China Environmental Model Cities Plan. NGOs are also working in international environmental cooperation, but the number of such NGOs is still small. More of this kind of cooperation should be promoted in the future.

According to MOFA, the amount of money disbursed per person engaged in ODA in Japan was $4.89 million in 1996, which was considerably larger than the figures in other countries: $2.96 million in the UK, $2.37 million in the USA, and $1.88 million in Germany (Ministry of Foreign Affairs 1997, p. 123). Japan's ODA, however, has been too heavily focused on the supply of money rather than human resources. In the future, it will be necessary to foster the development of more experts who can aid in implementing cooperation projects in diverse fields. They will need to acquire new skills and expertise specific to the countries they are to work in as Japanese experiences and methods may not always prove effective. At the same time, Japan must improve the social conditions domestically that will ensure that a sufficient number of Japanese are willing to work in such overseas settings.

The technologies that proved effective in Japan may not easily transfer to other countries. When transferring technologies, it is necessary to take into consideration the advantages and disadvantages such technology transfer may pose to societies and the environment. Situations may differ from country to country, and in some cases, the use of indigenous technologies may be more appropriate. Japan must study the possibility of developing locally suitable technologies instead of simply transferring technologies that were initially designed for Japan.

Among developing countries, the least developed face particular difficulties addressing environmental problems because they have serious shortages of funds, technologies, and human resources. Although Japan and other countries provide grant aid for infrastructure development to solve these problems, the recipient countries often do not have sufficient funds to maintain or manage the facilities provided through aid. Moreover, it is often difficult for these countries to utilize technologies provided to them unless their costs are low and they are easy to use. A lack of adequate laws and personnel adds to the difficulty of addressing environmental problems in these places. These are challenges which Japan and other developed nations must address in the future.

7. Environmental Policy Instruments

Hidefumi Imura

INTRODUCTION

Policy instruments are the tools used to enforce behavioral change. There is growing interest in understanding the variety of policy instruments at play in different countries as governments become less enchanted with strictly regulatory approaches and attempt to find more cost-efficient and effective means of improving environmental conditions or limiting pollution. Japan has long employed a variety of policy instruments, ranging from regulations, to administrative guidance, to voluntary mechanisms, and increasingly a variety of economic instruments, which are becoming popular in other countries as well (Hatch 2005; Sterner 2002; Golub 1998). This chapter begins with an overview of different types of environmental policy instruments, including regulations, economic measures and voluntary approaches (Carraro and Lévêque 1999, pp. 1-3). Voluntary approaches considered here include pollution control agreements, environmental management systems for industry, environmental plans at the national and local levels, environmental impact assessments, education, and information. The chapter surveys the changing use of environmental policy instruments in Japan and the reasons behind those changes.

ENVIRONMENTAL POLICY INSTRUMENTS

Policy instruments refer to the tools that are used for the enforcement of environmental policy, with the objective of achieving a certain environmental target or goal. For the protection of human health and ecosystems, there are some toxic pollutants, hazardous substances, and highly environmentally disruptive activities that simply need to be prohibited. In these cases, direct regulation and control is necessary and appropriate. Regulations make use of various standards, such as ambient air and water quality standards, allowable emission levels of pollutants, process standards, and prohibition of special types of land use.

In Japan, as in other countries, for economic and administrative reasons regulatory instruments have been used as the primary policy instrument to force industries to take environmental countermeasures. Japanese companies and citizens are accustomed to being ruled by laws which clearly define the standards that companies must comply with; they have traditionally been quite indifferent to the use of economic instruments although this is slowly changing (Imura 1992a).

There has been much discussion about the advantages and disadvantages of various policy instruments. A classical question regards the superiority of the command and control approach based on regulatory laws and standards versus economic instruments, such as taxes, charges, and emission permits. After comprehensive discussions, the Organization for Economic Cooperation and Development (OECD)'s Environmental Committee concluded that neither approach was superior, but rather the approaches were complementary and mutually reinforcing (Organization for Economic Cooperation and Development 1984, pp. 105-34 and 1991, pp. 8-18). The challenge, thus, is to find an efficient mix of the two approaches.

There is also growing attention to a third instrument, the 'voluntary approach'. A variety of voluntary approaches have been developed in OECD countries (Organization for Economic Cooperation and Development 1999, pp. 45-98). The definition of voluntary approaches is broad: they may encompass different forms of commitments, agreements, or contracts whereby polluters agree to achieve specific environmental objectives, possibly above or beyond current regulations. The use of voluntary approaches reflects the search for greater flexibility and a reduced regulatory burden. Japanese enterprises and local environmental authorities created a unique voluntary approach known as 'pollution control agreements (PCAs)' in the 1960s. PCAs have been extensively used to encourage businesses to control pollution. There are also new business initiatives, such as Keidanren's Voluntary Action Plan (VAP) and the voluntary environmental actions of individual enterprises under the International Standard Organization's (ISO) environmental management series, ISO 14000.

Other policy instruments include environmental plans, environmental impact assessments (EIAs), and environmental education and information. New instruments are being developed and used because of the changing objectives and targets of environmental policy.

This chapter tries to identify the major characteristics of the policy instruments adopted in Japan, focusing mainly on Japanese-style command and control approaches and the instruments developed for pollution control and energy conservation. There is also some discussion of policy instruments as they have been employed in response to climate change.

ACTORS AND POLICY INSTRUMENTS

Environmental Governance and the Role of Government

Approaches to environmental governance are influenced by the social culture of a nation. Japanese society has traditionally believed in and relied upon government in contrast to the prevailing Western idea that the 'market is better than government' (Imura 1992a).

Japan has a market economy, but its economic and environmental policies have to a large extent relied upon planning together with market forces. Since the Meiji Restoration, when Japan strove to rapidly catch up to the West, the government has used governmental guidance to promote industrial development (Johnson 1982). Government guidance and control are exerted through various channels: regulations, informal administrative guidance, and financial incentive systems. Government ministries have developed various financial tools such as the budgets for public works projects and the subsidies provided to local governments and private enterprises.

The Japanese government has made use of a combination of regulatory instruments and government guidance and support. The government has guided businesses in subtle ways to coordinate their interests and social objectives. When the government plans to institute new regulations on industries, it carefully negotiates with industrial leaders and political lobbies (Samuels 1987).

When stricter environmental regulations were adopted, government and industry kept dialogues going, exchanging views about the feasibility of meeting new standards. Most regulations were put into force only after assessments were made of the availability of control technologies. These assessments were made in close negotiations among government, industry, and politicians, many of whom were members of the environmental committees of the House of Representatives or the House of Councilors of the Japanese Diet. The burden on industry was often eased through the use of financial measures such as special loans, subsidies, and reduced tax burdens. In other words, environmental investment by the public sector was financed out of the government budget, through treasury loans, public investment schemes, and government banks. By bringing industry into the discussions, the government could improve the likelihood that laws and regulations would be strictly implemented once they were put into force.

Government planning and intervention facilitated the development of Japanese industries when they were in their infancy. Today, however, there are growing criticisms against interventionist government policies. Japan is being pressured to reduce the role of the government to go beyond the 'limits of prosperity in the ultimate industrial society' or what has also been referred to as an 'industrial monoculture society' (Sakaiya 1993, pp. 266-77).

Growing deficits are also making it increasingly difficult for both the central and local governments to provide financial support to private activities and bear the large cost necessary for construction activities and improvement of public infrastructure. Therefore, the government has shifted its policy emphasis to privatization and private sector initiatives. For example, the government enacted a law in 1999 to facilitate public financial initiatives (PFIs) in public infrastructure projects. The basic idea of this law is similar to the PFI that was introduced in the United Kingdom in the early 1990s (Yamauchi 1999).

The Role of Administrative Guidance

Administrative guidance has both positive and negative aspects. It is advantageous because it can be applied more flexibly than laws. Moreover, it can be used to push businesses to take stronger actions than required by law. It can provide quasi-official guidelines to businesses even when relevant legislation does not exist. The government may opt to rely on the efforts and knowledge of specific sectors or firms that have greater technical potential and financial capacity rather than try to legislate standards. On the other hand, administrative guidance may result in the protection of smaller firms and weak industrial sectors, thereby causing economic inefficiency. Moreover, it might prove inefficient due to bureaucratic sectionalism and conflicts among different ministries and departments. For example, the Ministry of Economy, Trade and Industry (METI) can exert its influence upon manufacturing and electric and gas utilities sectors, but its influence is relatively weak in the areas of transportation and construction.

A fundamental limitation of traditional administrative guidance is that its structures are producer-oriented. It does not work well in dealing with individual consumer behavior where instead local authorities must take the initiative, using information and environmental education campaigns that encourage the participation of citizens and non-governmental organizations (NGOs). In addition, Japan's interventionist industrial policy has been internationally criticized as a form of protectionism that lacks transparency. In sum, while administrative guidance and industrial policy played positive roles in the transformation of Japan into an economic giant, today there is a growing view that the government should minimize its intervention into private business activities.

A MIX OF ENVIRONMENTAL POLICY INSTRUMENTS

Japan developed what could be considered a national environmental management system based on national minimum standards. National environmental laws clarified the roles of national and local governments. The national government applied regulations nationwide. Local governments implemented environmental monitoring and day-to-day dialogue with factories. Industry was given the responsibility of monitoring and reporting their emissions.

Also important was the organizational and technical responses by industry. Industry, which at first did not pursue pollution measures with enthusiasm, implemented aggressive measures in response to local citizen and government demands for industry to be socially responsible. The business community invested in pollution control in order to encourage the active development and deployment of pollution control technologies. High levels of capital investment and investment in technology development, both of which supported rapid economic growth, made this possible. Further, the national government devised tax and policy finance measures to support pollution control investment.

Engineers were trained to support the development and deployment of pollution control technologies. Technological measures are indispensable for pollution control, and efforts were made at first for the development of 'end-of-pipe' control technologies such as flue-gas desulfurization technologies, and then various 'cleaner production technologies'. In air pollution control, the presence of engineers with abundant experience in heat control and energy conservation enabled the implementation of pollution control through the use of technologies, such as combustion control for boilers. Finally, large public investment was made in urban environmental infrastructure, including the construction of modern sewage systems, sewage collection pipes, and final water treatment plants. The national and local governments spent 70 trillion yen for the improvement of urban sewage systems between 1960 and 2000 (see Chapter 10).

The Regulatory Framework for Air and Water Pollution Control

Air pollution control has been one of the most important themes of Japanese environmental policy. Throughout the 1960s and 1970s, control of sulfur dioxide (SO_2) was especially important as it caused health problems, such as Yokkaichi asthma. Tighter regulation was enforced stepwise by the government, while allowing a certain lead-time for the development of control technology. Industry was constantly encouraged to find technical breakthroughs in order to comply with regulatory standards that were tightened step by step.

The Basic Law for Pollution Control established ambient air quality standards for SO_2, nitrogen dioxide (NO_2) and suspended particulate matter (SPM). These ambient air quality standards are not compulsory standards but their maintenance is strongly encouraged for the protection of human health and the conservation of the living environment. The standard for SO_2, as amended in May 1973, specified that the daily average of hourly values for SO_2 shall not exceed 0.04 parts per million (ppm), and hourly values shall not exceed 0.1 ppm. Mandatory emission standards are specified for each facility and are supplemented by area-wide total pollutant load control standards, which apply to factories located in heavily polluted areas. In addition, fuel standards are stipulated with regard to the allowable sulfur content of fuel oil used in facilities located in areas where seasonal air pollution is largely caused by diffuse and small and medium-sized sources (Kato 1989, pp. 263-99).

The emission standard for SO_2 sources is called the 'K-value regulation', under which a maximum permissible volume of emission per hour of SO_2 is specified in terms of the 'effective stack height,' the sum of actual stack height, and smoke ascent. A parameter called the K-value is then specified for each area. Regulations are stricter when there is a smaller K-value. With the aim of achieving ambient air quality standards, K-values were revised eight times step by step from 1968-76. Special K-values are prescribed for new construction or expansion of facilities in areas where emission sources are concentrated and a significant degradation of air quality is likely to occur (Committee on Japan's Experience in the Battle against Air Pollution 1997, pp. 63-4).

The regulatory framework for water pollution is more complicated than for air pollution, as it must control effluent from factories, the monitoring of rivers, lakes and sea waters, improvement of municipal sewage systems, and so forth. Regulatory targets are divided into those that are part of the 'living environment' (e.g. those requiring biological oxygen demand or chemical oxygen demand) and those that are 'health' matters, such as heavy metals and toxic chemicals (Ministry of the Environment 2001d). The Ministry of Environment (MOE) sets the environmental standards, while the Ministry of Land, Infrastructure and Transport conducts water quality monitoring of rivers and harbors and improvement of urban sewage systems, among other activities.

Area-Wide Total Pollutant Load Controls

Historically, SO_2 control began with outlet concentration controls that were revised and reinforced numerous times. Nevertheless, pollution remained serious in some areas where a number of factories were concentrated. In response to this, Mie Prefecture (home to Yokkaichi City) enacted an ordinance specifying total pollutant load controls in 1972; the national government followed with its own version in 1974. In 1974, 11 area-wide total pollutant load control areas were initially designated and the number of areas was later increased to 24. In these areas, prefectural governors in designated areas were required to prepare a plan to reduce total pollutant emissions. Large emission sources were required to stay within permissible emission levels, which were individually determined. New factories were subjected to more severe regulatory standards than existing ones. In addition, fuel standards (sulfur content ranging from 0.05 per cent to 1.02 per cent) were set for smaller factories.

A similar area-wide total pollutant load control was adopted in 1978 for the three coastal areas of Tokyo Bay, Ise Bay, and the Seto Inland Sea to address water pollution. Reduction targets based on chemical oxygen demand load were set with a five-year attainment timeframe for meeting the targets.

Regulation and Technical Challenges

In the late 1960s and early 1970s, a number of new laws to control environmental pollution and to protect natural ecosystems and habitats were enacted. Government interventions and guidance in industrial activities helped stimulate competition among industries in the development of technology to be used in controlling industrial pollution. Most of the environmental technologies such as flue-gas desulfurization and denitrification, computerized monitoring techniques and automobile exhaust control technologies were developed from a combination of government control and competitive market conditions. Advanced pollution control technologies were developed and disseminated. Sophisticated monitoring networks were established. Thanks to these efforts, Japan's environmental quality improved dramatically, particularly as far as ambient concentrations of pollutants, such as SO_2 in the atmosphere and heavy metals in water were concerned.

Decentralized Approach Supported by Technical Experts

Japan has used a decentralized approach to the enforcement of environmental legislation, regulations and standards. The center makes national uniform standards, but it is local governments that actually implement them. Local governments can set their own standards, but they must be in conformity with national schemes. Typically, national regulations apply to large factories and plants while local government legislation applies to smaller ones.

To deal with the need to implement the new regulations developed in the 1970s, local governments established inspection systems; local environmental administrators make regular and sometimes impromptu and unsolicited visits to factories to measure pollutant emissions and check the operation of machines and equipment. They are authorized to stop the operation of factories that violate the law. Most are technical officers, who have acquired a high level of knowledge and experience concerning production processes and environmental technologies. Industry also has its own special engineers, or 'pollution control managers'. In the postwar recovery period, Japan emphasized science and technology education and the establishment of engineering faculties in a number of universities, making it possible for factories and local governments to hire qualified environmental control technical experts.

Cost Benefit Analysis Versus Non-economic Policy Approaches

In contrast with the situation in the USA, cost benefit analysis has not been a major policy instrument in Japan. In the USA citizens are attracted by arguments of economic efficiency. Japanese society pays more attention to environmental effectiveness and social acceptability (Imura 1992a). The Japanese generally try to avoid economic approaches and monetary solutions and feel aversion to the monetary valuation of human health and lives. This aversion may be rooted in Japanese culture and religion as well as in the country's experience with life-threatening pollution. In Japan, there is a concern that if cost benefit analysis is employed this can become an excuse for industries to avoid taking action to control pollution.

The first OECD assessment of Japan's environmental policy pointed out that Japan had not attempted to balance costs and benefits. Instead, it suggested that in Japan pollution abatement is considered a 'moral obligation' (Organization for Economic Cooperation and Development 1977, pp. 19-20 and 85). Indeed, pollution control was basically considered a 'must' that was backed by strong political pressures. The government took stringent measures with only limited knowledge of dose-response relationships and economic costs and consequences.

This does not mean that cost benefit analysis has no history in Japan. The Environment Agency's (EA) first cost benefit analysis was conducted in 1976 in preparation for a revision of the emission standard for nitrogen oxide from automobile exhaust gas. Michio Hashimoto, the Director-General of the Environment Agency's Air Quality Bureau and one of the pioneers of Japanese environmental policy, initiated the study (Hashimoto 1988, p. 236; Environment Agency 1977a). In the same year, the EA developed a macro-economic model to analyze the macro-economic implications of environmental policies for its long-term plan for environmental preservation (Environment Agency 1977b). The model, however, failed to predict the drastic structural changes in the national economy as a result of the two oil crises. As a result, the EA hesitated to put additional resources into such economic studies. Strikingly, no notable economic studies of environmental measures were conducted by the government until the 1990s.

There is now somewhat greater interest in cost benefit analysis in Japan. In 1991, for example, young officials in the EA formed a Global Environmental Economics Study Group. This group published a booklet on Japan's Pollution Experiences, which attempted a cost benefit analysis of the government's response to pollution. As it was not an official EA publication, they were able to state conclusions that might have been difficult for the EA to make. They concluded that the cost of abating pollution after it had reached serious proportions was far higher than it would have been had action been taken earlier (Chikyu Kankyo Keizai Kenkyukai 1991). The objective of their study was to share lessons from the Japanese experiences with pollution abatement with other countries, especially rapidly industrializing economies in Asia.

A Non-economic Approach: Punishing Polluters

The OECD described Japan's approach to environmental protection as 'uneconomic' or even 'non-economic' (Organization for Economic Cooperation and Development 1977, p. 20). One important non-economic policy instrument that came to play an important role was a variant of the polluter pays principle (PPP) (see Chapter 4). The PPP was an economic principle introduced by the OECD to prevent the use of government subsidies to private firms, but it was interpreted quite uniquely in Japan. The objective of the OECD's PPP was to prevent the distortion in trade that government assistance to polluting industries might cause. In Japan, however, the PPP came simply to mean that the polluter must bear the cost for clean up and damage compensation: the 'punish polluters principle' (Organization for Economic Cooperation and Development 1977, p. 20). It led to the formation of the health damage compensation system.

The Health Damage Compensation System

One important objective of Japan's environmental policy was to settle the disputes between polluters and victims and relieve patients suffering from pollution-related diseases. This resulted in the development of a health damage compensation system based on the principle of no-fault indemnity liability. Emitters were charged to raise revenue to compensate victims.

Air and water pollution caused many health victims. The Law Concerning Special Measures for the Relief of Pollution-related Patients was enacted in 1969. The scope of the law was limited to 'relief' measures such as assistance in the form of medical care allowances to patients. In 1973, a more comprehensive law was formulated that recognized the extent of human suffering and the liability of polluters: the Pollution-related Health Damage Compensation Law. The law was premised on the principle of civil liability for damage compensation prescribed by the Civil Law and provided monetary compensation for health victims of air pollution. A drastic revision of the law was made in 1987 when the certification of new victims of air pollution was terminated (Environment Agency Research Group 1988, pp. 65-71).

The law set up two classes of regions, which became eligible for compensation. 'Class I' regions were regions designated by Cabinet Order as being regions where marked air pollution had arisen as a result of business or other human activities and where designated diseases due to the effects of such air pollution were prevalent. The diseases designated for Class I regions were chronic bronchitis, bronchial asthma, asthmatic bronchitis, pulmonary emphysema, and their complications. These diseases are 'non-specific diseases' in the sense that they could occur even in the absence of air pollution (Environment Agency Research Group 1988, pp. 11-12). A Cabinet Order also designated 'Class II' regions. Diseases pertinent to Class II regions were 'specific diseases' in the sense that they were caused by a pollutant with a direct link to the disease, such as with Minamata disease.

Certified patients of pollution-related diseases were categorized under one of four classes according to the degree of suffering they experience in their daily lives and the degree to which they have lost their ability to work. Amounts of compensation were determined by multiplying 'standard monthly indemnities' by percentages of coverage fixed for the four ranks of victims. The 'standard monthly indemnities' amounted to as much as 80 percent of the average wages of salary earners (Environment Agency Research Group 1988, p. 202).

All those who lived in Class I regions for more than a certain period of time and who suffered from one of the diseases could be certified as victims of air pollution. But it was theoretically impossible to distinguish between patients who became ill because of air pollution and those who became ill because of other causes, such as smoking or indoor pollution. When SO_2 pollution was still significant, the system was introduced on the presumption that the dominant cause of disease in the designated regions was air pollution. The system was also based on a legal principle that all air polluters should collectively share the liability and compensate the health damages of certified patients (Environment Agency Research Group 1988, pp. 13-18).

In August 1974 when the system started, there were 14,355 certified patients in 11 Class I designated regions. The total number of the certified patients had increased sharply to 98,694 (in 21 designated regions) as of March 1987. During this time, the ambient air quality in the designated regions markedly improved. As the air had become cleaner, questions were raised about why there were increasing numbers of certified patients. Thus, after extensive discussions, involving central and local governments, medical and legal experts, and interested citizens, the law was amended in September

1987 and the designation of all existing Class I regions was terminated in March 1988. New certification of patients was stopped, but compensation payment and other care for existing patients was continued (Environment Agency Research Group 1988, p. 86).

Compensation Payments to Certified Health Victims

It is not easy to estimate the damage cost of air pollution. The amount actually spent for payments to certified health victims could be used as an indicator. It should be noted, however, that the payments do not cover damages to property, forestry, and ecosystems, or the health damages of people who are not certified by the authorities. Moreover, there are various questions concerning the cause and effect relationship of air pollution and health damages. Still it can be helpful to translate the damage caused by air pollution into monetary terms.

In 1987, each patient received an average of 1,054,000 yen per year. Asthma and other diseases designated by the Compensation Law are chronic diseases and it generally takes a long time for patients to recover. This means that patients once certified will receive a similar level of payment until they recover from the disease or they die. From 1974-87, a total of more than 1 trillion yen was spent on compensation (Environment Agency Research Group 1988, p. 206). Taking into account the average life expectancy and the average rate of a patient's recovery from the diseases, it is expected that a similar payment level will be required for the compensation of existing patients into the coming decade. A rough estimate of the total cost of health damage payments as measured by the total amount of compensation payments to certified victims will amount to more than 2 trillion yen.

A more specific study of Yokkaichi was conducted by the Research Group on Global Environmental Economics (Chikyu Kankyo Keizai Kenkyukai) of the EA. In order to have a basis for comparison, the study assumed that had no control actions been taken, then the worst possible air pollution problems would have persisted in the city. Extrapolating from 1960s' health survey data, then 17,600 inhabitants, or 7.27 per cent of the 242,000 inhabitants of the city in 1974 might have suffered from pollution diseases. An even higher degree of damages would have been observed among patients. In contrast with these hypothetical numbers, the number of actual certified patients peaked at 1,140 in 1975 (0.47 per cent of the total population), and thereafter gradually decreased. Total compensation payments to the patients in Yokkaichi equalled 1.3 billion yen. If the same compensation scheme had applied, in the absence of pollution control measures, the total amount of payment from 1974-89 would have amounted to 21.0 billion yen (in 1989 yen). The actual cost of air pollution control was estimated to be 14.8 billion yen. Actual costs included investment and operation costs (the latter being assumed to be 30 per cent of the former) of plants and equipment shared by private business firms located in the city as well as the administrative cost shared by the public sector (e.g. the cost for installation of monitoring systems) (Chikyu Kankyo Keizai Kenkyukai 1991, pp. 34-5).

Incentive Effects of the SO_2 Emission Charge

In general, a distinction should be made between incentive charges and revenue-raising charges (or financial charges). The SO_2 emission charge was a financial charge. Revenue from the emission charge was earmarked for compensation payments to certified patients of air pollution.

Somewhat paradoxically, in the case of compensation payments for diseases that are not tied to a single pollutant (i.e., asthma and other respiratory diseases), the charge rate was increased over time even though emissions declined. Owing to strict regulation, total emissions decreased; nevertheless, the number of certified patients continued to increase. Thus, the rate of the charge had to be increased in order to finance the expanded compensation payment, and this served as an economic incentive to further reduce pollutant emissions. Thus, the higher rate had an economic incentive effect to reduce air pollution, while accelerating the increase in the charge rate for emissions.

The actual reduction achieved, however, cannot only be attributed to the SO_2 emission charge. Even more important were the combined effects of changes in industrial structure, oil prices, regulatory standards, and other factors. Nevertheless, the SO_2 emission charge proved effective in reducing pollution, even though it was economically inefficient as the charge rate was increased beyond the incentive level (Imura 1993, pp. 12-15).

Growing Disparities and Termination of the Designation of Class I Regions

The designation of Class I regions was given to regions where there was significant air pollution over a large area within the region and where diseases caused by air pollution were prevalent. The Central Council for Pollution Control in 1974 defined the criteria for significant air pollution in terms of SO_2 levels. The relationship between diseases and air pollutants other than SO_2, especially nitrogen oxide (NO_x) and SPM, was discussed but specific criteria were not presented mainly due to insufficient scientific data and evidence (Environment Agency Research Group 1988, pp. 19-54).

Air pollution with respect to NO_x and other pollutants has grown worse especially in large metropolitan areas such as Tokyo and Osaka. As a result, there was the possibility that the rising number of patients was linked to NO_x

and SPM from mobile sources rather than SO_2 emissions from stationary sources, which had declined substantially (Environment Agency Research Group 1988, p. 44).

Since 1983, the Central Council for Pollution Control has made extensive studies of the scientific, legal, and economic grounds of the compensation system (Environment Agency Research Group 1988, pp. 46-54). In 1987, the Council prepared a report, which stated that a quantitative causal relationship could not be found between the improved ambient air quality and the prevalence of the non-pollutant specific diseases. It stated that the continuation of Class I regions would go beyond the scope of the Compensation Law, and it would be reasonable to terminate the designation of Class I regions and stop the certification of new patients. The report also presented a new direction for the system, suggesting that the system should be shifted from a monetary compensation for the health damage of 'individual' persons to 'collective' or public environmental health measures (Environment Agency Research Group 1988, pp. 69-71).

On the basis of this report, the Compensation Law was amended in 1987 and the new system was put into force in the next year. As a result, designation of all existing Class I regions was terminated and certification of new patients was ended. But the provision of Class I regions is still valid and there remains room for certain regions to be designated again if air pollution in these regions significantly worsens in the future.

Framework Regulations and Action Plans and Programs for Promoting Collective Action by Government, Businesses, and Citizens

Framework regulation
Since the enactment of the Basic Environmental Law in 1993, Japan has been increasingly setting collective targets and guideposts and encouraging voluntary actions by businesses and citizens. These approaches have also been adopted in the Law for Promoting Measures to Cope with Global Warming and the amended Energy Conservation Law.

Framework regulations are established to advance new policy goals and new policy directions. In establishing framework regulation, the government sets targets to be achieved, but does not regulate or prohibit strictly citizen or industrial actions as it does with, for example, the control of hazardous pollutants. Instead, the government establishes laws that require relevant entities to achieve targets by taking appropriate, but voluntary measures. Here, 'framework' means the goals or targets that a relevant group as a whole should achieve. Groups are left the freedom to choose the most suitable method for achieving the target. A similar principle was adopted by the Japan Federation of Economic Organizations (Keidanren) in its voluntary action plans. Under this system industry-wide collective targets are set, but each company is allowed to choose which method to adopt to meet the target.

The Energy Saving Law, for example, adopts the so-called 'top-runner' method. The government sets energy conservation targets for electric appliances, cars, and other energy-consuming products. Then the names of companies that have achieved the highest level of performance are publicized. It is assumed that this will encourage other companies to make further efforts. Companies cannot be punished under the law.

The role of government plans

In Japan, government policies often take the form of plans. The government has used a planning system to promote industrial activity and exercise central control over the country. Various laws require the government to prepare long-term plans to promote relevant policy measures.

In the field of the environment, for example, the Basic Environmental Law of 1993 led the following year to the formation of the Basic Environmental Plan. Other examples of national plans are the Consolidated National Land Development Plan, the Basic Plan for Environmental Preservation of Seto Inland Sea, the National Land Use Plan, and the Long-term Energy Demand and Supply Plan.

In addition to plans, the government issues what are known as basic directions. Examples include the Basic Direction of the Preservation of Natural Environment and the Basic Direction for the Promotion of Measures to Cope with Global Warming. These plans and directions typically require that the government in formulating and implementing programs take into consideration the opinions of relevant Councils, such as the National Land Council, the Council for Environmental Preservation of the Seto Inland Sea, the Land Policy Council, and the Industrial Structure Council.

In some cases, the government decides plans as Ad Hoc Cabinet Decisions. For example, the Action Program to Arrest Global Warming was prepared as a Cabinet Decision in 1990.

In preparing a national plan, the competent ministry prepares the draft, consults with other ministries to obtain their consent, and finally submits it to a cabinet meeting for approval. The plan is then published in the name of the prime minister. As an example, the EA drafted the Basic Environmental Plan, but it was the government that after hearing the opinions of other ministries and agencies approved and issued the plan. This is an important mechanism for promoting a degree of coordination and consensus building among different ministries.

There is a difference between ministerial goals and visions and national plans. The EA's long-term environmental vision (Environment Agency 1987), for example, represented a goal of the agency; it did not have a legal basis or any binding effects on the policies of other ministries and agencies.

In contrast, the Basic Environmental Law mandated the formulation of the Basic Environmental Plan. As a result the policies of all ministries and agencies are required to be consistent with the Plan. When other ministries prepare their plans, the MOE can express its opinions and comment on them as well. This is a typical internal government process used to coordinate the policies of different ministries and integrate environmental considerations into various national policy plans on land development, land use, long-term energy supply and demand, and construction of infrastructure, including highways, airports, and municipal sewage systems.

Most national plans are in effect general policy guidelines that outline policy targets and measures to be taken to achieve them. The most important role of national plans is to indicate long-term future prospects and publicize basic directions of government policy. Local governments are also frequently asked in plans to take actions similar to those being taken at the national level. Plans usually do not bind private activities, but they may exercise influence upon them through various financial and other tools.

Development plans and programs
Development ministries draw up development plans that include policy targets, timeframes, and discussion of methods for achieving goals. Broadly speaking, there are two different types of development plans. The first are the comprehensive plans, which provide an umbrella for sectoral policies. The second are the plans for the realization and implementation of specific projects. The Consolidated National Land Development Plan is a good example of a comprehensive development plan. Specific plans include the Five-Year Plans for infrastructure projects.

When the government decides on a plan, the Environment Minister can express his opinions from the viewpoint of environmental protection. In this way, MOE can participate in the decision making of other ministries and integrate environmental considerations into development plans and programs.

Large-scale development projects are subject to an EIA according to the 1997 EIA Law (Chapter 8). However, there is not a formalized scheme for examining the environmental implications of policies, plans, and programs at early stages of their formulation. The MOE has started a study on strategic environmental assessment (SEA), an approach which has been instituted in some countries, such as the Netherlands and Canada. Many prefectures have also started to study SEA and some have revised their EIA schemes in order to ensure that they include environmental assessments of plans and programs.

Insufficient Land Use Planning and Control

Planning has been more effective in some policy areas than others. Land use planning is essential for controlling the environmentally unfavorable use of land. It is especially important in Japan, where population density is high and extremely intensive economic activities must be conducted in a limited land area. Land use planning, however, has been difficult to implement due to high land prices in large cities and the special economic role of land in the economy. Land has been a target of investment, thus, any modification of land use regulations could seriously affect the national economy. The government has had difficulty enforcing strong and systematic land use planning and control.

Land use planning is enforced at the national, prefectural, and municipal levels. The national government enacted the National Land Use Planning Law in 1974, when the country was suffering from a boom of speculative investment in land and the extreme rise in land values. According to the law, the national government is to make a national land use plan, and then prefectural governors and mayors are to make local land use plans that are in conformity with the national plans. The competent national ministries and agencies and prefectural governors decide the areas where land use is to be regulated for pollution control and nature conservation. Prefectural governors can also take various measures to prevent the rise of land prices, such as the designation of land price control areas.

The City Planning Law also provides land use zoning schemes and regulation of land use within the framework of city planning. The law covers details related to approval, permission, and licensing for the construction of facilities in urban areas. In general, however, land use control in Japan has been less strict than in some European countries, such as Germany and the United Kingdom. Citizens' participation and initiatives in city planning have been rather weak (Organization for Economic Cooperation and Development 1977, pp. 57-8; Hanayama 1989, pp. 415-36).

NATIONAL ENVIRONMENTAL PLANS

Japan makes use of national environmental plans. An example is the Action Program to Arrest Global Warming, which was decided on by the Cabinet in October 1990. The Action Program spelled out emission control measures, and set a goal of stabilizing carbon dioxide (CO_2) emissions at 1990 levels by 2000. However, the Action Program did not work effectively, because it did not have a clear legal basis. Ministries did not take serious implementation measures fearing that they would have adverse effects on the national economy. Thus, the Action Program proved to be little more than a guideline outlining general policy directions and possible technical options.

The Law for Promoting Measures to Cope with Global Warming (hereafter, Global Warming Law), which was enacted in 1998 and amended in 2003 when Japan ratified the Kyoto Protocol, called for a new national plan to achieve the targets set under the Kyoto Protocol.

The Basic Environment Plan

The most important national plans are known as Basic Plans. The Basic Environmental Plan, approved by the Cabinet in 1994, and revised in 2001, outlines the Japanese government's basic environmental policy. The Basic Environmental Plan promotes comprehensive and programmatic measures for environmental preservation. It includes guidelines for comprehensive and long-term measures, calls for national environmental management plans, and requires prefectural governors to develop their own plans. Under the Basic Environmental Plan, local governments are empowered to adopt special financial measures for the implementation of regional pollution control programs. In return, they are eligible to receive the special rate applied to national government subsidies for pollution control projects.

The Basic Law and the Basic Plan significantly upgraded the actual status of the EA. Before the Basic Law, the Agency did not have effective instruments to coordinate the policy measures of other ministries and agencies. After the Basic Law was enacted, the Agency was authorized to establish a comprehensive national plan, which all government departments must follow. The Basic Environment Plan has four main elements. It advocates the establishment of an 'environmentally sound material cycle'. The idea behind this is to re-examine the underlying foundation of the country's socio-economic system in order to minimize environmental burdens. This means looking hard at means for moving away from mass production systems, mass consumption, and mass disposal. A second goal is the promotion of 'harmonious coexistence' between nature and humans for the sake of both present and future generations. The third objective is enhancing stakeholder participation on a voluntary basis in environmental conservation activities. This means getting business firms, citizens, and private organizations involved. Finally, the plan promotes international cooperation for environmental protection (Ministry of the Environment 2001a, pp. 13-19).

The Basic Environment Plan stipulates targets for future environmental policies. Although it does not create new specific standards, it is more comprehensive than was the old Basic Law for Pollution Control and does include measures for limiting CO_2 emissions, recycling of resources, and international cooperation. Moreover, in contrast with previous plans, such as the long-term environmental plan of 1976, the Basic Environment Plan has a clear legal basis. Still, as it is premised on voluntary action, as is the case with all national plans, there is the risk that it will be little more than a paper wish.

Follow-up Reviews and Preparation of a New Plan

The Central Environmental Council in December 1995 started its first review of the Basic Environment Plan. Public hearings were held in order to reflect the views and opinions of citizens and other actors in the report. Hundreds of opinions were also received by mail and other means. The first review report was submitted to the Prime Minister in June 1996, and a detailed evaluation of the plan by the Central Environmental Council was published. The evaluation included item-by-item reviews of measures taken. The report contains data about government budgets, environmental quality, emissions of pollutants, and the like (Environment Agency 1997a).

In June 2000, the Prime Minister asked the Council to revise the Basic Environmental Plan in order to serve as a guide for national environmental policy in the new century. The Revised Plan was published in January 2001.

Local Action Plans: Consensus Building and Public Participation

Local governments also make comprehensive development and basic environmental plans. In some cases, relevant national laws request prefectural governors and mayors to prepare plans similar to national ones. As is discussed more below, the Global Warming Law requests prefectures and municipalities to prepare action plans that are to be in accordance with the basic directions established by the national government. In other cases, local governments prepare plans according to their own needs and initiatives. In the 1980s, a number of prefectures and municipalities prepared regional environmental management plans. Following the lead set by Yokohama, a number of prefectures and municipalities prepared special programs for the control of traffic-related pollution.

Chapter 28 of Agenda 21 stipulates that each local authority should enter into a dialogue with its citizens and private enterprises and adopt a Local Agenda 21 (United Nations 1992). It pointed out the importance for local authorities of learning from citizens and businesses and other organizations through consultation and consensus building. Many prefectures and municipalities have published a Local Agenda 21.

In the process of planning, consultation, and consensus building among diverse entities are necessary, but this is difficult to achieve in the central decision making structure of the national government. National ministries can hear opinions of relevant councils and sometimes hold public hearings, but it is not easy to ensure broader public participation in national decision making. Local decision making can be much more flexible and better to promote the participation and collaboration of citizens, businesses, and NGOs. In local areas, citizens tend to be more familiar with the environmental issues facing their areas. Japanese businesses recognize that their future is closely bound to the communities in which they are located and that they must keep up good relations with residents and local governments. Although businesses tend to be cautious about central government regulatory actions, they are generally more supportive of and willing to cooperate with local government initiatives.

Government Control versus Voluntary Action by Business

Businesses in general prefer to avoid government regulation and intervention. They prefer to act on their own initiative. Keidanren (now Nippon Keidanren), one of the largest business associations in the world and the largest in Japan, published a Global Environmental Charter, including 11-point guidelines for corporate action. In relation to energy conservation, the charter states that 'companies shall actively work to implement effective and rational measures to conserve energy and other resources even when such environmental problems have not been fully elucidated by science' (Keidanren 1991a).

Following enactment and amendment of the Energy Conservation Law in March 1993, the Ministry of International Trade and Industry (MITI) advised that businesses should prepare 'voluntary plans' for protecting the global environment. In May 1993, the EA also published a report on environment-friendly corporate actions, which was intended to serve as a guideline for businesses. Businesses feel this kind of government initiative is obtrusive and unnecessary, and there is a struggle for leadership between the government and business. Businesses prefer to emphasize their own initiatives such as 'responsible care programs' and 'self-regulatory guidelines'.

The Role of Voluntary Approaches

Progress in pollution prevention in Japan has been driven by the adoption of strict standards and the use of technologies (Organization for Economic Cooperation and Development 1977, pp. 84-7). At the same time, nationwide standards and local ordinances were supplemented by pollution control agreements concluded between prefectural or municipal government and industry. The agreements were pioneered by local environmental authorities and were extensively used to help adapt efforts to local conditions. Since the 1990s greater emphasis has been placed on the enhancement of partnerships, collaboration, and voluntary actions among various entities. Voluntary action plans have been published by a number of industrial associations and are summed up in the Keidanren Voluntary Action Plan.

According to Carraro and Lévêque (1999, pp. 2-3), voluntary approaches can be classified into three types: unilateral commitments, public voluntary schemes, and negotiated agreements. The PCAs in Japan can be considered to be negotiated agreements. The voluntary action plans (VAPs) are unilateral commitments by industries. More than 40,000 PCAs have been put into effect in Japan since the first such agreement was concluded in 1964 (Imura and Sugiyama 2002). Compare this with the European use of such systems, which only began in the late 1980s. Voluntary action plans have played an important role in Japanese environmental protection efforts (Imura 1998a). Japanese experiences with PCAs, therefore, may provide good examples of how and when voluntary schemes can be effective.

The PCAs are quite different from the voluntary action plans that have recently come into use, such as Keidanren's 1997 Voluntary Action Plan (VAP), a program that was influenced by the voluntary climate change approaches adopted in Europe.

Pollution control agreements and VAPs are different in terms of scope and background. Pollution control agreements have been used to prevent conventional pollution problems, while the VAPs established by industries have been a response to global warming, waste disposal, environmental management (ISO 14000), and environmental conservation in overseas business activities. The PCA approach was created at the initiative of local governments; the VAPs are independent of government intervention. Pollution control agreements generally receive positive evaluations because they are applied without intervention by the central government and take into account specific local conditions and the opinions of local residents.

As local governments are involved in the establishment of PCAs, it can be asked whether PCAs are truly 'voluntary' or not. Often local governments use PCAs as a tool to impose on industries more stringent controls than the ones enacted in national ordinances and laws. Furthermore, PCAs may be concluded under the pressure of administrative guidance emanating from local governments, raising some questions about their legitimacy.

Voluntary Action Plans for Coping with Global Environmental Issues

There has been growing criticism from both outside and inside the country of the Japanese government's intervention in the economy and social structures. It is increasingly argued that while government intervention and guidance in industrial activities was important to Japan's economic growth, changed economic circumstances require a move away from interventionist government policy and greater deregulation. This shift in attitude has been affecting environmental policy as well. With concerns about the government's capacity to regulate global environmental protection, greater attention is being paid to market-based approaches and voluntary schemes rather than command-and-control methods for environmental protection.

In July 1996, Keidanren published its Appeal on the Environment, which encourages industrial circles to deal with environmental challenges more concretely through measures to counteract global warming and by creating a recycle-based society. In addition, Keidanren issued a call to the business community to produce VAPs. In response to this call, 36 industries drafted plans in cooperation with 137 industrial organizations ranging from manufacturing and energy to distribution, transportation, finance, construction, and foreign trade (Keidanren 1997). The steel industry, to give one example, set a target of reducing energy consumption by 10 per cent of 1990 levels by 2010 and the volume of byproducts (slug, dust, sludge) needing disposal by 75 per cent of 1990 levels in the same timeframe. A target for recycling 75 per cent of all steel cans produced by 2010 also was included (Organization for Economic Cooperation and Development 1999, p. 74).

The VAPs fall into four main areas: combating global warming; improving waste management; introducing environmental management systems, such as the ISO 14000 series; and promoting environmental conservation in overseas business activities. The priority of measures taken differs across industries. Energy and resource consuming manufacturing industries tend to put emphasis on energy saving and CO_2 emission reductions and the three 'R's' of waste recycling: reuse, reduction, and recycling. Service industries are more likely to pursue certification under the ISO 14000 environmental management series. Measures to combat global warming have attracted the most interest.

Keidanren argues for the VAPs because they are voluntary and based on actions which industries themselves consider to be best given economic and political conditions. Many of the VAPs establish quantitative targets for greenhouse gas emissions reductions or waste reduction goals. They also involve a wide range of industries, including manufacturing, energy, distribution, transportation, construction, foreign trade, non-life insurance, and many others.

Keidanren puts the VAPs through an annual review process, and makes the results public (Keidanren 2003). The periodic reviews serve as a mechanism that pressures industrial circles to meet their targets and improve their goals.

Evaluation of VAPs

VAPs can be seen in both a positive and a negative light. VAPs are expected to play a big role in reducing greenhouse gas emissions in Japan. METI's Industrial Structure Committee has called upon industries to report their achievements in energy conservation and emission reductions of CO_2. Furthermore, some NGOs such as People's Forum 2001 (*Shimin Forum 2001*) and the Climate Change (*Kiko Hendo*) Network have worked actively on climate change issues, including evaluations of Japan's climate change policies and Keidanren's Voluntary Action Plan. Government and NGOs are carefully watching the implementation of these unilateral commitments by industries. Still, although Keidanren describes the targets set by industries as 'ambitious', and requires the best efforts of member associations and firms, it is very difficult to judge from the outside whether the targets are really very tough. The targets are set by each industry based on negotiations among member firms. This means that the targets may lean towards the minimum common denominator and may not take into account the best available technologies, or may be lax in order to accommodate weak firms.

There is also the problem that VAPs tend to be limited to the larger business firms as these are the members of Nippon Keidanren. Even though the largest portion of the total environmental load can be accounted for by their activities, a large number of small and medium-sized enterprises are exempted from taking action.

Voluntary action plans prescribe a review process that is conducted by industries themselves. The annual review enables Nippon Keidanren and its member industrial associations to adjust their objectives and actions, and to improve voluntary schemes after reviewing their own achievement. This, however, raises concerns about transparency. Each company reports its performance to the industrial association it belongs to, and then the aggregated report goes to Nippon Keidanren. Thus, the performance of each company is not necessarily made public, and there may be free-riding. Moreover, there are no sanctions against non-attainment of targets as the VAPs are unilateral commitments.

A weakness of VAPs is that they are simply unilateral commitments. Keidanren describes its plan as a 'social contract' and is proud of its own historical efforts towards environmental protection. It assures that industries will work to achieve their targets, regardless of their legal status. However, it is natural for many people to raise questions about the compatibility of capitalistic business interests and voluntary environmental efforts.

In order to ensure that businesses live up to their promises, mechanisms need to be established so that their actions can be judged by those affected by their activities. Mechanisms, such as eco-audits, that ensure public access to business information are indispensable in order to assure the credibility of businesses' environmental programs. A growing number of Japanese companies, including power generation companies, car manufacturers, and retailers have started to publish periodic environmental reports.

Environmental Management and ISO 14000

Since the mid-1990s, there also has been much interest among Japanese firms in the International Standard Organization's 14000 environmental management series. Environmental management systems that are in accordance with the standards of the ISO 14000 series have been widely adopted by Japanese business firms. The number of ISO 14000 accredited sites is very rapidly increasing, exceeding 12,000 as of July 2003 (ISO World 2003). More than 100 local government offices obtained accreditation in 2003. In addition, in recent years, many companies have adopted and publicized environmental statements, in which they commit themselves to work for environmental protection.

Increasing the Role of Economic Instruments

In the past, the main targets for pollution control were local level industrial activities. Polluters and victims were clearly identifiable. Emissions of pollutants from factories and plants could be monitored and controlled. Technologies could also be developed and applied to reduce pollutant emissions. Today, however, we are confronted with more complicated environmental problems that are taking place on continental and global scales. These are problems that are linked to our culture, technological preferences, and social values; their solution requires revolutionary restructuring of our economic system and society. People have realized that many environmental problems have their roots in affluent lifestyles and consumption (Princen, Maniates and Conca 2003), and the reform of the market is necessary in order to integrate the economy and environment more efficiently.

Japan also has come to pay more attention to the economic efficiency of environmental policies. This shift in attitude has been stimulated in large part by climate change concerns and international discussions pertaining to the use of economic instruments in environmental policy.

For global environmental problems, collective and cooperative actions between government and industry may still be necessary. However, this traditional Japanese approach to pollution control has relied very heavily on technological countermeasures, and thus, also has limitations. It is neither efficient nor practical to apply 'command-and-control' policies to regulate energy use and change high consumption lifestyles, both of which will be necessary to address climate change. Instead, greater attention will have to be paid to social breakthroughs. There will need to be a major reform of economic and social systems and changes in behavioral patterns of businesses and individuals. Citizen participation and the role of NGOs, as well as environmental education and information, will be essential. Greater use of market-based economic instruments, such as environmental charges and taxes, will also have to be considered. As is the case with other countries, Japan will need to find an appropriate mix of technological and socio-economic measures to help create an environmentally friendly society and to address major problems like climate change.

A good example for making the case for the need for a new policy paradigm in Japan is air pollution. Air pollution in industrial cities has improved remarkably, and thus has not been a priority concern. Nevertheless, air pollution in large cities such as Tokyo and Osaka has worsened in relation to particulate matter (PM) and NO_x. This is due to increasing car ownership and traffic volume. Regulatory standards for automobile exhaust gas and improvement of fuel economy reduced the emission of pollutants from automobiles, but increasing traffic volumes offset these reductions. Automobiles do not only cause local atmospheric pollution but have global impacts through the emission of CO_2. A new mix of policy instruments will be necessary if traffic-related pollution is to be adequately addressed in the future.

Problems such as traffic pollution, increasing wastes from households, and global warming originate largely from our daily lives. In these cases, polluters and victims are not clearly distinguishable. Not only industry but also citizens, or society as a whole, are responsible for causing and solving these problems. Regulation and control technology alone cannot solve them. Rather, fundamental reform of our economic system is imperative (Daly 1987). All members of society should pay the social cost for protecting the global as well as local environment. Environmental charges or taxes may be the most practical means to achieve such an economic reform.

Establishing a Global Warming Law

As host country of the Kyoto Conference and one of the world's largest economies, reducing greenhouse gas emissions is a leading environmental priority of the Japanese government. The government and society consider it important for Japan to be serious in its implementation efforts in order to gain the trust and commitment to action of other countries. In order to meet its Kyoto target of reducing greenhouse gas emissions by 6 per cent of 1990 levels by 2008-12, the Japanese government and industry have introduced a variety of policy measures and instruments.

The challenge for Japan to meet its commitment is great. Japan's CO_2 emissions increased by 9 per cent from 1990-96. The rising emissions made it essential for the government to start taking action immediately once the Kyoto Conference negotiations were concluded. As one of its first policy measures, the Prime Minister's office set up the Global Warming Prevention Headquarters. In May 1998 the headquarters proposed the Guideline for the Promotion of Measures to Cope with Global Warming (Ministry of the Environment 2003a, p. 94). Then, in October 1998 the government promulgated the world's first law created for the express purpose of preventing global warming, the Law Concerning the Promotion of the Measures to Cope with Global Warming (Global Warming Law). The Global Warming Law, which went into affect in 1999, promotes measures to be taken by national and local governments, businesses, citizens, and NGOs to reduce greenhouse gas emissions. It requires the national government to monitor climate conditions and the related health of ecosystems and promote measures to reduce emissions resulting from government activities.

The law also required the government to prepare a Guideline of Measures to Cope with Global Warming, prescribing basic actions to be taken by national and local governments, industry, and citizens to reduce their emissions. The Minister for Environment was authorized to designate a Center for Promoting Activities to Arrest Global Warming in order to raise awareness and disseminate information nationwide, carry out research to promote climate friendly lifestyles, and provide information for consumers about climate-friendly goods. The law further stipulated that prefectural and municipal governments should prepare plans for how they will reduce their greenhouse gas emissions and make public their actions. Prefectural governors were authorized to appoint voluntary advisors to promote awareness of climate friendly lifestyles and designate an organization to be a Prefectural Center for Promoting Activities to Prevent Global Warming (Ministry of the Environment 2001a, pp. 21-5).

When the Diet ratified the Kyoto Protocol in 2002, it amended the Global Warming Law. This was considered necessary given that emissions were still rising. A main aim of the amendment is to strengthen local initiatives. Local governments have been instructed to set up local consultation committees comprised of local governments, businesses, and citizens to develop strategies to reduce their emissions and have been empowered to appoint advisors for promoting activities to cope with global warming. It is important to note, however, that the law is not binding. It simply urges all stakeholders (government, industry, NGOs, and citizens) to make voluntary efforts to mitigate climate change through the formulation of plans and to report their actions. It does not set quantitative national emissions targets or targets for emissions from individual sources. The Global Warming Law, thus, cannot be considered to be a strong regulatory law.

The Guideline for the Promotion of Measures to Cope with Global Warming was also amended in 2002. The revised guideline includes numerical targets and a rich menu of measures to be taken to achieve Japan's reduction target by 2010 (Ministry of the Environment 2003a, pp. 91-3). The guideline sets the following reduction targets relative to 1990 levels:

- Reduction of CO_2 from energy sources (± 0.0 per cent). Sector specific targets are:
  Industry (- 7 per cent)
  Commercial and residential (- 2 per cent)
  Transportation (+ 17 per cent).
- Reduction of CO_2 from non-energy sources, methane and nitrous oxide (- 0.5 per cent).
- Reduction of emissions through the development of innovative technologies and others efforts by all groups (- 2.0 per cent).
- Restraining the increasing use of the three chlorofluorocarbon (CFC) alternatives with high global warming potentials hydrofluorocarbons (HFCs), perfluorocarbons (PFCs) and sulfur hexafluoride (SF_6) (+ 2.0 per cent).
- Sequestration by forestry and other vegetation and the use of biomass (- 3.9 per cent).

The guideline was established by Cabinet decision. This means that while it represents a national commitment to act to fulfil the Kyoto Protocol, it is also not legally binding. Given the voluntary nature of these policy measures, whether the country can successfully achieve its Kyoto Protocol targets or not remains a matter of debate.

The industry sector is expected to achieve a substantial reduction in its CO_2 emissions. The Keidanren Voluntary Action Plan has been important to this process in the industry sector. Emissions from the transportation, commercial, and residential sectors, however, are expected to continue to rise due to increased use of vehicles. It should also be noted that there is some controversy regarding the - 3.9 per cent sequestration target because of concerns about the scientific reliability of the data upon which the target is based.

The Use of Economic Instruments in Climate Policy

The Kyoto Protocol presented several new policy instruments, known as flexibility mechanisms, including emissions trading, activities implemented jointly, and the clean development mechanism (CDM). These were introduced into the Kyoto Protocol in order to enhance the variety of instruments states could employ to meet their reduction targets (World Meteorological Organization and United Nations Environment Program 2001, pp. 365-71).

Emissions trading refers to the buying and selling of pollution permits that are allocated by a government or other central authority to polluting entities. The idea behind emissions trading is that it places a price tag on emissions and, thus, gives firms that can reduce their emissions at relatively low cost an incentive to do so in order to sell off their permits. Activities implemented jointly or simply, joint implementation, is a system that was established to allow entities in developed states to gain credit for reducing emissions in transition economies. The CDM is a similar kind of mechanism that permits developed countries to obtain credit towards their own emissions reductions by involvement in projects in developing countries that lead to emissions reductions. The rationale of joint implementation and the CDM is that greenhouse gas emissions are a global pollution problem and, thus, it makes sense to reduce emissions in the most cost-effective manner. Typically reducing emissions in developing countries is cheaper than doing so in developed states. Japanese industries have shown considerable interest in the flexible mechanisms of the Kyoto Protocol and especially in CDM. Reflecting the business culture of Japan, there has been comparatively less discussion about the use of tradeable permits. Japanese businesses have a preference for developing technical solutions to pollution problems rather than depending upon market mechanisms. Citizens are also eager to have firms abide strictly by pollution control standards and dislike the idea of giving firms the 'right' to emit pollutants (or buy them) when effective control technologies are available (Imura 1992a). This may change, however, if the challenge of reducing CO_2 proves too formidable. The Japanese government and industries could be pushed to adopt instruments that have not been used with traditional air pollutants in order to deal with greenhouse gas emissions. In August 2004, the MOE publicized its plan to start experimental implementation of greenhouse gas emissions trading among domestic sources.

The Japanese government and industry are counting on the use of flexible mechanisms to make it possible for Japan to meet its greenhouse gas emissions reduction target. They have not yet, however, adopted carbon taxes. In spite of a number of economic models that indicate that carbon taxes are among the most effective way of reducing emissions, there has been some reluctance in Japan about unilaterally introducing environmental taxes. There is little prospect that internationally harmonized economic measures that include the United States of America, Europe, Japan, and other major economies will be put into force in the foreseeable future. The MOE and Ministry of Economy, Trade and Industry have both acknowledged the potential benefits of environmental taxes on fossil fuels for reducing greenhouse gas emissions, but they have failed to reach a consensus on an actual scheme. Considering the nation's political and economic situation, other measures for reducing emissions, such as strengthening the fuel economy standard of cars and establishing stricter building codes for poorly insulated houses, may be more realistic options.

Energy Conservation Policy

As a result of the two oil crises of the 1970s, the Japanese government and industries have worked hard to improve energy efficiency. Much of this was done under the Law Concerning the Rational Use of Energy (Energy Conservation Law). The Energy Conservation Law predates the climate change issue, and thus does not specify greenhouse gas mitigation as a direct objective. Nevertheless, it provides a strong basis for Japan to enforce measures to control CO_2 emissions by achieving higher energy efficiency in electric appliances, cars, buildings, and industrial production processes. Energy conservation made a significant contribution to the reduction of air pollutants (Environment Agency 1981) and helped restrict the growth of Japan's CO_2 emissions. As energy conservation provides firms with economic benefits, especially when oil prices are high, Japanese industry has been relatively supportive of conservation measures.

Energy Conservation Initiatives under the Energy Conservation Law

The Energy Conservation Law provides tax incentives and financial subsidies to firms which adopt conservation measures. The law established a tax system designed to accelerate reforms in the energy supply-and-demand structure by encouraging investment in energy-saving facilities. Systematic development of energy-saving technologies also was promoted. Thanks to these efforts, energy consumption per unit of gross domestic product (GDP) dropped by a dramatic 35 per cent in 1995 relative to 1973, the year of the first oil crisis (Energy Data and Modelling Center 2002, p. 31). Most of the conservation occurred in industries, which were motivated to act by high fuel prices. Since the late 1980s, however, demand for energy has increased rapidly. Lifestyles have changed and become more energy intensive and for much of the decade oil prices were relatively low. Thus, in the 1990s, improvements in Japan's energy consumption per unit of GDP slowed and CO_2 emissions began to rise. The need to address climate change has instilled in government and industries and among citizens new motivation for achieving higher levels of energy efficiency.

Enforcement of Energy Conservation in Industry

The oil price shocks led to the government implementing policies that would promote the rational use of oil and other energy resources. This has become an integral component of national energy plans. Standards were established in relation to the energy conservation performance of factories and plants as well as for the energy efficiency of machines and appliances. These standards played an important role in suppressing CO_2 emissions into the 1980s. The need to reverse the rising CO_2 emissions trend of the past decade has forced the government to amend the law several times in an effort to reinforce energy conservation measures.

The Japanese system for promoting energy saving in the industrial sector combines regulatory and financial assistance measures. This system is very similar to that which was adopted to control industrial pollution. The effectiveness of the regulatory measures has depended upon the administration's ability to monitor and inspect industry compliance with standards and targets. In Japan's case information and reporting requirements for factories were established and there was regular monitoring and inspection of industrial activities.

The amended Energy Conservation Law of June 1998 requires managers of designated factories consuming more than a certain quantity of energy a year to report how much energy they consume and how they use it. It authorizes competent agencies to make a recommendation or issue an order to companies that are not in compliance with government policies. Companies can be ordered to improve their use of energy, and when they do not comply, disciplinary actions can be taken against them. The Energy Conservation Law requires business offices to take measures comparable to those required or imposed on factories. In addition, the government has established energy conservation standards and required manufacturers of designated products, such as fluorescent lamps, televisions, and copying machines to label products with their energy efficiency ratings. The Energy Conservation Law offers financial and tax incentives to companies that undertake their own projects designed to rationalize energy use or utilize recycled resources (Resources and Energy Agency, 2000, pp. 114-9; Resources and Energy Agency, 1999, pp. 8-33).

Regulation of Automobile Fuel Economy and Taxation on Fuels

In most industrialized countries, including Japan, the transportation sector accounts for approximately a quarter to one-third of the nation's total energy requirement. Convenience is a major factor behind the increase in passenger and freight traffic and in the popularity of home delivery and just-in-time systems. Improvement of vehicle fuel efficiency, traffic avoidance and the reduction of the miles travelled by passengers and freight through the expanded use of public transportation are critical for Japan if it is to control its traffic-related CO_2 emissions.

A viable tool for improving vehicle fuel efficiency is the enforcement of fuel economy regulations. The Energy Conservation Law of 1979 set fuel economy targets for vehicles that were to be met by 1985; the standards were met but then remained unchanged until 1992. As a result, while the fuel economy of newly registered passenger cars in Japan showed a notable improvement from 1973-84, it declined in the late 1980s. With growing concern about climate change, in the 1990s, stricter target values were set and fuel economy levels again increased substantially (Resources and Energy Agency 1997, p. 95 and Resources and Energy Agency 2000, p. 103). The Energy Conservation Law as amended in 1998 urges Japan's automobile makers to improve the fuel efficiency of their cars an average of 22.8 per cent by 2010. Emissions from mid-sized cars must be cut by between 24 and 30 per cent according to the new law (Resources and Energy Agency 1999, pp. 382-5).

Some argue that the vehicle fuel improvements are the natural response of the marketplace to rising fuel prices and that the regulation has had little effect. Others claim that the market is unlikely to respond strongly to gasoline price changes (World Meteorological Organization and United Nations Environment Program 2001, pp. 358-9).

There has been some argument in Japan that the tax placed on automobiles and fuels should be raised taking into consideration the social costs of driving, including the damage costs associated with air pollution and global warming. A Panel of Experts on Auto-related Environmental Taxes was organized by the EA published a report on the use of Auto-related Taxes in Environmental Policy in July 1999 (Environment Agency 1999). The report examined the current tax rates and tax amounts imposed on different types of vehicles and fuels. After comparing the absolute taxes placed on vehicles in Japan with those in other countries, the report concluded that in Japan the taxes associated with driving a car are relatively low, but for possession of a car are high. The report urged a re-examination of the fuel-related tax system and establishment of taxation levels that would aid in preventing global warming and air pollution. To date, however, these recommendations have not been adopted.

Another controversial argument relates to the use of revenues from taxes on gasoline and diesel fuels for vehicles. Under the current system, the bulk of the revenues are earmarked to the special budget for road construction and improvement with only some of the revenues being used for other purposes. Environmentalists have argued that a part of the revenues should be spent for improvements in the mass transportation systems, but there is strong resistance to this idea from political lobbies. Before such a change can occur, it will be necessary to win over the Liberal Democratic Party politicians who form the 'road tribe' in the Diet, that is the group of politicians that exercises strong influence on the use of this budget by the Ministry of Land, Infrastructure, and Transport.

Deregulation for Energy Conservation and Environmental Protection

In many fields, skewed economic incentives and outdated regulatory structures have encouraged business activities that do not encourage energy conservation or environmental protection. The Electric Utilities Law regulates electricity generation at dispersed plants, such as waste incineration factories and households. Ensuring the stable supply of electricity is a major objective of the law, and it provides various control measures against the activities of the electric utilities industry. It also protects utilities by controlling entry into the utilities business and regulating the electricity generation of non-licensed entities. To encourage the development of small-scale dispersed power plants and the use of photovoltaic systems and fuel cells, regulations governing the connection between a utility's electricity system and dispersed, small-scale plants have been relaxed.

In many countries, existing regulation encourages the building of large power plants, where nearly two-thirds of a fuel's energy content is vented to the atmosphere as waste heat. Relaxation of the existing regulation on the construction of power plants would encourage the return to more efficient cogeneration plants, which use waste industrial steam to produce electricity, and district heating plants. The new policy objectives of energy conservation for CO_2 emission control, however, sometimes conflict with existing environmental requirements. In Japanese cities, for example, the building of cogeneration plants, which would be beneficial for reducing greenhouse gas emissions, has been restricted by air pollution control policies. Similarly, while the use of diesel-engined vehicles has been promoted for energy efficiency reasons, they are causing air pollution problems in large metropolitan areas.

These kinds of contradictions are being solved through technological innovation. Such technological development has made it possible to maintain high fuel economy while controlling exhaust gas (Japan Society of Atmospheric Environment 2000, pp. 659-63).

CONCLUSION

The Japanese government has used regulatory methods to control pollution, although its regulatory approach is distinct from that employed in other countries. In Japan, administrative guidance has led to considerable government industry cooperation in pollution abatement. The government has provided considerable financial assistance to industry to promote environmental protection and energy conservation. Industry, in turn, has invested heavily in technological innovation that has been beneficial for environmental protection and energy conservation.

For the past 40 years, the government has made use of decentralized monitoring and inspection systems. These have proven quite effective in ensuring industrial compliance with targets and laws and also a rather efficient means of assuring relatively high levels of success with policy implementation. In addition to traditional standards, the government also introduced some innovative measures to promote pollution control, such as the area-wide total pollutant load control system.

With the emergence of new environmental problems and the internationalization of industry, there are signs that Japan's approach to pollution control is changing. The government is relying more upon market forces and less upon government planning. The new environmental policies that have followed the passage of the Basic Environmental Law attach greater importance to the use of economic instruments and voluntary approaches than was the case in the past.

In 2002 the OECD sent a team to evaluate Japan's environmental policy performance. The team concluded that Japan's regulations are for the most part strict, well enforced and based on strong monitoring capacities and that the mix of instruments used to implement environmental policy is highly effective (Organization for Economic Cooperation and Development 2002, p. 22). Nonetheless, the report also points out that important gains in cost-effectiveness could be achieved through wider use of economic instruments. It recommends that Japan should strengthen and extend the use of economic instruments; make voluntary agreements more transparent, effective and efficient; and continue to assure appropriate enforcement of regulatory measures.

8. Case Studies of Environmental Politics in Japan

Fumikazu Yoshida

INTRODUCTION

Does economic development expand social liberties? Amartya Sen argues that the growth of gross national product (GNP) or individual incomes is very important as a means of expanding freedom: 'development can be seen as a process of expanding the real freedom that people enjoy' (Sen 1999, p. 3). Sen lists five distinct types of 'instrumental freedoms': political freedom, economic facilities, social opportunities, transparency guarantees, and protective security. However freedom also depends upon social and economic arrangements and political and civil rights. In the light of Sen's argument, this chapter examines Japan's development and environmental policies and their relationship to freedom in society. It reviews national level development goals and policies and the tools used to implement those goals. It further examines case studies of local outcomes, highlighting the implications for democracy at the local level. The relationships among national development goals, policy tools, and local outcomes can be illustrated by using several specific policy cases. This chapter does this by examining four policy areas: national/regional land development, energy, waste management, and environmental impact assessments (EIAs).

NATIONAL DEVELOPMENT OBJECTIVES AND POLICY TOOLS

In the 1960s, Japan's economic policy was formulated in accordance with the famous 'income-doubling policy' and was motivated mainly by growth of income targets. Japan achieved its 'income-doubling' goal and the gap between the rich and the poor narrowed. However, authorities gave relatively low priority to such considerations as the quality of life, culture, amenities, leisure facilities and opportunities. The main focus of health and safety policies has been to 'react and cure' (rather than prevent). A Japanese proverb sums up the situation nicely: 'Only *gaiatsu* (pressure from abroad) and human tragedy can bring about changes in Japanese policy'. As a result, those cases in which development has had a negative effect on the environment but did not directly harm human health were given low priority.

One of the tools used to reach national development policy goals, particularly public works schemes, has been governmental subsidies. Japan's percentage rate of general government fixed capital formation in terms of GNP is two to three times higher than that of other Organization for Economic Cooperation and Development (OECD) countries. This means that governmental expenditures on public works projects have had an enormous effect on the Japanese economy. One side-effect of large subsidies is the standardization and uniformity of urban planning and road construction at the local level, which tends to overlook regional amenities and demolishes traditional landscapes. Publicly subsidized works lack flexibility and tend to go over budget. Governmental subsidies also can lead to shorter facility life spans. There is also a strong link between public works projects and political power. Critics point out that since many local councilors are members of construction-related industries, there is 'grass-route conservatism' (this is not a misspelling, but a typical Japanese verbal joke, a pun, taken from the English term 'grass-roots democracy'). Inevitably, the main interest of local council members is to get hold of and spend the subsidies allocated for development projects.

Policy and Democracy at the Local Level

National level development policies and policy tools have had some impact on the nature of democracy at the local level. After World War II, the Japanese political and economic systems were obliged to become more democratic, but this has been more successful at the local than the national level. At the regional level, authorities set up local governments and elections for mayors and prefectural governors. Ever since, local governments, supported by citizens' movements, have been relatively more successful in implementing strict environmental regulations than the national government. There are many cases in which national level development policies have thwarted local practices and damaged local environments.

The central government has retained its old bureaucratic habits. Factionalism (as well as sectionalism) of ministries and agencies is rampant, which has led to a lack of coordination in overall governmental policy. Another result of nationally dictated policies has been that development and environmental planning processes have been open neither to the general public nor to the Diet, where they were not featured on the agenda for discussion. Therefore, there has been little public debate, formal review, or scrutiny over development plans. Nor have the citizens who are likely to be affected by projects been permitted to take part in the real planning process (Miyamoto 1973, p. 231). Somewhere along the line, the idea of local democracy seems to have been misplaced. Increased attention needs to be paid to how national development plans and the policy tools used to implement them influence policy outcomes and democratic processes at the local level. The following sections discuss in detail specific cases in several policy areas, beginning with development planning.

NATIONAL/REGIONAL LAND DEVELOPMENT POLICIES AND THE ENVIRONMENT

Agencies and ministries seem to act independently in a spirit of competition rather than working together in a fully co-operative way. (Organization for Economic Cooperation and Development 1994a, p. 113)

Japan has a relatively bad record when it comes to the integration of its development and environmental policies. In several cases, plans for development have not included environmental considerations. Consequently, development projects often have disturbed severely the environment. Examples of this are the ill-considered National Consolidated Development Plans. Soon after the end of World War II, the government designated a number of locations as part of a regional development plan (*tokutei chiiki kaihatsu*). The goals of the plan included building huge industrial complexes in various locations and utilizing Japan's water resources to provide hydro-electrical power. The construction of these industrial complexes severely damaged the environment and the construction of dams and reservoirs resulted in the flooding of valuable land in many rural areas.

First and Second National Consolidated Development Plans (1962-77)

In 1962, the government launched a New Consolidated Development Plan based on the 'growth pole strategy' (*kyoten kaihatsu shugi*). The plan envisaged a string of large-scale petrochemical plants as well as iron and steel manufacturing complexes along Japan's Pacific coast, an area which would embrace the areas of Yokkaichi, Chiba, and Sakai. The plan proposed the creation of 15 new industrial cities and six development areas (Honma 1991, p. 7).

The resulting policy outcomes, however, have not been benign. Harmful consequences have included: 1) the disruption and pollution of the environment in the vicinity of these complexes; 2) a deterioration in the quality of neighborhood agriculture and a weakening of small businesses; 3) a crisis in the budgets of local governments; and 4) a weakening in the autonomy of local governments as a result of their dependence on national subsidies (Miyamoto 1973, pp. 22-52).

These harmful consequences can be traced back to several specific factors. First, capital investment was mainly devoted to strengthening the industrial infrastructure, and much less attention was paid to the prevention of pollution. Second, overall, local governments could only reap paltry tax revenues because they had to offer tax reductions in order to attract industrial complexes to their localities. Third, resources budgeted to cover 'social welfare' costs simply went to pollution prevention equipment. Fourth, there was a destructive delay in distributing resources to pay for desulfurization equipment, for low sulfur oil, for high stacks, and for greenbelts around the plants. One case, the Yokkaichi Industrial Complex in Mie Prefecture, is a typical case that illustrates these problems. It is noteworthy because the conflict between the industries of the complex and victims of their pollution had to be settled in a court of law.

Critics have argued that the first plan was a failure since it was based on short-term economic targets and was never intended to enhance or enrich the quality of the people's lives, their culture, or education and health. Unfortunately, the lessons learned during the first plan were not applied to designing the Second National Consolidated Development Plan in 1969.

Like the First Plan, the Second Plan called for the development of gigantic industrial complexes throughout Japan. Again the plan aimed for the full realization of national land potential, but there was little concern for preserving a harmonious balance between human beings and nature. The national government initiated immense projects, such as those in Mutsu-Kogawara (Aomori Prefecture), East-Tomakomai (Hokkaido), and Shibushi (Kagoshima Prefecture), backed up by interest groups and parliamentary politics. At the same time, the government of Prime Minister Kakuei Tanaka initiated a campaign called 'The Plan for Remodeling the Japanese Archipelago', which was designed to stimulate the construction of roads and infrastructure throughout Japan. Planners worked to create blueprints for the establishment of a national network system to link cities across Japan with bullet trains. Unfortunately, since strict regulations concerning land policy were not enforced, the plan also encouraged private companies to speculate in land investments. Examination of a specific case study will show how the application of national plans at the local level can lead to disastrous consequences.

Case Study: The Failure of Mutsu-Kogawa Development Project

The project for Mutsu-Kogawara industrial complex was launched in 1969 as a part of the Second Consolidated National Plan. The Report on the Location of Japanese Industrial Centers, published in 1969, proposed the building of an enormous complex that would include facilities for the production of iron, steel, petrochemical goods, and nuclear power. The project failed on many counts because the original proposal was premised on the supposition that there would be a huge demand (both at home and abroad) for such goods. In addition, it failed to consider a number of vital issues. The plan treated the region as if it were an unoccupied space and ignored the fact that people lived in the area. The plan failed to consider the local industries of agriculture and fishing. The plan showed no consciousness of the need for parallel development of industry and agriculture. No steps were taken (or even suggested) to prevent unregulated land speculation.

Under the project, a dual system of project management was implemented. While Aomori Prefecture set up a public corporation to manage the development, an organ of the central government, Keidanren (the Federation of Economic Organizations), and the Hokkaido-Tohoku Development Corporation established a special committee to oversee the project. Consequently, no one was sure who actually had overall responsibility for implementing the plan.

At the same time, just after the plan was made public, there was a flurry of large-scale and unregulated land speculation that helped the project to be doomed. Speculators did not consider industrial investment in the context of Japan's overall economy. In 1973, during the first oil crisis, a local people's protest movement began to gather force to protest development; however, they did not influence the project. Even after 1974, when the economic situation worsened, speculators continued to buy up the land. This only ensured that the debts incurred by the public development corporation grew bigger and bigger. At the same time, farmers who had sold their land lost all chances of re-employment since the proposed industrial plants remained un-built. Such farmers became known as 'refugees of development' (*Kaihatsu nanmin*) (Funabashi, Hasegawa and Iijima 1998, pp. 11-41).

During the 1970s, only the plan to build oil storage plants was actually realized. By 1983, the government had borrowed about 139 billion yen. Despite this huge debt, in 1984, the national government launched a new national project to build several plants designed to reprocess nuclear fuel and to process uranium. In 1985, the two bodies responsible for the plants, the Federation of Electric Power Companies and the Public Development Corporation, reached an agreement over the location of only one of these facilities. Bad debts linked to the project totaled 140 billion yen. The money had to be borrowed in order to purchase land from farmers and to compensate for losses sustained by the fishing industry (Funabashi, Hasegawa and Iijima 1998, pp. 43-72). By that time, public opinion in Aomori was deeply divided between those for and those against the installation of nuclear facilities.

The defects of the Mutsu-Kogawara industrial complex and its ultimate failure have the following root causes:

1. The short term allowed for the decision-making process (13 months).
2. The autocratic behavior and inflexibility of the Aomori Prefecture Government, which had no intention of listening to the opinions and troubles of the local people and failed to reconsider the project in light of local conditions.
3. The vagueness of purpose in the department of the central government responsible for the process.
4. The overextensive reach of the petrochemical complex project.
5. The lowering of the basic living conditions of the people residing within the development area, and the serious breakup of social relationships among local communities.
6. The uncritical acceptance of 'unfavorable' and dangerous facilities and the fiscal dependency they created.
7. The failure to consider Japan's overall economic context in implementing plans.
8. The failure to prevent land price speculation, leading to Japan's 'bubble economy'.
9. The failure to correctly estimate costs and the accumulation of bad debts incurred by the Public Development Corporation (the corporation went bankrupt with debts of 240 billion yen in 1999).
10. The plurality of agencies responsible for development (Funabashi, Hasegawa and Iijima 1998, pp. 93-119).

The plan for a huge industrial complex overestimated the demand for products (iron, steel, and petrochemical goods). As a result of further changes in the industrial structure after the oil crises of 1973 and 1979, the whole plan lost its feasibility. Yet although this was clearly going to cause serious problems, officials postponed reconsidering the original plans.

In the cases of East-Tomakomai and Mutsu-Kogawara, the original plan was eventually scaled down, but it was not fundamentally changed. Consequently, large areas of land that were bought for industrial development have remained unused and it has not been possible to recover the mountain of bad debts incurred in purchasing the land. Repayment of the debts fell on the taxpayer.

In response to critics of the project, the person in charge of the National Consolidated Plan, the Deputy Secretary of the National Land Agency, was quoted as saying that 'development policy is a process of trial and error' (Honma 1991, p.78). The question, however, remains: who is to be held responsible for the harm caused by such error-prone hit-and-miss development policies, and how should such persons be held accountable?

The Third Consolidated National Development Plan (1977)

In 1977 the national government implemented the Third Consolidated National Development Plan, and in 1983 the government introduced The Law for Promoting the Development of High Technology Integrated Regions (Technolpolis Law) to promote the location of high-tech industry in designated areas. The government had designated 26 trial locations under the Technolpolis Law as of 1989 (*Yuhikaku Dictionary of Economic Terms* 1998, p. 856). The main targeted industries included those in the areas of lightweight and high value-added products, and those with intensive research and development costs, such as electronics, semiconductors, optics, and computer software. Inland development was supported by new transportation systems (highways, airports). Authorities reduced some smokestack industrial pollution, but caused new pollution problems with the development of high-tech industry.

'High-tech' industries, such as optics and semiconductor manufacturing, have helped to lead Japan's economy over the past two decades and have been widely credited with helping Japan move toward an environmentally more benign industrial structure. Despite their clean image and their undisputed low emissions of conventionally monitored pollutants, such as sulfur dioxide into the air or heavy metals into surface waters, it has been clear since the late 1980s that high-tech industries have caused serious pollution problems. Hazardous organic chemical compounds, such as trichloroethylene, from high-tech industries have polluted the environment, especially groundwater. Below seven cases are introduced in which pursuit of economic development through the promotion of high-tech industries has caused very serious pollution problems and expensive cleanup problems.

Case 1. Taishi City: denying responsibility

In Taishi City, Hyogo Prefecture, in 1984, authorities discovered that a large area of groundwater had been contaminated with trichloroethylene. The suspected source was the Toshiba Taishi Plant, where trichloroethylene was used to clean cathode ray tubes. The underground water aquifer was the source of drinking water for a nearby town.

The pollution in the groundwater was caused because trichloroethylene had been stored deep underground (more than 7 m) for a long time. Early remediation through soil removal would have limited the damage. As it was, workers found trichloroethylene concentrations measuring about 8000 parts per billion (ppb) in the deep wells, which is more than 200 times the standard of 30 ppb. The even more toxic *cis*-1,2-dichloroethylene was detected in nearby wells (Japan Water Pollution Research Association 1986, pp. 116-42 and 149-83).

Authorities solved the problem by switching the source of drinking water. After discovering the contamination in the wells, the affected area was aerated and treated with activated carbon. The water supply was converted from private wells to centrally piped tap water, although some contaminated wells are being still used for bathing. Although the Toshiba Taishi Plant refused to take official responsibility for the pollution, it made a 'donation' to cover the costs of switching from the use of private wells to centrally supplied tap water (Hyogo Prefecture 1995, p.53).

Case 2. Kimitsu City: a pioneer in cleanup

In 1988 authorities announced that organic compounds had polluted the groundwater near the Toshiba Components Plant in Kimitsu City, Chiba Prefecture. This plant produces semi-conductors and employs about 500 workers. It had used trichloroethylene as an organic solvent to clean silicon chips. Neither the central government nor the local government carried out a systematic investigation of the trichloroethylene problem at the site, so the initiative to conduct a study fell to Kimitsu City and the Chiba Geological Environment Research Laboratory. By boring holes in 34 places, they mapped the aquifer and delineated seven highly polluted 'hot spots'. They then developed a new cleanup technology to address the problem.

Basically the process consisted of three parts. First, waste substances and contaminated soil were removed and then subjected to heating and air-drying treatment. Second, a shield of steel-tubing sheet pile was installed to create a barrier well system. Third, to remove the contaminated substances, the cleanup operation sought to pump, aerate, and use the water of public wells. The total cost of the investigation and the cleanup operation has so far amounted to no less than 1.2 billion yen, of which only 50 million yen has been supplied by the city (Kimitsu City, Department of Environment 1993).

The Kimitsu groundwater pollution case gave impetus to an amendment of the Water Pollution Control Law in 1989 and had a great influence on the way high-tech pollution all over Japan was handled. The cause and effect relationship of high-tech pollution was disclosed for the first time in this case, and the cleanup technology developed by Kimitsu came to be widely known in Japan.

Case 3. Yamagata Prefecture: industrial park pollution

Kyushu is a scenic island with abundant water; however, the area is economically lagging. It therefore has a ready supply of relatively low-wage labor. These two factors, combined with accommodative local governments, have made it an attractive location for high-tech industries. Many semi-conductor manufacturing plants have been built in the Tohoku district, in the northeast of the island. The government of Yamagata Prefecture developed the Omori Industrial Park, where 16 companies have located, including a number of high-tech manufacturing factories. A local government survey in 1992 detected trichloroethylene near the industrial park in concentrations as high as 2000 ppb.

The five plants that used trichloroethylene as an organic solvent and, thus, were the suspected sources were Yamagata Casio, Higashine Shin Dengen, Yamagata Sanken, Yamagata Fujitsu, and Yamagata Kinseki. With a total workforce exceeding 3000, these plants have a large impact on the local economy. Although the local government has already confirmed contamination of soil strata at the sites of three of these business establishments, it has not yet revealed how the contamination was caused or to what extent corrections have been made (Yamagata Prefecture 1995, pp. 33-4).

Case 4. Hadano: Japanese superfund system
Hadano City, with 160,000 residents, is located at the foot of the Tanzawa Mountains in Kanagawa Prefecture. Most of its tap water (now nearly 65 per cent) has been supplied by groundwater since the city set up a water supply company in 1890. The discovery of groundwater pollution in 1989 forced the city to install aerators in four places in its water distribution system (Hadano City 1993, p. 78).

Hadano's industrial park, where many business establishments continue to use chlorinated chemical substances, is located directly over the center of the city's groundwater recharge basin. As a result, ground water pollution is spread over an area of 12 km^2. The local authority conducted a basic survey of 63 companies, occasionally using test borings, from 1991-94. In 1992 it was reported that 60 m-deep wells were polluted by trichloroethylene (95-866 ppb) and tetrachloroethylene (19-143 ppb). In response, 44 of the 63 companies undertook detailed investigations at their own expense and subsequently initiated cleanup activities on their own. Approximately 9 tons of organic solvents were obtained from 22 companies, including 2 drycleaners.

To resolve the pollution problem, Hadano also established a Groundwater Use Cooperative Fund System for the preservation of groundwater and has taken the opportunity to check groundwater pollution. It has led the country in enforcing the Groundwater Contamination Control Cleanup Ordinance, also known as the 'Japanese Superfund', established in 1993. The Hadano case has been a rather good example of the polluter pays principle (PPP) (Hadano City 1996, p. 87).

Case 5. Fukushima and Tochigi: pollution at all levels
Generally speaking, high-tech products are made up of many parts that are manufactured by widely dispersed subcontractors. Many of these firms appear to be polluting the groundwater outside the big cities throughout

Japan and in much of the rest of Asia. Within Japan, evidence comes from Fukushima Prefecture, where subcontractors of precision machinery for optical lens production have been the objects of a groundwater cleanup enforcement operation including 36 cases. In addition, tetrachloroethylene appears to have leaked into the groundwater at the large (1500 workers) Canon Fukushima plant (Chuman 1992, pp. 19-30).

Tochigi Prefecture offers additional examples. The groundwater of Tochigi City and Tsuga Town is partially contaminated by trichloroethylene, and the same chemical was detected at concentrations of up to 4400 ppb in a drain from a ditch running alongside the Electrolysis Condenser Company. In 1990 trichloroethylene was detected in groundwater at Kanuma, also in Tochigi, whose local product, Kanuma Soil, is prized for gardening use. According to an investigation by the prefecture, the relatively small Canon Kanuma Plant (220 workers), located upstream of the aquifer, was identified as the suspected pollution source. The plant used 240 tons of tetrachloroethylene per year as an undiluted solvent for grinding lenses for copy machines and cameras. The used solvent was stored in six underground waste liquid tanks and was collected by an industrial waste disposal business. Leaks from both the cleaner waste liquid tank and the distillation reprocessing apparatus appeared to be the cause of the pollution (Tochigi Prefecture 1994, p. 208).

Commentary on the High-tech Development Schemes

The above cases illustrate the worrisome levels of pollution from high-tech plants, including subcontractors, that has spread throughout Japan. Of special concern is that most of the known groundwater pollution incidents have not yet been fully made public. One reason for this is that local authorities have responded to the pollution cases in different ways. Some are active in identifying polluters and enforcing cleanup, whereas others are reluctant to explore or reveal pollution sources. These differences may be due to a number of factors, including the nature of relations between authorities and the relevant enterprises, variations in the degree of public dependence on groundwater, and local legal provisions exemplified by groundwater pollution control ordinances.

Because of the failure to take local conditions and environmental realities into consideration, it will be crucial in the future to proceed with groundwater cleanup according to the amended Water Pollution Control Law (amended in 1996), although enforcement is likely to be costly and difficult. Some enterprises refuse to admit responsibility for pollution officially but pay some of the cleanup expenses as a 'contribution'. Although some local authorities have raised funds to provide companies with loans for cleanup, this money is derived from public funds, in violation of the polluter pays principle. It is indispensable to make clear the cleanup responsibility of an enterprise identified as a pollution source. It is also vital that information regarding pollution sources and purification measures be made available to the public.

The Fourth Consolidated National Development Plan and Resort Development (1987-present)

Ever since the central government's attempt to implement the New Consolidated National Development Plan of 1962, it also has been promoting schemes to encourage tourism. However, it was not until Japan passed the 1987 Fourth Consolidated National Development Plan and the Resort Law that tourism became the target of large-scale development throughout Japan. The tourism push was part of the government's plan to revitalize the private sector and to increase money flow throughout the country.

The Resort Law encourages private company initiatives to develop resorts in natural areas. It permits the radical deregulation of farmland for diversification into other purposes. It promotes the opening of natural forest areas to resorts. It also provides for government subsidies and tax breaks to encourage resort development (provisions 1, 14, and 15) (Sato 1990, pp. 82-132).

As a result of the Resort Law and the subsequent rush to develop resorts, land price speculation was rampant. As soon as the Resort Law was passed all 47 prefectures immediately initiated resort projects (by 1990, these were 900 ventures). About 20 per cent of all Japan's total landmass was earmarked as areas for resort development. This movement stimulated land speculation and a sharp rise in the price of land. This speculation was one of the causes of Japan's 'bubble economy' of the late 1980s and early 1990s.

How the land law promoted land price speculation is worthy of further examination. In order to qualify for the central government's subsidies and tax reductions, local governments drew up plans to acquire the permission of landowners to develop land while inviting private companies to invest in the land's development. The private companies borrowed money from banks in order to invest in the construction of golf courses, ski resorts, and holiday hotels. Since most specific projects were administered as a third sector system in which local governments and private developers were jointly involved, the development of private resorts was in part treated like governmental public works. Also, the responsibility and the control of each of these third sector projects tended to be vague. The combination of the Consolidated National Development Plan and the Resort Law was therefore the main cause of rampant land speculation and the immediate cause of the 'bubble economy'.

Environmental Policy in Japan

After the bursting of the bubble, Japan was left with widespread environmental degradation and acres of half-developed, abandoned land, while the burden of paying off all the bad debts fell upon the shoulders of the taxpayers. We are obliged to point out that the originators of the initial plan that led to this mess are the shortsighted lawmakers, and it is they who should be held responsible.

The Fourth Consolidated Development Plan fell victim to many of the same problems that plagued the First, Second, and Third Plans: 1) the secrecy of decision-making processes, which were open only to members of the cabinet but were closed to both the general public and the Diet; 2) the absence of any official review processes for the plans, which tended to overestimate the demand for industrial goods and overlooked the changes that were occurring in the structure of industry and the economy; 3) the initial failure to designate a responsible ministry or agency to implement the plan led to a failure of accountability and responsibility (although, after 1974, the government did set up the National Land Agency); 4) the blind promotion of the plan encouraged speculators to invest overhastily in land development; 5) the lack of strict regulations on land price speculation and the acquisition of private land led to inflated real estate prices and overdevelopment; 6) a failure to include as central parts of the plan any measures designed to protect the environment.

'Local Development' as an Alternative to Consolidated Development Plans

Strategies of 'local development' offer an alternative to the traditional development patterns that have prevailed in Japan. The traditional Consolidated Development Plans were directed by national interests, did not consider local conditions, and caused serious negative environmental consequences. In contrast, many regions of Japan have eagerly sought alternative ways of regional development. One style of self-directed development, known as local development, includes a number of distinguishing features. First, it is not dependent on subsidies from the central government or sponsorship by big companies, but is based upon the region's own natural resources, industries, and culture. Being independent of the national government encourages local areas to learn to develop and manage their enterprises by themselves. Second, a local perspective ensures that more attention will be paid to environmental preservation and that there will be regard for each region's natural environment, landscapes, and amenities. Concern for the local environment leads to more sustainable development. Third, the local economy benefits because local development seeks to construct a complex industrial structure with close and multiple relationships among local businesses, thereby ensuring a greater percentage of profits will be kept within the local area. Local development ensures a high-quality local economic structure. Fourth, local development encourages meaningful citizen input; it institutionalizes citizen involvement and promotes grass-roots democracy (Hobo 1996, pp. 221-8).

There are many examples of local development throughout Japan. In Oita Prefecture, there is an initiative to foster the idea of 'one village, one specialty' (Hobo 1996, pp. 205-68). Kanazawa City preserved its historical heritage by encouraging the development of traditional industries and crafts. In Hokkaido, Ikeda Town created its own winery. Some mountainous regions have initiated various programs. There are programs which garner support of urban residents for people living in mountainous regions, encourage the trade and exchange of local agricultural and forest products, promote investments in forested areas through development of real estate (for second houses or health resorts), establish extended cooperative agreements among linked communities, and organize agricultural cooperatives.

ENERGY POLICY AND THE ENVIRONMENT

Japan's national energy policies after World War II had a deep impact upon the environment because they supported the development of numerous power generating plants at the local level, from hydroelectric power-generating dams, coal and oil power-generating stations, to nuclear power stations. Each type of generating station has caused numerous pollution and environmental degradation problems. The main vehicles utilized to support the development of power plants were three laws: the Law for Promotion of Electric Power Resources, the Special Account Law for Promoting the Development of Electric Power Resources, and the Law to Manage the Areas Surrounding Electrical Power Facilities. These laws allowed the national government to award subsidies, funded by tax revenues, to local areas for developing power production plants. The government passed these laws to promote development of power sources against the background of citizen movements opposed to the construction of power stations, especially nuclear facilities.

Subsidies for Siting Power Stations

In 1973, the government of Kakuei Tanaka, which had already introduced an automobile fuel tax to pay for road construction, introduced the three laws noted above to promote construction of power-generating stations by using a tax levied on the consumption of electricity. Resources drawn from the Power Resources Development Levy, partly intended to protect the environment, were used to subsidize public works projects, such as the construction of roads leading to and from power stations (Miyamoto 1989, p. 238). The subsidies were basically compensation or bribes to appease local citizens. A pamphlet issued by the Resources Energy Agency explains the purpose of the three laws in these terms:

> since power generating stations employ fewer people than do other industries, and because the energy is not utilized at the sites near the stations but is relayed to metropolitan areas, we have to be able to answer the complaints of local people who see no merit or gain to themselves in siting the stations in their locality.

The subsidies came from tax revenue and were dolled out according to how the prefectures structured the energy development plans, among other factors. For example, in the early 1980s, one citizen user paid 1000 yen per year as a resources tax. From 1974-84, the total amount of tax revenue used to fund the subsidy system amounted to 266 billion yen. Every year about 300 billion yen was granted; however over 100 billion yen became surplus (Miyamoto 1989 pp. 239-40). Subsidies were divided between educational and cultural facilities (29 per cent), road construction (25 per cent), sports and recreational facilities (15 per cent), and agriculture and fishery facilities (8 per cent). The Prefectures that received the largest proportion of the subsidies were those in which nuclear facilities had been sited: Fukushima and Fukui Prefectures. Consequently, nuclear power-generating stations are concentrated locally in Fukushima, Fukui, and Niigata prefectures.

The subsidy system has several problems. Revenue from subsidies swells the temporary budget of the cities, towns, and villages that are targeted and supports the building of unnecessary facilities. These unneeded facilities require continuous maintenance expenditures for their upkeep. At the same time, the fixed assets tax revenue derived from power-generating facilities decreases over time. Nevertheless, the cities, towns, and villages in which the facilities are located tend to accept additional facilities. Also, local residents do not consume much of the energy produced at the local level. Instead, it is shipped to metropolitan areas where people do not know where the energy comes from. They are not aware of the risks involved with power generation and often use energy wastefully. This means that a good deal of energy is not used efficiently, and urban dwellers need not weigh the risks and benefits of using nuclear energy in their daily lives because the risk is transferred to generation plant locales.

Nuclear Power Facilities and the Environment

Japan is home to 51 nuclear power plants and their related facilities, and while these plants generate one-third of the electricity used in Japan, they also pose specific risks. Nuclear power plant management and safety is not regulated by the Environment Agency. Instead, the Science and Technology Agency and the Resources Energy Agency of the Ministry of International Trade and Industry (MITI) regulate the industry. Since the early 1970s, when commercial nuclear power stations began to come into operation, many small-scale accidents have occurred at nuclear power plants around the country including steam leaks and feed water pump cracks due to metal fatigue. Recently, however, more serious accidents have occurred. In 1997, there was a serious accident at the experimental fast breeder reactor (Monju) operated by the Power Reactor and Nuclear Fuel Development Corporation in Fukui Prefecture. In 1999, there was an accident at the conversion plant (Japan Nuclear Fuel Conversion Company (JCO) at Tokai-mura in Ibaraki Prefecture.

Japanese nuclear policy aims at a complete reprocessing and nuclear fuel cycle. The small-scale plant at Tokai-mura houses a unit for reprocessing, while a bigger reprocessing plant is now under construction at Rokkasho-mura (Mutsu-Kogawara). Although the reprocessing plant is in operation, much spent fuel is still being transported and reprocessed in the United Kingdom (UK) or France. The government proposes to build a fast breeder reactor (FBR) that will be able to use plutonium. However, the major accident at Monju indicates that the successful (and safe) development of the FBR may remain elusive. Nevertheless, the reprocessed plutonium that has been returned from the UK and France is being stockpiled, and the government is planning to use plutonium in a light water-type reactor (pluthermal).

Of special note is that both the responsibility for the safety of nuclear plants and related facilities and the responsibility of the planning and operation of the facilities rests with the same authority. A nuclear safety committee is attached to the Science and Technology Agency, but it only has a staff of 30 people. The responsibility for ensuring that safety regulations are observed also falls within the purview of the Science and Technology Agency and the Resource Energy Agency. Now two organizations have been unified into one organization, Genshiryoku Hoan-in (Nuclear Safety Agency). This arrangement differs from that of the United States Nuclear Regulatory Commission, where the agencies for regulation and development are kept separate.

The management of nuclear waste also remains a huge problem. There are no formal laws that regulate the storage of high-level radioactive waste. Nor does the national government offer any guidance on how to select sites at which to deposit high-level radioactive waste. At Rokkasho-mura, which is still under construction, high-level radioactive waste is already being stored in glass canisters. It is not only the management of nuclear waste that is a problem; the management of solid waste still remains a huge headache.

WASTE MANAGEMENT POLICY AND THE ENVIRONMENT

One of the biggest environmental problems facing present-day Japan is the issue of waste and waste disposal. Needless to say, many of the safety hazards that have resulted from the siting of waste disposal sites and the conduct of waste companies remain a present danger to Japan's environment and people. Much of the environmental pollution is the result of a number of related factors: the choice of landfill disposal sites and disputes over siting; the shortage of suitable sites; the burden of disposal sites on local government capacity; emissions of specific pollutants; such as dioxin Polychlorinated dibenzo-*p*-dioxins, Polychlorinated dibenzo-furans (PCDDs/Dfs) which arise from the use of domestic waste incinerators; and finally, poorly designed laws and policies, such as the newly introduced 'Law for the Promotion of Sorted Recycling of Containers and Packaging' (Yoshida 1998, pp. 23-48).

Wastes are classified roughly into two types: municipal solid (domestic) waste and industrial waste. The domestic consumption of raw materials and resources amounts to about four tons of waste (including municipal waste and industrial waste) per person annually. In 2000, industrial waste amounted to about 400 million tons, which accounted for between 80 to 90 per cent of the total quantity of waste. Nineteen kinds of industrial waste have been classified, and those that are classified as 'injurious to human health and the living environment' are located in specially managed sites. Unfortunately, the 19 specified items do not cover every kind of industrial waste. The list ignores a number of different waste streams, for example, the pollution of surplus soil.

The official figures given for industrial waste in 2000 were listed under three headings: sludge 46 per cent, animal excrement 22 per cent, and construction waste 15 per cent (Ministry of the Environment 2003b, p. 50). In fact, the amount of construction waste is greater than this since the figures do not take into account the weight of dehydrated sludge. About one-fifth of all the industrial waste produced is disposed of. The amount of waste recycled has reached a ceiling of about 40 per cent.

In recognition of the differences between waste streams and disposal facilities, landfill sites are divided into three types: 1) least controlled landfill sites, of which Japan has 1,611; 2) controlled landfill sites equipped with a liner, of which there are 1025; and 3) strictly controlled landfill sites encased in concrete, of which Japan has 41 (Ministry of the Environment 2004b).

Over the last few years, the differences in landfill criteria have sometimes been rendered meaningless. For example, although a 1997 revision of the Waste Disposal and Public Cleansing Law prohibits the disposal of municipal solid waste in sites without a liner or a wastewater treatment facility, old landfill sites that had been established before the revision have not yet been properly regulated.

Teshima: Illegal Dumping of Waste and Environmental Pollution

The illegal dumping of a massive amount of waste at Teshima Island in the Seto Inland Sea brought the issue of accountability to the fore. The Teshima case highlights the problems associated with finding those responsible for illegal dumping, proving causation for the environmental pollution, and getting them to bear the cleanup costs. An investigation by the Environmental Dispute Coordination Commission discovered that the waste illegally dumped at Teshima Island contained such hazardous materials as lead, polychlorinated biphenyl (PCB), and dioxins (PCDDs/DFs). The affected area covers 460,000 m² and 87 per cent of this area falls outside the limits established for the permitted dumping of hazardous waste. At the same time, not only lead and benzene but also dioxin was found in the groundwater in quantities exceeding the legal criteria of permitted levels. Although no obvious traces of pollution in the subsoil or in the creatures living on the seabed have been detected, there can be no doubt that hazardous waste matter has been leaching through to groundwater and then flowing out to the sea (Hanashima, Takatsuki and Nakasugi 1996, p. 4).

The origins of the illegal dumping at Teshima Island can be traced back to 1975 when the company responsible applied for permission to operate a hazardous waste management disposal business. In 1977, the company modified its application so that it could operate an intermediate disposal business in order to cultivate earthworms in the sludge for the production of a soil conditioner. In 1978, the Kagawa prefectural government granted the company permission to do this. In 1983, the Prefectural Public Safety Commission also gave the company permission to organize a scrap metal business authorized to haul shredder dust, waste oil, and sludge as well as to run landfill operations and carry out open burning. The company, however, also carried out open burning of unauthorized waste. As the volume of waste being hauled to the site continued to increase, the Hyogo Prefectural Police became suspicious that the company was violating the Waste Treatment Act of 1990, which had been designed to end the excessive movement of wastes, improper disposal, and open burning.

Although the company complied with the orders of the Kagawa Prefectural Government to remove the dumped waste and install prevention equipment to prevent the outflow of litter, a good deal of waste matter was left behind. Five hundred and forty-nine inhabitants of Teshima Island requested the right to question 21 producers of waste. In 1993 the Kagawa Prefectural Government asked the Environmental Dispute Coordination Commission to mediate between the company and the residents who were asking not only for the removal of wastes but also for compensation for damages. In 1996, the Takamatsu District Court decided in favor of the local residents (Yoshida 1998, p. 25).

At issue in this and other cases is which party should be held liable for the damages, the producers of the waste, the waste disposal company, and/or the local government? In the above case, the original Waste Disposal and Public Cleansing Law proved inadequate as a means to counter the waste disposal company's attempts to evade the issue by arguing that shredder dust was not industrial waste since it still contained valuable products. Such inadequacies in the law left room for the administration to interpret its terms in an arbitrary manner. In July 1997, however, the Kagawa Prefectural Government did come to an intermediate agreement, and admitted that they had made a mistake in giving permission to the waste service company, while expressing their regret at what had happened. At the same time, they made a decision in favor of the intermediate disposal of waste. This, however, did not satisfy the local inhabitants who had asked for the complete removal of waste. The residents were not pleased that there was no mention of the generators' responsibility for what had happened. Also, there was no recognition that the free offer of land by the local government had been a precondition for the establishment of the disposal facility site in the first place. With financial help from the national exchequer, the Kagawa Prefectural Government proposed to spend more than 15 billion yen for the cleanup.

Complicating the case was the fact that the waste producers hired an unauthorized waste disposal company, despite their prior knowledge of the situation. The generators of the waste had nevertheless hired the unauthorized disposal business because of its lower than average charges. The hiring of an illegal disposal company is not the salient issue. On this point, the wording of the law is clear: 'force the solvent generators to bear the burden'. The problem is getting the numerous waste generators to fork over the necessary capital to get the job done although, in this case, most of the 21 generators expressed their intention to bear part of the disposal costs on the pretext that it was 'settlement money'. However, their 'contribution' will fall short of paying for the cleanup (Yoshida 1998, p. 25).

Revision of Waste Disposal Laws and a Framework for the Future

The fundamental law regarding the disposal of waste in Japan was originally passed in 1971, but was revised once in 1991 and again in 1997, making it more stringent. For example, the revised law mandated that disposal sites must go through an EIA process. According to this provision, the disposal facility must investigate the influence of the facility on the surrounding environment. The local governor must publish the results of the investigation and hold a hearing to consider the opinions of all those affected. All of the stakeholders must come to some agreement before the state will give permission to construct a landfill. Another provision stipulates that the management record of the disposal facility must be made public. The law also requires the government to strengthen the penal regulations regarding the illegal dumping of industrial waste; it called for a maximum fine of 100 million yen to be imposed upon anyone judged guilty of illegal dumping. The law requires that industry and the government must donate/create a fund to cover the expenses for the disposal of industrial waste for which no liability can be assigned to a specific company (Yoshida 2004, pp. 55-80).

The revised law has been criticized, however, on several counts. First, some argue that the responsibility of the generator of the waste has actually been reduced, rather than increased. The fund to restore land damaged by illegal dumping depends entirely on voluntary contributions. Second, interested parties the local government, the affected parties, and specialists are granted no more than a hearing. In other words, there is no mechanism to incorporate their opinions. Third, there are no specific provisions regulating the siting of landfills. Fourth, 60 per cent of all local governments consider the revised law useless when it comes to its ability to reduce the number of disputes over siting decisions. So, although the law has been significantly revised, others and I argue that the existing law and the general administration of waste control process by the Ministry of Health, Labor and Welfare is fundamentally flawed.

Under the direction of the Ministry of Health and Public Welfare, the Japanese government's administration of public sanitation has focused on the prevention of infectious diseases, which has led to an increase in the use of incineration to dispose of wastes. Large-scale incineration operations carried out by public sanitation agencies have led to increased dioxin pollution.

Because Japan gets many of its raw materials from abroad and because it has relatively lax waste disposal regulations, there has been little need to conserve depleting resources or to reduce pressure on the environment. Despite the fact that Japan's landfill sites are overflowing, it has made little progress in the reduction or recycling of waste matter. To overcome this situation, some have proposed that raw materials should be taxed and that recycling should be subsidized. These proposals are similar to the American Resource Conservation and Recovery Act, Superfund (the Comprehensive Environmental Response, Compensation and Liability Act (CERCLA), and the German Soil Protection Law (Bodenschutz Gesetz) (Yoshida 2004, pp. 55-80).

In summary, Japan needs to build a better framework regulating waste management. Strict criteria for the construction, operation, and maintenance of disposal facility construction need to be established. Also, a system to clarify the responsibilities of the waste producer/generator must also be established. This has to be done to protect the soil and the groundwater, as well as to reduce waste. Once this framework has been put into place, it will be necessary to integrate the present Japanese waste administration systems under coordinated administrative control. For example, the Ministry of Health, Labor and Welfare oversees the implementation of the Waste Disposal and Public Cleansing Law, while the Ministry of Economy, Trade and Industry (METI) administers the Recycling Law and the Law for the Promotion and Utilization of Recyclable Resources. This makes it difficult to integrate waste management and recycling processes.

Japan's Laws for the Promotion of Collection and Recycling of Containers and Packaging

Several factors have made it increasingly necessary to incorporate recycling practices into waste management plans, but Japan's current laws fall short of the task. The modern practices of mass production, mass distribution, and mass consumption, plus the need to attract customers by the use of fancy, but superfluous packaging, has led to a shocking increase in the amount of packaging waste. Since nearly half the volume of domestic waste in Japan consists of containers and packaging including, cans, bottles, polyethylene terephthalate (PET) bottles, and paper packages, the government passed a law in April of 1997 to promote recycling. However, the new 'Sorted Collection and Recycling of Containers and Packaging' Law was immediately contested. The Tokyo Metropolitan Government and 12 other cities called for the law's reconsideration because of the excessive burden that its provisions would place on local government finances (Yoshida 2004, pp. 83-121).

French and German Influence on Japan's Recycling Laws

In some respects, Japan's recycling laws have been influenced by the French and German experiences. The German system, the Dual System Deutschland (DSD), stipulates that the collection and classification of waste should not be carried out by local authorities but by a separate organization. The DSD is responsible for recycling goods marked with a 'green dot', and the manufacturing enterprises and sellers of goods marked with a 'green dot' pay the DSD the costs of collection. The French system, on the other hand, requires the local government to take on the responsibility for collection while a private company, the Eco-Emballage Company, manages the actual recycling, financed by container manufacturers. Container manufacturers must also guarantee to take back recycled goods. The Japanese government adopted a system closer to that of the French but with some differences In Japan, local government and citizens have joint responsibility for the recovery of resources (Yoshida 2004, pp. 101-4).

The main Japanese law regulating recycling is the Law for the Promotion of Sorted Collection and Recycling of Containers and Packaging, which was sponsored by the Ministry of Health, Labor and Welfare. The law received important support from the All-Japan Prefectural and Municipal Workers Unions, local government, and labor unions that agreed to cooperate with the policy as a means of maintaining and expanding a directly managed union workers' job. The law stipulates a number of conditions. First, a city, town, or village must establish classificatory criteria for the sorting and sacking of different kinds of waste matter according to their constitution (for instance, whether biodegradable or non-biodegradable). Also, localities must specify the types of sacks to be used by the consumer, and must collect the waste thus sorted at set times. Second, domestic (and other) consumers must participate in recycling processes by sorting and sacking separately the various kinds of waste. Third, the manufacturers and users of containers must ensure that the recycling businesses remarket the material as recycled goods, but the law does not require manufactures to guarantee the lowest price for recycling the goods (Yoshida 2004, pp. 91-2).

A Heavy Burden on Local Governments and Tokyo's Solution

The most serious burden imposed on local governments by the new recycling system is the exceedingly heavy cost of collection. For instance, while local governments must use public tax revenues to pay 25-30 yen per PET bottle for collection, the manufacturers were only expected to pay 10,000 yen per ton, the equivalent of no more than 1 yen per 10 g for recycling. At the same time, the local government faces supplementary expenses incurred by the criteria for sorted refuse including costs for cleaning, condensing, and the prevention of remixing. The amount local governments must pay for associated services must be equal to the expenses of maintaining a 10-ton truck.

For these reasons, Tokyo and 12 other cities requested that the new law should be reconsidered. Tokyo, indeed, has enacted its own Tokyo Ordinance, which asks the enterprises concerned to undertake voluntary collections that are not required by the national law. The Tokyo Ordinance outlines three 'requests'. First, it seeks to promote voluntary collection by container manufacturers. Second, it requests that distributors install a collection box and asks all enterprises to collect container materials as recovery resources. Third, it requests collectors and distributors of sorted materials to set up collection boxes and requests that the container and content makers carry out intermediate treatment and recycling. Finally, it requests local governments to take temporary responsibility for the delivery of materials to the intermediate disposal facilities. In October 1997, the Tokyo municipal government and the makers of PET bottles reached an agreement that the PET bottle manufacturers should take the responsibility for establishing a recycling facility and that the Tokyo Municipal Government should rent out property to PET for storing the collected goods before onward transportation. The other 12 cities that had reservations about the new recycling law instituted similar voluntary measures (Yoshida 2004, pp. 114-6).

Weak Incentives for Reducing Plastic Wastes

In Japan, in contrast to Germany, recycling regulations do little to discourage the use of plastic containers. The German DSD system requires the enterprise to pay the cost of container and packaging disposal. The cost of recycling plastics is about 20 times higher than the rate for the recycling of glass. This effectively discourages the manufacture of plastic containers, which are difficult to dispose of. In Japan, on the other hand, the use of plastic bottles has rapidly increased, mainly due to the great increase in the sale of mineral water (by more than three times during 1996-97). In expectation of the 'Law for the Promotion of Sorted Collection and Recycling of Containers and Packaging', the makers of PET bottles actually lifted the voluntary self-control on the manufacture and use of such bottles. This is a great weakness of the Japanese. The cause of this weakness is the priority placed on the recycler and not on source reduction.

The 'Law for the Promotion of Sorted Collection and Recycling of Containers and Packaging' stipulates that returnable glass bottles are to be collected by the enterprise, but in fact the bottles are not reused immediately. In Sapporo, they are smashed into cullet (gobbets of glass which can then be remolded). This is part of a scheme instituted by the Sapporo Municipal Government that asks residents to sort cans, glass bottles, and PET bottles separately from 'flammable garbage'. Residents pack the sorted wastes into specified transparent bags, which are collected once or twice a week. At the same time, the majority of the rapidly increasing number of PET bottles on the market become pure waste since only about 30 per cent, at the highest estimate, are collected. Therefore, the absolute volume of PET bottles that are neither recycled nor reused has increased rapidly (Yoshida 2004, pp. 83-6).

The Problem with Recycling: An Imbalance of Supply and Demand

An imbalance of supply and demand in paper and plastic recycling business weakens the overall recycling system in Japan. Currently, excessive stocks of used paper are burnt because of a shortage of storage space (stockyards). A similar imbalance between supply and demand is likely to occur in the recycling of containers and packaging. The new act provides that the competent ministers from the Ministry of Finance; METI; the Ministry of Health, Labor and Welfare; and the Ministry of Agriculture, Forestry and Fisheries should decide on the structure of the recycling program. City, town, and village authorities must establish plans for collection processes. As of 2002, no more than 50 per cent of the PET bottles sold had been recovered. With regard to other plastics (polystyrene foam, vinyl chloride, wrapping foil, and such like) –which from the fiscal year 2000 are to be collected separately – no likely technology for their recycling is on the horizon. Even Germany faces the problem of coordinating supply and demand. A major task for the future is the development of technology and the product market development of recycling. It is particularly urgent to prepare stockyards (that is, to allocate storage space) for household-sorted and collected container and packing wastes.

Chlorinated Dioxins and Related Compounds

Japan is now more polluted by dioxins and related compounds than any other country in the world. The amount of dioxins generated by local government waste incineration facilities is now as much as 5 kg per year. An investigation is being conducted to understand which industries are the major sources of dioxins. A list of the usual suspects includes facilities that dispose of chlorinated organic compounds, waste oils, medical wastes from hospitals, as well as iron manufacturing plants. Often, the concentrations of dioxin in the air near these facilities have been as high as $0.6 pgTEQ/m^3$ (pico gram toxicity equivalency quantity/m^3) in big metropolitan and residential areas, when compared with background areas (without artificial pollution) that have an average of 0.05 to $0.06 pgTEQ/m^3$.

Dioxins can affect the human body in a variety of ways, from acute toxicity to chronic toxicity, carcinogenity, and changes to the thyroid gland. It has recently been noticed that it can also induce reproductive toxicity. In the past, dioxin has usually entered the human body through the consumption of fish, particularly shellfish, so that it is especially alarming to learn that a baby can be infected with dioxin through its mother's milk. In fact, 51 pico gram (pg) fat concentration of dioxin was found in the milk of an Osaka mother, the highest concentration yet noted in a Japanese subject (Miyata 1999, p. 27).

Polychlorinated dibenzo-*p*-dioxins (PCDDs) are in general often dealt with as a type of dioxin, as are polychlorinated dibenzo-furans (PCDFs). The toxic mechanism of Coplanar PCBs is similar to that of dioxins. Dioxins have had a bad reputation ever since the Americans used it as a defoliant during the Vietnam War. In Japan, it is well known that PCDFs and Coplanar PCBs are responsible for the Kanemi Oil Disease (Miyata 1999, pp. 37-61).

An estimated 70 per cent of all the world's garbage incinerators are located in Japan and the incinerators, which burn municipal solid waste are the principal sources of dioxins (Yoshida 1998, p. 40). Although no complete investigation has yet been made of the incinerators and small-sized furnaces that burn industrial waste, there can be no doubt that the pollution for which they are responsible is likely to be intensely hazardous. Nor can there be any doubt that the present high level of dioxin pollution in Japan's environment is an inevitable result of the dogmatic adherence to the practice of waste incineration in local incinerators.

In spite of the fact that Japan is the country with the world's highest levels of airborne dioxins, the measures Japan has taken to control incinerator pollution lags far behind those of other countries. In June 1996, the Ministry of Health and Welfare did finally set a limit to the daily intake of dioxins considered harmless to human health: 10pgTEQ/Kg/day. At the same time, the Ministry's revised 'Air Pollution Control Law Enforcement Ordinance' and the Waste Disposal Law Enforcement Ordinance set out to regulate standards for the emission of dioxins from incinerators. For a newly built incinerator, less than 0.1 to 5ngTEQ/Nm^3 (nano gram toxicity equivalency quantity/normal m^3), and in the case of an old incinerator, 1 to 10 ng, these levels to be achieved over a period of five years, or 80 ng to be achieved over the period of a year (Yoshida 1998, p. 41).

The most fundamental measure necessary to reduce dioxin pollution must be a reduction in the amount of waste incinerated. During incineration, it will be necessary to completely prevent the production of dioxins, by means of the 3Ts (temperature, time, and turbulence). Although the mechanism by which dioxin is produced is in general understood, certain problems still need to be resolved. Researchers need to learn more about the toxic effects of vinyl chloride, disposed electric appliances, waste wood, chlorinated fire retardants and antiseptics, products which include copper (which undergoes the catalysis of dioxin in a recomposite reaction), and salty waste foods. If plastic wastes were to be strictly sorted and perfectly collected, if all food waste were to be reduced to compost, and if cast-out home electrical appliances were to be strictly recycled according to the provisions of the Sorted Collection and Recycling of Containers and Packing Law, then there would be a huge reduction in the amount of waste that needs to be incinerated. In fact, Sweden and Germany have placed a temporary moratorium on the building of new incinerators, and for newly constructed incinerators they have set the strict standard of 0.1 ng emissions of dioxin: these steps, as well as reducing dioxin, have also succeeded in reducing waste (Yoshida 1998, p. 41).

EIA PROCESSES

History of the EIA Law

Environmental impact assessment has been a key component of many nations' efforts to protect ecological systems in the face of population and development pressures. The USA introduced environmental impact assessment requirements for federally funded projects in its 1969 National Environmental Policy Act (NEPA). Influenced by these developments, the Japanese Government also introduced the idea of EIA in 1972 when the Cabinet approved the guideline, On Environmental Conservation Measures Relating to Public Works. In contrast with the US NEPA, however, which was a law, in Japan's case only guidelines were passed. Moreover, the Japanese guidelines did not describe any specific EIA procedures. In an effort to introduce a uniform method of conducting EIAs, the Environment Agency prepared a new bill on EIA procedures in 1974, but it met with considerable opposition within the government and from business. It took many years of extensive studies and discussions within government circles before the Environment Agency and other ministries agreed on the contents of an EIA bill. The Cabinet submitted this bill to the House of Representatives in 1982. However, because the bill did not come up for a vote before the House of Representatives was dissolved in November 1983, legislative procedure required that the bill die. Business interests, and especially power generation companies, were reluctant to see the bill passed, fearing that it would fuel the anti-nuclear protest movement.

The need for EIA, however, was difficult to ignore. Not only did national development plans tend to overestimate the future demand for new facilities, but they also often failed to predict the negative environmental consequences that could accompany facility development. For years, there was no formal assessment system for national development plans and no room for reconsideration of a plan once it was given the go-ahead. Consequently it was often not clear who should be held accountable when individual projects or entire plans went wrong. This problem was a fundamental issue of transparency in the workings of Japanese democracy.

With the national government failing to move, a number of local governments established or began planning to institute their own EIA schemes. Responding to these pressures and the urgent need for a national EIA procedure, the Cabinet finally decided to set up an EIA system although still not with the power of law, but rather as a form of administrative guidance. In 1984 the Cabinet approved guidelines for a uniform EIA procedure, entitled 'On the Implementation of Environmental Impact Assessment'. These guidelines prescribed specific rules to be followed for large-scale development projects in which the national government was involved. Since that time and until EIA legislation was passed in 1997, EIAs were conducted under the 1984 guidelines, as well as under such specific laws as the Public Water Area Reclamation Law and more specific administrative guidelines, such as MITI's guidelines for EIAs on power plant construction. Locally, as of February 1998, 53 of 59 prefectural governments and designated large cities had carried out EIAs according to their own EIA regulations and guidelines (Environment Agency 1998, p. 257).

An EIA Law eventually was enacted after more than 20 years of efforts by the Environment Agency to have one introduced. In the 1970s and 1980s, a strong industry lobby succeeded in opposing EIA legislation. After the United Nations Conference on Environment and Development in 1992, however, national circumstances changed drastically. It was pointed out that among industrialized countries Japan was the only country that did not have an EIA law. This was despite the fact that according to OECD Council Recommendations EIA was to be applied to aid projects. As a result the Overseas Economic Cooperation Fund (OECF, now the Japan Bank for International Cooperation (JBIC)) began in 1988 to conduct EIA studies prior to making decisions on providing loans or grants for aid projects in 1988. It proved uncomfortable for Japan's political leaders that although an advanced industrialized country, Japan had never institutionalized EIA in its national law.

The 1993 Basic Environment Law provided impetus for reconsidering existing EIA systems. It required the national government to take necessary measures so that developing projects that may exert severely adverse effects on the environment are subject to advance surveys, predictions or evaluations regarding their environmental impact. In July 1995, the Environment Agency established the Environmental Impact Assessment Systems Study Commission, an ad-hoc research group. After examining EIA systems in Japan and abroad, the commission published a report in June 1996, listing various points for improving Japan's EIA procedures (Environment Agency 1997, p. 247).

Responding to the commission report, the prime minister requested that the Central Environmental Council, the official consulting body for national environmental policy, submit to him a report recommending a national EIA system for Japan. The council engaged in intense internal discussion. It also held national and regional public hearings, as well as requesting public opinion via postal mail, facsimile and email. The council then compiled a report and submitted it to the prime minister in February 1997. The report specified major elements of a national law to be enacted pertaining to EIA procedures in Japan. The Cabinet submitted a bill on environmental impact assessments to the National Diet in March 1997. The bill was voted into law by the Diet in June 1997, without any amendments and entered into force in June 1999 (Environment Agency 1998, pp. 256-9). Compared to the previous schemes based on the Cabinet Decision of 1984, the new law provides more flexibility in determining the projects which must be subject to EIA ('screening') and the items and methods of impact studies to be conducted ('scoping').

Screening of projects subject to environmental impact assessment

The 1997 EIA Law prescribes the procedures for conducting EIAs on large-scale projects (or projects which change the contours of the land or construct new facilities) that may have significant impact on the environment. Projects subject to the EIA Law are large-scale projects implemented, authorized or approved by the national government that may exert severe effects on the environment. There are two classes of projects:

1. 'Class-I Projects' are projects of a certain scale, for which EIAs must be conducted.
2. 'Class-II Projects' are projects that may have environmental effects comparable to that of Class-1 Projects, but for which determination of whether or not EIAs are to be conducted is carried out on an individual basis.

For the development of new urban residential areas, for example, projects over 100 ha (approximately 220 a.) or more in area fall into Class I, while those between 75 and 100 ha might be subject to EIA as Class-II projects. Similar rules apply to other projects. The governmental bodies that provide licensing and authorization of projects determine whether or not EIAs must be undertaken for Class-II Projects ('screening'). They must first listen to the views of the relevant prefectural governors and take into consideration the characteristics of the projects and regional circumstances (Harashina 1996, pp. 34-40).

Scoping

The impact exerted on the environment by a project differs depending upon the characteristics of the particular project and the environmental circumstances of the region in which the project is implemented. For this reason, the techniques for conducting surveys, forecasts, and evaluations are not stipulated in advance, but rather a scoping procedure is adopted which determines the most appropriate methods.

The developer seeking to implement a project subject to the EIA Law is required to prepare a scoping document which compiles the environmental items to be studied and the techniques to be used for conducting the relevant surveys and other activities. The developer must respond to the views of the prefectural governors, mayors, and the public, in developing the final methods for conducting the EIA (Harashina 1996, pp. 34-40).

Draft and final environmental impact statements
The results of the EIA conducted by the would be developer and their study on environmental preservation measures has to be compiled in what is known as a Draft Environmental Impact Statement (Draft EIS). The Draft EIS must include: a compilation of the results of the surveys, forecasts and evaluations for each item; a progress report on the study of environmental preservation measures; and, surveys and other measures taken after the start of construction. The would be developer has to compile all the views received concerning the Draft EIS and must amend them accordingly. This might mean including additional surveys, forecasts, or evaluations. Once the developer has a completed EIS, the Environmental Minister and the administrative bodies which are responsible for providing the necessary licensing and authorization for the project comment on the EIS and may require alterations. The administrative bodies can reject the project or attach conditions regarding environmental preservation to the project, via the handling of the licensing and authorization procedures. Once completed an EIS must be opened for public viewing and comment (Kurasaka 2003, pp. 283-95).

Limitation of environmental impact assessments
While the EIA Law is an improvement, there are limitations to its applicability and effectiveness. First, it is applied only to large-scale projects, of which there are not many, even if Class-II projects are included in the calculation. Many smaller-scale projects are left to the EIA processes stipulated by local ordinances and guidelines. Second, EIAs are only conducted after specifications of the project, such as location, scale, and design have been completely determined. In many cases, there is little room to change the plan. It is usually very difficult to secure a large land area necessary for a big project, so there is very little flexibility in land use planning. Moreover, many development projects are public works projects for which plans are decided by central and local governments. When local governments are eager to promote projects, it is difficult to stop the projects. EIAs are considered to be the central tool for preventive environmental policy, but in reality, it has been left to central and local authorities to approve projects (Suwa 1997, pp. 164-72).

   The Ministry of the Environment (MOE) has started a study to address the limitations of EIS with a view to establishing a system that would address the larger issue of the policies that lie behind development projects. The MOE is considering a 'strategic environmental assessment' of policies, plans, and programs which would incorporate public participation in decision making (Sadler and Verheem 1996; Comprehensive Study Group on Strategic Environmental Assessment 2000).

CONCLUSION

The introduction to this chapter raised the intriguing question of whether development has expanded social liberties in Japan? How has development influenced the freedoms held in Japanese society and the functioning of democracy? The case studies present a mixed picture. While Japan has achieved remarkable growth over the post-war period, this was often done at high costs to the natural environment and human health. Issues related to land development may be one of Japan's weakest areas from an environmental perspective. Industrial development has often taken priority over environmental preservation, at times scarring the environment. This can be seen in ill-conceived land development schemes and promotion of leisure developments. It is evident in the government's provision of subsidies to local communities in return for their accepting large-scale power plants that might have substantial negative environmental effects. The failure of the government to deal adequately with the illegal dumping of waste continues to be a problem. Yet another indication of the priority given to land development over ecological concerns was the difficulty the Environment Agency had in introducing EIA.

There are, however, signs of change that suggest the development of more democratic and participatory approaches to land use issues. Increasingly, local governments are working on development projects that are independent of the national government and focus on promotion of local culture, natural resources, and industry. They tend to be more sustainable than many of the large consolidated development plans that have emanated from the national government.

The introduction of an EIA Law is another important indication of a more participatory and transparent process for land use. The EIA process has been introduced at the national level to deal with problems arising from industrial development, including major construction projects and the building of power plants. Nevertheless, Japan still needs a more comprehensive overall social assessment of public works, since too often public projects have a negative effect on the environment. Many project designs ignore the democratically expressed will of the people at the local level and nationally dictated projects often go over budget.

It can be argued that Japan needs an 'environmental new deal' or what could be called public works for environmental restoration. The 'environmental new deal' could spur the cleanup of contaminated soil in metropolitan and rural areas and the removal of traces of heavy metal, organic solvents, and other toxic substances from groundwater sources and the atmosphere.

It is also the case that there needs to be an overhaul of Japan's subsidy system. Rather than providing subsidies simply for development, subsidies could be granted to prevent pollution by both central and local governments. There have been cases where such subsidies for pollution control have been applied. For example, in response to *itai-itai* disease that broke out in Toyama Prefecture as a result of a mining operation, tax reductions and special depreciation systems were made available to the mining firm to deal with the pollution even though this example runs somewhat counter to the PPP of the OECD. In the future, the possibility of a subsidy system for pollution prevention should be considered.

It is also necessary to move beyond questions of technology to a consideration of what kinds of changes must be made to the social system itself. To protect the environment there must be changes in governmental attitudes and greater attention toward the needs and well being of society. This will require greater citizen input into policy decisions. Increasing information flows between the state and Japanese citizens would create more transparency in decision making about development questions.

9. Local Government, Industry and Pollution Control Agreements

Yu Matsuno

INTRODUCTION

It is widely acknowledged that local governments in Japan played a vital role in combating pollution problems during the country's rapid economic growth period. Regional legislators introduced pollution control ordinances as early as the 1940s when national legislation to fight pollution had not yet been enacted. They pioneered a compensation system for pollution victims and introduced stricter emission control standards than those prescribed by national law in the 1960s. Local governments innovated the total pollution load control system in the 1970s. The local governments' compensation system and total pollution load control systems were later adopted by the national government and became national environmental policy standards. This chapter will focus on pollution control agreements (PCAs), which are widely used by local governments in Japan. This analysis is therefore confined to the pollution control aspect of environmental policy.

STRUCTURE OF LOCAL GOVERNANCE IN JAPAN

Japan's structure of local governance is twofold. There are 47 prefectures under the national government and as of 1 April 2003 there were 3,213 municipalities under prefectural control Ministry of Public Management, Home Affairs, Posts and Telecommunications (MPHPT).[1] These are made up of cities, towns, villages and special wards in Tokyo. Citizens directly elect their governors, mayors and the members of local assemblies at each level every four years. Each level of local government is given some degree of discretionary power by national law under the constitution. The 12 largest cities, whose population exceeds one million, are designated by cabinet order to be given greater legal power, and 25 additional cities, whose population is over 300 000, are also given more regional power than those smaller towns. Tokyo has a population exceeding ten million. In contrast, the 48 smallest villages have populations that are less than a thousand. This means that the expressions 'local governance' and 'local government' address a very wide range of entities.

LOCAL GOVERNMENT VERSUS NATIONAL GOVERNMENT IN ENVIRONMENTAL POLICY MAKING[2]

Japan's national government put more emphasis on economic growth than on any other social value after the end of World War II. This resulted in serious damages to the environment and human health. The national government was reluctant to take measures to abate pollution. It was not until the summer of 1970 when Prime Minister Eisaku Sato unexpectedly set up the Central Anti-pollution Measures' Headquarters that national steps were finally initiated to fight pollution. It was probably the surge of public opinion against the national government for not resolving pollution problems, which brought about this action. Another motive for Sato's switch to an environmentally friendly attitude from a purely economic one could have been his desire to take steps in concert with the US government, which had already changed its approach earlier that year.[3] Six new and eight amended environmental bills were passed by the Pollution Diet in 1970, and this had important ramifications for local governments as well.

Many local areas with dense concentrations of industrial facilities suffered from serious pollution problems. No effective legislation or standards were in place to limit or control this pollution. With the adoption of new laws, greater legislative power was allocated locally. For example, local governments at the prefectural level were permitted to set and impose stricter emission standards on sources of pollutants than those set by the national government. Prior to this time, although local governments had introduced some standards, it was not clear whether they had legal authority to enforce them. The national environmental policy changes of 1970 clarified local government authority. Prefectural governments were officially allowed to impose stricter regulation on polluters with ordinances that were more restrictive than those at the national level. In practice, municipalities were also allowed to do so as long as their ordinances restricted polluters' activities in different manners than did national laws. A survey on PCAs conducted by Matsuno and Ueta in 1999 found that it was not lack of power as much as lack of manpower and funds and the growing complexity of environmental problems that were regarded as the biggest difficulties faced by local governments (Matsuno and Ueta 2002, pp. 123-5).

There is a basic division of roles between the national government and local governments. The national government sets ambient and emission standards while the local governments implement them. In Japan, desired ambient standards are stipulated, and the government is then expected to try to attain them. Ambient standards, in other words, are not compulsory. Emissions standards are basically uniform across the country and are not supposed to impose excessive burdens on industry. When the burden imposed by emission standards is deemed to be excessive by business, several kinds of subsidies, such as tax benefits and favorable interest loans can be introduced by economic ministries and, in particular, the Ministry of Economics, Trade and Industry (METI, formerly the Ministry of International Trade and Industry (MITI) described below) (Terao 1994; Matsuno 1997, pp. 110-20). The emission standards set by the national government are national minimum standards. When the ambient standards are not attained in local areas, the national government is often criticized by the press and people in those areas negatively effected (*Asahi Shimbun,* 21 February 2000, p. 4). The government, however, is not legally required to take immediate action to guarantee that standards will be attained. Instead, local governments are expected to clean up the problem. This means that local governments, which are the ones that are most aware of local environmental, economic and social conditions, need to be given power to do this. One way they have found such power is through PCAs.

DEFINITION OF A POLLUTION CONTROL AGREEMENT

A PCA is an agreement which is concluded between a polluter and a local government located in the area where the pollutants emitted may cause detrimental effects to the residents living there. A PCA covers the emitter's pollution prevention measures and other relevant matters, though it is important to note that the agreement is not required by law. Parties to a PCA on each side can be single or multiple. For example, parties to a PCA might be a local government and several businesses. Alternatively, several local governments and one business can establish a PCA. This is only natural as it often happens that the smoke emitted by one factory affects several municipalities and prefectures and that several businesses operate collectively. A local government is sometimes obliged to conclude a PCA with a residents' group as a polluter, usually as the operator of a municipal waste incineration facility, landfills or sewage works. PCAs are also called memorandums, pollution control contracts or environment preservation agreements (Matsuno and Ueta 2002).

PCAs usually include some or all of the following clauses:

1. Obligating businesses to make general efforts to prevent pollution.
2. Stipulating emission standards of pollutants, including types of fuel burned to be flue-gas.

3. Giving local government rights of on-site inspection.
4. Obliging business to report environment-related matters.
5. Stipulating sanctions in the case of a violation of the PCA. An example of this would be the temporary suspension of operations.
6. Stipulating a liability rule in the case of damage.
7. Stipulating residents' participation in the administration of a PCA.
8. Obligating a business enterprise to take care of its immediate surroundings, for example, with a requirement to plant trees around a facility (Environment Agency 1990, pp. 19-26; Matsuno and Ueta 2002, pp. 75-8).

According to our survey, the most contentious issue in negotiating a PCA is the level at which to set an emission standard. Emission standards are at the core of most PCAs. PCAs are contracted most typically when a new factory is being sited or when facilities are expanded. Many PCAs have also been created on existing business sites.

HISTORY OF PCAs

The first recognized PCA is thought to be the one established between Shimane Prefecture and two businesses that established new factories in the prefecture in 1952. There may well have been PCA-type agreements earlier than this as Japan has several centuries of experience with pollution from the mining industry, but none are known to the author. PCAs became popular after one was concluded between an electric power company and the Yokohama city government in 1964 when the company wanted to build a new thermal power plant in the already heavily polluted city.

The Yokohama case is often cited as the first PCA (Ueta 1996, p. 136; Kitamura 2003, p. 55). It is interesting to note that it is different from most PCAs in that the city government had to negotiate first with the national government for its arrangement. The electric power industry was heavily regulated by the MITI. The concerned electric power company had been established by law and the national government retained most of its stock; the new location plan was part of the national government's energy policy for coal. This meant that Yokohama city did not have the authority to impose regulations upon the company itself; it had to turn to the MITI to get a PCA established. In general, city governments had no power to influence decisions regarding the construction of power plants, but in this case, the city government had some grounds to be involved in the matter.

The power plant was to be built on the site of another electric company, which the government had reclaimed and then sold on the condition that future transfer of the site to a third party would need the city government's approval. The MITI was at first reluctant to accept the city government's demand that it should guide the company to take pollution prevention measures and adopt the more stringent emission standards proposed by the city government than were required under national laws. MITI eventually had to accept the claim of the city government, however. The reason for MITI's acceptance of Yokohama's demands can be attributed to the shock that MITI felt in 1964 when residents' movements in Mishima and Numazu were successful in opposing the plans to build industrial complexes that MITI had planned and supported. The ministry is believed to have recognized the potential power of residents' movements in Yokohama as well as the need for stringent pollution prevention measures. Once MITI's approval was given, the city government and the electric power company negotiated and concluded the PCA (Saruta 1971; 1981; 1999). In spite of the importance attributed to the Yokohama PCA today, it took several years for the general public, the press and other local governments to fully understand the implications of this new governance mechanism. Yet, looking back, it is possible to say that the Yokohama PCA was precedent setting. As Figure 9.1 illustrates, slowly after this time, it became common for electric power companies and other regulated industries, such as the petroleum industry, to conclude PCAs with relevant local governments before permission was given for the construction of new plants by the national government (Hashimoto 1988, p. 76; *Asahi Shimbun*, 2 May 1969, p. 4).

In 1968, the Tokyo government publicly proposed to the Tokyo Electric Power Company (TEPCO) to conclude a PCA in relation to a new thermal power plant. The Tokyo government threatened not to sell land to the company even though the government had reclaimed the land in order that the very power plant could be built there. There were several rounds of negotiations, and finally the company agreed to conclude a PCA. The PCA required TEPCO to take very stringent pollution prevention measures, measures that went beyond the level prescribed by national law. At the same time that these negotiations were being reported in the press, the Yokohama PCA case and some preceding cases were also referenced. This helped make the term 'pollution control agreement' well known throughout the nation. In both the Yokohama and Tokyo cases, the mayor and the governor were newly elected reformists supported by socialists and communists, then (and most of the time since) minority parties in the National Diet. PCAs are considered to be one of the greatest achievements made by local governments supported by reformist political parties that had not only local, but also national consequences. These initiatives pushed a reluctant national government to create and enforce stringent pollution control policies (*Asahi Shimbun*, 15 August 1968, p. 15; 4 September 1968, p. 1; 11 September 1968, pp. 1 and 5; Mitsuo et al. 1970; Kobayashi et al. 1970; Matsuno 2000, pp. 77-84).

Figure 9.1 The Number of Newly Concluded PCAs Per Year

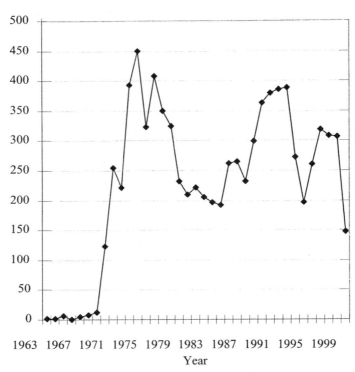

Notes: The data represented here is of currently valid PCAs by year of their creation. The survey data show that 51 per cent of those local governments responding to the survey had concluded PCAs. The total number of PCAs was estimated to be 30 000.[4] Seventy-five per cent informed us of the year when their PCA was concluded. The actual number of PCAs concluded each year is believed to be about three times larger than the survey results showed. Because a small portion of PCAs are abolished every year, the first peak is possibly a little higher (Matsuno 2001, pp. 3 and 5; Matsuno and Ueta 2002, pp. 43-4 and p. 82)

TEPCO is the largest electric power company of the ten regional monopolies in Japan and supplies electricity to Tokyo and several other prefectures around it. The conclusion of a PCA between Tokyo Prefecture and TEPCO initiated a ripple effect and led other local governments to create PCAs as well. The governor of the prefecture of Chiba, for instance, expressed his displeasure that TEPCO promised Tokyo better conditions than they had in Chiba, especially because power plants in Chiba supplied Tokyo with electricity but caused pollution in Chiba. The governor in Chiba thus declared that he would refuse any more new construction of power plants in the prefecture, including one that was already in the planning stage.

Referring to the Tokyo PCA, Kanagawa Prefecture, in which Yokohama city is located, also requested that TEPCO enforce stringent measures to combat pollution. Two months after the conclusion of the Tokyo PCA, the council on pollution prevention of Osaka reported to the governor that construction of new units of a thermal power plant in the prefecture could be permitted only when the total emissions of sulfur oxides from the plant were reduced (*Asahi Shimbun*, 7 September 1968, p. 15; 10 October 1968, p. 14; 19 November 1968, p. 7).

In 1969, 5 out of 20 newly built and existing integrated steelworks concluded PCAs (Matsuno 1997, pp. 107-9). This was important because a large integrated steelworks, which produces products from iron ore, consumes roughly 1 per cent of total national energy. It is often the case that they are the single largest source of local pollution (Matsuno 1997, p. 102). By 1973, 17 integrated steelworks (that is almost all the steelworks owned by the five leading steel companies) concluded PCAs with local governments. One of the five integrated steelworks which concluded a PCA in 1969 is located in Kitakyushu, a city with heavy industry and politically more conservative than Yokohama or Tokyo. In Kitakyushu MITI worked jointly with the city and businesses to facilitate a PCA contract based on scientific assessment (Matsuno 1997, pp. 107-9; Fujikura 1998, pp. 237-9).

History has shown that once a company accepts a stringent request by one local government and if that request is made public, it should expect to receive similar requests from all other local governments. Moreover, the same requests are immediately made to other businesses in the industry, and restrictions typically would apply both to new and existing facilities. These measures, in turn, would then be extended to other businesses in the area. One PCA, in other words, can result in many other PCAs. These PCAs often encompass a wide scope of environmentally sensitive material and, therefore, the environmental agreement can enforce restrictions between private enterprise and local government.

In the past, PCAs often required the use of technology which was not yet fully developed, so PCAs are believed to have contributed to the rapid development of pollution prevention technology in Japan. The number of newly concluded PCAs grew rapidly after 1968 and peaked around 1974. They were suddenly reduced around 1979-80, started to grow again around 1985, and made a second peak from 1989-92.

PCAs in the 1960s and 1970s were mainly concluded with manufacturing sites related to the chemical, electric power, iron-steel and mining industries. In the 1980s and 1990s, PCAs were negotiated with other industries as well (including agriculture, construction, transportation and industrial waste management). These PCAs grew both in number and in proportion. The scale of the sites that concluded PCAs in the 1960s and 1970s was relatively large, sometimes with more than 1,000 workers, but those in the 1980s and 1990s were smaller, sometimes with only 1 or 2 workers. This reflects the fact that local governments concluded PCAs with the most polluting sites first and then moved on to other sites, and that the focus of environmental problems changed in the course of time. In the 1980s, newly recognized threats to the environment came from high-tech industry research institutes and factories. The local governments which created PCAs were becoming smaller entities. Factories, the sources of traditional pollutants, were often located in or close to large cities, partly because these factories created employment and partly because they chose locations close to consumers. After the 1970s, guided by the national government industrial facilities shifted operations away from densely populated places, in order to alleviate pollution problems in these areas and also to activate local economies. Some facilities such as golf courses and landfills have tended to locate in local areas because of the low price of large portions of land.

PCAs in Chiba Prefecture

It is instructive to examine how and why a prefecture pursued PCAs. Chiba Prefecture first concluded PCAs with 41 businesses owning industrial complexes, including TEPCO in 1968. Since then the prefecture has gradually changed from simple PCAs in the early days to more comprehensive ones today. PCAs have been renewed every five years since 1980. Chiba has been the most active prefecture in using PCAs. Initially only sulfur oxide was targeted, but later PCAs were formulated which addressed other air pollutants, water pollutants, noise and odor from stationary sources and nitrogen oxides from vehicles. Basic PCAs came to be accompanied by specification agreements which stipulated the emission standards of each pollutant and required measures for pollution prevention including waste disposal and chemical safety. In addition there were interpretation agreements, which stipulated the reporting formats for measurement results and methods of measurement. Beginning in the 1970s, relevant cities where the concerned factories were located joined PCAs. Counterparts to PCAs have been expanded to 65 sites owned by 57 businesses (as of July 2003). Emission standards have been renewed and made more stringent (Chiba Prefecture 1994; 2000a; 2000b; telephone inquiry of Chiba Prefecture by the author 3 July 2003).

As a result of such efforts, targeted pollutant emissions have been reduced drastically. The prefecture has an ordinance which stipulates more stringent emission standards than the law requires. PCAs that are concluded with the largest businesses operating in the prefecture have emission standards above those legally mandated. In addition to emission standards, the businesses are required to submit annual plans for pollution prevention which are reviewed by local government. They are also required to consult with the government about the construction of new facilities. Businesses are required to install automatic emission measuring devices using remote data communications at smokestacks. The data is then transmitted to the relevant government officials. Smaller businesses without PCAs are given guidelines (*yoko*) made by the government. For sulfur oxides, nitrogen oxides and particulate matter, functions are defined to calculate emission standards based on the amount of fuels and materials used at the site, but the exact emission standards are negotiated between the relevant governments and each business. Some inequity exists and the governments do not make the level of standards imposed on each business public so that businesses cannot be compared with each other. Accordingly, businesses have not criticized such inequities. Instead most businesses mostly complain about the cumbersome procedures involving PCAs. About 90 per cent of businesses claimed that the procedures for renewals and the administration of PCAs were too complicated and should be simplified according to a survey made by the prefecture in 1993 (Chiba Prefecture 1994). In response, the procedures were adjusted by the government. With regards to the merits of PCAs, about 60 per cent of respondents say that PCAs create smoother relationships with governments. About 70 per cent say that the contents of PCAs do in fact reflect their thinking (Chiba Prefecture 1994).

The prefectural government explains that most pollutants are emitted from a relatively small number of large facilities in Chiba, which is not true in neighboring prefectures, such as Tokyo and Kanagawa, and that is the reason why PCAs are effective policy tools for the prefecture and are actively used (telephone inquiry of Chiba Prefecture by the author 16 October 2000).

THE RESPONSE OF THE JAPANESE NATIONAL GOVERNMENT TO PCAs AND THE LEGAL STATUS OF PCAs

Japan is a very centralized country and the national government influences local governments through its power and control of finances. It is very difficult for local governments to act without the permission of the national government and local governments are usually averse to challenging the national government.

As noted above, MITI was initially reluctant to administer PCAs, but at the same time it was forced to recognize the need for them because of the Mishima-Numazu shock. MITI admitted the need for PCAs in 1964. After this point, MITI actively encouraged the conclusion of PCAs between local governments and businesses. Since the 1960s some local branches of MITI have participated as witnesses in PCAs between local governments and electric power companies (Matsuno 2000, pp. 77 and 81).

The Ministry of Health and Welfare (MHW) was responsible for the regulation of pollution until the creation of the Central Anti-Pollution Measure Headquarters in 1970 and the Environment Agency (EA) in 1971. The national newspaper, *Asahi Shimbun*, reported in 1968 that MHW evaluated the PCA between the Tokyo prefectural government and TEPCO as very desirable (*Asahi Shimbun*, 11 September 1968, p. 5). In 1969 MHW along with MITI referred to a PCA in Yokkaichi, a city notorious for its serious air pollution as a model case for the nation (*Asahi Shimbun*, 15 May 1969, p. 5). The White Paper on Pollution, which was published by the Central Headquarters in 1971, said that PCAs had spread as an effective preventive instrument of pollution (Prime Minister's Office 1971, p. 381).

White Papers on the Environment have been published by the EA since its foundation in 1971. They have assessed the number of PCAs every year and analyzed the reasons for their increase in number (Environment Agency 1971-2000; Ministry of the Environment 2001-2003). The EA has also worked to spread news about PCAs. In 1990, for example, the EA sent local governments, as reference material, data of PCAs concluded among local governments, residents and businesses which managed golf courses (*Asahi Shimbun*, 12 July 1990, p. 30). Also in 1990, the EA edited *The PCA Collection of Different Industries* (Environment Agency 1990).

In June 1970, the Ministry of Home Affairs (MHA), which took charge of local governance, made public their *Outline of Pollution Control Measures* (Ministry of Home Affairs 1970). The outline stated that MHA would guide local governments in concluding PCAs with businesses before new facilities were to be built as a preventative pollution control measure and that MHA would draw up a model PCA (although this appears never to have happened). They explained the outline in a series of articles in a journal for local government officials: the national government should encourage better diffusion of PCAs, PCAs should be contracts made under public law that give birth to rights and duties, and in order to oblige businesses to conclude PCAs for such instances as when they are establishing new locations, local ordinances should be established (Katayama 1970a, p. 14; 1970b, p. 8). MHA edited the *Collection of Pollution Control Ordinances and Agreements* in 1971. The EA later became a co-editor and is still working on the collection of data (Ministry of Home Affairs and Environment Agency 1971).

Although today MITI, EA and MHA say that PCAs are made voluntarily between local governments and businesses and that they are neither involved in, nor do they specifically encourage the creation of PCAs, the facts described above clearly indicate otherwise. Only the EA, which is legally recognized as being in charge of these matters, describes PCAs as *positive* instruments and admits that that is why they provide local governments with information on PCAs. Encouragement from the national government should be considered a catalyst for the quick diffusion of PCAs among both relatively large reformist local governments and local governments more generally (Matsuno 2000, pp. 82-4).

In sum, when the national government changed its attitude toward pollution problems and started establishing a system of environmental laws at the beginning of the 1970s, the experiences of local governments in this field was far advanced than that of the national government. Essentially, the national government adopted a system utilizing, though implicitly, what local governments had already pioneered; in other words, leaving it untouched.

In the early 1970s, there was no uniformity in how ministries of the national government interpreted the legal status of PCAs. A MITI bureaucrat said that PCAs were a form of administrative guidance while an official from MHA said that PCAs should be seen as a contract under public law (Mitsuo et al. 1970, p. 13; Katayama 1970a, p. 14; 1970b, p. 8). Today national government officials are united in answering that they are not supposed to know and interpret the strict legal status of PCAs, but that it also is not necessary for PCAs to have such status for them to be effective (Matsuno 2000, pp. 78-80). Legal scholars have debated the question of whether or not a PCA is simply a 'gentlemen's agreement' which does not establish concrete rights and duties, or a contract which does offer concrete privileges and responsibilities. Today the majority of judicial precedents and legal scholars seem to have reached an agreement that PCAs represent legal contracts (Ministry of Home Affairs and Environment Agency 1971, Volume 8, pp. 105-6; Kitamura 2003, pp. 62-3; Harada 1994, pp. 168-78; Abe 1995, p. 58). However, because a contract is valid only when it is concluded voluntarily by both parties, and because businesses seem to have been often forced to conclude PCAs, some scholars question the validity of PCAs as legal contracts (Sugiyama and Imura 1999, p. 131). According to our survey, only 3 per cent of local governments which had proposed a PCA to a business said that they had ever received a refusal. Moreover, only 23 per cent of local governments which already had valid PCAs with businesses said they had ever made concessions in the negotiations to conclude PCAs with businesses (Matsuno and Ueta 2002, pp. 72-3 and 89).

Most business owners and executives believe that it is more beneficial to conclude PCAs in order to ensure the smooth operation of their business in the area than to have conflict with local governments and residents. Businesses tend to avoid conflicts with governments in Japan for reasons analyzed later in this chapter. In countries like the USA, businesses file law suits. In Japan where court processes are slow, in contrast, generally there is an aversion to filing law suits.

Some Japanese businesses proudly advertise their practice of enforcing stringent PCAs in their environmental reports as a proof of their environmentally friendly business practices. It is worth noting that the statistics above also show that some PCAs are voluntary contracts and not the products of unilateral coercion. According to a survey done by the Chiba prefectural government in 1993, 68 per cent of businesses which had concluded PCAs with the government said their concerns were taken into consideration when renewing PCAs (Chiba Prefecture 1994, p. 105). In 1980, the Osaka prefectural government and Kansai Electric Power Company (KEPCO) renewed their PCA, first concluded in 1974, covering six power plants in the prefecture. KEPCO demanded that the limit on the amount of fuel that could be used and the utilization rates of generating plants be lifted. The Osaka prefectual government accepted KEPCO's demand on condition that it would install flue-gas denitrification equipment at the plants, and the deal between them was realized (Osaka Prefecture 1980, pp. 211-12). This suggests that while businesses cannot easily refuse the conclusion of a PCA, some of them have been able to effectively influence the content of PCAs.

EFFECTIVENESS OF PCAs

PCAs can be divided into two groups: those which impose additional regulations upon businesses and those which do not. By *additional regulation* we mean more stringent regulation for businesses in some sense. For example, it may stipulate more stringent emission standards than laws or ordinances do, or it may impose regulations upon facilities which are exempted from regulations by laws or ordinances because of their small scale. Such clauses may also target pollutants which are not regulated by laws or ordinances because of their (seemingly) relatively low risk to human health and the environment or because of a lack of scientific research on their possible effects. According to our survey, 91 per cent of local governments said that businesses either 'perfectly' or 'very well' observed PCAs while only 4 per cent said businesses did not 'very well' or 'at all' observe them. Five per cent of local governments said they did not know. It can be concluded that PCAs are usually observed by businesses. We can also draw the conclusion that imposing additional regulations upon businesses should improve the state of the local environment (Matsuno and Ueta 2002, pp. 58-9).

Emission standards for sulfur oxides stipulated by the PCAs of 11 thermal power plants of TEPCO in 5 prefectures are 14-100 per cent stricter than those stipulated by laws and ordinances. Some PCAs literally stipulate zero emission, which is only possible when liquefied natural gas is used as a fuel (Ajia Shakai Mondai Kenkyusho 1991, p. 162).

As an example, the PCA between KEPCO and Osaka Prefecture specified limitations for hourly particulate matter emissions, annual sulfur oxides emissions, annual nitrogen oxides emissions, daily sulfur oxides emissions, sulfur content of fuel, the amounts of fuel used, the utilization rates of generating plants and wastewater. The stringency of limitations placed on the emissions of sulfur oxides, which were the most important air pollutant addressed by the PCA, were more stringent than those specified by law even though Osaka already had among the most stringent emissions limitations by law in the country. The Compensation Law for Pollution-related Health Damages imposed a levy on industry based upon their sulfur oxide emissions beginning in 1974, and this also contributed to the reduction of sulfur oxide emissions in industrial areas throughout the country in the 1980s when the rate of the levy soared. However, for the large power plants in Osaka Prefecture, the emissions limitations specified by the PCA were even more stringent than the levy. For relatively smaller power plants, emissions limitations have been specified more loosely than those for larger power plants, and for these power plants in the 1980s the levy seems to have been more stringent than the PCAs. The concentration of sulfur oxides was reduced sufficiently in the 1970s to attain the national ambient standards almost everywhere in the country including Osaka. Thus, the additional reduction achieved by the levy was both unintended and excessive (Matsuno and Ueta 2000).

Most, if not all, thermal power plants have concluded PCAs with local governments. As a result, pollutant emissions by the electric power industry, which had been the most polluting industry in terms of sulfur and nitrogen oxides emissions (having occupied about 30-40 per cent of total emissions in Japan for at least the last three decades), have been reduced substantially. As for the iron steel industry, whose emissions of traditional pollutants were second to those of the electric power industry, 18 out of 21 integrated steelworks had concluded PCAs with relevant local governments by 1984. The remaining three were rather small operations or shrunk their production. Most traditional pollutants were emitted by these huge steelworks. It was not until the arrival of PCAs that traditional pollutant emissions were drastically reduced in this industry (Matsuno 1997; Environment Agency Research Group 1988, pp. 216-17).

Other problems, including noise and water pollution, also have been addressed by PCAs. Many major industries, including chemical, ceramic-stone-clay and paper-pulp, have formulated PCAs. Of various policy instruments used, it was mainly the limitations specified in PCAs that brought about the reduction of traditional pollutant emissions from large industrial facilities, which emitted the largest amount of traditional pollutants. Other policy instruments, such as the pollution control regulations, stipulated by national laws and local ordinances, established national and local minimums in cases where effective PCAs were absent.

Although PCAs concluded with small and medium businesses are large in number, because these businesses' contribution to traditional pollution problems has been relatively small, studies of PCAs concluded with small and medium businesses are still incomplete and insufficient to draw up an adequate picture of their contribution. According to our survey, 14 per cent of PCAs were concluded with businesses with less than 10 employees and of these, 25 per cent imposed additional regulations. Fifty-five per cent of PCAs involved firms with 10-99 employees, and 42 per cent of these imposed additional regulations. While only 28 per cent of PCAs are with firms with 100-999 employees, 55 per cent of these PCAs included regulations above those required by law. Finally, only 4 per cent of PCAs are with firms with more than 999 employees, but 70 per cent of these imposed additional regulations. The smaller the business is, the less frequently additional pollution control measures are demanded by a PCA concluded with the local government. These findings suggest the need to consider the function of PCAs when they do not impose additional requirements upon businesses. This point will be discussed in the next section.

COMPARISON BETWEEN PCAs AND OTHER INSTRUMENTS[5]

In addition to PCAs, local governments often use two other policy instruments to control businesses: regulation by ordinance and administrative guidance with guidelines (*yoko*). Ordinances must be passed by the local assembly; they are the official instrument of local governments to implement policies. Japanese local governments are frequently criticized for enjoying too much discretionary power because of their use of administrative guidance. While administrative guidance is often based on guidelines that are set by the local administration, this is often done without the approval of the local assembly. They are not legally binding.

It is useful to compare the features of PCAs with those of other instruments in order to understand why they are employed. In our survey we asked local governments to evaluate the relative advantage of each instrument with regard to 18 features that could be considered advantageous by local governments. These included such features as whether the instrument had binding force, was based on democratic procedures, did not lead to inequity among those targeted by the regulation, and so forth (see Table 9.1). We asked the local governments to evaluate the fit between the features and the policy instrument using a four-point scale. Then we analyzed their evaluation statistically and arrived at ranking of instruments (Matsuno 2001, pp. 11-16; Matsuno 2002, pp. 50-5). PCAs are given the highest ranking (1) alone for features 7 (makes it easy to gain residents' understanding for new construction or for the expansion of a business), 8 (can be used to collect information about pollution control technology), 13 (does not require consultation with the national government), 15 (makes it easy to adapt regulation to the financial condition of each business), 17 (makes it easy to adapt regulation to the economic situation of the area) and 18 (makes it easy to adapt regulation to the topographical, geographical and meteorological conditions of the area).

It should be noted that only larger local governments, that is, governments of prefectures, designated cities and core cities, were asked to make these rankings found in Table 9.1 across policy instruments due to our limited research budget. Other local governments were asked to evaluate features only in relation to PCAs. Features 8, 13 and 15 are evaluated highly by larger local governments but not by smaller governments. On the other hand, though PCAs are given the worst ranking (2 or 3) alone for feature 3 (does not produce inequity among regulated businesses), and feature 5 (no negotiation with business is necessary), smaller governments evaluate PCAs as not being so inequitable. The most widely accepted advantageous features of PCAs over other instruments are features 7, 17 and 18. The most widely perceived disadvantageous feature of PCAs is feature 5, that is, the need to negotiate with businesses. In the 1960s, the PCA's most useful feature was regarded as feature 16 (makes it possible to introduce needed regulation when national laws are deficient). This is because local governments could regulate polluters with PCAs even when they had no legal powers to officially do so. Because local governments gained some regulatory power in the environmental field in the 1970s, feature 16 now is ranked as an equally applicable feature for PCAs and guidelines. Feature 18 suggests that the given instrument makes it easy to adapt regulation to the topographical, geographical and meteorological conditions of the area.

Environmental economists and those advised by them frequently recommend the use of market-based instruments such as emission taxes and emission permit trading rather than command-and-control (CAC) instruments such as emission standards and technology designation for reasons that they are deemed to be more cost-effective (Intergovernmental Panel on Climate Change 2001, p. 401; Organization for Economic Cooperation and Development 2002, p. 22). There is no such thing as pure efficiency in maximizing social net benefit because of the difficulty of measuring the value of the environment, human health and life in monetary terms. Cost-effectiveness here means minimization of the abatement costs of detrimental activities. Market-based instruments do this by making the marginal abatement costs of polluters uniform. The rationale is that if they are not uniform, we can always decrease total abatement costs, making polluters with low marginal costs abate more and those with high marginal costs abate less. This argument can be applied to 'well-mixed' pollution

Environmental Policy in Japan

Table 9. 1   Comparison of Ordinances, Guidelines and PCAs

		Ordinance	Guideline	PCA
1.	Has binding force	1	3	2
2.	Is based on democratic procedures	1	3	2
3.	Results in no inequity among regulated businesses	1	2	3
4.	Establishment process is transparent	1	2	2
5.	No negotiation with business necessary	1	1	2
6.	Promotes environmental consciousness in regulated businesses	1	2	1
7.	Makes it easy to gain residents' understanding for new construction or expansion of business facilities	2	2	1
8.	Can be used to collect information about pollution control technology	2	2	1
9.	Allows for experimentation with new regulations	2	1	2
10.	Inspires innovation of pollution control/ environmental preservation technologies	1	1	1
11.	Does not take a long time from proposal to implementation	3	1	2
12.	Does not have to be approved by the local assembly	2	1	1
13.	Does not require consultation with national government prior to introduction	3	2	1
14.	Easily results in cooperation of regulated businesses	1	2	1
15.	Makes it easy to adapt regulation to financial conditions of each business	3	2	1
16.	Makes it possible to introduce regulation when national laws are deficient	1	2	1
17.	Makes it easy to adapt regulation to economic situation of the area	2	2	1
18.	Makes it easy to adapt regulation to the topographical, geographical and meteorological conditions of the area	2	2	1

Notes: Low numbers represent evaluations of better fit than high numbers. Instruments can tie in their ranking when the difference of evaluations for instruments is not statistically significant.

problems such as global warming and ozone layer depletion, where a given amount of pollutant emissions contributes an equal amount of damage no matter where the polluter is located. For traditional regional pollution problems, the location of the source of pollutants matters.

For example, if a large source of air pollutants is located close to a densely populated residential area, the amount of damage it does is larger than when the source is located far away. This kind of regional pollution problem is very common throughout the world, but is especially problematic in densely populated countries such as Japan, where residential areas and industrial areas are often close to each other or are mixed. In these cases, the usual policy goal is to lower the concentration of pollutants beneath some standard. This can only be achieved cost-effectively by assigning the amount of abatement necessary source by source, taking into account the locations of sources and natural conditions that might affect the flow of pollutants. This flexibility is not possible either with market-based instruments nor CAC instruments unless the policy tool is unusually complicated.

In these instances PCAs are necessary. With PCAs local governments can assign source by source the amount of pollutant abatement needed while not imposing excessive burdens upon businesses although this can result in inequities among businesses.

The score of 1 for feature 18 in relation to PCAs suggests that local governments, consciously or unconsciously, apply cost-efficient thinking in their decisions regarding the most appropriate policy instrument. Since local governments do not appear to pursue optimal resource allocation in the way economists do, it might be more appropriate to suggest that cost-effectiveness is instrumentally pursued to attain stability in the local economy.

A similar argument applies to feature 15 (makes it easy to adapt regulation to the financial condition of each business) and 17 (makes it easy to adapt regulation to the economic situation of the area). Adapting regulations to the financial condition of each business or economic condition of the area is not possible or difficult with usual market-based or CAC instruments, but is possible and easier with PCA-like instruments which assign the amount of emission abatement source by source. This feature is linked to the stability of the local economy. Local governments do not want to see businesses shut down or moving from the area.

Next we will examine feature 7 (makes it easy to gain residents' understanding for new construction or for expansion of business facilities). PCAs are ranked as 1 on this feature probably because they are concluded with specific businesses and designed to control their specific operations. Businesses mainly seek residential understanding of their operations. Japanese businesses seem to have learned that need for residential acceptance of their operations. Residential opposition can make it difficult or risky to start or continue an operation as was the case with Mishima-Numazu. In some cases as in Minamata where businesses already operated, angry residents participated in physical destruction of business facilities. Businesses and citizens also learned through major suits around 1970 that suits could be effectively used against businesses. Law suits, of course, disturb business activities and can cost businesses more than what they gain from their polluting activities. Since the mid-1960s, businesses in regulated industries were essentially obligated to show the national government they had local approval in order to gain permission to operate. PCAs were regarded as the most suitable signal of this approval.

Gaining residential understanding is also important for local governments. If local governments are not responsive to residential opposition to the siting or operation of a business, governors, mayors and members of local assemblies can lose votes in the next election, even if the siting or operation of a business is technically legal. If local governments give procedural permission to a business opposed by residents, local governments can be blamed and may even be targeted for law suits by residents contending that government procedures were wrong and illegal. As a local government has to care about not only the environment but also the stability and prosperity of the local economy, residential understanding is important. To look at the matter in institutional terms, the following components are critical: a local democratic system that residents directly elect, a judicial system which allows for citizen appeal, and the freedom for residents to run anti-business and anti-government campaigns. In Japan, citizens had only restricted rights or at times no such rights at all before the World War II.

To help facilitate residential acceptance, or to alleviate residential anxiety, businesses may find it reasonable to agree to additional regulations that have a positive impact on the well-being of the environment and residents' lives by improving the environment beyond the level national law or local ordinances demand. In addition, it is also emotionally persuasive because it appeals to a resident's sentiment by making businesses pay more than 'officially' needed. A business has to show that it is not a cold-blooded entity seeking profits over human health. This kind of association of evil images with businesses has been persistent among the Japanese people since the 1960s. Since large businesses need to care about their reputation, they typically set aside funds which can be used to take additional pollution prevention measures.

In the case of smaller businesses, the trends are different. When the scale of a business is small, it is less likely to have a negative image. Indeed, small businesses are generally regarded as enterprises that deserve help. Smaller businesses, moreover, often lack funds to take additional measures or even to take the measures required by existing laws or ordinances. This seems to be why additional regulation has been less frequently imposed upon smaller businesses by PCAs.

PCAs often include clauses calling for general pollution-control efforts, on-site inspection, sanctions, resident participation, liability and enhancing a facility's surroundings. Sanctions, resident participation and (probably) liability clauses are more frequently included in PCAs of smaller local governments than in those of larger ones. This suggests that local governments are trying to gain citizen understanding and approval by including such clauses in PCAs.

Local governments will not always require a small business to enforce additional measures on top of basic laws and ordinances because they are somewhat sympathetic to the financial position of many small businesses. Small businesses may not have the funds to cover all the costs for such enforcement. Even though the government may be lenient in this sense, they are usually more rigid in insisting that these businesses abide by previously established laws and ordinances. Local governments often develop a strategy involving the local residential community to participate in a PCA in which all parties are more or less satisfied with the outcome. It is important to involve the local community because they need to feel comfortable with the location and general operation of a business.

When the population of a community is less than about 10000, people often know each other. They may even know the mayor, members of the local assembly and possibly people from the relevant business. In these cases, negotiations can be more informal. It is probable that negotiating with a local government and signing a PCA will improve businesses' environmental consciousness even without additional regulation. The fact that residents participate in the negotiation or the administration of a PCA indicates that communication will be strengthened among businesses, governments and residents. Because requiring additional measures needs convincing scientific rationale, the inability to form that rationale may be one of the reasons why PCAs of smaller local governments less frequently impose additional regulations upon businesses.

The feature for which PCA is ranked worst is feature 5: local governments do not have to negotiate with businesses. It is natural for PCAs to be ranked as the worst in this feature. The costs of negotiating with businesses, or transaction costs, increase as the number of businesses increase. PCAs can best be used when it is necessary only to regulate a relatively small number of businesses. Indeed the Yokohama city government, the pioneer of PCA, established guidelines for traditional pollutant regulations (such as sulfur oxides) based on experiences accumulated using PCAs on larger sources to regulate smaller sources, but later ceased to conclude new PCAs all together (Yokohama city 1976, pp. 13-20; Yokohama city 1997, pp. 175-6). According to our survey, among local governments with PCAs, 62 per cent have fewer than 11 PCAs, 78 per cent less than 21 and 92 per cent less than 51 PCAs. Twenty per cent of local governments had only one PCA. So the argument is consistent with the survey results. At the same time, some local governments have easily concluded PCAs with numerous businesses. For example, 2.6 per cent of local governments have more than 100 PCAs. Local governments with a relatively large number of PCAs tend to keep transaction costs low by formatting the contents of the PCA and/or by carefully negotiating over only a small number of large pollutant sources and negotiating more briefly with a large number of smaller emitters (Matsuno and Ueta 2002, pp. 44-5; Matsuno 2001, pp. 5-6). In the latter case, they tend not to impose additional regulations.

PCAs are different from ordinances and guidelines in that the content of PCAs are sometimes not disclosed to the general public. Ordinances and guidelines are always disclosed. According to our survey, about half of all PCAs are disclosed to the general public. When the content of a PCA is made public and it is considered *not* stringent enough, relevant local government and businesses will be criticized by residents. In instances where PCA contents are disclosed, a local government may also be challenged by businesses faced with stringent PCAs regarding inequities the PCA causes among businesses. When the content of a PCA is made public and it is stringent, the business may be forced to conclude similarly stringent PCAs with other local governments. This was the case concerning the PCA established between Tokyo and TEPCO. It also risks being blamed by other businesses for accepting the stringent PCA since they too may be required subsequently to accept similar restrictions. Today's trend of increasing disclosure of governmental information in Japan may make PCAs more stringent (Matsuno and Ueta 2002, pp. 75-7). Disclosure of PCAs will also improve risk communication as residents are supplied with information on business operation and can express their opinions on the PCAs even when they are not allowed to participate in the direct negotiation of PCAs.

CONCLUSION

The use of PCAs rather than other policy instruments appears to be related to the compatibility of the instrument to the pollution prevention goal, the local economy's stability and the local society's stability. A PCA-like instrument which makes discretionary source-by-source regulations may be what governments all over the world will want to use. They may want to use this kind of policy instrument not only for regional pollution problems, whose quality and quantity of damage is affected by the spatial arrangements between polluters and victims, but also for more mixed pollution problems such as global warming. For example, if the national government assigns a specific amount of greenhouse gas reduction to local governments, those local governments may want to use a PCA-like instrument for the local economy's stability. However, our study suggests that the necessary conditions for this kind of instrument to be effective can be too demanding for some countries. These conditions include:

- Politicians being willing to take the initiative to start the very first PCA.
- Discretionary power of a local government or existence of local governance.
- The national government's positive attitude to a PCA when local governments are weaker in relation to the national government.
- Capability, knowledge and funds must be available to local governments to negotiate with businesses about the science of the environment and pollution control technology and to oversee their actions.
- An ethical bureaucracy.
- Residential support for a PCA which makes it beneficial for businesses to observe its contents.
- A corporate culture open to government cooperative intervention.
- A national atmosphere that accepts ambiguous legal legitimacy.

It is difficult to compare Japanese PCAs with environmental agreements between governments and businesses in European countries, as both are diverse. The apparent difference is the large number of PCAs in Japan compared with the few that are in existence in Europe. This difference relates to such conditions as corporate culture, national atmosphere and an environmental regulatory structure where the national government leaves to local governments the responsibility for protecting and cleaning up the environment. Local governments are also more adept at coordinating the relationships between businesses and residents than is government at the national level. This paper has focused on PCAs, but it is important to remember that local governments in Japan use PCAs along with other policy instruments such as regulations by ordinance and administrative guidance with guidelines. Ordinances are superior to other policy tools under the rule of law because they have binding force. It is, however, costly for local administrations to introduce them. Guidelines are quicker to introduce than others policy instruments though they are inferior to other methods in terms of legitimacy and binding force. Japanese local governments integrate all of these methods on a case-by-case and complementary basis.

ADDENDUM: EXAMPLES OF POLLUTION CONTROL AGREEMENTS

I. Yokohama case: the first PCA[6]

Agreement between Yokohama city government and the Electric Power Development Company (letters exchanged between the government and the company).

(A) Letter from the government to the company to require it to take pollution prevention measures.

FY39ei No.1070
1 December Showa 39 (1964)

Yoshida Kakuta
President
Electric Power Development Company

Asukada Kazuo
Mayor of Yokohama city

On Pollution Prevention at the Isogo Thermal Power Plant

In regard to your company's use of part of Tokyo Electric Power Company's reclaimed land in Negishi Bay, which was requested of us by your company, we are obliged to cooperate with you, considering that this matter forms a part of the national government's coal policy.

We have been deliberately examining (possible) pollution problems (associated with the project), especially because the land is located adjacent to residential areas.

As a result, we submitted a request to the national government for (a list of) necessary points concerning this matter, to which we received their (positive) reply. Therefore, we are now requesting your company to observe the points which are listed on the attached sheet. We will notify TEPCO of our consent upon receipt of your company's agreement to our request.

We would also like to remind you that the proposed power station shall be required to strive for the mutual prosperity of the citizens of Yokohama as long as it is situated within our municipal boundaries and, therefore, we expect your company's public announcement of its intention to actively cooperate with the pollution control measures adopted by the Yokohama city government.

Requests Concerning Pollution Prevention at the Electric Power
Development Company's Isogo Thermal Power Plant

1. As the meteorological observation data obtained by the Yokohama city
government and the wind tunnel test results established by your company are
extremely important, the design of the new power plant will fully take into
account all implications of those data and results.

2. As the meteorological conditions are an influential factor in air pollution,
the Electric Power Development Company (hereafter, EPDC) will install its
own anemoscope, anemometer and the like to obtain meteorological data
with a view to its use to control air pollution. The EDPC will fully cooperate
with air pollution surveys conducted by Yokohama city government.

3. Yokohama city government understands that EPDC plans to achieve a
total dust collection efficiency of not less than 98 per cent, with the
combined use of a multi-cyclone dust collector and Cottrell precipitator. This
level of efficiency will be observed and all necessary arrangements will be
made to effectively deal with accidents.

4. Yokohama city government understands that the planned chimney stack
height is 120 meters and that the discharge velocity and temperature of flue
gas are thirty meter per second and 130 degrees Celsius, respectively at the
rated load. These conditions will be strictly observed and proper
arrangements will be made to prevent down draft and any other undesirable
flue gas effects.

5. Yokohama city government understands that the fuel coal for the planned
new power plant will be pulverized Hokkaido coal with low ash and sulfur
content. EPDC is required to continuously use high quality coal, that is coal
with low ash and sulfur contents. The heavy oil which will be used as
auxiliary fuel will also have a low sulfur content.

6. The Yokohama city government understands that, given facilities
equipped as described above and making use of the fuel listed above, the
dust density measured at the outlets of chimney stacks of Isogo coal thermal
power plant will be 0.6 grams per normal cubic meter. A density equal to or
less than this level will be continuously maintained. Similarly, as the
emissions concentration of sulfur dioxide is estimated to be 500 parts per
million, the concentration will not exceed this level at any time.

7. All units and equipment will be installed indoors to minimize noise
pollution in the neighboring area. Should the outdoor installation of some

equipment be found to be necessary, a silencer shall be provided for each piece of equipment to minimize noise. The necessary measures aimed at maintaining the noise level of the Isogo coal thermal power plant at the current forty phons or under in neighboring residential areas will be introduced.

8. Proper waste water treatment systems will be introduced to treat the waste water from the steam condenser, cooling water, blow water from the boilers and miscellaneous other waste water discharged from the premises. An oil separator will be introduced to remove the oil and grease used for machinery and equipment from the waste water in order to prevent the contamination of sea water. All necessary precautions will be taken to prevent pollution of the sea by coal transport vessels.

9. Scattering of the ash collected by the dust collectors and hopper and the like will not be allowed, and proper care will be taken in its transportation for disposal.

10. All necessary arrangements will be made and care taken to prevent spontaneous ignition and dust dispersion at the coal yard. Prior consultation with the Yokohama Fire Service will be required to introduce all necessary measures for preventing fires and other disasters and all subsequent instructions by the Service will be strictly observed.

11. Regular measurements and analysis of the fuel constituents, soot and smoke concentrations, dust collection efficiency, noise level, waste water and the like will be conducted. The measurement and analysis records will be submitted to the Yokohama city government whenever such data is requested by the government. EPDC will permit city officials responsible for pollution control entry to the Isogo coal thermal power plant to conduct any necessary inspections or surveys when deemed appropriate by the Yokohama city government as long as 'such inspections and surveys do not disrupt the normal operation of the power plant.

12. Should any occurrence of pollution by the Isogo coal thermal power plant be predicted, EPDC will swiftly take necessary measures under the instructions of the Yokohama city government as established through consultations between both sides.

13. Should any of the above conditions not be observed by EPDC or should actual damage occur due to the operation of the Isogo thermal power plant, the Yokohama city government may apply the necessary pollution control

measures through consultations with EPDC. All expenses incurred in applying such measures will be borne by EPDC.

14. Should EPDC wish to contest any of the pollution control measures applied by the Yokohama city government pursuant to Clause 13 above, a third party committee will be requested to rule on the issue.

The title, composition, operation and scope of activities of this committee will be separately determined through consultations between both sides. Should the committee find the measures applied by the Yokohama city government to be inappropriate, all expenses relating to said measures will be borne by the government.

(B) Letter from the company to the government accepting its request:

Thermoelectric No. 317
1 December Showa 39 (1964)

Asukada Kazuo
Mayor of Yokohama city

Yoshida Kakuta
President
Electric Power Development Company

On Pollution Prevention Measures at
our Company's Isogo Thermal Power Plant

We would like to express our utmost gratitude for your kind understanding of our project to construct the Isogo coal thermal power plant.

In regard to the pollution prevention measures requested in your letter (FY39ei No. 1070), we are pleased to announce our readiness to introduce pollution prevention measures in line with your request.

We are fully aware of the special aspects of the site in that it is adjacent to residential areas. We are fully prepared to make every effort to establish positive understanding and trust between ourselves and the local residents during the construction, as well as operation, of this power plant and we would like to humbly request the full cooperation of the Yokohama city government.

We hope to commence preparatory work, including the construction of temporary structures, as soon as possible in order to complete the construction of the new power station on schedule. Please allow me to thank you in advance in your kind consideration of and assistance in the matter concerned.

II. The Tokyo Case Described Below Helped to Make PCAs Well-Known.[7]

Agreement between Tokyo prefectural government and Tokyo Electric Power Company

Memorandum on Pollution Prevention at Thermal Power Plants

The governor of Tokyo Prefecture, Minobe Ryokichi, and the president of Tokyo Electric Power Company (TEPCO), Kikawada Kazutaka, have agreed upon the pollution prevention of TEPCO's thermal power plants located in Tokyo Prefecture as found in the memorandum below. There are two copies of the memorandum and both parties are to be given possession of one of these copies.

1. Plan for reducing SO_2 emissions: In the Oi thermal power plant, which TEPCO plans to build, TEPCO will procure and use ultra low sulfur crude oil. In existing thermal power plants, TEPCO will use good quality oil and reduce SO_2 emissions every year and the total SO_2 emissions from both new and existing plants will be half of FY 1967 levels in FY 1973. Further, TEPCO will make efforts to reduce SO_2 emissions from FY 1967 on.

2. Improvement of fuel: In its thermal power plants in Tokyo Prefecture, TEPCO will use good quality Minas heavy oil and desulfurized heavy oil. As a result, the sulfur content will be, in existing thermal power plants 0.25% for coal and 1.0% for heavy oil, and in Oi thermal power plant 0.1% for Minas crude oil.

3. Use of ultra low sulfur crude oil in Oi thermal power plant: TEPCO promises to use ultra low sulfur crude oil at all times in the future in the Oi thermal power plant.

4. Procurement of ultra low sulfur crude oil: In regard to the ultra low sulfur crude oil to be used in Oi thermal power plant, TEPCO will conclude long term contracts with oil companies to procure the oil directly immediately upon the making of a decision on the construction of the power plant.

5. Pollution prevention measures for soot and smoke and waste water: In order to prevent pollution, in addition to the use of ultra low sulfur crude oil TEPCO will take the following measures:

    a. Measures for addressing soot and smoke:

        1. Although Aviation Law limits the height of the Oi thermal power plants' smokestacks to under one hundred meters, the outlets of the smokestacks will be united in order that their emissions will go higher.

        2. In order for emissions to be diffused and diluted, the temperature and the velocity of emissions will be 130 degrees Celsius and 30 meters per second, respectively.

        3. TEPCO will equip the power plant with a high-performance electric dust chamber and filter fine dust to make the emissions cleaner.

    b. Measures for addressing waste water:

        1. All acid and alkali water discharged from the pure-water producing machine, and all water used to wash machinery and oils used for machinery will be passed through neutralization settling tanks and oil filtering tanks to make waste water clean.

        2. General waste water on the premises will also be passed through oil separating tanks.

6. Measures to prevent fire and explosion:

    a. Measures concerning crude oil facilities: In regard to safety measures to prevent fire, explosion and the like in crude oil facilities, pipes will be welded together to prevent oil leaks and all possible preventative measures will be taken, including adoption of explosion-proof systems and leak detectors.

    More specifically, 'danger areas' on the premises will be determined according to the recommendation of the American Petroleum Institute, which is currently the most authoritative voice on this issue, and the facilities inside these areas will be equipped according to the technical guideline of the Industrial Safety Institute of the Ministry of Labor – 'Explosion-proof Guideline for Factory Electric Equipment'.

    b. Measures concerning fuel oil storage equipment: Oil storage tanks and oil supplying equipment will be designed to be sufficiently secure following the provisions of the 'Cabinet Order on Regulation of Dangerous Materials' and will be designed to be sufficient to withstand an earthquake even more serious than the Great Kanto Earthquake. Distances between tanks will be farther than what is prescribed by law,[8] and an oil embankment will be built around each tank.

In regard to fire fighting facilities, tanks will be equipped with water sprinklers and a sufficient quantity of high foam bubble-type fire extinguishing agent will be ready to use at all times. To provide against emergencies, the plant will be equipped with remotely controllable fire fighting facilities run by diesel engines.

During operations, tours of inspection will be conducted strictly and maintenance will be perfect.

c. Measures concerning the transport of crude oil: In regard to transporting crude oil, TEPCO will be guided by the Vessel Bureau of the Ministry of Transportation and by the Coast Guard, and will take all possible measures to assure safe transport to the plant.

TEPCO will use tankers with high-performance controllability and double shelled bodies. They will also be equipped with steam/carbon dioxide fire extinguishing equipment and the like, in addition to the usual fire extinguishing equipment.

Regarding tankers entry and departure from the port, times when sea traffic is heavy will be avoided. All measures will be taken to assure tankers can safely cross sea routes to get to shore and to enter safely into sea routes when leaving the port. Fire fighting nets will be put under the pilot's supervision.

7. Analyses of fuel contents and related matters: Analyses of fuel contents will be conducted periodically and necessary points required by Tokyo Prefecture will be always reported. In regard to waste water inspection, there are still no legal standards so inspections will be done according to the outcome of discussions involving both parties.

8. Management of change and other related matters in the construction plan of Oi thermal power plant: Consent of Tokyo Prefecture will be needed before changes can be made to the basic plan for the Oi thermal power plant. In order that construction may begin, all necessary matters will be fully discussed between both sides and TEPCO will be sure to adhere to instructions given by Tokyo Prefecture.

9. Measures in case of pollution, disaster and the like: In the case that there is pollution or a disaster occurs, or in case there is the possibility of either, both sides will discuss the situation and necessary measures will be taken. The costs of these measures will be borne by TEPCO.

10. Establishment of the 'Tokyo Prefectural Committee for Pollution Prevention': TEPCO agrees to the establishment of the 'Tokyo Prefectural Committee for Pollution Prevention' (hereafter, 'Committee') to promote pollution prevention measures in Tokyo.

11. Members of the 'Committee': The 'Committee' will consist of a certain number of members. They will be officials of the Urban Pollution Department of the Capitol Affairs Bureau of Tokyo Prefecture and of the Institute of Pollution Research of Tokyo Prefecture, as well as experts and the like who will be commissioned by Tokyo Prefecture.

12. Investigations to be conducted by the 'Committee': The 'Committee' will investigate the status of pollution prevention measures in thermal power plants run by TEPCO in Tokyo Prefecture. Visits to power plant facilities for this purpose will be made at a time when it does not hinder the business of TEPCO. Those who visit the facilities will be officials from the Urban Pollution Department of the Capitol Affairs Bureau and of the Institute of Pollution Research of Tokyo Prefecture.

13. 'Principle of disclosure': Matters related to this memorandum will be treated according to the 'principle of disclosure' except for commercially confidential matters.

14. Future measures: TEPCO will take the best pollution prevention measures in its thermal power plants in Tokyo Prefecture at all times in the future.

15. Specifications: Necessary specifications to implement this memorandum will be decided based on discussions between both sides.

10 September, Showa 43 (1968)
The Governor of Tokyo Prefecture Minobe Ryokichi.
The President of Tokyo Electric Power Company Kikawada Kazutaka.

III. Chiba[9]

The format of the basic pollution control agreements made between Chiba prefectural government, relevant city governments and relevant companies is renewed every five years. Below is the latest version of this agreement, which was last renewed in 2000. The same agreement applies to each of the 57 businesses which run 65 factories in Chiba Prefecture (as of July 2003). This basic agreement is accompanied by a specifications agreement which is five to six times longer than this basic one.

Agreement on Pollution Prevention

Chiba Prefecture, _ _city (hereafter X) and _ _ Co. Ltd (hereafter Y) agree upon prevention of pollution caused by Y's construction and operation as follows:

1. Idea of pollution prevention: X and Y recognize that environmental disruption due to pollution is a threat to the achievement of a healthy and cultural life for the inhabitants of the prefecture, that overcoming this is an urgent and important task, that businesses have a social responsibility to prevent pollution caused by business activities, and that preventing pollution to assure the local people's health and the soundness of their living environment is an important task of local governments. Based on these understandings, X will guide Y and Y will always make maximum efforts to observe laws and this agreement.

2. Specification agreement:
    a. Y will take pollution prevention measures appropriately and sufficiently to observe the specifications agreement that is concluded between X and Y.
    b. When the specification agreement needs to be renewed and X requests Y to revise the agreement either because ambient environmental standards concerning air pollution, water pollution and the like are not being attained with the pollution prevention measures taken by Y even when observing the specification agreement; pollution control technology advances; or for other reasons, Y will comply with the request.

3. Annual plan:
    a. Every year Y will submit the annual plan of pollution prevention measures (hereafter the annual plan) to be taken in the next fiscal year.
    b. When the annual plan submitted by Y according to the above clause is regarded inappropriate by X, X will instruct Y to change it and Y will comply with the instructions.
    c. If Y is to change the annual plan during said year, Y will submit the new plan beforehand. The previous item is applied to this case correspondingly.
    d. Y will observe quantities of emissions for flue gases, waste water and the like, as well as pollution prevention measures written in the annual plan according to the previous three items.
    e. Prior consultation on expansion and the like of production facilities and the like: If Y is to construct, expand, or change production facilities and pollution prevention facilities (Including those written in the annual

plan. Hereafter, production facilities and the like.), Y must consult with X beforehand and must be given X's consent.

f. Measures in case of occurrence of pollution and the like: When pollution is expected to occur or it occurred, in spite of measures taken according to previous three clauses, and when X recognize that Y is responsible for that, Y will fulfill its own responsibility to take necessary measures without no delay and will report the measures taken to X immediately.

g. Measures in case of emergency:

1. When a state of emergency as defined by Clause 23 of the Air Pollution Prevention Law and Clause 18 of the Water Pollution Prevention Law is expected to occur or has occurred, Y must immediately take necessary measures as instructed by X.

2. When the situation defined by X is brought about by a worsening of air, water, or other pollution that threatens the health of local people and the soundness of their living environment, Y must take necessary measures as stipulated by X.

7. Curtailment of operations: When the air, water, or other pollution situation does not improve as a result of the measures taken according to the previous two clauses and when the situation threatens to seriously damage people's health or the soundness of their living environment, and when X instructs Y to take additional measures beyond those required by the previous two clauses, to take full   prevention measures, or to suspend operations of part or all facilities which emit soot and smoke and the like, Y must comply with what is instructed.

8. Measures in case of accident:

a. When an accident, such as a breakdown or damage to facilities occurs and it is related to pollution, etc., Y must take temporary counter-measures immediately and report the situation to X.

b. In the case of the previous item, if X instructs Y to take necessary counter-measures to prevent an expansion or repetition of the accident, Y must comply with those instructions.

c. X can instruct Y to suspend or take other measures related to the operation of said facilities until the counter-measures determined by the previous item are taken completely by Y.

9. Related businesses:[10]

a. Y will guide and supervise its related businesses (except for those which have concluded a pollution control agreement with either or both

Xs) located on the premises and on the adjacent site according to the purport of this agreement.

b. X regards the production facilities and the like owned by the related businesses described in the previous item as those owned or taken charge of by Y in applying this agreement to those facilities. Y is fully responsible for applying this agreement to the said facilities.

10. Guidance and the like for subcontracting businesses: Y will actively guide and supervise its subcontracting businesses located on the premises on their pollution prevention. If these businesses cause pollution problems, Y will deal with them with sincerity.

11. Compensation for damage:

a. When pollution occurs around Y's factory, and when investigations reveal that Y is responsible for the occurrence, Y must compensate victims for the damage.

b. In making compensation as required by the previous item, X will act as intermediary between Y and the victims.

12. Measures in the case of violations:

a. When Y violates this agreement or the specifications agreement, X can instruct Y to take necessary measures for improvement in a certain period of time or to suspend completely or partially the operation of facilities related to the violation until Y resolves the violation.

b. When Y violates Clause 4 of this agreement, X can instruct Y to cancel the construction of production facilities and the like related to the violation or to suspend completely or partially Y's operations, no matter what the previous item stipulates.

13. Reporting and inspection: X can request Y to make a report when needed and can conduct inspections on Y's premises to the extent that the inspection is necessary for the enforcement of this agreement.

14. Disposal of waste: Y must make efforts to reduce the amount of waste generated by its business activities and must dispose of the waste appropriately, according to its responsibility for preventing contamination of the environment.

15. Improvement of immediate surroundings and the like: Y will improve its immediate surroundings willingly by planting trees on the premises and surroundings and the like. Y will also actively cooperate with X to create and preserve green tracts of land and the like.

16. Improvement of pollution prevention facilities and the like:

a. Y must actively make efforts to develop pollution control technology and improve pollution prevention facilities and the like in order to reduce emissions of air and other pollutants beyond the level prescribed in the specification agreement.

b. X will actively cooperate with Y in regard to the previous item.

17. Miscellaneous: When matters not dealt with in this agreement must be dealt with, or when questions arise in regard to matters dealt with in this agreement, X and Y will settle the matter based on consultation between both sides. In order to prove the conclusion of this agreement, three copies of the agreement have been made and X and Y will each be given one.

Year/Month/Day

X1 Ichibacho 1-1, Chiba-city, Chiba Prefecture,
  Chiba Prefecture,
  Governor of Chiba Prefecture, Signature

X2 Address of the city,
Name of the city, Mayor of the city, Signature

Y Address of the company,
Name of the company, President of the company, Signature

NOTES

[1] Ministry of Public Management, Home Affairs, Posts and Telecommunications, www.soumu.go.jp/english/.

[2] Here 'national government' means the administrative body that includes national ministries and agencies, which are led by the cabinet, and whose members are appointed by the prime minister. The prime minister is elected by the Diet from among its members. 'Local government' is used to refer to an administrative body led by a governor or a mayor who is elected by local constituents. Though the national government is led by politicians and they sometimes make important decisions as Sato did in 1970, most concrete bills and policies are prepared by bureaucrats. In fact, it is often said that the government is virtually governed by bureaucrats. Governors and mayors who are elected directly by the people are relatively more powerful in their local governments than are ministers in the national government.

[3] Sato was in a weak position in relation to the USA because he could not restrain the export of textile goods from Japan to the USA, which he had promised to President Nixon in return for the USA having returned Okinawa to Japan in the previous year (Kissinger, 1979; Wakaizumi, 1994). Moreover, in 1970 the Nixon presidency started advocating a new way of thinking, that is, that producing low-priced goods without taking the necessary measures to control pollution caused by their production is unfair business (Nixon, 1970). See also Matsuno (1994, pp. 59-62).

[4] The Environment Agency's estimate based on their survey of prefectural governments is 32 000, which is very close to ours and heightens the credibility of both surveys.

[5] 'Policy instruments' are classified by the ways they are introduced, that is, through approval of

local assembly, decision solely by administrative body or negotiation between local government and business, and not by the contents of what is introduced, such as command-and-control measures or emissions taxes. They can be called administrative instruments.

6 A translation of the Yokohama case can be found in EX Corporation (1996, Annex 18). The translation used here is a revised version of these documents made by the author edited by Rachel Howser and Miranda Schreurs based on Saruta (1971, pp. 108-11) and Denki-Sangyo-Shimbunsha (1973, pp. 250-1). Examples of other PCAs can be found in Gresser, Fujikura and Morishima (1981, pp. 399-404) and Yamanouchi and Kiyohara (1989, pp. 237-45). The former contains a PCA between a residential group and a business and also one for a nuclear facility.

7 The translation is based on the document found in Denki-Sangyo-Shimbunsha (1973, pp. 92-4).

8 The 1923 earthquake occurred just to the west of Tokyo. Close to 100 000 people died and 40 000 people went missing. The earthquake's maginitude was 7.9 on the Richter scale.

9 The translation is based on the original document given to the author by Chiba Prefecture.

10 A 'related business' here means a 'subsidiary business'.

10. Japan's Environmental Policy: Financial Mechanisms

Tomohiko Inui, Akira Morishima and Hidefumi Imura

INTRODUCTION

This chapter provides an overview of environmental finance mechanisms in Japan. Since the 1960s, the Japanese government has developed various financial mechanisms to promote environmental protection in Japan. The central government has developed financial mechanisms to help local governments build important environmental infrastructures in their localities. The national government has also developed unique economic incentive schemes to encourage private companies to invest in pollution control and environmental protection technologies. These mechanisms have played an indispensable role in promoting pollution control and environmental protection in Japan.

FINANCIAL ARRANGEMENTS FOR POLLUTION CONTROL INVESTMENTS IN LOCALITIES

Japan's Basic Environment Law provides the national government with authority to identify localities with serious pollution problems, require them to develop 'Pollution Control Programs,' and submit their pollution control plans to the central government. Each designated region sets quantitative environmental targets and describes measures to achieve them. The regional plan also includes estimates of public and private expenditures to implement the measures and achieve the goals (Japan Environmental Sanitation Center 1986 pp. 1-2). Submission of the regional Pollution Control Program is a prerequisite to receive special financial assistance from the national government. The term of the program is five years and it is renewable. As of 2001, 34 regions have been designated. The designated areas include all major industrial cities and large metropolitan areas in Japan. In total, the 34

Environmental Policy in Japan

designated regions cover 8 per cent of the nation's land area. Fifty-three per cent of the population lives in these regions, and 52 per cent of the manufacturing product shipments come from these areas (Ministry of the Environment 2003a, p. 244).

Table 10.1 Special Rates for Local Governments for Pollution Control Projects

Type of project		Ordinary rate	Special rate
Specific public sewage system		1/3	1/2
Municipal sewage system		4/10	1/2
Final treatment facilities in the public sewage system		2/3-3/4	(1/2)*
Buffer green belts		1/3	1/2
Waste treatment facilities	Night soil treatment facilities	1/3	1/2
	Municipal garbage treatment facilities	1/4	1/2
	Industrial waste treatment facilities	0	1/2
Public primary and junior high schools	New construction, enlargement, reconstruction	1/3	1/2 - 2/3
	Pollution prevention works	1/3	2/3
Urban rivers		1/3	2/3
Harbors		0	1/2
Agricultural facilities	Mining pollution	65/100	2/3
	Industrial pollution	55/100	2/3
	Others	55/100	55/100
Agricultural land	Soil improvement	1/2	2/3
	Others	1/2	1/2*
Monitoring and measurement equipment		1/3	1/2

Notes: *As of 1985. Even if there is no increase in the rates for national subsidies, local governments can enjoy other benefits. They are allowed to issue local bonds for special pollution control purposes beyond the control limits designated by the central government.
Source: Japan Environmental Sanitation Center (Nihon Kankyo Eisei Center): Report on the Analysis and Survey of Pollution Control Programs (Kogai Boshi Keikaku Kaiseki Kento Chosa), 1986, p. 6.

Typically, each designated region covers a geographic area consisting of several cities and towns. The program may include multiple projects, such as improvement of sewage systems, construction of new environmental infrastructures (e.g., buffer zones, waste disposal facilities), land improvement, dredging and water induction and establishment of monitoring systems. Enlargement of existing factory sites and construction of new sites are usually restricted in the designated areas, while relocation of existing factories to more suitable industrial locations is often encouraged.

Following the submission of the Pollution Control Program to the central government, the locality receives special financial assistance from the central government. The Law on Special Financial Arrangement by the Government for Public Projects of Pollution Control specifies types of special financial assistance available to designated localities. They include:

1. Greater cost sharing by the central government and application of special national subsidy rates to local pollution control efforts (Table 10.1);
2. Relaxation of national government control on local bonds to increase the number of eligible projects; and
3. Relaxation of the national government control on the fiscal policy of local government to allow local government to include the redemption money for the local bonds in its basic fiscal demand account.

In 1995, the 34 designated regions spent a total of 3.6 trillion yen (US $300 billion) on pollution control programs: 2.5 trillion yen for pollution control projects and 1.1 trillion yen for projects related to pollution prevention. The amount of subsidies that the designated regions received from the central government through the special subsidy rate program was 38.6 billion yen. Recent data show that the special subsidy rate program has been particularly helpful in building municipal garbage treatment facilities. In 1995, 579 billion yen was allocated to the construction of municipal garbage treatment facilities in designated regions. In addition, designated regions received a 'bonus' budget of 44.9 billion yen from the central government through the special subsidy rate program (Environment Agency 1996, pp. 277-9).

MUNICIPAL SEWAGE SYSTEMS

Both nationally and locally, the construction and improvement of municipal sewage systems has been regarded as the single most important pollution control project in Japan. A large amount of money has been spent on developing municipal sewage systems. In 1960, only 5 per cent of the total Japanese population received the service of municipal sewage systems, that is, collection of waste water by pipes and treatment of waste water before discharge. To improve the situation, the central government enacted the first five year plan for improving sewage systems in 1960. Since its enactment, the first five year plan has been renewed every five years (Ministry of the Environment 2003a, p. 244).

Thus far, more than 70 trillion yen (The total budget for the first through eighth five year plans plus the budget for fiscal year 2001 and 2002.) has been spent on construction and improvement of municipal sewage systems (Table 10.2). As a result, by March 2002, the percentage of the national population receiving sewage treatment services reached 63.5 per cent while the rate was as small as 44 per cent in 1990 and 30 per cent in 1980 (Japan Sewerage Association). In large cities with populations of over a million, almost every household receives sewage treatment services. In small and medium-sized cities, however, there remain households without effective municipal sewage systems (Table 10.3) (Nihon Gesuido Kyokai 2002, pp. 26-7).

For the fiscal year 2000, a total of 3.41 trillion yen was appropriated for the central and local government projects related to the construction and improvement of municipal sewage systems. The central government provides subsidies to local governments, which cover 1/3 (or 1/2 in the designated areas) of the project costs. Operation and maintenance of the system is also very costly. In 2000, 2.3 trillion yen was spent for this purpose.

Table 10.2 Expenditures for Municipal Sewage Systems

Phase	Period	Total actual expenditure (billion yen)	Population ratio with service (per cent)
1st Five Year Plan	1963-66	296.3	20
2nd Five Year Plan	1967-70	617.8	23
3rd Five Year Plan	1971-75	2,624	26
4th Five Year Plan	1976-80	6,387	30
5th Five Year Plan	1981-85	8,478	36
6th Five Year Plan	1986-90	11,693	44
7th Five Year Plan	1991-95	16,711	54
8th Five Year Plan	1996-2000	23,700	62
Total	1963-2000	70,507	

Notes: Based on five year plans.
Sources: Suido Sangyo Shimbunsha 2001, Annals of Sewage Work (*Gesuido Nenkan*) 2000, Tokyo: Suido Sangyo Shimbunsha, pp. 60-68; Nihon Gesuido Kyokai (Japan Sewage Works Association), www.alpha-web.ne.jp/jswa/ accessed 21 June 2004; Nihon Gesuido Kyokai 2002, p. 28.

Seventy per cent of the 2.3 trillion yen budget was spent on the redemption of local government bonds. The revenue from user charges covered 39.4 per cent of the operation and maintenance costs (Nihon Gesuido Kyokai 2001).

FINANCIAL ARRANGEMENTS TO PROMOTE ENVIRONMENTAL INVESTMENT

The Japanese government has developed two major financial assistance mechanisms to encourage environmental investment in the private sector. The first is taxation. The other is based on government-established, 'policy-based' financial organizations that provide financial resources for environmental protection efforts in the private sector.

Table 10.3 Improvement of Municipal Sewage Systems

City size	1985	2002
Designated large cities (with a population greater than one million)	80.6	98.0
Cities with a population from 300 thousand to one million	42.1	72.1
Cities with a population from 50 to 300 thousand	29.9	61.6
Cities with a population less than 50 thousand	8.5	33.4
Towns and villages	3.2	25.1
Country as a whole	35.9	61.7

Notes: Population ratio with service (per cent).
Sources: Suido Sangyo Shimbunsha 2001, *Gesuido Nenkan* 2000, pp. 60-8; Nihon Gesuido Kyokai 2004; Nihon Gesuido Kyokai 2001, p. 28.

Tax Benefits

The Japanese government has been using taxation primarily as a means to encourage private companies to invest in environmental protection. Instead of punishing polluting industries by requiring them to pay additional taxes, the Japanese government has been using tax benefits to encourage private investment in pollution control and energy saving. For example, tax exemptions are given to companies that install new pollution control devices. This policy is one of the main reasons that pollution control technologies diffuse rapidly in Japan. Another important tax mechanism is the Exceptions to the Corporate Tax Law Act, which allows companies with pollution control equipment or facilities to use accelerated depreciation rates in calculating their taxes. The most important tax incentive is a 50 per cent special depreciation in the first year for pollution control equipment and devices. Other available depreciation or reduction methods include a 'shortened depreciation' rate for waste-water treatment equipment and a 'special reserve fund' for enterprises with especially large pollution control costs or large reductions in profits due to large environmental expenditures. Other special tax incentives include reduced commodity tax rates for low pollution automobiles and reduced customs duties on desulfurized imported oil.

Policy-based Financial Institutions

The national government began to establish 'policy-based' financial institutions in the early 1960s to make low interest loans available for private companies interested in investment in pollution control. The Japan Development Bank began providing low interest loans for investing in pollution control in 1960, the Small Business Finance Corporation in 1961, and the People's Finance Corporation in 1963. Then the Pollution Control Service Corporation (PCSC, renamed Japan Environment Corporation (JEC)) was established in 1965, in order to meet the increasing demands for pollution control investment in small and medium-sized enterprises. In addition to these national schemes, local governments have also created environmental finance institutions to provide low interest loans for local enterprises. As of 1970, 37 out of 47 prefectures and 48 cities already had such institutions (Environment Agency 1971, p. 386). The number of local governments with such a financial system further increased to 45 out of 47 prefectures as of 1997 (Environment Agency 1997a, pp. 172-4).

The Fiscal Investment and Loan Program (FILP)
These policy-based financial institutions procure most of their necessary funds through the FILP. FILP was established by the central government to provide financial resources for public institutions that contribute to national policy objectives. The government draws funds for this program from different kinds of financial sources: 1) the Trust Fund Bureau Fund; 2) the Postal Life Insurance Fund; 3) the Industrial Investment Special Account; and 4) Government Guaranteed Bonds. It then combines and allocates these funds to institutions that implement national policies, such as policy-based financial institutions, local governments and public corporations. Figure 10.1 shows the scheme of FILP and the outstanding balance at the end of FY 1998. FILPs includes the following components:

Trust Fund Bureau Fund. This Fund is the core of the FILP's financial resources. Public funds including postal savings and employee and national pension reserves are deposited in the Trust Fund, where they are managed by the Trust Fund Bureau. In FY 1998, they totaled 436 trillion yen: 58 per cent from postal savings and 32 per cent from pension funds. Out of the Fund, 316 trillion yen was allocated to the FILP. It represented 79 per cent of the balance of the FILP (Yano Tsuneta Kinenkai 2003, pp. 386-92).

Postal Life Insurance Fund. This fund is accumulated through the postal life insurance business and is classified as a public fund like the Trust Fund Bureau Fund. More than half of the Postal Life Insurance Fund is utilized by the FILP.

Industrial Investment Special Account. The resources of this account are dividends from Nippon Telegraph and Telephone Corporation, Japan Tobacco, Inc. stocks and payments to the government by the Japan Bank for International Cooperation. The account handles the investment portion of the FILP plan.

Government-guaranteed bonds. FILP-financed institutions, such as the Japan Highway Public Corporation, issue bonds in the financial markets. With the government guaranteeing their bonds, the institutions can smoothly procure funds.

'Policy-based' financial institutions played an important role in pollution control efforts in Japan during the 1960s and 1970s. At that time, the ratio of owned capital to total capital was much lower in Japan than in other countries, and Japanese enterprises were dependent upon banks for investments. Commercial banks, however, were not particularly interested in granting loans for pollution control investments. Low interest loans from the specialized financial institutions were, therefore, very useful and in many cases necessary. Without these special low interest loan programs, a number of enterprises would have found it difficult to finance pollution control projects. One way to measure the impact of low interest loans on environmental investment in the private sector is to estimate the amount of savings that the loan recipients would have enjoyed had the benefits been given in the form of subsidies. This 'subsidy equivalent' was estimated to be a little more than 10 per cent of the amount of loans granted or 1.3 per cent of total pollution control investment in 1975 (Organization for Economic Cooperation and Development 1977, p. 75).

Availability of low interest loans has led to the establishment of a constant market for companies manufacturing anti-pollution devices. The market for anti-pollution devices rapidly expanded during the early 1970s. In 1975, investment in anti-pollution devices reached an annual total of nearly one trillion yen, or 17.7 per cent of combined capital spending (Figure 10.2).

The expansion of the market for pollution control technologies intensified the competition among manufacturers and accelerated the development of new anti-pollution technologies. Market competition was also increased by anti-pollution studies carried out by the Science and Technology Agency and Ministry of International Trade and Industry.

Figure 10.1   The Scheme and Balance of FILP in FY 1998

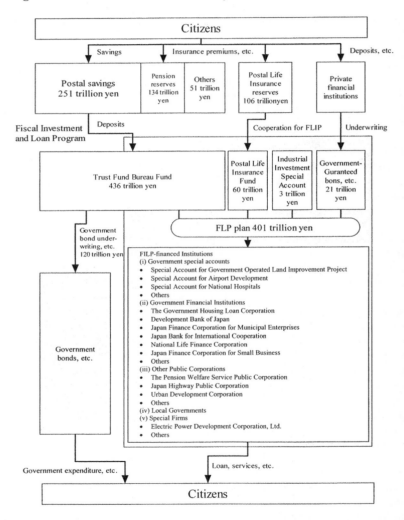

Source: Financial Bureau of the Ministry of Finance, 'Fiscal Investment and Loan Program 99,' November 1999.

Growing central and local government budgets for the construction, operation and maintenance of urban environmental infrastructures (including sewage systems and municipal waste plants) created a large market for environmental technologies. As a result, the pollution control industry developed rapidly in Japan. The rapid development of pollution control technologies has allowed Japan to contribute greatly to pollution prevention efforts throughout the world. Japan's contribution has been particularly significant in the field of air pollution control technologies.

Figure 10.2 Pollution Control Investment in Japan

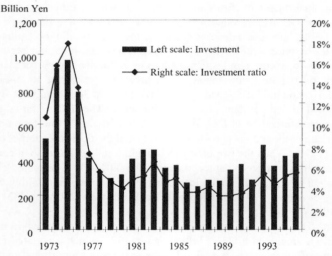

Source: Data from Ministry of International Trade and Industry, 'Business Investment Plans of Major Japanese Industries.'

The rest of this chapter focuses on the activities of the Japan Development Bank (JDB) and the JEC because these institutions have played unique roles in supporting the pollution prevention activities of Japanese firms. The primary function of the JDB is to offer loans to large corporations in Japan. The function of the JEC was to provide both technical and financial assistance to private companies and local governments for addressing pollution control problems.

Japan Development Bank

The JDB has played an important role in facilitating anti-pollution and energy conservation efforts in Japan by extending loans to environment-related investments. The JDB was established in 1951 and the emphasis of the activities conducted by the JDB has changed as the Japanese government's policy role has changed. Shortly after the JDB's establishment, the government's overriding policy priority was supporting economic reconstruction. The JDB thus targeted its finance operations to support vast investments by basic industries such as electric power, coal mining, ocean shipping, iron and steel. In the early 1970s, when industrial pollution became an important policy issue in Japan, the JDB's loan activities changed accordingly. The JDB started to focus more on investment projects that involve improvement of the living environment, including pollution control.

In 1960, the JDB introduced its first anti-pollution loan program to support investment by firms in sewage treatment facilities. In subsequent years, the JDB also introduced several other anti-pollution programs. In the early 1970s, Japanese industries needed to install anti-pollution equipment to meet the requirements of the newly established anti-pollution regulations. For energy-consuming industries, such as oil refineries and power plants, the burden of required investment was heavy. For example, to install one desulfurization unit, a company had to invest almost 30 billion yen. The JDB responded to their demands for affordable loans. The JDB's first target was smoke desulfurization (1970). Its focus then shifted to waste treatment, the prevention of air and noise pollution (1971) and the denitrification of exhaust gases (1976). When the two oil crises brought a sudden increase in corporate investment in energy-saving technologies, the JDB further promoted efficient utilization of energy through a loan scheme for companies installing energy-saving devices (1975) (Development Bank of Japan 2002, pp. 331-2 and 398-400).

The JDB loans for anti-pollution measures and other environmental provisions amounted to 205.5 billion yen in 1975, which accounted for 26.8 per cent of all loans for the period – the maximum proportional outlay for anti-pollution loans to date (Table 10.4). There was a high concentration of loans in this sector over the four-year period from FY 1973 to FY 1976. This amount declined over time during the latter half of the 1970s as companies finished installing expensive end-of-pipe measures. More recently, an annual total for anti-pollution loans has been around 30 to 40 billion yen, and despite slight fluctuations due to varying interest rates, the capital requirement has been relatively stable.

Two immediate effects of the JDB loans are the accommodation of capital availability and the provision of investment incentives through low interest loans. The accommodation of capital availability arises directly from the allocation of JDB loans and indirectly because JDB loans induce private-sector loans. This indirect effect is known as a 'cow bell effect.' Several empirical studies have been conducted to examine this 'cow bell effect.' They stress the role of JDB loans in increasing the capital stock and

Table 10.4 JDB Loans for Environmental and Energy Conservation Projects

Fiscal year	Total amount of JDB's loan	Loan for environmental projects		Loan for energy conservation projects	
	Billion yen	Billion yen	Per cent	Billion yen	Per cent
1965	199.7	1.5	0.7		
1970	314.9	3.1	1.0		
1971	425.1	24.3	5.7		
1972	460.5	42.2	9.2		
1973	543.9	76.1	14.0		
1974	631.7	162.7	25.7		
1975	766.2	205.5	26.8	4.3	0.6
1976	760.8	190.2	25.0	7.7	1.0
1977	673.2	102.1	15.2	7.1	1.0
1978	992.4	131.7	13.3	8.6	0.9
1979	948.9	85.7	9.0	16.0	1.7
1980	973.4	112.8	11.6	15.8	1.6
1981	1,077.5	85.8	8.0	28.0	2.6
1982	1,161.5	86.1	7.4	36.4	3.1
1983	1,154.0	94.2	8.2	46.5	4.0
1984	1,162.4	116.3	10.0	34.4	3.0
1985	1,105.0	82.9	7.5	22.2	2.0
1986	1,091.7	71.3	6.5	28.7	2.6
1987	1,283.5	53.6	4.2	12.9	1.0
1988	1,353.5	60.0	4.4	4.7	0.3
1989	1,409.1	60.6	4.3	3.9	0.3
1990	1,492.6	57.7	3.9	9.1	0.6
1991	1,927.1	68.6	3.6	15.7	0.8
1992	2,586.8	76.0	2.9	28.2	1.1
1993	2,742.5	60.9	2.2	30.6	1.1
1994	2,292.3	61.7	2.7	52.4	2.3
1995	1,819.4	23.0	1.3	12.1	0.7
1996	1,738.7	40.5	2.3	1.5	0.1
1997	1,900.5	31.3	1.6	5.8	0.3

Source: Development Bank of Japan 2002, pp. 840-5.

production levels of specific industries and corporations (Horiuchi and Sui 1993, pp. 441-65). Particularly in the 1970s when companies had to involve themselves actively in environmental investment, many companies were not in a position to invest in activities that did not return a profit such as pollution prevention. This was partly due to an immature long-term financial/capital market and partly due to the significant drop-off of economic growth since the end of the 1960s (Development Bank of Japan 2002, pp. 331-2; Cruz et al. 2002, p. 42). Under these circumstances, the JDB helped private companies acquire the necessary capital funds to install anti-pollution devices. By offering loans at reduced interest rates, the JDB has consistently played a role in relieving the financial burden placed on companies that must comply with environmental provisions. This in turn has accelerated the installation of environmentally sound technologies in Japan.

Table 10.5 Trends in Energy Conservation Investment in Major Industrial Sectors

Fiscal Year	Cement	Paper & pulp	Petro-chemical	Steel	Auto-mobile	Power-generation	Total
1979	20.4	6.0	6.4	94.2	6.1	9.6	195.6
1980	4.2	8.8	19.1	165.4	17.9	12.2	326.0
1981	8.4	9.5	37.6	210.7	20.6	28.5	447.6
1982	14.1	6.2	38.4	227.2	10.0	53.4	440.8
1983	12.3	12.4	31.0	155.5	13.2	64.8	374.6
1984	9.5	28.1	18.6	114.9	10.8	49.5	305.6
1985	14.5	48.5	12.6	92.6	13.2	22.7	297.2
1986	11.6	25.9	9.8	115.8	8.7	30.2	266.0
1987	8.9	12.7	23.3	108.3	6.8	24.1	229.4
1988	7.5	19.2	18.0	42.9	13.5	18.8	159.4
1989	9.2	22.7	17.3	37.6	13.7	15.2	156.4
1990	12.6	58.9	11.1	65.3	10.2	48.5	258.2
1991	12.0	36.0	36.1	173.4	13.9	38.7	369.1
1992	5.5	12.3	52.0	192.1	14.0	92.9	458.2
1993	8.7	22.6	42.3	147.6	21.3	225.2	535.4
1994	3.8	9.2	9.5	129.9	10.0	182.3	410.1
1995	4.7	35.4	8.9	161.2	6.8	170.6	452.3

Notes: In billion yen. The total includes other sectors.
Source: Data are from Ministry of International Trade and Industry, *Business Investment Plans of Major Japanese Industries*, annual reports.

Energy-saving investment and JDB loans

The government's energy conservation policy helped industries to promote energy-saving investments. In 1979, the *Law Concerning the Rational Use of Energy* was enacted, with detailed guidelines for energy-saving equipment and building standards. The government also provided long-term, low-interest loan programs through government financial institutions such as the JDB.

The JDB contributed to environmental protection through its energy-related loans. In the late 1970s, energy-related loans accounted for more than 40 per cent of all JDB loans. The primary aim of these loans was for energy security, but they also contributed to rational use of energy, resulting in less pollution and lower carbon dioxide emissions. Shortly after the second oil crisis, between 1980 and 1981, capital spending on energy-saving technology increased sharply. In 1981, the annual total of loans for installing energy-saving devices was just under 30 billion yen. In 1983, the figure reached 46.5 billion yen. A general downshift in investment followed and continued until 1990. Then, increases in energy-saving investment in the iron and steel and electric power sectors reversed the downward trend (Table 10.5). In 1993, the energy conservation investment loan reached a new high of 52.4 billion yen (Table 10.4), partly due to the creation of new loan schemes prompted by the enactment of the Energy-saving and Recycling Law (Energy Conservation Law) in 1991 (Development Bank of Japan 2002, p. 599).

DEALING WITH GLOBAL ENVIRONMENTAL ISSUES

In the 1980s, global environmental problems, such as global warming and ozone depletion, became important policy issues in advanced industrial countries. In response, the JDB began to introduce new loan schemes to deal with global environmental issues. A new loan scheme focusing on freon gas emissions reductions was introduced in 1988. Nitrogen oxide emissions reductions were added as a new target in 1989. The year 1995 saw a significant revision of JDB's loan schemes: a shift in focus from 'pollution prevention' to 'global environmental projects.'

The JDB merged with the Hokkaido-Tohoku Development Finance Corporation to form the Development Bank of Japan (DBJ) in October 1999. The DBJ is in the process of identifying new environmental loan schemes in areas such as renewable resources and recycling. It is also seeking to extend its lending and investment programs to projects contributing to greenhouse gas emissions reductions. In addition, DBJ is planning to introduce a new credit policy that takes into account environmental aspects of projects in making loan decisions (Development Bank of Japan 2002, p. 776).

Environmental issues have evolved over the years from control of hazardous pollutants to energy conservation to global environmental concerns. Business investment decisions have changed accordingly (Hamamoto 1998, p. 24). The investment focus has shifted from end-of-pipe, pollution control technologies to energy-saving technologies to more diversified activities such as development of recycling and renewable energy technologies. The DBJ has responded to these changing investment needs by introducing and developing new loan schemes. The DBJ has been one of the most important financial institutions for environmental investment in Japan.

The Japan Environment Corporation

The Japanese government established the PCSC, the predecessor to the Japan Environment Corporation in 1965 under the Law Establishing the Pollution Control Service Corporation. The PCSC's primary mission was to provide both technical and financial assistance to private companies and local governments in addressing pollution control problems. Many considered the establishment of the PCSC to be an innovative and unique approach to supporting environmental investment efforts by small and medium-sized enterprises (SMEs) and local governments.

The law that established the PCSC was amended in 1992 to address better the changing nature of environmental issues, which have evolved from industrial pollution problems to larger, more complex environmental issues. This amendment led to the establishment of the JEC. Its main supervising authority was the Environment Agency, and its major funding sources were the FILP program and subsidies from the central government. The JEC had three major programs: 1) Construction and Transfer (CAT) Program; 2) Loan Program; and 3) Global Environment Program for the conservation of the environment (Morishima 2004, pp. 324-58). In 2004, JEC was abolished and its activities were succeeded by the Environmental Recovery and Conservation Agency (ERCA), which was created by merging JEC and the Environmental Health Compensation and Prevention Association.

Construction and Transfer (CAT) Program
Under the CAT Program, the JEC builds pollution prevention facilities, and thereafter transfers these facilities to its 'customers' on favorable terms. Its 'customers' are mainly SMEs and local governments. Many SMEs and local governments have difficulty building or improving pollution control facilities by themselves because they lack the financial and technical resources necessary to do so. The CAT Program is available for constructing the following five types of pollution prevention facilities: 1) Factory Complexes; 2) Buffer Green Belts; 3) Green Parks to Abate Air Pollution; 4) Industrial Waste Disposal Facilities and Green Parks; and 5) Composite Facilities at National and Quasi-national Parks. The JEC's favorable loan conditions make the CAT Program attractive to SMEs and local governments with few financial and technical resources. A 'customer' pays 5 per cent of the construction costs as a down payment, and JEC takes care of the remaining 95 per cent, using a government loan (i.e. FILP). Program recipients are allowed to make loan payments over a long period (normally 20 years), and rates are low and fixed.

Loan program
The JEC offers low-interest government loans to private enterprises and local governments in order to stimulate pollution control investment efforts. An applicant submits a loan application to the JEC, and the JEC assesses the application from both credit and technical viewpoints. Loan applicants do not have to pay for administrative services because the JEC's administrative costs are fully funded by the central government. Once approved, public entity applicants (e.g. local governments and associated entities) receive loans *directly* from the JEC through its 'direct loan system.' Private entity

applicants, on the other hand, receive funds *indirectly* from the JEC through its 'agency loan system.' Instead of dealing with private entity applicants directly, the JEC uses private banks as its 'agents' to accommodate their loan needs. Many private banks have nation-wide networks with branch offices all over Japan. This 'agency loan system' is more convenient and suitable for dealing with numerous private loan recipients (Morishima 2004, pp. 350-4).

Three principles of the CAT and Loan Programs
As a 'policy-based' financial institution, the JEC makes its funding decisions in accordance with policy priorities set by the national government. Loan applications are examined according to the following three principles:

Priority by subject. Preference is given to SMEs and local governments in deciding loan periods and interest rates. Loan periods are longer and interest rates are lower for SMEs and local governments than for large enterprises (LEs). An interest subsidy from the national account is used to supplement the interest differences.

Priority for cooperative projects. Preference is given to projects that involve cooperative or joint pollution control technology. It is more economical for several companies to build and operate a pollution control facility jointly than for a single company to set up a facility and use it exclusively. Interest rates are lower and loan ratios are higher for projects involving cooperative pollution control efforts.

Priority based on urgency. Priority is given to environmental projects that require immediate attention. For example, in the late 1990s, dioxins from waste incineration plants became a serious pollution problem in Japan. To address this issue, in 1998 the Ministry of Health and Welfare adopted stricter dioxin standards. To meet the new standards, many waste incineration plant operators had to invest a significant amount of money to update and improve their facilities. The JEC's loan program responded to their investment needs by raising the loan ratio and lowering the required collateral coverage.

Evolution of the CAT and Loan Programs
The annual budget for the CAT Program in the 1990s ranged from 35 billion yen to 55 billion yen (15 to 30 projects per year). Five hundred and fifteen projects received funding between 1967-98, amounting to total project costs of 786 billion yen. Forty per cent of total project costs came from Factory Complex (factory relocation) projects. Among many CAT projects, the Joint Pollution Control Facilities projects were particularly effective in stimulating pollution control investments in the early stages of pollution control, when

waste water and air pollutants from industrial facilities were the major cause of pollution problems in Japan (Morishima 2004, pp. 345-50).

The JEC's loan activities peaked in 1975 at 127 billion yen. During the 1970s, heavy industries were the main recipients of JEC loans, when their need to install air pollution control equipment was particularly strong. As heavy industries' investment needs for pollution control dropped, the overall loan figures began to decline. The flow of loan applications from SMEs, however, remains constant. In the 1990s, JEC loans for industrial waste treatment facilities rose sharply. The annual budget for the Loan Program in the 1990s ranged from 20-40 billion yen (30 to 100 cases per year). Between 1966-98, approximately 4,000 environmental investment projects received funding from the JEC through its loan program; the total amount of JEC loans amounted to 1 trillion yen.

The JEC has played an important role in supporting environmental investment efforts in Japan through its CAT and Loan Programs. The JEC's successes and accomplishments can be summarized as follows.

Mobilization of private market funds

Government loans provided by the JEC and other public financial institutions played a very important role in early pollution control efforts in Japan. Initially, private financial institutions were reluctant to invest in pollution control technologies since their profitability was quite uncertain. Encouraged by the JEC's earlier successes, however, private lending institutions began to show more interest in investing in environmental projects. The JEC succeeded in mobilizing private market funds by demonstrating the feasibility and profitability of environmental investment.

Small and medium-sized enterprises

SMEs have benefited tremendously from the JEC's loan activities. Many SMEs could not have installed the pollution control equipment necessary to comply with regulatory standards without JEC loans. Since 90 per cent of private enterprises in Japan are SMEs, JEC's achievement in this area is significant.

Technical guidance and advice

Aside from being the major 'policy-based' financial institution in the area of environmental finance, the JEC plays an important role as a leading environmental research institution. Both the CAT and Loan Programs involve research projects and technical analyses conducted by the JEC's technical advisory team and specialized experts. Through its research activities, the JEC has contributed significantly to the development of industrial pollution control technologies.

CONCLUSION

This chapter examined environmental finance mechanisms in Japan. The national government played a central role in developing environmental finance mechanisms in Japan. Special financial schemes and subsidy programs were developed to help local governments build environmental infrastructure in their localities. Tax benefits and 'policy-based' financial institutions helped many companies to invest in pollution control technologies in their earlier environmental protection efforts. Institutions such as the JDB and the JEC played a particularly important role in the 1960s and 1970s, when private lending institutions were still very skeptical about the feasibility and profitability of environmental investment. The early successes of the JDB and the JEC have encouraged private financial institutions and as a result more private funds have become available for environmental investment projects in the private sector. Public financial institutions, however, remain important in helping SMEs and local governments in their environmental investment efforts.

The FILP system in Japan played an essential role in improving Japan's economic infrastructure and helping private firms to make investments in pollution control technologies and environmental protection. In the 2000s however Japan must rely more on market forces and private initiatives. The reform of policy-based financing and the FILP system are top policy priorities. The JEC, in particular, has largely finished its role in aiding SMEs with pollution control measures. Once it was reorganized as ERCA, its activities shifted to hazardous waste treatment and resource recovery from wastes.

11. Environmental Industries and Technologies in Japan

Hidefumi Imura, Ryota Shinohara and Koji Himi

INTRODUCTION

Improvements in environmental performance require not only regulatory action but also environmental products and services. The role of environmental industries is to make technologically sophisticated environmental products and services available to enterprises, consumers and public authorities at competitive prices. The definition of environmental technology used here is broad, including not only 'end-of-pipe' (EP) clean-up technologies, but also 'cleaner production' (CP) technologies and those which improve energy and resource efficiency at the source. Regulations of emissions of harmful substances can stimulate the development of EP technologies and may also encourage the development of CP technologies that are more efficient both economically and environmentally. As the environment becomes a more central issue for businesses, environmental considerations are becoming internalized in a growing range of sectors. Environmental industries can be found in the manufacturing, banking, insurance, consulting, transportation, wholesale and retail and information and communication sectors, among others.

The 'greening of industry' is a main goal of environmental policy. This chapter looks at one aspect of the greening of industry, examining the environmental industries and technologies that played an essential role in Japan's battle to clean up air and water pollution. Environmental technologies are indispensable for developing countries, which in many cases are expanding their industrial production without simultaneously adopting proper technical control measures. Developing countries must nurture their own environmental industries by improving their technical, financial and human resource capabilities. This chapter takes up technological issues related to the development of clean cars, waste disposal and recycling, issues that will be increasingly important in the twenty-first century as nations are forced to shift in the direction of becoming resource recycling societies with sustainable urban transport systems.

THE ROLE OF ENVIRONMENTAL TECHNOLOGIES

In Japan's case, economic development had two opposing effects. On the one hand, it caused environmental degradation; on the other, growth enabled industries to develop and introduce advanced control technologies. In the fight against extreme pollution in Japan, various technologies were developed and utilized, largely irrespective of their cost. Such an approach was made possible by the availability of EP technologies. The country owed its economic and environmental successes largely to the strong desire for technological innovation and competitive market conditions that prevailed in its industries. Japan, however, was criticized internationally for 'pollution dumping,' exporting industrial products at low prices and sacrificing environmental protection. In the long run, however, circumstances changed and technical breakthroughs in environmental pollution control proved requisite for Japanese industries to survive in the international market.

Demand and Supply of Environmental Technology

In order to promote environmental industries, governments can adopt two different types of measures: those that stimulate the demand of environmental technologies and those that encourage their supply.

Governments have various policy tools to expand the size of environmental technology and service markets. One is the application of stringent regulations and standards. Another involves the use of economic incentives and market forces. The government used a combination of regulation and subsidies to encourage private sector investment in environmental control devices and equipment. Growing central and local government budgets for public environmental projects, such as for the construction, operation and maintenance of urban environmental infrastructures, including sewage systems and municipal waste incineration plants, created a large market for environmental technologies (Imura 1983).

On the supply side, the government used subsidies to assist research and development (R&D) in the private sector. For the development of renewable energy sources, the government created the New Energy Development Organization (NEDO) to promote energy R&D. Research institutes of government ministries and agencies have also undertaken basic R&D in environmental science and technology. In general, however, the most crucial effort for the development of key control technologies was made by private sector initiatives stimulated by government environmental regulation and market competition. A good example of the role of market forces in the development of control technologies was the development of automobile exhaust gas control devices such as catalytic converters (Himi 2000b) (See Box 11.1. In spite of the conflicts between regulatory and business interests, the government and industry maintained a dialogue in an attempt to strike the best balance possible between environmental requirements and technical feasibility.

Financial mechanisms were necessary to support the large investment costs of installing pollution control devices and equipment and for R&D into new technologies. The Japan Development Bank (which later became the Development Bank of Japan) played a key role as a financial supporter of such industrial efforts. The Pollution Control Corporation (later the Japan Environmental Corporation) also played a key role in assisting the efforts of small and medium-sized enterprises. These two institutions were created by the government, and have operated out of government treasury loans and investment schemes. These governmental financial institutions created low-interest rate loan systems to raise investment capital (Organization for Economic Cooperation and Development 1977a, pp. 73-6; Environment Agency 1976). At the same time, the government adopted supporting measures like tax incentives that approve special amortization methods for the depreciation in the value of anti-pollution equipment. Thus, private anti-pollution investment rapidly increased in the 1970s, peaking in 1975 (Imura 1983; Committee on Japan's Experience in the Battle against Air Pollution 1997, p. 77).

Regulations for Environmental Technology

The 'Air Pollution Control Law' of 1968 introduced a control scheme that defined controlled areas, established emissions criteria for those areas, determined the acceptable height of stacks and chimneys and authorized the government to order improvements and impose penalties. Despite the introduction of the law, sulfur oxides (SO_x) and nitrogen oxides (NO_x) emissions continued to rise. In response, the regulations were reinforced through the enlargement of controlled areas nationwide, the authorization of local governments to set additional emission criteria and the establishment of penalties for the violation of the emission standards.

An important element of this process was that the government examined the actual technical situation of industries and used this information to set higher standards for pollution control. In a ratcheting-up process, once these initial standards were met, the government set yet higher standards. In parallel with this, the government took leadership in the technological development of accurate and practical measurement techniques, methods and equipment for monitoring of the environment and source management. This was important in order to ensure the scientifically reliable enforcement of regulations (Committee on Japan's Experience in the Battle against Air Pollution 1997, pp. 59-65).

Box 11. 1   Automobile Exhaust Emission Gas

The standards for automobile exhaust gas control for newly produced automobiles were revised to include a grace period that would allow automobile manufacturers to make timely technical modifications.

In 1975-76, the USA planned to tighten its control over automobile exhaust gas emissions according to the standards stipulated by the Clean Air Act. This movement in the USA triggered the Japanese populace to make similar demands of their government in order to enforce standards as stringent as those in the USA. Thus, in 1976 a new standard was introduced: less than 2.1g/km for carbon monoxide (CO), less than 0.25g/km for hydrocarbon, and less than 1.2g/km for NO_x. These figures were set in response to the report of the Central Council for Pollution Control. Although automobile manufacturers claimed that the standards would be impossible to achieve, the standards stimulated technical competition among manufacturers. Soon afterwards, two Japanese car manufacturers announced that they had succeeded in developing control technology to meet the targets. Their success was due to their exhaustive technical development efforts and their recognition that this was a good chance for them to flaunt their technical superiority. The new standards were implemented as the regulations for the fiscal years 1975-78. Japan won international attention for its success at reducing its emissions by more than 90 per cent.

The stringent emission controls were based on basic and intensive studies on the fuel combustion mechanisms of engines, and these studies enabled car manufacturers to produce more fuel-efficient engines. Thus, contrary to what the skeptics predicted, successful emission controls proved to be compatible with improved fuel economy, a win-win for customers and the environment. Japanese automobile manufacturers have remained internationally competitive while continuing to be pressured by stringent pollution control standards. They have done this by making continued improvements in engines and body structures, and developing emission gas purifiers (Japan Society of Atmospheric Environment 2000, pp. 945-59).

These government initiatives further stimulated the development of environmental monitoring and measurement technologies. The government introduced subsidies to promote the maintenance and introduction of measuring equipment and the installation of telemeter systems by prefectures and municipalities, since they are the ones actually implementing the regulations. The telemeter systems enabled local environmental authorities to collect the pollutant emissions and meteorological data automatically from factories and monitoring stations (Organization for Economic Cooperation and Development 1977a, p. 23; Ministry of the Environment 2003a, pp. 129-30). Development of EP control devices was also promoted.

The anti-pollution techniques of the 1960s were far from satisfactory, and R&D of new control devices was delegated to national research institutions of the Ministry of International Trade and Industry (MITI), now the Ministry of Economy, Trade and Industry (METI). At the same time, desulfurization techniques were developed as a part of large-scale joint pollution control projects being conducted by the government and the private sector. The government also provided subsides and tax measures for R&D into pollution control techniques by private industries.

Human Resources: Pollution Control Managers

Engineers were behind the development of technical solutions to policy mandates. The Law Concerning the Improvement of Pollution Prevention Systems in Specific Factories obligated companies to establish effective organizational structures for pollution control in their factories and plants to ensure compliance with regulations. The law required that factories and plants with facilities designated as polluting facilities have a 'pollution prevention general manager' and a 'pollution control manager' to be in charge of practical management of technical matters regarding pollution control. These managers are responsible for the maintenance and management of pollution prevention facilities as well as the implementation of necessary measures in accidental or emergency cases. Would-be pollution control managers must pass a national examination for pollution control or complete a lecture course to earn their qualifications (Japan Environmental Management Association for Industry 2002, pp. 683 and 885). As of the end of 1998, the total number of those who had passed the national examination or earned the qualification was more than 470,000. These individuals have contributed significantly to the voluntary anti-pollution efforts of private industries.

Heat management in factories was another area where human resources were critical. Heat management lies at the heart of factory air pollution control measures. Adequate heat management kills 'three birds with one stone' by reducing energy expenditures and energy consumption per unit of production, decreasing air pollutant exhaust volumes and improving product quality. Heat management measures can include supplementary pollution prevention equipment, including flue-gas desulfurization facilities and dust-collecting devices. The large number of technicians and skilled heat workers at factory sites were integral to the implementation of Japan's air pollution measures (Japan Society of Atmospheric Environment 2000, p. 453).

A Win-win Approach: Energy Saving and Air Pollution Control

Energy consumption has strong relevance to environmental pollution. The improvement of energy consumption by enhancing thermal and energy efficiency proved effective not only for economic efficiency, but also in the total volume control of air pollutants. As a result of drastic energy conservation measures triggered by the two oil crises of the 1970s, Japan achieved close to a 35 per cent reduction in energy demand relative to gross domestic product (GDP) in 1997 compared to 1973. Reduction of fuel use through energy conservation contributed to SO_x emissions reductions. While SO_x emissions reductions were also due to a switch to low sulfur content oil, the desulfurization of heavy oil, and the desulfurization of smoke came through energy conservation. It is important to realize that smoke accounted for approximately 25 per cent of pollution from 1973-79 (Environment Agency 1981; Committee on Japan's Experience in the Battle against Air Pollution 1997, pp. 86-7).

Economic growth must be achieved while decreasing, or at least not significantly increasing, the use of fossil fuels. Far greater efforts will have to be made to improve energy efficiency and utilize renewable energy. The Japanese government has promoted technical developments for energy conservation through low interest rate loan systems and tax incentive measures. The government also now requires that offices designated as 'large energy users' by the 'Law Concerning the Rational Use of Energy' employ 'energy managers' (who have passed the national examination) in order to be qualified to manage the use of energy and to plan for the rational use of energy. Such systems for energy conservation measures at factories and plants are very similar to those adopted for industrial pollution control. They are examples of how governments can take measures to guide industrial efforts in conserving energy and protecting the environment.

LESSONS FROM JAPANESE EXPERIENCES

Technical measures for environmental control were implemented with the use of EP approaches for pollution control. Historically, the solution to air and water pollution problems came largely from the development and diffusion of EP technologies. The rapid dissemination of such control technologies is of vital importance to developing countries where industrial activities without proper discharge control are causing significant air and water pollution problems. Technology transfer in this field is a central priority for development assistance programs.

The conventional EP approach, however, may not necessarily be the best or only technical solution available. The environmental soundness of a certain technology must be assessed according to its long-term compatibility with sustainability objectives. Moreover, cost-effectiveness should be considered. In some cases, sophisticated but expensive technologies may not be recommendable. This is especially the case for developing countries where advanced technologies are not economically feasible, or where there is a deficiency in technical expertise rendering them unable to handle such technologies. More important than EP approaches may be the development of production processes and products designed to minimize environmental impacts by reducing resource use, maximizing resource efficiency and minimizing waste generation. In line with this idea, both developing and developed countries must recognize that industrial technologies must be substantially reformed in order to achieve sustainable development.

Fossil fuels often worsen air pollution. Control technology such as flue-gas desulfurization can abate the emission of air pollutants such as SO_x, help countries solve local air pollution problems and enhance the health of their citizens. The pollution-ameliorating aspects of this technology, however, require energy; thus, the technology may have unintended consequences, such as encouraging the use of fossil fuels and thereby increasing the emission of the greenhouse gas, carbon dioxide (CO_2). Moreover, control technologies may generate large amounts of by-products; gypsum, for example, is a by-product of desulfurization. By-products cannot always be effectively used, and if they result in waste, they may have environmentally hazardous impacts (Japan Society of Atmospheric Environment 2000, pp. 471-2). Thus, the control of certain pollutants can multiply other problems or have other unintended implications. The environmental soundness and appropriateness of a technology cannot be judged based on a single criterion.

Control Technologies

Low-sulfur oil and flue-gas treatment technologies

A good example of control technologies in pollution abatement is the technical measures used for SO_x emission control: the shift to low-sulfur content fuels and the application of flue-gas desulfurization.

Approximately two-thirds of Japan's primary energy is provided by petroleum. The average sulfur content of imported crude oil for refining is now about 1.5 per cent. Since 1967, desulfurization plants have been built to reduce the sulfur content of heavy oil. As a result, the sulfur content of the cleanest heavy oil (class A) was reduced to as low as 0.5 per cent. The total consumption of heavy oil decreased while the share of low-sulfur A-oil in total heavy-oil consumption increased. Thus, the average sulfur content of heavy oil for domestic consumption dropped from 2.6 per cent in 1965 to 1.09 per cent in 1990. Together with the shift to low-sulfur content oil, import of sulfur-free fuels such as liquid natural gas (LNG) and liquid petroleum gas (LPG) has been expanded.

As regulations were tightened, measures to change fuel sources proved insufficient. Many factories, therefore, also chose to install flue-gas desulfurization plants. In the late 1960s, the flue-gas desulfurization technology was still in the R&D stage. But stricter regulations stimulated the R&D of such technology, and in the mid-1970s it spread over the country very rapidly (Japan Society of Atmospheric Environment 2000, pp. 465-520). The most remarkable increase in the total treatment capacity of plants was observed in the 1970s when Japan was still pursuing rapid economic growth, but continued to steadily increase thereafter, as well. In 1974, the number of flue-gas desulfurization plants was already 994. By 1989 it was 1846 units and today there are approximately 2000 in operation, with a total processed volume exceeding 200 million m^3/hour. The total processed volume for all flue-gas desulfurization facilities in the world is estimated at about 700 million m^3/hour, with Japan, the USA and Germany alone accounting for over 90 per cent of this amount (Committee on Japan's Experience in the Battle against Air Pollution 1997, p. 70-1; Ministry of the Environment 2003a, p. 114).

For smaller-scale sources in urban areas that could not install flue-gas desulfurization equipment, the use of much cleaner fuels such as kerosene and natural gas were promoted. This was done in accordance with the regulations and guidelines of local environmental authorities in prefectures and municipalities. Flue-gas denitrification technology was commercialized approximately five years later than flue-gas desulfurization. The number of denitrification units steadily increased throughout the 1970s and 1980s. In 1989, 434 flue gas denitrification units were installed for removal of NO_x from power plants, industrial boilers and other stationary sources of air pollutants. There were 1439 units in operation in 1999 (Ministry of the Environment 2003a, p. 113). Even small-scale boilers were equipped with desulfurization units. The widespread use of desulfurization technology and cleaner low-sulfur fuels also was partly facilitated by SO_x emission charges. These charges were fines placed on individual sources and were used to finance compensation payments to certified health victims of air pollution. The rate of charges became extremely high in some areas, such as Osaka, and functioned as an economic incentive for industry to further reduce the emission of air pollutants (Imura 1993).

Improvement in ambient air quality
As of 1990 there were about 1,700 ambient air quality monitoring stations all over the country. Concentrations of sulfur dioxide (SO_2), nitrogen dioxide (NO_2), suspended particulate matter and other pollutants in the atmosphere were recorded at these stations. As a result of this measuring activity, the

national total amount of SO_2 discharged into the atmosphere decreased from 4.8 million tons in 1970 to 0.7 million tons in 1990. This means that the SO_2 discharge per unit of GDP achieved a 14-fold decrease over the same period. The highest average annual concentration of SO_2 measured at the 15 air pollution monitoring stations, for which consistent data has been available since 1967, was 0.059 parts per million (ppm). After this record level was recorded in 1967 there was a consistent decline in SO_2 levels to 0.01 ppm in 1986 (Ministry of the Environment 2003a, p. 107).

Successful reduction of SO_x emissions can be illustrated by the figures available for some cities. The total annual emission of SO_x in Yokohama decreased from 104,500 tons in 1968 to 5,260 tons in 1985, while in Osaka levels went from 96,000 tons in 1970 to 5,600 tons in 1985. In these cities, emissions decreased to about one-twentieth of their earlier levels.

Environmental Expenditures: Cost of Control Technologies

At its peak, investments by large firms in air, water and noise pollution control plants and equipment totalled 950 billion yen, or 17.6 per cent of the total investment by the private sector in 1975. Since 1977, however, investment levels have remained relatively small at about 300 to 400 billion yen, or 3 to 4 per cent of total private investment. The total investment cost for pollution control over the decade from 1965-75 amounted to about 6 trillion yen. It was predicted at the beginning of the 1970s that another 20 trillion yen would become necessary over the decade from 1975-85, and that it would have a significant macroeconomic impact (Environment Agency 1977b, p. 26). But this prediction proved to be an overestimation. The energy consumptive industrial structure was changed due to increased energy prices. Control plants and equipment became available at moderate prices as they were widely disseminated (Study Group on the Global Environmental Economics, 1991, pp. 49-53).

The annual sale of pollution control devices and equipment is shown in Table 11.1. This covers the supply of devices and equipment to both private and public sectors. The share of water pollution control devices and equipment has been consistently large. In the early 1970s, the share of air pollution control was also large, as major investments were made in control plants and equipment, including precipitators and flue-gas desulfurization and denitrification equipment. Since the mid-1990s, the share of recycled solid waste is increasing sharply in accordance with the new policy priorities given to resource recycling and the formation of a 'sound material-cycle society'(*junkan-gata shakai*).

There are no statistics available regarding the costs of operating pollution control plants and equipment, but they can generally be assumed to be about 30 per cent of total fixed costs (Chikyu Kankyo Keizai Kenkyukai

1991, p. 35). Thus, these figures provide a rough estimation of the cost required to retrieve and maintain clean air and water in the country. While the cost was large, and may have had severe impacts on some specific economic sectors or industries, the effect on the total national economy was not very large. In the 1990s, the priority in environmental control technology shifted to the treatment and recycling of solid wastes, and recycling is becoming an important business sector in the national economy.

Table 11.1 Annual Sales of Environmental Devices and Equipment

Year	1970	1975	1980	1985	1990	1995	2000
Total (billion yen)	195	683	655	653	785	1,418	1,531
Share (%)							
Air	41.20	45.70	24.40	22.60	19.60	19.80	8.80
Water	47.10	43.30	53.80	49.40	49.40	37.80	40.00
Solid waste	11.40	10.70	20.80	27.40	29.60	41.70	53.00
Noise	0.27	0.23	0.99	0.58	0.83	0.60	0.22

Source: Japan Industrial Machinery Association 2001, pp. 18-19.

The Role of Cleaner Production Technology

The concepts of EP and CP

Generally, pollution control technologies are known as EP technology, which are used for the final treatment of wastes in the production process. At first Japanese industry was not willing to introduce EP technology voluntarily, as it increased the fixed costs of production. Likewise, economic difficulties have prevented developing countries from implementing pollution control measures. Unlike post-production EP technology, however, CP technology is a preventive treatment emphasizing resource and energy conservation, enabling more efficient use of resources and wastes based on recycling and the closed, cyclical use of materials and energy.

In the 1970s, Japanese industry had to meet strengthened environmental regulations while surviving the two oil crises. It was achieved by promoting resource and energy conservation, changing manufacturing methods, reusing waste products and developing cleaner technologies that did not impact productivity. Although those technologies were not adopted in a systematic manner, it quickly became obvious that primary CP technology was promising to improve productivity while protecting the environment (Ichimura 1992; Huisingh 1989; United Nations Environmental Programme 1993).

In 1975, the United Nations Environment Program (UNEP) established an Industry and Environment Program Activity Center in Paris. Japanese companies, however, were reluctant to disclose CP technologies as they were regarded as an expertise that heightened their competitiveness. The UNEP International Environmental Technology Center (UNEP-IETC) was established in Osaka in 1992 to facilitate dissemination of CP and other environmental technologies. Osaka Prefecture and Osaka City created the Global Environmental Center (GEC) to support the activities of UNEP-IETC. The GEC has developed a database of environmental technologies to facilitate technology transfer to developing countries. Included is information regarding technologies for air and water pollution control and continuous monitoring, waste management, on-site green technique, cleaner production, energy-saving at business-related buildings, soil and groundwater contamination surveys and countermeasures and advanced environmental equipment. GEC also provides training to developing country experts.

Application of CP technology to hazardous chemical substances
In Japan, CP technology now plays an important role in many industrial activities such as paper production, steel making, oil refining, sugar manufacturing, nonferrous metal manufacturing, metal plating and leather tanning (Kagaku-Kogyo-Nippo-sha 1991, pp. 13-98).

A good example of conversion to CP technology was in the production process of sodium hydroxide to prevent the use of mercury. The old mercury process was switched to the diaphragm process, and then to the ion-exchange membrane process, which is a CP technology. For changing from the mercury process to the ion-exchange membrane process, 421.4 billion yen was required, 334 billion yen of which was for system replacement, and 87.4 billion yen for pollution control. The Japanese government and the Japan Development Bank financially assisted companies to make this investment (Environment Agency 1974).

Industrial pollution control technology suitable for developing countries
From the viewpoint of business, pollution control technology is generally perceived as non-productive. Industry usually resists investing sufficient funds and personnel into pollution control. However, improving treatment efficiency can reduce the cost of environmental measures. If the cost of treatment technology does not add to the production cost, it will be more readily accepted by industry. In many cases, CP technology is more effective than EP technology. Unfortunately, the transfer of CP technology to developing countries is still very limited. It is essential for promoting technology transfer through multiple channels including not only official development assistance, but also through foreign direct investment and market-based pathways.

Introducing CP technology in developing countries

CP technology requires technical know-how. A close review of each CP technology is necessary to promote its transfer. A major concern here is the high initial cost, which often is an obstacle to the adoption of CP technologies in developing countries. Moreover, the operation and maintenance of CP technology requires technical expertise in such areas as chemistry, engineering, energy management and business administration. There are very few experts who possess these skills, even in developed countries. It is an urgent task for international technical cooperation to set up training programs for experts on CP technology in developing countries.

Strategic promotion of CP technology is a key for developing countries to achieve both production efficiency improvement and attainment of environmental goals. Pollution control experts in governments and companies, however, tend to think that EP technology is more reliable than CP technology for meeting effluent standards. This is because EP technology can be distinguished from other parts of the entire production system, and its environmental objectives can be differentiated from others. The CP technologies, however, can also lead to the modernization and improvement of production processes with positive environmental benefits.

The improvement of production lines is the first step to CP technology implementation. Even simple measures can achieve energy and resource saving, and waste reduction. The expenses required for such measures often can be recouped in a year or so. The introduction of the CP technology in the construction of new plants or the improvement of existing plants and production processes is relatively easy and inexpensive. Clean production technology should be introduced in planned stages. As an initial step, a new evaluation system (that includes the taking back of invested costs) to assess the value of raw materials and energy reduced through the CP technology should be adopted. The internationalization of environmental measures can be an encouragement to pioneering companies in CP technology, as cleaner suppliers will be more competitive in international markets.

The Basic Law for the Formation of a Sound Material-cycle Society

The central issues of concern in Japan's environmental policy have changed as new problems have emerged. Since the late 1980s, in particular, the volume of solid waste has expanded rapidly. People began to reflect upon the connections between their affluent lifestyles and the increase in the volume of wastes. They became concerned about the 'throwaway culture' in which the 'one-way-use' of products generates formidable amounts of waste and contributes to the rapid filling of Japan's very limited landfill space. Moreover, a number of improper landfill sites were discovered, where hazardous industrial wastes were being illegally dumped without necessary treatment, posing health risks to the people living in the vicinity.

Thus, transformation of our economic and social systems to a sound material-cycle society (*junkan-gata shakai*) became one of the top priorities of Japan's environmental policy, together with measures to prevent climate change due to the use of fossil fuels. National and local governments, as well as companies, are investing more in the development of technologies related to the recycling, reuse and recovery of resources, although these downstream measures alone are not sufficient. The Basic Environmental Law of 1993 took up the concept of recycling as a basic policy direction, and in June 2000, the government enacted the Basic Law for the Establishment of a Sound Material-cycle Society. At this time, five relevant laws also were amended (Ministry of the Environment 2003b, pp. 88-98). The management of municipal and industrial solid wastes is viewed as an urgent matter for both national and local environmental policy agendas. In terms of priorities, the law states that the 'reduction' at source should first be encouraged followed by reuse, material recycling, and thermal recycling.

In the development of a sound material-cycle society, it is necessary to encourage the establishment of production technologies that make the most effective use of energy and materials and take into consideration the whole life cycle of a product. Examples of new production technologies that do not require great investment in plant or equipment, and thus, should be developed are resource and energy-conserving processes, long-life products, recycling systems, maintenance technologies to extend equipment life and efficient physical distribution systems based on smaller transport mileage for materials.

Environmentally sound technologies for a sound material-cycle society

Until the central government reform in 2001, the Ministry of Health and Welfare (MHW) and MITI shared government administration of solid waste management. These two ministries dealt with the issue from different angles: MHW focused on public cleansing and safe disposal of municipal solid waste from households while MITI focused on the effective treatment and utilization of industrial waste. With the birth of the Ministry of the Environment (MOE), the municipal waste administration of MHW was moved to MOE's Department of Solid Waste and Recycling. MOE deals with solid waste issues with the aim of developing a sound material-cycle society.

Because of its limited landfill space, Japan adopted the incineration method for sanitary treatment and volume reduction of municipal wastes from households. It has about 1,715 modern incineration plants, which is the largest number of plants of any country in the world. In comparison, France has 260 and the USA 150 (Sakai 1999, p.8). Waste incineration, however, results in the release of dioxin. Dioxin is toxic and has been detected in the air and soil near incineration plants. This information led the public to question the appropriateness of solid waste treatment by incineration. In response, the MHW proposed that small-scale incineration plants be replaced with more advanced large-scale ones, which cannot only eliminate dioxins, but also are equipped with gas turbines for power generation and heat recovery.

In order to cope with the increasing volume and variety of waste, the increased difficulty of processing and the shortage of landfill space, there should be a fundamental change in waste disposal policy. Previously, waste disposal mainly consisted of 'burning and burying'. Currently, policy is being changed in order to transform the socioeconomic structure of Japan to recycling, by controlling the production of waste, recycling as much as possible of the waste that is produced and recovering the thermal energy from waste when it is burned (Ministry of the Environment 2003b, p. 154).

MUNICIPAL WASTE AND RESOURCE RECYCLING

Municipal Waste

Under the Waste Disposal Law, waste is divided into two major categories: general waste and industrial waste. The former type includes 'municipal waste', that is, household rubbish and other waste generated from individuals' and businesses' activities in cities. In Japan, municipal waste disposal had been regarded as the responsibility of municipalities. Now to some extent Japan follows the principle of 'extended producers' responsibility', the idea that producers should take care of the whole life cycle of their products, as a result of new recycling laws (Asano and Ori 1999). The Container Packaging Recycling Law, for example, lays down that producers should be responsible for the disposal of wastes derived from their products, but it requests municipal governments to provide collection service before wastes are handed over to the disposal by producers. Thus, most of the work related to collection and disposal of municipal waste still falls to municipalities.

The fundamental principles of municipal waste disposal are that the volume of waste should first be reduced by recycling, and then disposed of in a sanitary fashion so as not to harm the environment. Household waste is normally collected and transported by collection truck, and finally buried at landfill sites, either directly or after intermediate processing at incineration facilities. Intermediate processing is obligated in order to reduce the volume of waste and render it stable and harmless. In Japan, most intermediate processing is done in the form of incineration processing. In 2000, 94.1 per cent of waste received intermediate processing. As a result, the volume of waste buried at final disposal sites was 10.5 million tons, or about one-fifth of the total collected, which was 52.3 million tons. The rate of resource recovery from waste was a mere 14.3 per cent, or 7.9 million tons (Ministry of the Environment 2003b, p. 48).

A variety of costs are involved in waste disposal, from the salaries and wages of those involved in disposal to the cost of purchasing collection trucks and the cost of building intermediate processing and final disposal facilities. In 2000, these costs were about 2.38 trillion yen, and the per-person cost of waste disposal had risen to about 18,700 yen a year (Ministry of the Environment 2003b, p. 68). Costs are being driven up by rising construction and maintenance costs attributable to the deterioration of incinerators due to increased volume of waste with high calorific value, such as paper and plastic and the introduction of high-level processing for special environmental measures such as the control of dioxins.

Although the amount of waste buried has been reduced thanks to intermediate processing, the capacity of landfills is still inadequate and landfills in large metropolitan areas have few years of life left (Ministry of the Environment 2003b, p.75). It is extremely difficult to find land for constructing new landfills, because of the difficulty of gaining the approval of local residents. In the past, large cities located in coastal areas secured landfill sites in the sea. A huge area of land was created by dumping solid waste in coastal areas, such as around Tokyo Bay. However, because this caused the loss of wetlands, an important living environment for migratory birds and the degradation of the marine environment, it has become increasingly difficult to obtain public support for this method of waste disposal. In Nagoya City, for example, a landfill plan at Fujimae Higata presented by the municipal government was abandoned due to strong public protest in the late 1990s. The city changed its policy and enforced radical waste reduction measures such as segregated collection (Nagoya City 2001).

The Container Packaging Recycling Law

Because of changes in production, distribution and consumption structures that have accompanied changing lifestyles, not only is there more waste, but the makeup of waste has changed. Cans, bottles, plastic containers and other container and packaging waste make up about 60 per cent of the volume of the municipal waste stream and 25 per cent of its weight. Meanwhile, the resource recovery rate from municipal waste was only 14.3 per cent in 2000, a much lower level than for industrial waste, which has a recycling rate of about 45.4 per cent (Ministry of the Environment 2003b, pp. 48-50).

As of 1995, 65 per cent of municipalities practiced some form of source separation of recyclable wastes, and this ratio is increasing (Ministry of the

Environment 2003b, p. 52). The most frequently separated items are cans, bottles, PET bottles and other plastic. A barrier to the promotion of separate collection is that the cost to collect some recyclables may exceed income from their sale. Some businesses will not accept items (such as paper) for recycling unless the municipality is willing to bear the costs. The first reason for this low level of recycling is the difficulty of creating incentives for recycling and controlling waste production at the product manufacturing, distribution and consumption stages. Currently, most of the cost burden is borne by municipalities, which are responsible for waste collection. This means that the cost burden is not really borne by polluters.

There is a need to improve incentive systems in order to develop a sound material-cycle society (Ministry of the Environment 2003b, pp. 99-103). To this end, the Container Packaging Recycling Law of 1995 was enacted for promoting the recycling of container packaging, which is recyclable and represents a significant portion of the municipal waste stream. Under the law, responsibility for waste recycling is shared among consumers, municipalities and businesses, as a step towards having all parties cooperate actively in controlling waste production and promoting recycling (Ministry of the Environment 2003b, pp. 90-3).

Municipalities are in charge of collecting container packaging waste separately, and sorting, compressing and packing it into a form that is easy to recycle. The consumer is asked to cooperate with the municipality in source separation, by sorting recyclables. The law defines 'designated businesses' as those that use specific containers or those which are targeted for remerchandising, manufacture or import specific containers and use specific kinds of packaging. Designated businesses are responsible for remerchandising the container packaging waste collected by the municipalities to the extent that they use or manufacture such items. A similar rule for burden sharing among consumers, municipalities and businesses was adopted in subsequent legislation covering different types of products, such as home electric appliances and cars. In other words, consumers have to bear the cost of waste disposal while businesses are obliged to collect used products and treat them properly.

Waste disposal facilities
In order to promote recycling, various facilities have been established. They include recycling centers, recycling plazas and other recycling-related facilities where the source-separated cans, bottles and other recyclables collected by the municipalities can be sorted and compressed. For bulk waste disposal, national subsidies are provided for the establishment of facilities not only for crushing and compressing bulk waste, but also for sorting and reusing the recyclable items.

For promoting power generation by waste incineration facilities, public subsidies were expanded beginning in 1995 to include not only the energy consumed by existing facilities, but also electricity that is supplied to nearby public facilities and electricity generated in order to provide a stable supply to sell to electrical utilities. At all continuous-feed waste incineration facilities built from 1996 onwards, efforts have been made to establish electrical power generation capabilities (Takasugi 1999; Ministry of the Environment 2003b, pp. 68-70).

Industrial waste management

Disposal of industrial waste is the responsibility of the business that produces the waste. A business can either dispose of the waste itself, or contract with an industrial waste disposal company.

The total volume of industrial waste produced in 2000 was about 406 million tons, or about eight times the amount of municipal waste. And although the volume of municipal waste has begun to decrease, the volume of industrial waste remains stable or is even growing slightly. The volume of waste has been reduced by about 177 million tons (about 44 per cent) through intermediate processing. About 184 million tons (45 per cent) is recycled, and the remaining 45 million tons (11 per cent) is finally disposed of by burial or other means. The remaining life of existing final disposal sites for industrial waste was 3.9 years throughout the country as of the end of 2000, and only 1.2 years in the Tokyo Metropolitan Area, so the situation is much more urgent than it is for municipal waste (Ministry of the Environment 2003b, p. 75).

Meanwhile, illegal dumping and other forms of improper disposal continue to be rampant. Based on arrest records, the National Police Agency estimates that more than one million tons of industrial waste has been dumped illegally every year since 1990 (Ministry of the Environment 2003b, pp. 75-8). Such illegal dumping gives industrial waste a bad name, making it more difficult to secure disposal facilities and it is one factor standing in the way of a solution to the current landfill crisis.

Safe treatment of industrial waste

Industrial waste may contain harmful substances that are produced during manufacturing and processing. In order to prevent the environmental pollution that can accompany the production and disposal of such industrial waste, new standards have been enforced. Businesses that produce a large volume of industrial waste are being instructed by prefectural governors to develop disposal plans and a recycling designation system to promote smooth recycling by manufacturers and processors.

Establishment of industrial waste disposal facilities is difficult due to opposition from local residents. In many cases, people dislike the idea of

Box 11.2 The Kitakyushu Eco-Town Project

As an old industrial city, Kitakyushu retains vast land areas which were once developed for the siting of industrial facilities, but are almost abandoned today. The city also has an accumulation of technologies for the processing of metals, chemicals and other materials that can be applied to the development of resource recycling and recovery technologies. Examples include the gasification-melting technology developed from blast furnace technology. Kitakyushu presented a new urban industrial development policy to invite recycling and other eco-industries to its unused reclaimed land sites in the Hibikinada area.

In 1997, MITI launched the 'Eco-Town Project' to provide assistance to local governments, which were planning to achieve regional development through the promotion of environmental industry. Local governments are requested to make master plans. If the plans are approved by MITI, local governments can receive various forms of financial aid from the national government, including subsidies to private companies that agree to construct recycling and other facilities, and financial support for the exhibition of eco-technologies.

Kitakyushu is one of the first eco-towns to be designated by MITI. Its plan was centered on two projects: construction of an eco-industrial complex (or 'environmental kombinat'), and the research center for the verification of recycling technologies. The city provides various benefits to small and medium-sized companies for the incubation of diverse technologies. So far, recycling factories for PET-bottles, cars, electric appliances and construction materials have started operation in the Hibikinada area, and the number of factories is increasing.

The ultimate aim of the Kitakyushu eco-town is not only to develop recycling industries, but also to create a new industrial system in which resources are most efficiently utilized through the cooperation of production, distribution and resource recovery and recycling industries (Environment Agency 1998, pp. 81-95).

industrial waste and feel anxiety and distrust towards landfills and other disposal facilities and those who operate them, a classic 'not in my backyard' (NIMBY) problem. Meanwhile, illegal dumping and other forms of inappropriate disposal continue to be common, increasing the uneasiness that local residents feel about industrial waste disposal and making it even more difficult to secure disposal facilities. It is necessary to break this vicious circle in order to secure highly safe and reliable industrial waste disposal facilities. Central and local governments started an effort to comprehensively reform the industrial waste disposal system through measures aimed at ensuring disposal facilities that are safe and reliable, preventing illegal dumping and restoring dump sites to their original condition. The Kitakyushu Eco-Town Project, which is a model of industrial development based on recycling technologies and is promoted by METI is one such effort (Environment Agency 1998, pp. 81-95) (Box 11.2).

DEVELOPMENT OF CLEAN CARS

Automobiles are major consumers of oil and sources of air pollutants and greenhouse gases. Development of clean cars (*teikogaisha* or cars with lower pollutant emissions) is a big challenge for automobile manufacturers. Measures to be taken by the transportation sector include improving the fuel efficiency of gasoline and diesel engine cars and developing technology to reduce the emission of air pollutants. To achieve this goal, efforts are being made to improve internal-combustion engine-building technology (the adoption of a lean-burn engine of the direct injection type) and hybrid-electric cars (which are powered by a combination of an electric motor and a gasoline engine). Some carmakers have successfully developed these technologies for commercial application. In addition, attention is being focused on methods of dispensing with car idling and reducing drag on cars (the reduction of car weight) as a means to improve fuel economy.

The development of clean cars, such as electric, methanol, compressed natural gas, solar, hydrogen, gas-turbine and stirling-engine cars and cars that operate alternately on gasoline and LPG is also being promoted. The electric car has already entered the commercialization stage and other clean cars are under development (Ministry of the Environment 2003a, pp. 114-19; Ministry of the Environment 2003c). Emissions of CO_2 from railroad cars per ton of cargo are much smaller than that of motor vehicles. Therefore, efforts are being made under the initiative of the Japan Freight Railway to accelerate a modal shift from trucks to new types of locomotives, container freight cars and piggyback cars (Ministry of the Environment 2003a, p.119). Finally, steps are being taken to encourage the recycling of obsolete cars from the standpoint of efficiently utilizing resources and of curbing CO_2 emissions. In addition, tax incentives aimed at encouraging the use of clean cars are being considered.

Development of More Energy-efficient Cars

Both the Environment Agency (EA) and the Ministry of Transportation have published reports focusing on the reduction of CO_2 emissions from automobiles (Global Environmental Department 1992b; Committee on Transportation Policy 1999; Committee on Transportation Technology 1998). The reports list the development of clean cars as a policy measure of high priority to be taken over the short and medium term. They recommend that the development of technology for improving the fuel efficiency of gasoline- and diesel-engine cars to achieve the goal set by the Energy-Saving Law (the Law Concerning the Rational Use of Energy) be pursued vigorously. As policy measures for the medium term, they suggest the necessity of developing and spreading the ownership of hybrid-electric compact cars that run on electricity and gasoline and medium and large-size compressed natural gas cars (Ohta 2000).

Electric cars are environmentally friendly in that they emit only half as much CO_2 as diesel engines, even when the emission from electricity generation is taken into account. In addition, they emit very little NO_x. The main reasons why an increase in their ownership has not occurred are their low economic efficiency and limited driving range compared with gasoline and diesel cars. For similar reasons, the dissemination of clean cars has been slow. In order to provide greater incentives for clean car development, Prime Minister Jun'ichiro Koizumi decided in May 2001 that 7,000 cars owned by the government should be replaced by clean cars. According to the plan, the number of clean cars owned by the government should increase from a mere 316 in 2000 to 7,021 in 2004, 4,180 of which are to be hybrid cars. Following this initiative, METI, the Ministry of Land, Infrastructure and Transport, and Ministry of Environment (MOE) developed an Action Plan for Development and Diffusion of Clean Cars with a target of disseminating 10 million clean cars into the country by 2020 (Ministry of the Environment 2002a).

Recent government reports not only suggest the technology development for reducing CO_2 emissions by cars, but also propose policy measures to be taken in step with the technology development (Kashima 2000). They propose 'eco-conscious driving', such as automatic stopping of the engine rather than allowing the idling of parked cars, strict observance of speed limits on expressways, encouragement of shared riding to office and home, discouragement of loading cars with goods not immediately needed and the maintenance of air pressure in tires at prescribed levels. They also point out the necessity for educating drivers on eco-conscious driving on various occasions such as the acquisition and renewal of a driver's license.

CONCLUSION

Pollution control technologies require substantial investments and maintenance costs. But without such technologies, countries will not be able to modernize their industrial processes. With respect to the cost of new technologies, one can draw lessons from the Japanese experience in the development and dissemination of control technologies. In Japan where environmental pollution caused serious damages to human health, due to strong public pressure and eventual government adoption of regulations and other measures, various sophisticated pollution control technologies were applied despite high costs. At first it was felt that the use of such technologies as flue-gas desulfurization and denitrification would not be economically feasible. Costs, however, were reduced rapidly once technical feasibility was proven and the market for control technologies was expanded. The dissemination of environmental technology further accelerated technical innovation and made its production more cost-effective and resource-efficient.

Countries must choose the most appropriate technical options given their economic and environmental requirements. Developed countries should provide technical information and data to help developing countries determine the most appropriate technical options for dealing with environmental problems. The focus should be on the 'environmental soundness' of technologies, combining long-term economic objectives and environmental quality considerations.

Environmental measures that were once implemented locally are now being adopted on a global basis. In some instances, the establishment of laws and the development of treatment technologies have proven successful at reducing or eliminating pollutants produced by industrial activities. Still, much remains to be done. A good example is the need to develop effective technologies to reduce CO_2 emissions. Innovative environmental conservation technologies will be necessary for future generations. Clean production technologies should be employed for the conservation of energy and resources in the daily lives of citizens in all nations.

12. Japan's Environmental Management Experiences: Strategic Implications for Asia's Developing Countries

Yong Ren

INTRODUCTION

Japan was the first nation in the Asian region to experience rapid economic growth. This meant that Japan also was the first nation in the area to face serious industrial pollution problems. Japan eventually managed to control its industrial pollution achieving a kind of 'anti-pollution miracle' that followed upon its 'economic miracle'.

Japan's anti-pollution miracle can be attributed to its successful environmental management programs. The national government adopted and enforced stringent environmental regulations and made effective use of the cooperative relationship that exists between government and industry to promote pollution control. It also helped finance pollution control technology research and development and guide the shift to a more energy efficient economy. Part of the anti-pollution miracle was dealing with urban environmental pollution, a problem that is pervasive in Asia today. The Japanese government has made huge investments in urban environmental infrastructure development, including sewage treatment, waste disposal facilities and green buffer zones.

Many developing countries in Asia have been trying to duplicate Japan's economic success, and some have achieved rather significant economic growth rates. Unfortunately, these countries are now facing serious industrial pollution problems similar to the ones that Japan faced in the late 1960s and early 1970s. Asian countries should learn from Japan's relatively strong record since the 1970s in pollution control.

The main objectives of this chapter are to examine the reasons behind Japan's successful environmental management experiences and consider the lessons this history may hold for Asia's developing countries. In contrast with much of the environmental policy literature on Japan that is the work of scholars from developed countries, this study is done explicitly with developing countries in mind. Particular attention is focused on aspects of Japan's environmental history that are pertinent for developing countries.

The chapter consists of three sections. The first section provides a brief overview of environmental management programs in Japan making some comparisons with China, South Korea, Thailand and the Philippines. The second section examines factors that were key to Japan's environmental management success. The third section considers the strengths and weaknesses of Japan's environmental management approach and its applicability to developing countries.

ECONOMIC GROWTH, ENVIRONMENTAL POLLUTION AND ENVIRONMENTAL POLICY SYSTEMS IN ASIA

A wave of rapid economic growth swept over Asia, beginning with Japan in the 1960s, followed by South Korea and Taiwan. Economies of other Asian countries, including Thailand, Malaysia and Indonesia, grew rapidly in subsequent decades, and most recently, China joined the league, with a remarkable gross domestic product (GDP) growth rate of over 11 per cent per annum from 1990-96. Rapid economic growth accelerated industrialization, urbanization and the transformation to mass consumption societies. Serious environmental problems emerged as a result.

Because Japan was the first nation in the region to experience massive economic growth and resulting pollution problems, it also was the first nation in the region to establish national environmental management programs. As other countries in the region began to experience serious pollution problems as a result of rapid economic growth, they also began to create pollution control programs. Japan started its national response to industrial pollution in the mid-1960s, symbolized by the enactment of the nation's first environmental law, the 1967 Basic Law of Environmental Pollution Control. Most other countries in the region started to develop national environmental programs in the late 1970s or later. South Korea, one of the first nations that successfully followed Japan's economic success, enacted its first national environmental law in 1977. China, the most recent example of an Asian economic miracle, established a national environmental agency in 1982, 11 years after Japan established its Environment Agency in 1971 (Table 12.1).

Table 12.2 summarizes national environmental management systems in five Asian countries. It shows when each country enacted a basic environmental law, what environmental policies are in place to deal with various pollution and conservation issues, and whether there are additional mechanisms to address issues such as the effects of development projects, environmental finance, environment-related disputes and environmental research and development (R&D). It shows that Japan and South Korea have well-developed environmental management systems. Basic environmental regulations are already in place in China, Thailand and the Philippines. While these relative latecomers have developed some mechanisms to deal with pollution issues, in many cases there is not sufficient legislation in place or support in the form of environmental financing, R&D and dispute resolution systems, for environmental protection efforts to be very effective.

Table 12.1 Establishment of Environmental Governance Systems in Asia

Country	Establishment of national environmental Administration	First national environmental legislation	First local environmental regulation
Japan	1971	1967	1949 (Tokyo)
China	1982 (1988, 1998)	1979	No evidence before early 1980s
S. Korea	1980 (1990)	(1963) 1977	No evidence before 1975
Thailand	1975 (1992)	(1975) 1992	No evidence
Philippines	1977 (1986, 1997)	1977	No evidence

Source: The World Bank 2000; Japan Environmental Council 2000.

JAPAN'S ENVIRONMENTAL MANAGEMENT EXPERIENCES

Developing countries in Asia that followed Japan's lead in their quest for economic growth also have begun to feel the negative impacts of rapid economic growth. As Asia's developing countries learned a great deal from Japan's economic success, they also can learn important lessons from Japan's environmental management experiences.

Identifying factors that were key to Japan's success in environmental management requires a holistic approach. Jänicke and Weidner (1997, p. 4) argue that in order to understand why a nation succeeds or fails in managing environmental problems, one must consider a number of factors and their complex interactions. No single, isolated factor determines environmental policy outcomes. It is, for example, important to have strict environmental regulations, but the mere existence of regulations is not sufficient; rules must also be enforced by an effective and reliable enforcement agency. Similarly, the availability of funds and technologies also is important to effective implementation. The presence or absence of political interest in environmental protection can influence which regulations are formulated and aggressively implemented. Additionally, social norms and cultural values influence people's views about the environment, and the economic and technological development of a nation impacts environmental conditions. In short, a comprehensive view is necessary to understand how these factors interact.

Table 12.2 National Environmental Management Systems in Asia

Countries/Policies		Japan	China	S. Korea	Thailand	Philippines
Basic environmental policy		Yes (67, 93)	Yes (79, 89)	Yes (63,77,90)	Yes (75, 92)	Yes (75)
Env'l pollution control	Air	Yes (68)	Yes (87,95)	Yes (90, 99)		Yes (99)
	Water	Yes (70)	Yes (67,93)	Yes (90, 99)	Yes	Yes
	Sea	Yes (70)	Yes (82)			Yes
	Automobile exhausts	Yes (72,92)			Yes	Yes
	Soil	Yes (70)		Yes (95, 99)		
	Noise	Yes (68)	Yes (96)	Yes (96)		
	Solid waste	Yes (70)	Yes (95)	Yes (86,99)		
	Toxic materials	Yes (73)		Yes (90, 99)	Yes (92)	Yes (90)
	Sewage	Yes		Yes (66,99)		
Nature Conservation		Yes (72)		Yes (91,99)		Yes (78)
Environmental Impact Assessment (EIA)		Yes (97)		Yes (93,99)		
Financing		Yes		Yes		
Environmental disputes resolution		Yes		Yes		
Environmental R&D				Yes (94,99)		

Notes: [a]'Yes' indicates that there is a specific law in place and a number(s) in parenthesis ('93, 99') shows the year in which the law was enacted (and amended); [b]a 'blank' cell means that no specific law is in place, but there are relevant laws and/or regulations available to address the problem in question.
Sources: Japan Environment Council 2000; Institute for Global Environmental Strategies 1999 and 2000.

A holistic view of environmental management tells us that setting formal rules to structure and regulating complex relations among the many factors involved in environmental management is important. For example, an effective environmental administrative body must be established to oversee and coordinate activities. Formal rules and regulations are necessary to protect the environment from harmful industrial activities. At the same time, however, the issue of economic development cannot be ignored. A major challenge is figuring out how to balance environmental protection and economic development. Successful environmental management strategies include developing the necessary institutional capabilities.

A review of Japan's environmental management experiences tells us that the following four factors were key to Japan's success: the use of cooperative approaches in environmental governance; the integration of environmental protection with technological and economic development; the development and rigid enforcement of environmental policy and; large-scale investment in environmental technology development and environmental protection.

Strategic Implications of Japan's Environmental Management Experience for Asia's Developing Countries

Four major lessons for Asia's developing countries can be drawn from Japan's experiences with environmental management. To succeed in managing environmental issues, it is important to: 1) approach environmental issues in a cooperative manner; 2) balance economic development and environmental protection; 3) build an effective national environmental policy system; and 4) develop environmental finance mechanisms. This section examines each of these factors and their relevance for Asia's developing countries.

Cooperative Approach to Environmental Governance

The actors involved in environmental governance include national and local governments, business organizations, media, non-governmental organizations (NGOs), citizens and citizens' groups. Good environmental governance requires the involvement of all relevant actors and the development of cooperative relationships among them. Cooperation among actors can lead to collective actions for environmental protection. It can also help to develop shared environmental values. When cooperative decision-making structures exist, even when disagreement among actors is not resolved, the creativity of collective efforts can be enhanced (Loehman and Kilgour 1998, p. 5).

In Japan prior to the 1990s, environmental governance could be characterized as following a hierarchical model where environmental governance was largely viewed as an executive activity. While ministries and agencies were at the top of the hierarchy, there were also elements of what could be called a network model because there was some involvement in environmental decision making on the part of businesses, citizens and NGOs. Since the 1990s, more emphasis has been placed on developing partnerships among government, business, citizens, NGOs and other civil society actors. Thus, the hierarchical model has been weakened with time as Japan becomes more pluralistic in its decision-making processes.

Currently in Japan, environmental problems are tied to so many aspects of the society and the economy that many actors are involved in policy making.

There is deep involvement by both economic and public sector actors in environmental governance. This helps to assure that environmental matters are considered in industrial and general infrastructure development.

Inter-ministerial Conflict and Cooperation

Japan's administrative system is characterized by power sharing. Power sharing helps to bring all government agencies and departments together; it breeds both conflict and cooperation. While the Environment Agency (EA) assumed general responsibilities for policy development and coordination, the Ministry of International Trade and Industry (MITI), the Ministry of Construction and the Ministry of Health and Welfare contributed considerably to industrial pollution control, municipal waste management and urban environmental infrastructure construction. Indeed, only 2.78 per cent of the total national environmental budget from 1995-97 was allocated to the EA; the rest of the budget was distributed among other ministries and agencies. Inter-ministerial negotiations have been extremely important for dealing with conflict and encouraging cooperation in both policy making and enforcement processes in Japan. It should be noted, however, that power sharing often requires considerable time and energy to reach a consensus among relevant administrative agencies.

It would be wrong to portray environmental policy making in Japan as harmonious. There has been much conflict between relevant ministries and agencies, industries and environmental groups over issues relating to environmental management. Before the 1970s, such conflict was strong enough that some policy proposals failed. For instance, attempts to pass an environmental impact assessment law failed repeatedly because they met strong and persistent resistance from ministries representing industrial groups. As a result the EIA Law did not pass until 1997.

In an effort to deal with the kind of power imbalance that resulted in this kind of delay in environmental policy development, the Japanese government decided to take steps to strengthen environmental perspectives in the policy making process. The government restructured the Central Pollution Control Council as the Central Environment Council (CEC) in 1993 to create an additional venue for environmental policy coordination and consultation (Box 12.1). It also elevated the EA to the status of Ministry of the Environment (MOE) in 2001. The Environment Ministry should be in a better position than the EA was in terms of its negotiation power and its ability to act as an equal in inter-ministerial coordination efforts. This should help reduce the costs involved in consensus building.

In many developing countries, environmental power within the government is often quite centralized. South Korea's Ministry of the Environment (MoE) and the Philippines' Department of Environment and

Natural Resource (DENR), for example, have considerable responsibilities and power. South Korea's MoE is responsible not only for environmental protection, but also tap water supply, sewage treatment and solid waste management, policy areas that the Japanese MOE does not even have jurisdiction over. The Philippines' DENR's responsibilities include mineral resources, land, forest and ecosystems, protected areas, wildlife protection, pollution control, sewage treatment and solid waste management. This list is also broader than that covered by Japan's MOE.

Box 12.1   Central Environment Council in Japan

The 1993 Basic Environment Law established the CEC, which reports to the prime minister and the minister of the environment. The CEC provides a venue for policy consultations and negotiations. The CEC consists of 10 subcommittees and each subcommittee specializes in a major pollution category, such as air or water pollution. The CEC consists of representatives from Japan's academic research community, industrial groups, labor groups, citizens' organizations and retired government officials. Having a wide variety of groups represented in the council means that scientific, industrial and societal views are heard. Not only are economic and technological considerations considered, but also the social acceptability and equity dimensions of policy are analyzed. The CEC, thus, promotes both scientific and democratic policy making and societal understanding. Some CEC meetings are open to the public. In public hearings, the CEC explains policy proposals to the public and receives public comment on them. Following national example, local governments also have environmental councils to consult them.

Source: Ren 2000, p. 83.

A major advantage of a more power-centralized structure within the government for environmental protection (but that still is pluralistic in the sense that external actors have access to decision makers), such as Japan recently has moved towards with the creation of its MOE and exists in many developing countries in Asia, is that governmental responsibilities for environmental matters are more centralized and power relations among ministries more equal. In other words, compared with systems where environmental responsibilities are divided across many ministries and agencies, in a more power-centralized executive structure, the administrative body overseeing environmental affairs is subject to less influence from other ministries that may have other goals than protecting the environment. Such a system is better for promoting environmental protection measures.

The other side of the coin, however, is that the power-centralized system leaves less room for policy consultation and discussions with other government agencies and some outside bodies. Policy implementation and enforcement, therefore, is also less likely to be carried out in cooperation with others. A potential major disadvantage of this type of system is that available administrative resources are less likely to be utilized fully. By cooperating with other government officials, environmental officials can make use of the additional resources held by other government agencies. Policy ideas, professional and technical expertise and administrative skills are examples of additional resources that can be 'borrowed' from other agencies.

In light of Japan's successful experience and its cooperative approach to environmental management issues, it may be worthwhile for Asia's developing countries to reexamine their management styles and explore ways to cooperate more with other government agencies and/or outside groups.

National-local Government Cooperation

A relatively high degree of decentralization is desirable in environmental policy making. Local governments can contribute significantly to successful environmental management. First, local governments understand much more about their local problems and conditions than national governments possibly can. It is easier for them to formulate policy measures that suit their specific needs and conditions. Second, local governments are closer to citizens and know much more about their needs. Local governments can provide a practical venue for citizens, citizens' groups and NGOs to participate in their local affairs. Third, local governments are smaller and local rules are simpler. Many local governments have higher managerial efficiency and lower coordination costs. Effective and efficient local governments can play a leading role in environmental governance.

Decentralization implies that subnational units of government have substantial political, fiscal and administrative powers. Far more than the national government, local governments in Japan are the ones that have had to respond directly to pollution victims' and citizens' complaints about environmental quality. Since local leaders in Japan are democratically elected, they are influenced by public opinion. Thus, as local citizens' concerns with environmental degradation grew in Japan, local leaders had to pay more attention to the environment (Ren 2000, pp. 84-5). Perhaps as a result, it is not surprising that local governments have played a pioneering and leading role in local environmental governance since as early as the 1960s. They responded to industrial pollution control much earlier than the national government. For example, many local governments adopted proactive measures like the EIA before the national government started to consider adopting an EIA ordinance or law. Some progressive localities set environmental standards that were stricter than the national standards and many adopted pollution control agreements. Innovative localities have taken new initiatives, launching interesting and unique local environmental projects. The 'Eco-Town Project' in Kitakyushu is an example. Local governments have been more actively involved than the national government in local environmental management issues, including in relation to industrial development, urban planning and urban infrastructure construction.

Japan's national government has developed cooperative relationships with local governments to support their local environmental management efforts. Japan's environmental management experience involves considerable cooperation between the central government and local governments. The Japanese government has provided local governments with grants, subsidies and other financial assistance to help them build environmental monitoring facilities, engage in environmental R&D and carry out various local public works projects. These assistance programs have contributed significantly to increase local institutional capacities to deal with environmental problems.

Japan's environmental management experience suggests that joint efforts by national and local governments can contribute significantly to successful environmental management. In many developing countries local governments lack institutional capacities to play a leading role in local environmental management. Japan's experience suggests that financial assistance from the central government can help local governments develop institutional capacities for environmental protection. This includes financial aid, personnel training, transfer of policy know-how and development of technological expertise.

Of course, relations between central and local governments vary by political system type and level of economic development. In countries where local governments lack sufficient interest in environmental conservation because their primary concern lies with economic development, the national government's leadership and policy support are critical. In countries where local interest in environmental protection is weak, rapid decentralization can exacerbate environmental problems due to lack of environmental policy enforcement. This suggests that decentralization of environmental governance should be done gradually and as local capacities and interests in environmental protection expand.

Administrative powers and finance distribution have been notably decentralized in China since the 1980s. The local share of total public expenditures (55.6 per cent) and total tax revenue (51.4 per cent) is higher than it is in Japan, South Korea, Thailand or the Philippines. Still, in countries like China where grassroots pressures for environmental protection remain weak and local governmental environmental management capacity remains inadequate, top-down management by the central government remains necessary. This is the case even though in terms of managerial efficiency, it is more cost-effective when local governments and other actors play more active roles in environmental protection. An example of an effective top-down approach for environmental protection was China's national government's initiative to develop a quantitative environmental performance review system. The quantitative review system succeeded in generating interest in urban environmental management and contributed significantly to urban environmental improvement in many cities and towns (Box 12.2).

Box 12.2 Environmental Performance by China's Cities

To deal more effectively with urban environmental problems, China developed a quantitative environmental performance review system. Since 1989 the system has been used by the State Environmental Protection Administration (SEPA) to assess city governments' and their mayors' efforts and achievements in urban environmental management. Participating cities are annually ranked according to numerical standards set by SEPA. These include 26 indicators divided into four groupings: environmental quality, pollution prevention and abatement, environmental infrastructure and environmental governance. SEPA ranks 47 major urban areas, provincial governments, municipalities and communities in their jurisdictions. Results of the rankings are published in newspapers and SEPA's annual reports. Currently, 609 cities or 91 per cent of Chinese cities have been reviewed in this system. The publication of findings places great pressure on urban governments, mayors and citizens to improve their city's ranking.

Source: National Environmental Protection Agency, China, 1994.

Business Cooperation

Perhaps because the costs of avoiding pollution control in the 1960s ended up being so high, Japanese corporations now generally cooperate with governmental efforts to set environmental standards and comply with the nation's environmental regulations. From the outside, it appears that they are quite willing to monitor and regulate their own activities to ensure that their activities will not cause serious environmental problems. Many Japanese businesses now appear to view good environmental citizenship as necessary for their image or even to improve market share. Environmental auditing systems, life cycle assessment and International Standard Organization (ISO) 14000 environmental management series have been introduced in many companies. Keidanren issued a Voluntary Action Plan on the Environment in

1997. Following Keidanren's example, 32 federations and associations also published sectoral voluntary action plans.

Box 12.3   Japanese Corporate Culture and Environmental Performance

Japanese companies today still retain features of family-based companies. It is common, for example, for Japanese companies to make pronouncements stressing that their success must be honestly won with the best interests of society in mind. Japanese companies typically employ a line-of-command or 'do as ordered from the top' approach to management, which combines the concept of the household with modern business management. As a result, when top management decides to invest in environmental protection, it generally can do so quite effectively. Also important is that middle-management is typically technically skilled. This has aided in the introduction and operation of pollution control equipment and facilities.

Another characteristic of Japanese corporate culture is that many large corporations are affiliated with small and medium-sized companies in a network of common-interest-entities; there is considerable mutual stock holding among them. When the environmental behavior of the parent company in this kind of network changes, it often has a strong influence on its small and medium-sized subsidiaries and affiliated companies.

Source: Ren 2000, p. 87.

It is useful to distinguish between 'quasi-voluntary' and 'voluntary action'. Margaret Levi uses the term 'quasi-voluntary compliance' to describe taxpayers' behavior in a system where most taxpayers pay taxes even though they are not directly coerced by authorities. Compliance is 'voluntary' to the extent that individual taxpayers are not directly coerced when they decide whether or not to pay their taxes. Compliance is really only 'quasi-voluntary', however, because individual taxpayers also know that tax evasion is illegal and punishable (Ostrom 1997, p. 94). It could be argued that many Japanese corporations 'quasi-voluntarily' comply with environmental regulations and standards, because they know that regulators enforce regulations strictly and reliably, that society watches their actions and that non-compliance is not in their best interest. The potential costs of avoiding pollution control measures include suspension of business operations, paying the costs of compensating for pollution damage and decrease in product sales due to poor public image. Yet, there is also reason to believe that Japanese industries are shifting towards more genuine 'voluntary action'.

Japan's experience suggests that well-defined regulatory standards and strict and reliable enforcement mechanisms are keys to induce business corporations' 'quasi-voluntary' compliance with environmental regulations. Many Japanese companies have established pollution control departments, developed their own environmental management programs and hired pollution control managers to ensure compliance and avoid penalties (see Chapter 10). Social pressures such as public opinion, anti-pollution protests and citizens' claims for pollution damages have played an important role in inducing 'quasi-voluntary' compliance by businesses. Japan's corporate culture has also contributed significantly to businesses' quality environmental performance (Box 12.3). In addition, Japan's industrial associations have played a significant role in developing a cooperative government business relationship, exchanging information about environmental technologies and experiences, and coordinating private corporations' environmental management efforts (Box 12.4).

Box 12.4   Japanese Business Associations and Environmental Cooperation

Japan's industrial associations play a central role in coordinating pollution control efforts in the private sector. These associations, as representatives of a large number of Japanese manufacturers and producers, often negotiate with national and local government officials about policies that affect them, such as energy, regional development and pollution control programs. This helps ensure that national and local environmental policies are developed taking into consideration technical and economic feasibility concerns. Since the association negotiates on behalf of all member companies, this also means that the economic risk to a particular firm of taking costly pollution control measures is reduced since all members of the association must abide by the same regulations. Japanese industrial associations also play an important role in providing technical training to workers, facilitating information exchange and developing a better understanding of various rules and regulations at the local and national level. Keidanren, the largest economic association in Japan, has recently launched a voluntary environmental management program on behalf of Japan's industrial circle.

Source: Ren 2000, p. 88.

Many developing countries are struggling with the issue of non-compliance. Japan's experience suggests that strict environmental regulations and reliable enforcement mechanisms are keys to addressing non-compliance issues. Indeed, it is noteworthy that over 65 per cent of Japanese enterprises now have pollution control departments and there are approximately 23,000 pollution control supervisors and 40,000 pollution control managers in the country (Ren 2000, p. 86). It is also significant that in cases of serious or deliberate non-compliance with the law, they can be arrested. Well-defined standards and reliable enforcement mechanisms are necessary to induce private companies' 'quasi-voluntary' compliance with environmental regulations.

Public Cooperation

The public also has contributed significantly to Japan's improved environmental management performance. During the 1960s, when industrial pollution became a serious problem, pollution-related victims and their families and friends played an indispensable role in educating politicians, government and corporate officials and the general public about the negative health effects of industrial pollution (Ren 2000, p. 93). Citizens had personal incentives to monitor both polluters and regulators.

The industrial pollution problems of the 1960s also drew significant media attention. The media played a significant role in informing the public of the serious health consequences of industrial pollution. The media remains an important actor on the environmental management scene.

The Japanese government over the years has developed various formal rules and regulations to support public participation in environmental governance. Environmental dispute resolution and compensation systems have become more formalized and institutionalized since the end of the era of serious industrial pollution problems (the early 1970s). The establishment of the CEC in 1993 is a more recent example that illustrates the government's interest in public participation in environmental management. As discussed earlier (Box 12.1), the Japanese government established the CEC to further encourage public participation in environmental policy making. The Japanese government has also become more open to information disclosure. More data and information are now accessible to the public, especially environmental quality data. Areas that could still be made more open, even in Japan, are information about environmental policy making, the environmental performance data of both public and private sectors and information about major polluters and their pollutant discharge records.

Many countries in Asia also recognize the importance of public participation in environmental management. The constitutions of many Asian countries designate a healthy and clean environment as a citizen's right. Environmental quality information is increasingly accessible to the public. The Chinese government publishes a weekly report on environmental quality in China. The report has significantly increased the public interest in environmental protection. Another example is Indonesia's Clean Rivers Program. The Program publicized data on the volume of pollutants discharged by plants and factories in Indonesia. As a result of this program, pollution discharge into waterways came under the close scrutiny of the public; public pressure forced polluters to reduce their emissions. The total discharges from the 100 plants participating in the program were reduced by one-third between 1989-94 (World Bank 2000, p. 24). These are examples of how, through information disclosure, corporations can be persuaded to alter their behavior because of their concern about their image with consumers and stockholders.

BALANCING ECONOMIC GROWTH AND ENVIRONMENTAL PROTECTION

Impacts of Environmental Investment on the National Economy

One of the most valuable lessons we can learn from Japan's environmental management experience is that environmental protection does not necessarily retard economic growth. In fact, the Organization for Economic Cooperation and Development (OECD) (1994, p. 95) concluded that: 'During the last two decades, Japan had the largest economic growth among G7 countries, while substantially reducing emissions of a number of pollutants, notably air pollutants and containing the growth of others. For instance, while GDP increased by 122 per cent, SO_2 emissions decreased by 82 per cent and nitrogen oxide (NO_x) emissions by 21 per cent, the best performance among OECD countries. Such 'decoupling' is a necessary condition for moving economic growth towards sustainable development.'

The Japanese experience shows that from long-term and macro perspectives, environmental investment can promote social and economic development. New environmental regulations created incentives to innovate production and manufacturing technologies. New business opportunities arose as a result of an increase in environmental investment. Environmental facility manufacturing and related service sectors were born. Net job creation appears to have been neutral or slightly positive (Environment Agency 1994, p. 164).

Environmental facility manufacturing and related service sectors grew over the years. Today, air pollution control device manufacturers produce almost 200 billion yen worth of equipment annually (Figure 12.1). In the period from 1966-95, production of air pollution control devices amounted to 6.6 trillion yen or US $46.7 billion in 1990 dollars (Committee on Japan's Experience in the Battle against Air Pollution 1997, p. 76). According to this report, the annual production value of waste treatment facilities is about 600 billion yen. The annual production value of water treatment facilities doubled between the 1980s and 1990s, and now holds the largest share of environmental facilities' production value, standing at between 600 and 800 billion yen. In total, about 1.6 trillion yen worth of pollution control equipment and facilities is produced annually in Japan today. This accounts for 0.3 per cent of Japan's gross national product (GNP) or 0.8 per cent of annual industrial value-added (Figure 12.2). For some companies in Japan, environmental pollution control has become a profitable business opportunity.

As explained in Chapter 10, based on an econometrics model, the EA of Japan quantitatively analyzed both the negative and positive effects of pollution control investment in Japan during the period from 1965-75. The conclusion it reached was that there was no severe negative impact on the national economy during this period. In describing the overall impact of environmental investment on Japan's macro economy, the EA states as follows: 'Just as the period of high economic growth (was) achieved by concentrated investments, when the peak in pollution prevention investments coincided with the recession following the oil crisis, these investments reinvigorated slumping demand and supported capital investment and employment' (Environment Agency 1994, p. 164). An OECD study on Japan's environmental investment and its effect on the national economy reached a similar conclusion: 'the impact of pollution prevention investment against national economy is neutral or negligible' (Environment Agency 1992, p. 199).

Financial Impacts of Environmental Investment on Businesses

Japan's experience also shows that environmental investment can be quite burdensome at first for some industries but become less so over time. Financial impacts of environmental investment were quite significant for certain industry groups in the early years of Japan's pollution control history. Textile and steel industries had to invest heavily in pollution control and as a result experienced a significant profit reduction of over 90 per cent in the mid-1970s, peak years for pollution control investment. Other metal industries also experienced substantial losses. Since the 1970s, however, the impact of pollution control expenditures on production costs and profits have declined sharply, eventually becoming insignificant (Environment Agency 1992, p. 181).

Instead of avoiding investing in environmental technologies, many Japanese companies, especially large companies with significant resources, tried to minimize the financial impacts of environmental investment by improving their business operations. The experience of Japan's nine electric power companies shows that improvements in business operations could help absorb pollution prevention costs. They rationalized their production process, began offering value-added services, and improved the performance of pollution abatement facilities (Environment Agency 1992, p. 182). This example suggests that integration of pollution control and improvement of industrial production can minimize the financial risk of environmental investment.

Figure 12.1   Environmental Facilities' Production Value

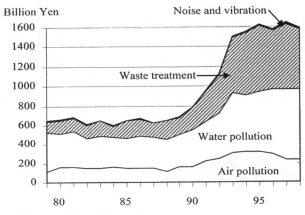

Notes: Translated from Japanese by the author.
Source: Federation of Machinery Industry of Japan 1999.

Figure 12.2   Environmental Facilities' Production as a Ratio to GNP and Industry Value-added

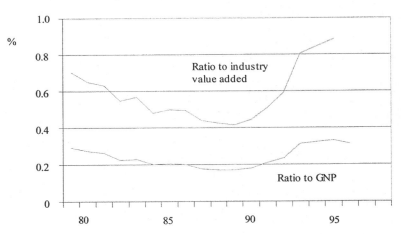

Notes: Translated from Japanese by the author.
Source: The Federation of Machinery Industry of Japan 1999.

Smaller firms tend to feel the brunt of pollution control investment more significantly than larger ones. To aid medium and small-scale enterprises that were less capable of bearing the cost of environmental investment, the Japanese government established various financial assistance mechanisms. The government's financial assistance programs included subsidies, tax breaks and low-interest loans. Other Asian countries can benefit from learning about the measures the Japanese government developed to help companies reduce the financial risk of pollution control investment.

Over the last 40 years, Japanese companies have continuously invested in more efficient production technologies and energy and resource conservation technologies. As a result, Japan has become one of the most 'efficient' nations in the world. Energy consumption per GDP declined 30 per cent from 1975-91, and sulfur dioxide emissions per unit of GDP declined by around 88 per cent from 1965-80 (Figure 12.3). For industrial water use in Japan, the recycled water usage as a percentage of the total volume of fresh water consumption was 36.2 per cent in 1965. By 1990, the recovery rate increased to 75.7 per cent.

Japan's Automobile Industry

In their efforts to meet strict environmental regulations and standards, many companies have invested in environmental technologies and, as a result, have become more efficient and productive producers. Their competitiveness and profitability have increased. In short, they have become more successful companies because of their investment in production and pollution control technologies. Japan's automobile industry is one of the most notable examples. Following the 1970 Clean Air Act Amendments in the USA, the Japanese government issued strict automobile exhaust regulations in 1972. Japan's automobile industry worked diligently to meet the newly established automobile exhaust regulations. The industry achieved its goal in 1978. Cars became cleaner and more efficient. Their engine performance also was much improved. The competitiveness of Japan's automobile industry in the international market increased as a result of these improvements (Ueta 1993, p. 41) (Figure 12.4).

In contrast, US automobile manufacturers did not respond quickly to the new standards set by the 1970 Clean Air Act Amendment. The US government thought that attaining the new standards would involve significant technological difficulties and that forcing automobile manufactures to meet the standards in a short period of time would be detrimental to the industry. Ironically, however, the attempt to protect the industry had the opposite effect. The delayed implementation of the Clean Air Act Amendment allowed US car manufacturers to continue to produce inefficient and dirty cars. This delay is considered partly responsible for a relative decline of US automobile manufacturers in the world market (Ueta 1993, p. 41).

Japan's success story suggests that environmental regulations can be used to foster technological innovations and improvements in industrial production. Japan's success story offers an attractive strategic option to Asia's developing countries. Innovative environmental regulations can play a major part in accelerating a shift from mass resource consumption and heavy pollution to high efficiency and less pollution.

Figure 12.3   Changes in Energy Efficiency and SO$_2$ Emissions

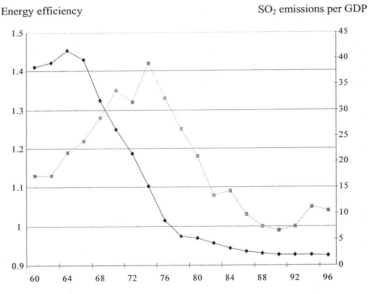

Energy efficiency   SO$_2$ emissions per GDP

‑■‑   Energy consumption per unit of GDP (TOE/million Japanese Yen)
‑◆‑   SO$_2$ emission per unit of GDP (Kg/million Japanese Yen)

Sources: World Bank Development Indicators 1998; Li Zhidong 1999.

National Environmental Policy System: Japan's Seven Environmental Policy Categories

Japan has a well-developed national environmental policy system that can be broken down into seven policy categories. There are groups of rules and regulations relating to: 1) basic policy; 2) administration and organization-building; 3) pollution control and nature conservation; 4) environmental dispute resolution, compensation and related issues; 5) finance and technology R&D; 6) integration of environmental protection and economic development and 7) global environmental issues. Since the enactment of the 1967 Basic Law of Environmental Pollution Control, Japan's legislature has passed or amended almost a hundred environmental laws. These seven categories of environmental policies constitute Japan's well-developed, holistic environmental management system.

Many of Asia's developing countries do not have as well-developed a national environmental management system as Japan's. Some have rules and regulations that cover the seven policy categories mentioned above, but they are typically less effective or weak compared to Japan's well-developed environmental regulations. Many of Asia's developing countries do not have well-developed environmental dispute resolution mechanisms or compensation schemes and lack adequate financing and R&D capabilities. They are also often poor at integrating environmental protection and economic development and tend to have little concern for global environmental protection.

Take China as an example. China has six environmental laws (see Table 12.3). These six laws and a considerable number of administrative rules are the main components of China's environmental policy package. Low standards and loose enforcement make China's environmental policy system less effective. Too many administrative rules also make China's system less effective, taking away necessary managerial resources from policy implementation and enforcement.

Figure 12.4 Shares of Exported Passenger Cars

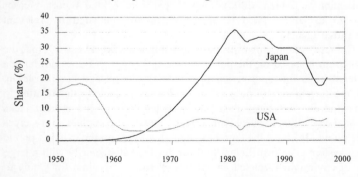

Notes: The figure shows the share of cars exported respectively by Japan and the USA relative to total passenger car exports of 13 major countries.
Source: Japan Automobile Manufacturers Association 1999.

Basic Environmental Policy

China's most fundamental, basic environmental law is the Environmental Protection Law, which was enacted in 1979 for trial implementation and amended in 1989 for formal implementation. The law concentrates heavily on issues associated with industrial pollution, and there is very little attention to issues such as nature conservation, household effluents and other issues relating to urbanization. The roles and responsibilities of the national government, local governments and other actors, including businesses and citizens, are not defined very well. Moreover, the law is an odd mixture of generalized principles and detailed rules and regulations, making it very confusing. An amendment to the law is necessary to make the law more effective and up-to-date.

Environmental Dispute Resolution and Compensation

Although China has ministerial-level regulations, there is no basic legislation relating to environmental dispute resolution and compensation. China utilizes its public reporting system to deal with citizens' complaints about pollution and other problems. This system, in conjunction with the normal judicial process, acts as a main channel for environmental dispute resolution. Citizens are also able to express their opinions, make suggestions, or voice complaints about environmental matters. In 2000, a total of 247,741 letters were written by complaining citizens, and 139,424 citizens brought their complaints directly to government offices (State Environmental Protection Administration of China, 2000). Only 1 per cent of the reported cases actually go to court; the rest of the cases are mediated by relevant administrative agencies.

The Chinese system, however, has some important weaknesses. First, the current system is based on the public reporting system and does not have a strong legal basis for environmental dispute resolution and compensation. Second, the current system does not have clear and detailed rules relating to compensation for damages caused by polluters. Third, the system lacks institutional capabilities to deal with a large number of complaints it receives from the public. In short, the current system that relies on the existing public reporting system is an insufficient tool for dealing satisfactorily with a large number of environment-related complaints. Perhaps it is time for China to formally establish a law related to environmental dispute resolution and compensation. As public environmental awareness grows, demand for such a law will increase.

Integration of Economic Development and Environmental Protection

One of the most important lessons we can learn from Japan's environmental management experience is that it is possible to balance environmental protection and economic development. To achieve both economic development and environmental protection goals, China has been trying to integrate its environmental protection and economic development strategies, guidelines, policies and plans. However, the integration is still insufficient, leading to ineffective outcomes. In particular, weaknesses are visible in areas such as energy use, industrial siting, clean production technology, transportation and urban infrastructure construction. As China experiences continued high economic growth, it is imperative that environmental considerations be incorporated into these sectoral policy areas. Otherwise, China will have to pay even high costs to abate pollution later.

Sanctions against Non-compliance

Since 1997, the Chinese government has closed about 70,000 small enterprises that were heavy polluters and made little business profits. This was done under special ordinance of the State Council and not because of regularized rules or regulations. The government can also suspend operations or close a heavily polluting plant that is not able to control its pollution.

As discussed earlier, to induce 'quasi-voluntary' compliance with environmental regulations, there must be reliable and effective enforcers of these rules and meaningful sanctions against non-compliance. Loose enforcement of environmental regulations has been a problem for China. In addition, there are few effective sanctions against non-compliance. Fines and pollution fees are charged against polluters who violate national pollution standards; however, since these fees and fines are set low, many factories opt to pay the penalties and continue to pollute the environment. As a result of amendments to the Penal Code in 1997, criminal penalties can be imposed, but only in the case where severe damages to health and property occur. The weak capacities and will of the judicial system to resolve environmental crimes is also a problem.

Financing and the R&D of Environmental Technologies

Another very important reason for Japan's environmental success is that Japan has succeeded in designing and developing strong environmental finance mechanisms. In many developing countries, environmental investment is seen as a major 'bottleneck' that has delayed the introduction of necessary pollution control technologies in their countries. This section reviews Japan's environmental finance mechanisms and considers what lessons Asia's developing countries could learn from Japan's successful experience.

In Japan, as of 1991, 87 per cent of environmental protection costs were being born by national and local governments (World Bank 1994, p. 80). The national government and local governments are responsible for investment in environmental infrastructure construction. Private businesses often share the costs for public pollution control projects, in addition to bearing the costs necessary to install and operate pollution control devices for their plants and factories. National financial institutions provide low-interest loans to private companies for their pollution control investments.

Local governments' major environmental infrastructure construction projects include public sewage, solid waste and human waste treatment plant construction. In 1991, local governments' environmental infrastructure expenditures accounted for more than 60 per cent of all environmental infrastructure expenditures. Local government funds covered about 20 per cent, commercial bank loans 30 per cent, and loans made available by the national government 20 per cent of the total expenditures. In addition, the national government provided local governments with direct subsidies. Approximately 20 to 30 per cent of local environmental infrastructure construction projects are supported by direct subsidies from the central government (World Bank 1994, p. 80).

Private companies finance their own pollution control projects based on the 'polluter pays principle' (PPP). In 1991, private enterprises' funds plus loans from commercial banks accounted for 71 per cent of the total industrial pollution control investments in Japan. National government-affiliated financial institutions and local governments provided 28 per cent of the costs in the form of low-interest loans. Subsidies from local governments provided 1 per cent of the total expenditures (World Bank 1994, p. 80).

In addition, the Law Concerning Enterprises' Bearing of the Cost of Public Pollution Control Works, which was enacted in 1971, calls for private enterprises to share costs of environmental pollution prevention projects. By the end of March 1993, 99 projects had been designated as environmental pollution prevention projects, and 46.8 per cent of these costs were paid by private enterprises (Environment Agency 1994, p. 445).

Much of the central government's environmental budget goes to environmental infrastructure construction. In the 1990s, environmental infrastructure construction accounted for 83 per cent of the national government's environmental budget. Only 11 per cent of the budget was allocated for nature conservation. Sewage piping and treatment projects account for 70 per cent of all environmental infrastructure projects. Noise prevention, domestic garbage disposal and sewage piping construction in rural areas account for approximately 8 per cent of all environmental infrastructure projects.

The Japanese government provides financial assistance to private companies to support their pollution control efforts. Three types of assistance are available: 1) low-interest loans provided by national-government affiliated financial institutions; 2) governmental preferential taxes; and 3) governmental direct subsidies. National government-affiliated financial institutions provided low-interest loans to corporations and this played an extremely important role in helping Japanese enterprises' early efforts to install pollution control equipment (see Chapter 5).

Government-affiliated financial organizations that provide Japanese companies with low-interest loans to support their pollution control efforts include the Japan Development Bank, Japan Environment Corporation (JEC), Small and Medium Enterprise Finance Corporation and People's Finance Corporation. Usually, these institutions set interest rates that are 1 to 2 per cent lower than commercial loan rates. From 1975-85, low-interest loans lent by all government-affiliated financial institutions accounted for 30 to 40 per cent of the total industrial investments in pollution control annually (Figure 12.5). The annual cost of these low-interest loans to the Japanese government in terms of the differential between these loans and commercial loans has been about 2.0-2.8 billion yen since the 1980s. When the budget for the JEC is added to this figure, the central government allocates about 4 billion yen annually to cover JEC operations. This amounts to approximately 3 per cent of the central government's total annual environment budget, a relatively small figure when compared to the contribution that has been made to reduce industrial pollution.

The JEC was established specifically to support small and medium-sized enterprises' pollution control efforts. Figure 12.5 shows that the JEC's low-interest loans account for 15 to 25 per cent of the total pollution control investments by private enterprises. Survey findings show that the cumulative investments in pollution control technologies by small and medium-sized enterprises accounted for approximately 27 per cent of the total investments by all private enterprises from 1986-91 (Fujikura 1999, p. 1413). It is estimated that JEC loans accounted for at least 50 per cent of pollution control investments made by these small and medium-sized enterprises during this period, playing a critical role in helping these companies to overcome financial difficulties associated with pollution control investment.

Environmental investment has always been part of Japan's comprehensive environmental management strategy. In comparison, many Asian developing countries have not yet developed viable environmental investment strategies. Japan's environmental finance experience strongly suggests the benefits of a joint-effort model that involves both the government and the private sector. The Japanese government developed financial mechanisms to provide financial assistance to private companies. Preferential tax treatment, subsidies and low-interest loans were provided to help them overcome

financial   difficulties   associated   with   environmental   infrastructure
investments.   Many   private   companies   responded   to   these   financial
incentives. They installed pollution control devices and improved production
technologies. Many developing countries could benefit from learning about
Japan's environmental finance mechanisms because lack of available funds
is one of the most significant factors that has delayed the introduction of
pollution control technologies in many developing countries. Encouragingly,
some of Japan's neighboring countries have set up environmental finance
institutions like the Japan Development Bank and JEC (see Chapter 10).
Thailand's Environmental Fund and South Korea's Special Environment
Account have played a positive role in improving environmental conditions
in their countries (Ren, Chang and Imura 2000).

Figure 12.5   *Low-interest Loans for Industrial Pollution Control*

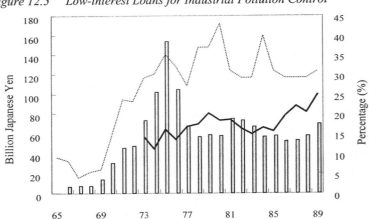

the amount of low-interest loans by JDB to the total investment in pollution
control by private sector (billion Yen)

Ratio of low-interest loans by JDB to the total investment in pollution
control by private sector (%)

Ratio of the total low-interest loans to the total investment in pollution
control by private sector (%)

Source: Japan Development Bank, Annual Business Reports of (various years).

COMPARING THE SITUATION OF JAPAN TO CHINA, SOUTH KOREA, THAILAND AND THE PHILIPPINES

It is useful to reflect upon the socio-economic conditions of other Asian
countries when considering the usefulness of the Japanese model. The

understanding of socio-economic, political and cultural processes is of central importance in dealing with environmental problems. Environmental governance is conditioned by national political-economic structures, the stage of economic development, social norms, cultural values and the severity of pollution problems. National approaches to environmental protection are influenced by a wide array of factors.

The extremely high population density and large economies of Japan and South Korea create great strains on natural resources and the environment. But something that Japan and South Korea have that many other developing countries lack is universal literacy and relatively high per capita incomes.

Table 12.3 Asian Countries' Socio-economic Context (1998)

	Japan	China	S.Korea	Thailand	Philippines
Surface area (1,000km²)[a]	378	9,597	99	513	300
Population (m.)	126	1,239	46	61	75
Pop. density (people/km²)	335	133	470	120	19
Urban population					
1997	78	32	83	21	56
2010[c]	80.6	43	91.4	27.4	
Adult illiteracy (% age 15 & older)					
Male		9	1	3	5
Female		25	4	7	6
GDP/cap US $	32,380	750	7,970	2,200	1,050
GDP/cap purchasing power parity (1996$)	23,158	3,363	13,193	6,873	3,415
GDP growth rate (% 1990-96)	2.2	11.6	7.7	8.6	2.8
Structure of output value-added as % GDP					
Industry	38[b]	49	43	40	32
Service	60[b]	33	51	49	50
GDP/unit energy use (1995$/kg)	10.5	0.7	3.0	2.2	2.1

Notes: [a] 1996, [b] 1995, [c] projected.
Source: World Bank 2000; Japan Environmental Council 2000.

Adult illiteracy in China stood at 34 per cent in 1995 and about 22.2 per cent of the population fell below the poverty line, defined as US $1 in purchasing power parity. Adult illiteracy was somewhat less in the Philippines (11 per cent), but 26.9 per cent of the population fell below the poverty line in 1994 (World Bank 2000, p. 237). Illiteracy inhibits efforts to improve environmental conditions through information dissemination. It also implies low levels of awareness about environmental pollution problems, the rational use of natural resources and environmental conservation. Poverty usually means that people's first priority lies with achieving basic sustenance. There is little room left over for environmental protection. These factors suggest some powerful limitations to the transferability of the Japanese model and also imply the need to deal with these critical developmental issues (Table 12.3).

There are still great barriers to overcome in the developing countries of Asia. Environmental protection and economic growth are still typically viewed as trade-offs. Non-compliance with regulations is a serious problem. The institutional capacity of regulators is low. Yet, on a more positive note, since the late 1980s there have been major changes in environmental governance structures throughout the region and there are signs of convergence in innovations in environmental governance.

Another important difference can be found in terms of the degree of diversity of countries in terms of geography and population. Japan, South Korea and Thailand have relatively homogeneous populations. There is not great cultural diversity within these countries. In comparison with these countries, China is highly diverse both in terms of its large number of ethnic groups and its geography. This suggests that in China environmental governance structures may need to be varied depending upon the region and the target population.

Table 12.4 Degrees of Decentralization

	Japan	China	S. Korea	Taiwan	Philippines
Subnational government share of total expenditures	30.5	55.6	49.1	9.6	16.2
Subnational government share of total tax revenue	37.8[a]	51.4	21.7[b]	5.5	16.4
Subnational elections 1999					
Intermediate[c]	Yes	No	Yes	No	Yes
Local[d]	Yes	No	Yes	Yes	Yes
Subsidies and other transfers as % of total expenditures	52[e]		49	7	18

Notes: [a]1990, [b] 1996, [c] state, province, region, department, or other elected entity between the local and the national government, [d]municipality or equivalent, [e]1980.
Source: World Bank 2000; Japan Environmental Council 2000.

There are also substantial differences in the political systems of Asia. Since the end of World War II, Japan has been democratic with elections at both the local and national levels. South Korea and the Philippines in the early 1990s could also be classified as democratic. In contrast, China and Thailand enjoy more centralized political regimes. It goes without saying that these political system differences influence greatly the applicability and transferability of environmental governance structures (Table 12.4).

Table 12.5 Environmental Performance: Sanitation

	Japan	China	S. Korea	Thailand	Philippines
Access to sanitation (urban population % 1995)	95	87	100	98	93
Sewerage connection %	58[a]	25.8[b]	39		

Notes: [a] 1996 [b] 1995.
Source: World Bank, World Development Report 1999/2000, 'The State of the Environment in Asia', 1999/2000.

Table 12.6 Urban Environmental Quality

	Tokyo	Beijing	Seoul	Bangkok	Manila
TSP	C	E	B	E	E
SO_2	A	C	B		B
CO	A		A	B	
NO_2	C	D	C	C	
O_3	C	C	B		
Pb			A	A	D

Notes: Total suspended particulates (TSP); sulfur dioxide (SO_2); carbon monoxide (CO), nitrogen dioxide (NO_2); oxygen (O_3); lead (Pb). Atmospheric concentrations of pollutants are relative to World Health Organization standards: A: under half; B: within standards; C: under two times the standards; D: under three times the standards; E: over three times the standards. Pb levels are roadside, all others are ambient air.
Source: World Bank, World Development Report 2000.

Finally, whereas Japan has been able to address pollution problems in stages, first tackling industrial pollution in the late 1960s and 1970s, then urban environmental problems beginning in the late 1970s, and global environmental protection and sustainable development issues since the 1990s, the developing countries of Asia are being asked to pursue all of these together. The developing countries of Asia will need to embrace a more holistic approach to environmental protection from the start than did Japan.

As Tables 12.5 and 12.6 suggest, the developing countries of Asia still have much to do in order to bring their environmental standards up to those of Japan. In particular, urban air quality remains a major issue (Tables 12.5 and 12.6).

China's transition to a market economy, deregulation and decentralization in Japan and elsewhere in the region, and democratization and localization in South Korea, the Philippines and Thailand are indications that Asia is on the move. As a result of various degrees of deregulation throughout the region, there is greater reliance and acceptance of flexible mechanisms, market-based mechanisms and voluntary approaches. Citizens, NGOs, the media and civil society have gained greater voice in decision making throughout the region. Environmental governance is gaining a greater grassroots' component in systems that in the past have been typified by top-down governance.

CONCLUSION

Japan's experiences with pollution abatement and environmental protection suggest that it is important to simultaneously manage social, economic and environmental changes. Japan's history with pollution control includes both successes and failures. While acknowledging the important political, social and geographical differences that exist among the Asian countries, because Japan has been a frontrunner in environmental protection in the Asian region, its experiences can provide important lessons for the countries of the region. The most important lessons to be learned are that there is much to gain from developing cooperative approaches among actors in environmental governance and economic development and environmental protection can be integrated. Japanese experiences can also provide useful examples of how national environmental policy can be structured and environmental pollution control financed.

Environmental management for sustainable development requires the development of good, holistic environmental governance structures. This means developing both formal environmental institutions (e.g. rules, laws and contracts and administrative structures) and encouraging the growth of informal environmental institutions (e.g. environmental values and social norms). There have been steps in this direction in Asia, but the challenge still remains large.

13. Environmental Policy-making in the Advanced Industrialized Countries: Japan, the European Union and the United States of America Compared

Miranda A. Schreurs

INTRODUCTION

In many respects the environmental programs, laws and institutions found in Japan resemble those of the United States of America (USA) and many European countries. This is not so surprising given that the advanced industrialized states have experienced many of the same pollution problems and environmental concerns as a result of industrialization, urbanization and agricultural modernization. For well over a century, they have introduced many similar laws and programs to deal with these problems learning from each other's experiences, scientific insights and policy solutions. There has been much policy convergence in the environmental field among the earlier industrializers.

For Japan, observing, analyzing and borrowing from the USA and European environmental research and policy programs is a long-established and well-accepted tradition. Cross-societal learning between Japan and the West in relation to the environment is evident as early as the Meiji Restoration, 1868-1912, when Japan began its first period of rapid industrialization and borrowing of policy ideas and practices from the West (e.g. Wilkening 2004). Examples include the spread of hygiene and sanitation measures, the introduction of measures to control the emissions of dust and soot in urban areas in the first half of the twentieth century and the development of a national park system in the 1930s. A second wave of policy diffusion began in the 1960s, when post-war economic growth resulted in a series of pollution tragedies and a search for a means of dealing with this pollution that had Japan's bureaucrats researching environmental policy approaches overseas. A third wave started in the 1980s and intensified in the 1990s as Japan entered a growing number of international environmental agreements and concern with international environmental problems and issues of sustainability led Japan's political leaders to once again consider ways to alter and improve their approaches to environmental protection. Still today there continues to be much information exchange and debate about environmental policy priorities, policy measures and instruments and governance strategies (Social Learning Group 2001). Nor has the learning been strictly unidirectional. Japan too has provided lessons to the West especially in regard to the control of air pollution and development of more energy-efficient technologies.

The importance placed on cross-societal policy learning in Japan has been institutionalized since the time of Meiji through the practice of sending Japanese bureaucrats overseas for one or two years to learn how things are done in other social and political systems and to foster human networks (Jansen 1995). In addition, much time and money is spent translating Western laws and writings about the environment into Japanese. Outsiders, moreover, have been allowed to play an important role in helping to foster Japan's environmental non-governmental organization (NGO) community by establishing environmental newsletters and setting up or helping to run and finance new environmental groups.

Importantly, Japan is now beginning to play a similar role in relation to developing countries in East and Southeast Asia as it hosts environmental researchers and engineers from the region to study and learn in Japan and supports environmental conservation activities and environmental infrastructure development in those countries. As interest in environmental protection expands in East Asia (Rock 2002), the Japanese government has also been actively consulting developing country governments about environmental management and disseminating information about best practices.

There are many similarities between Japan and other industrialized states in terms of their environmental policy successes and failures. Across Europe, North America and Japan, energy efficiency improvements have been dramatic, but they have been easier to achieve in industries than in households and have been offset by growing demand for energy as consumption levels rise. Air pollution from stationary sources has proven easier to control than from mobile sources, and emissions from ground and air transport are expected to be among the largest contributors to future greenhouse gas emissions. There is a growing interest in renewable energies, but they still hold only a small share of total energy supply. Recycling rates have improved dramatically, but recycling of finished products – especially cars and electronics – has proven difficult. Dealing with hazardous wastes remains a major challenge for the industrialized states (O'Neill 2000).

Despite such broad similarities, however, there are important differences among Japan, Europe and North America in terms of their policy performance and areas of environmental expertise (Jänicke and Weidner

1997; Lafferty and Meadowcroft 2000; O'Neill 2000; Vernon 1995; Schreurs 2002). The Japanese strength lies with developing technological solutions to control pollution as opposed to approaches which focus on nature conservation or wildlife preservation (Schreurs 2000; Barrett 2005). Comparatively speaking, Japan has out-performed the US and Europe in several environmental areas.

Because of technological advances, Japan achieved higher energy efficiency levels (energy intensity per unit gross domestic product (GDP)) than most other industrialized countries in the 1980s although the gap with many European countries has narrowed since the 1990s. Improvements in energy efficiency reduce energy import needs as well as harmful emissions. According to the International Energy Agency (IEA) and the Organization for Economic Cooperation and Development (OECD), 'Japan was leading all other countries in intensities reductions before 1990' (International Energy Agency and Organization for Economic Cooperation and Development 2004, p. 75). Japan ranks among what the IEA and OECD define as low-energy-intensity countries, along with Denmark, France, Germany, Italy and the United Kingdom (UK). The USA, Finland, Sweden and the Netherlands by comparison are medium-intensity countries and Norway, Australia and Canada, high-energy intensity countries. Since the 1990s, however, it should be noted that energy-intensity trends in the manufacturing sector in Japan have been moving in the wrong direction and have shown slight increases, possibly a response to the recession and lower investments in energy-efficiency improvements by industry (International Energy Agency and Organization for Economic Cooperation and Development 2004, pp. 69-75). As a result of the improved energy efficiency levels in Japan in the latter 1970s and 1980s and pollution control abatement efforts, Japan was able to reduce its classic air pollutant levels substantially and earlier than most other industrialized countries. It also became a leader in the use of air pollution control technologies (Moore and Miller 1995; Weidner 1996) although it ranks third in pollution control exports behind Germany and the USA.[1]

Use of public transport in Japan is much higher than in the USA and or the UK. The 2000 US Census indicates that close to 88 per cent of Americans commute to work by car, truck, or van (Reschovsky 2004, p. 3). The Department of Transport in the UK reports that approximately 80 per cent of all distance travelled in the UK is by car.[2]   In the fall of 2001, 70 per cent of the UK's 24 million employed were travelling to work by car.[3]   In contrast, the Ministry of Land, Infrastructure and Transport in Japan indicates that of the 1.3 million kilometers that were travelled per year by road or rail in Japan in 1997, 861,000 or 65 per cent were done using private transportation; the remaining 35 per cent were by train or public road transport.[4] According to one recent, albeit not representative survey, of 351 Japanese respondents, 44.4 per cent commuted to school or work by train,

9.4 per cent by bus, 13.4 per cent by bicycle, 6.8 per cent by walking and only 16.8 per cent by car and 6.2 per cent by motorcycle. In comparison, of the 307 US and Canadian respondents to the survey, 52.1 per cent commuted by car. Public transportation was primarily by bus (19.2 per cent) with only 4.2 per cent using trains. The remainder walked or cycled. The 187 European respondents from 8 western European countries used public transportation much more than Americans (27.3 per cent bus, 19.3 per cent car), but less than their Japanese counterparts. Cars were relied upon by 26.7 per cent of the respondents.[5]

As has been described in considerable detail in other chapters, Japan also performed well in reducing harmful air pollutants. The cumulative impact of the energy-efficiency improvements, promotion of public transportation, and pollution control measures implemented in Japan was to turn a terrible air quality situation around. While there is room for further improvement, relatively speaking for such a densely populated and highly urbanized society, air quality in Japan is relatively good. Given the extreme air pollution in Asia's many large urban and industrial centers, the Japanese case certainly deserves close scrutiny for the lessons it may hold.

Where Japan has traditionally been weaker is with efforts to protect natural environments domestically and overseas. In an effort to control flooding, Japan's rivers have been dammed, straightened and covered in concrete. Coastlines have been lost to urban and industrial development. Although Japan is heavily forested, much of the forest is monoculture, and thus, lacks great biological diversity. Construction projects have resulted in a maze of highways and tunnels cutting through Japan's mountainous terrain, the building of thousands of golf courses in remote mountain villages, airports that at times threaten sensitive marine environments and landfill projects that fill in wetlands (Kerr 2002; Karan 2005). Certainly, this is in part a result of Japan's very limited size relative to its rather large population, but it is also a result of the relative power of competing interests in Japan. Environmental activists who have struggled against these tendencies are considerably weaker than the industrial and construction interests who have been able to drive and shape the Japanese political economy.

Japan's domestic strengths and weaknesses in relation to environmental protection have been mirrored in its overseas activities. Relative to other aid donors, Japan has placed much emphasis on the development of environmental infrastructure, especially with regard to clean water, sewage and energy efficiency. The USA, in contrast, appears to focus more efforts on altering governance mechanisms through, for example, fostering NGO activities in developing countries and major European donors on nature conservation.

Japan has done especially much for basic infrastructure improvement and environmental service development in East and Southeast Asia. Much public and private investment is targeted at finding technological solutions to freshwater problems, air pollution problems and energy needs. Where the Japanese government and industries have been most criticized in their overseas activities are in contributing to the destruction of natural areas, old growth forests and traditional life styles or to the endangerment of wildlife species.

There are also far fewer international environmental agreements in Asia than it is the case in Europe or North America. The Center for International Earth Science Information Network (CIESIN) has compiled a database of international environmental agreements. This data base indicates that in April 2004, Japan was party to 114 agreements and was signatory to 5 more. This compares with 272 for Germany (of which it was party to 237) and 162 for the USA (of which it was party to 130).[6] Thus, there may also have been fewer international regulations controlling investment and development in Asia.

There are, however, numerous signs of change in Japan that suggest a growing appreciation for the importance of nature conservation and international environmental protection (Karan 2005). Japan has joined the European Union (EU) in signing the Kyoto Protocol controlling greenhouse gas emissions, the Convention on Biological Diversity, the Cartegna Protocol on Biosafety, and the Basel Convention on the Control of Transboundary Movements of Hazardous Wastes and Their Disposal despite the failure of the USA to join these agreements. Japan also shows similar concerns to many European countries about the use of genetically modified organisms. Japan and the EU are arguably doing more to address climate change through emissions' controls, energy-efficiency improvements and flexible mechanisms than the USA, which is arguing for a longer-term technologically driven approach of changing society in a less greenhouse gas-intensive direction. Japan in recent years has followed the EU's efforts to promote recycling and introduce renewable energies. Japan is a leader in the use of solar power. It has also adopted waste minimization, collection and recycling schemes similar to those found in northern Europe.

In some areas, Japanese policies continue to cause considerable controversy. Japan has resisted the adoption of strict preservationist approaches to international wildlife species protection in favor of limited-use programs. This has resulted in considerable international criticism in relation to Japan's support of whaling and its begrudging agreement of an international moratorium on the export and trade of ivory (Miyaoka 2004). Although there are some signs of improvement, Japan is also frequently criticized for its contribution to tropical deforestation (Bevis 1995; Dauvergne 1997 and 2001) and depletion of marine wildlife. Japan's status as one of the world's largest producers of nuclear energy (the USA is the largest producer) also elicits debate.

The most important reason for the differences between Japan and other industrialized countries in their approaches to environmental governance derive from their social and political institutions and political cultures. Changes in these institutions and in the political culture in the past decade or two also help explain why Japan's approach to environmental governance is growing closer to that found in the EU.

In Japan there is a kind of neocorporatist relationship between the state and industry that is institutionalized in processes such as *amakudari* (literally, 'descent from heaven,' referring to the retirement of bureaucrats into lucrative positions in industry and in public corporations) and *gyousei shido* (administrative guidance), a practice which refers to government bureaucrats guiding, persuading, or negotiating with industry about economic matters (Johnson 1982). Usually because the government consults with industry prior to establishing new regulations and industry is able to influence the shape of policy, once a policy decision is reached, there is generally high success with implementation. Voluntary agreements have become ubiquitous in Japan, both at the local level and increasingly at the national level as industries, responding to government guidance (and perhaps seeking to deflect the establishment of new regulations), establish emissions' targets and resource reduction goals that are higher than national requirements. These agreements may work in Japan because of its political culture. They are somewhat similar in form to the 'covenants' found in the Netherlands (Glasbergen 1998) although in Japan environmental groups have had comparatively little voice in the shape that the voluntary agreements take.

Compared with Europe and North America, environmental policy making in Japan since the 1970s has been far more top-down and centered in the bureaucracy than was the case in northern Europe or the USA where environmental groups and green parties have played a large role in influencing policy developments and implementation outcomes. Japan is more like northern European countries in the more limited extent to which the courts are relied upon for settling grievances than is the case of the USA where plaintiffs relatively quickly turn to the courts for redress and environmental groups take the government to court for failing to implement environmental legislation (McSpadden 1997). Instead, in Japan the courts are seen as a last resort and efforts are made to resolve disputes, for example, over the siting of a new facility, through negotiation, persuasion and compensation (Haley 1991; Lesbirel 1998).

Many of the differences seen between Japan and other industrialized countries are an outgrowth of their historical experiences with pollution and destruction of nature. Thus, there are notable differences in the extent to which the focus of policy efforts is on pollution control for health purposes or the protection of natural areas for conservation or preservation purposes.

They also reflect distinct social and political institutional arrangements, which influence which actors are the primary wielders of power, and cultural understandings of nature. In order to better understand the unique aspects of Japan's approach to environmental governance, this chapter begins with a brief historical overview of environmental policy formation in Japan as compared with Europe and the USA. It then compares the institutions and programs that were formed to deal with environmental problems. There is also discussion of how environmental policy making is both converging and diverging across the triad as new environmental problems challenge traditional approaches to environmental protection.

Early Industrialization and the Rise of Anti-Pollution and Conservation Movements

Environmental policy learning is something that has been occurring across the advanced industrialized states for over a century. During the nineteenth century, protest against the human health impacts of industrialization and urbanization began to emerge. The UK, the first country to industrialize, led the world in the introduction of pollution control measures. The 1834 Poor Law Commission's report led to a revolution in sanitation. Parliament approved legislation in 1853 aimed at reducing the level of smoke emitted by coal-burning furnaces and in 1863 issued the Alkali Act requiring factories to remove 95 per cent of the hydrochloric acid emitted in the production of soap, glass and textiles. Water pollution was addressed when the stench of the River Thames, which had basically become an open sewer, became so bad that it made it almost impossible for Parliament to conduct its business. In 1876, Parliament approved the Rivers Pollution Prevention Act (Vogel 1986, p. 32).

Germany and Japan, which were late industrializers, began to follow suit towards the end of the nineteenth century as their efforts to rapidly industrialize began to intensify their pollution problems. In 1877, Prussia forbade the use of rivers for the dumping of sewage and introduced licensing requirements for polluting firms as a way of addressing air pollution (Wey 1982, pp. 27-32). Sanitation and hygiene reform began in Japan after the 1868 Meiji Restoration.[7] The Meiji Restoration was a period when Japan's political leaders traveled to the West in order to learn about Western political, social and economic institutions and then to selectively adopt those that seemed most appropriate to Japan's conditions. In the realm of health and hygiene, Japan borrowed from UK experiences. Some decades later, following US and European examples, local governments in major urban areas in Japan issued ordinances to address air pollution by trying to control the siting of plants and regulating smoke emissions.

Pollution Protest, Conservation and Wildlife Preservation Groups

Japan has a long history of forest management that emerged in response to the loss of forests near castle towns, where wood was used for building and firewood, and forests were cleared for agriculture. Japan's relatively sophisticated forest management system meant that 70 per cent of the country was still forested at the time of Japan's opening to the West (Totman 1989; Barrett 1997, p. 10). Japan also has a relatively long history of citizen mobilization in response to severe local pollution. There are numerous examples of villages protesting about the pollution of rivers and rice paddies from runoff from mining activities and the soil erosion caused by deforestation around mines (Huddle, Reich and Stiskin 1975; Gresser, Fujikura and Morishima 1981; McKean 1981; Broadbent 1998; Wilkening 2004). The most famous is the Ashio Copper Mine pollution case that was described in Chapter 2.

In contrast with Europe and the USA, however, no formal environmental movement formed in pre-war Japan. In the nineteenth century, the emergence of preservation and conservation movements in the USA and Europe led to the eventual birth of numerous environmental groups, several of which still exist today. Preservationists believed in the intrinsic worth of nature and fought for its preservation on those grounds. Conservationists argued for the protection of nature in order to ensure its continued value for resource extraction purposes or recreation. Private voluntary organizations for protection of open spaces began to form in the second half of the nineteenth century. In the UK the Commons, Open Spaces and Footpaths Preservations Society formed in 1865. In 1891, Mrs Robert W. Williamson established the Royal Society for the Protection of Birds. In 1895, the National Trust was established to preserve places of historical interest and natural beauty. Paralleling this, in the USA, the Audobon Society and the Sierra Club were created. In Prussia (and later Germany), state governments sponsored the formation of nature conservation agencies in response to the growth in nature tourism caused by urbanization and the growth of railroads. Associations for nature conservation such as Bund für Vogelschutz (1899) and the Bund Heimatschutz (1914), an umbrella organization of 250 affiliated nature conservation groups, formed (Wey 1992). Although Japan's largest environmental group, the Wild Bird Society (*Nippon Yacho no Kai*), formed in 1934, this was an exceptional case. In contrast with the many groups that formed in Europe and North America, an organized environmental movement did not really take root in Japan in the pre-war period. This is important to consider given the comparatively late development in Japan of a national environmental movement in the post-World War II period.

National Park Movements

While national environmental groups and associations did not gain much of a foothold in Japan in the first half of the twentieth century, it is interesting to consider that Japan was relatively early in its introduction of a national park system. Trends in the USA influenced Japan. In the USA, growing concerns about the need to preserve and conserve land that was rapidly being changed due to the march to the west of European settlers led to the establishment of the world's first national park at Yellowstone in 1872. Initially national parks were established only in the vast western frontier of the USA. Then, in the early twentieth century calls to establish national parks in the more densely populated eastern areas grew. A National Park Service was established in 1916 and the first three national parks established on the east coast were formed between 1919 and 1926 (National Geographic Society, p. 14). The first countries to follow the lead of the USA were all relatively unpopulated: Australia (1879), Canada (1885) and Sweden (1909) (Table 13.1).

Table 13.1 Year of Establishment of First National Park

USA	1872
Australia	1879
Canada	1885
Sweden	1909
Japan	1934
UK	1949
France	1963
Spain	1969
Austria	1992

Japan's first national parks were set up in the mid-1930s. Although this was 50 or more years after the USA, Australia, Canada and Sweden established national parks, Japan was well ahead of many European countries in forming a national park system. In much of Europe, where little nature remained in its natural state, historical preservation and conservation initiatives found many supporters, but it proved difficult to introduce national parks because there was little undisturbed nature that remained. Thus, while France passed a Law on the Conservation of Natural Sites and Monuments in 1930, it did not establish a National Parks Law until the 1950s and did not set up its first national park until 1963. And while the UK was a leader in the establishment of historical monuments and parks, it only set up its first national park in 1949. Spain created its first national park in 1969.

While few Japanese consider themselves to be religious, most are married in Shinto shrines and are brought to rest in Buddhist temples. The essence of

Shintosim is harmony with nature and Buddhism places a high value on all forms of life. As a result of these religious traditions, certain places of tremendous natural beauty have been revered as almost sacred places throughout Japanese history. This is true of the cultivated gardens of Buddhist temples and the more natural aesthetics of Shinto shrines in cities like Kyoto, Nara and Kamakura as well as natural formations, such as many of Japan's volcanic mountains.

The first effort to preserve land in Japan appears to have been a 1911 petition brought by concerned citizens calling for the protection of Nikko, a beautiful forested area where the Shogun Tokugawa Ieyasu had a splendid, albeit somewhat ostentatious temple erected for his memorial. Two years later a National Parks Association was created and in 1931 Japan passed a National Parks Law. Between 1934 and 1938, 15 areas were designated as national parks. These developments suggest that even without a strong national environmental movement due to foreign example and local pressures some notable environmental victories have been won.

As was true everywhere, World War II brought a temporary stop to the establishment of national parks, but soon after the war ended, a movement began to designate yet more areas for preservation. By 1955, six more national parks had been added and in 1957 a more comprehensive National Parks Law replaced the 1931 legislation (Sutherland and Britton 1995). Currently, Japan has 28 national parks, 55 quasi-National Parks, 300 prefectural parks and 6.8 per cent of its land categorized as protected.[8]

The effects of these different early experiences with protection of natural areas still can be seen today. In comparative terms, Japan is closer to the USA and Canada in terms of setting aside extensive tracts of land for strict nature preservation (World Conservation Union (IUCN) categories I-III) than the major European states. The total area of national territory under some form of protection recognized by the IUCN (categories I-VI), however, ranks low in Japan compared with other industrial states, and especially the USA, Germany and the UK (Table 13.2).

Resource Extraction in Developing Countries

In Japan's race to catch up with the West and to prevent domination by it, great emphasis was placed by the Meiji leadership on strengthening the military. *Fukoku kyohei*, literally 'rich country, strong army' was the slogan of the day (Pyle 1996). Well aware of China's fate and its semi-colonial status under a series of unequal treaties that were forced upon it by the UK, Germany and the USA, Japan's leaders determined that Japan should not too become a colony of the West and should instead free Asia of Western influence and become a colonizer itself. Japan won its first colony (Formosa (Taiwan)) and made Korea a protectorate after the Sino-Japanese War of

1894-5. In the 1930s, it turned Manchuria into a puppet state and during the height of the Pacific War, conquered Singapore, Indonesia, large parts of China and Southeast Asia. Japan's colonies became important sources of natural resources (primarily fuel and minerals) and agricultural products. Thus, much like is true for many European countries and the USA, during its initial phase of rapid industrialization, Japan was able to benefit from the natural resources and labor acquired in less developed countries.

Table 13.2 Major Protected Areas (IUCN Management Categories I-VI)

	Total area (km²)	% of terri- tory	ha/ 1,000 capita	By IUCN Category in percentage terms (a)					
				I(b)	II (c)	III (d)	IV (e)	V(f)	VI(g)
Canada	953103	9.6	3146.9	3	42	0	42	10	3
USA	1988444	21.2	742.7	20	13	3	20	6	38
Japan	25590	6.8	20.3	1	51	0	19	29	0
UK	50001	20.4	20.4	0	0	0	6	94	0
France	55723	10.1	95.1	3	5	0	6	86	0
Germany	96193	26.9	117.2	0	0	0	5	94	0
Italy	22037	7.3	38.3	0	17	0	12	71	0
Korea	6838	6.9	14.9	0	0	0	5	95	0
Mexico	159759	8.2	162.6	8	5	0	13	19	56

Notes: a) IUCN management categories I-VI. National classifications may differ; b) Strict nature reserves/wilderness areas: protected areas managed mainly for science/wilderness protection; c) National parks: protected areas managed mainly for ecosystem protection and recreation. Natural monuments: protected areas managed mainly for conservation of specific natural features; d) Habitat/species management areas: protected areas managed mainly for landscape/seascape conservation and recreation; e) Protected landscapes/seascapes: protected areas managed mainly for landscape/seascape conservation and recreation; f) Managed resource protected areas: protected areas managed mainly for the sustainable use of natural ecosytems.
Source: Organization for Economic Cooperation and Development, OECD Environmental Data Compendium 1999 (Paris, Organization for Economic Cooperation and Development: 1999), p. 115.

Although defeat in World War II meant that Japan was forced to give up its colonies, the legacies of this period influenced economic and environmental policy developments in the post-war period throughout parts of Asia where Japan had had a presence. On the one hand, the ties built up over many decades of colonization and years of experience in East and Southeast Asia meant that Japanese companies were able to move into the region with relative ease once the Japanese economy began to grow again in the post-war period. For a second time, Japan began to rely heavily on East and Southeast Asia (and this time also the Middle East) for natural resources and energy to feed its rapid post-war industrialization. This time, however, it was not military might, but rather economic might that made it possible for Japan to obtain resources from other regions. Japan has been a major importer of timber, oil, gas, minerals, marine and agricultural products from Asia since the 1960s.

On the other hand, Japan's colonization and occupation of much of Asia left bitter memories that forced Japan to pursue a pacifist foreign policy and find non-military means of making foreign contributions. This has been an important factor behind some of the resentment towards Japan that remains in the region. It also explains Japan's emergence as a leading donor of official development assistance (Potter 1996; Kato 2002) and its growing emphasis on foreign environmental assistance.

Environmental Movements and Environmental Activism

World War II brought conservation initiatives throughout the world to a halt and war added to the rapid destruction of nature that industrialization had begun. In Japan, the military used national parks as military practice ranges. At the end of the war, environmental protection was not on the agenda of any government. Rebuilding cities destroyed by bombs, feeding hungry populations and creating employment opportunities were the primary issues of the time.

In Europe conservation groups slowly began to reestablish themselves after the war. The International Union for the Protection of Nature (later, renamed the IUCN-World Conservation Union) was set up in 1948 in the UK and the Deutscher Naturschutzring formed in Germany as an umbrella organization of conservation groups in 1950. In France the Société Nationale de Protection de la Nature was formed in 1958 (Prendiville 1994). There were also a few such efforts in Japan. In 1949, for example, volunteers formed the Oze Marsh Conservation Union to protest against the building of a hydroelectric dam, which would destroy marshland where birds nested and fed. This group became the basis for the foundation of the Japan branch of the Nature Conservation Society in 1951.

The 1950s and 1960s were growth years in the USA, western Europe and, especially, Japan. Because of the importance placed on economic development in all of these countries, industrial pollution and infrastructure development was treated as a nuisance that simply had to be tolerated. Only in a few instances did pollution become serious enough to gain political attention – as occurred in the UK after the 'killer smog' caused by an air inversion in London in 1952 led to an estimated 4,000 deaths. Parliament reacted by passing the Clean Air Bill in 1956 (Vogel 1986, pp. 38-9). The US Congress followed the UK lead several years later with the passage of the Clean Air Act in 1963. More dramatic changes to institutional structures and the introduction of sweeping environmental reforms did not occur until later in the decade and into the 1970s as environmental movements sprang up across the industrialized world.

The character and the timing of the rise and fall of the movements varied somewhat between Japan and other industrialized countries. Japan's environmental citizens' movement emerged relatively early. It focused on the health problems that started to plague the country. Because of Japan's extreme population density and the proximity of industrial facilities to urban residential areas, pollution and health became quickly intertwined. *kogaibyo* (pollution diseases) became a focus of national media and political attention by the end of the 1960s as more and more people came to learn of the Minamata and Kumamoto mercury poisoning cases, the *itai-itai* ('it hurts, it hurts') cadmium poisoning cases in Toyama Prefecture, the asthma problems associated with poor air quality in Yokkaichi, and the severe urban pollution and related health scares affecting communities in Tokyo, Osaka and other major urban areas.

By the early 1970s, there were thousands of environmental citizens' movements protesting a wide array of pollution and quality of life concerns. These groups were an important force behind the environmental policy changes that were made in Japan between 1967 and just after the oil shock of 1973.

Environmental activism continued in Japan after the early 1970s but its character was distinctly different from that which took shape in either the USA or northern Europe. Most of the protest movements of the early 1970s disbanded once their grievances were addressed. By the 1980s, the environmental movement in Japan had diminished in size and in political influence. There were still local environmental citizens' movements that continued their protest activities and objected to construction projects, such as airports, dams and US military facilities that threatened environmentally sensitive areas or the quality of life in residential communities. There were groups that worked to better urban environmental conditions through the greening of urban space or the cleaning up of urban waterways. Another important development was the *seikatsu seikyo* (consumer cooperatives) that formed across the country and began selling locally produced organic foods and eco-friendly products and encouraging their members to recycle milk cartons and to turn waste cooking oil into soap. Once they recognized that the key to safer living conditions was in influencing local politics, they also formed a national network and began sponsoring green-oriented politicians to run in local elections (Lam Peng Er 1999). Not until the late 1980s and early 1990s, however, did more than a few very small national environmental groups form and there were no independent environmental think tanks.

This is a major contrast with the situation in Europe and the USA in the 1970s and 1980s and is arguably one reason why environmental policy in Japan took on such a strong technological orientation and remained somewhat limited in the range of issues that were addressed. In the USA, numerous new environmental groups and think tanks formed in the 1970s, including Greenpeace, Friends of the Earth, the Natural Resources Defense Council, World Resources Institute and Resources for the Future. These and older groups, such as the Sierra Club and World Wildlife Fund, became central players in environmental policy formulation with most establishing offices near Capitol Hill in order to lobby and educate Congress and the media. In Europe too, national and international environmental groups, including Greenpeace and Friends of the Earth, formed and began launching campaigns. In addition, the citizens' movements that formed to protest infrastructure development that was destroying rural landscapes or to demonstrate against nuclear and coal power plants began forming national networks to strengthen their political power. The largest to form in Germany was the Bundesverband Bürgerinitiativen Umwelt.

Most dramatic is that in the parliamentary systems of Europe, green parties began to form. When the sit-ins, demonstrations and protests of activist groups (who were concerned about not only environmental protection, but also gender equality, nuclear energy and nuclear proliferation and the possibility of a breakout of a war between the USA and the Soviet Union on European soil) failed to bring about the kind of policy changes they desired, environmentalist decided to work to change policies from within the system. Activists formed green parties in an effort to change politics from within the system. France led the way when an environmental candidate stood for election in 1973. The success of green parties in winning representation in national parliaments and in some cases being invited to be coalition partners in government has made them a force to contend with in Europe (Bomberg 1998; O'Neill 1997). It has brought environmental policy matters directly into the legislative process in a way that is not paralleled in Japan or, for that matter, in the USA. In the June 2004 European Parliament elections, the green party grouping won 40 of the 732 seats. The German Green Party/Alliance 90 won 8.6 per cent of the seats in the Bundestag in the 2002 elections. There the party has helped to instill a greater awareness of environmental matters in the Social Democratic Party and Christian Democratic Union as well. There is some interest among environmentalists in Japan in the possibility of establishing a green party. The Green Network is trying to get an environmental party established in Japan.[9] To date, however, the network appears too weak to win seats at the national level.

It is interesting and important to consider why in Japan's parliamentary political system despite the emergence of numerous political parties, no green party has ever been elected to the Diet. While no definitive answer is possible, one can speculate that it has to do with a combination of factors, including lack of organizational leadership within Japan's environmental movement; lack of funds within the community and the absence of any outside support possibilities; a local as opposed to a national consciousness about the environment among most groups; and a highly competitive electoral system that is candidate-focused as opposed to party-focused. In the USA and Europe environmental groups were able to obtain funding for their operations from a combination of member donations, government grants or direct support (the case in some European countries) and foundation or church support. In addition, they could relatively easily obtain non-profit status and enjoy the ability to attract tax-deductible donations. As a result environmental groups were able to professionalize and hire staff. In contrast, in Japan until the late 1990s, there were huge hurdles that faced groups wanting to incorporate as non-profit organizations (NPOs), what in the West are usually called NGOs. Even those that have managed to get legal status as NPOs still have difficulty obtaining sufficient financial resources to hire full-time staff due to the problems of building up membership and obtaining donations. Japan lacks the large churches and private foundations that have helped fund civil society in Europe and North America. Nor as is the case in many European countries did the government provide environmental groups with any financial assistance although this is now changing.

As a result, Japan's environmental movement at the national level remains extremely small and weak when compared with the situation in the USA and northern Europe. Environmental policy formulation remained far more exclusively in the hands of bureaucrats and industry than was the case in either the USA or Europe. This, no doubt, influenced the range of environmental issues that were debated within Japan and the nature of policy solutions that were adopted.

Japanese Environmental Laws in Comparative Perspective

The latter 1960s and the 1970s were an explosive period of social movement activism in Japan and the West. While much of the unrest had to do with other issues – Japan's renewal of the Treaty of Mutual Cooperation and Security between Japan and the United States of America, the Vietnam war, women's rights (more the case in Europe and the USA than Japan) and civil rights, pollution problems and nuclear energy became rallying points in many societies. Citizens began to demand greater governmental accountability and an opening of political processes to greater citizen involvement. In the USA this led to the passage of the Freedom of Information Act in 1966, which was amended in 1974 after the Watergate scandal. In the 1960s the demands of a rapidly growing environmental movement resulted in the expansion of the rights of citizens in the USA to go to court not only when they themselves suffered damages from pollution but also in instances of damage to landscape, public health, or recreational opportunities. They also led to the landmark 1969 National Environmental

Policy Act (NEPA) mandating environmental impact assessments for all projects receiving federal funding and the 1970 amendments to the US Clean Air Act and Clean Water Act, which established strict new limitations on a range of pollutants (Jones 1975; Bryner 1995). In addition, the Environmental Protection Agency was established, following the lead of Sweden.

Legislative changes in Japan were influenced in no small way by developments in the USA. In Japan, the Pollution Control Basic Law of 1967, one of the first such laws in the world, was amended in the 1970 Pollution Diet when numerous laws and amendments addressing air and water quality, nature conservation and noise pollution similar to those in the USA were passed. The Environment Agency was established in 1971. Much of the pollution legislation that was introduced in Japan during the early 1970s was based on legislation introduced in the USA. Noticeable exceptions were that Japan did not expand the right of standing of citizens or environmental groups so that they could sue for protection of nature, introduce environmental impact assessment requirements as were mandated by the NEPA in the USA (Barrett and Therivel 1991), establish a freedom of information act that facilitates citizens' abilities to monitor government decision-making processes, or introduce regulations or procedures that would facilitate the formation of non-profit organizations (such as allowing tax deductible donations to non-profit groups).

Thus, while Japan joined the USA and Europe in introducing regulations requiring industry to meet emission standards, and in the case of emissions from automobiles established stricter standards than existed in either the USA or Europe (Nishimura 1989), the Japanese government was less open to the idea of passing legislation that would have made decision making more transparent or pluralistic.

Instead, the regulations that were introduced focused on the establishment of standards that were considered safe from a human health perspective and would make Japan more efficient in its use of resources. The government worked closely with industry, providing support in various ways, to facilitate the introduction of pollution control technologies and cleaner production methods. Both government and industry were pressured to ensure that the policies were in fact implemented by a public that had been made acutely aware of the threat of pollution to human health and a judicial system that had taken an untypically activist role in response to several major pollution disease cases that were brought before it (Upham 1987; Gresser, Fujikura and Morishima 1981). Notably under this pressure, the ruling Liberal Democratic Party passed a Pollution Victims' Compensation Law, which required industries in designated pollution zones to pay into a fund for pollution victims regardless of whether or not they as individual firms were responsible for the damage.

The extent to which pollution resulted in human suffering in Japan shaped in very important ways the focus of subsequent environmental protection efforts. The Japanese government's environmental protection priorities were heavily focused on the reduction of emissions that were hazardous to human health (Gresser, Fujikura and Morishima 1981). These were coupled with energy policies that would make Japan less dependent on energy imports. The result was a highly technologically oriented approach to pollution control, but one that proved quite effective in doing what it was intended to do – reduce targeted emissions and improve energy efficiency. Areas that fell outside of this area of focus, and especially those that threatened to restrict the powerful construction industry, did not meet with as much success. There was also little attention given to environmental conservation issues outside of Japan, which largely explains why Japan found itself being criticized quite strongly in the 1980s and early 1990s for its role in environmental destruction of the global commons (through, for example, overfishing, importing of endangered species, or tropical deforestation in Southeast Asia) (Dauvergne 1997; Dauvergne 2001; Bevis, 1995).

The pluralism that came to characterize the environmental policy field in the USA, Canada and northern Europe and that fostered important debates about environmental priorities and policy instruments was far more limited in Japan because of the weak role of environmental think tanks, environmental NGOs and environmental expert groups. In western Europe and the USA, environmental groups, think tanks and expert groups have played a very important role in bringing public and political attention to environmental threats and to developing and disseminating new ways of thinking about the environment. To give a few examples, Milieu Defensie (1992) and later the Wuppertal Institute in Germany were key developers and promoters of the ideas of ecological space and ecological footprints (Wuppertal Institut für Klima, Umwelt, Energie 1998). Environmental Defense in the USA played a key role in promoting the concept of emissions trading. They worked closely with the George H. W. Bush administration in the formulation of the 1990 Clean Air Act amendments that led to the introduction of a sulfur emissions permit trading system (Bryner 1995). Greenpeace Germany helped to develop the prototype of a refrigerator that does not consume ozone-depleting chlorofluorocarbons (CFCs) (Cavender-Bares and Jäger 2001: 75).

In Japan, environmental groups were too small to really play this kind of role, nor were they really welcomed or encouraged by the government to aid in policy formulation or the development of new policy instruments. And while there were a handful of politicians in the Diet who showed a strong interest in environmental issues, no political party emerged as a champion of the environment. Moreover, there were no independent environmental think tanks such as World Resources Institute, Resources for the Future, or the Max Plank Institutes. Environmental bureaucrats, who were eager to promote environmental causes, were themselves in a relatively weak position within a national government that even after the pollution problems of the 1960s and early 1970s remained predominately concerned with maintaining economic growth. In order to strengthen their positions in inter-ministerial negotiations and in policy formulation, these bureaucrats often turned to the outside – looking to the USA and Europe – for information about new environmental problems, policy ideas and policy instruments. They also looked to the west to apply pressure on the Japanese government to change policies that they did not have sufficient strength to change by themselves.

To the extent debates emerged about policy instruments and approaches, it came to a large extent from local governments that in many cases took the lead in pressuring the national government to act by taking matters into their own hands – passing emissions standards when the national government failed to act, introducing local freedom of information ordinances and establishing voluntary pollution control agreements with industry to assure that not only would they comply with national standards, but would also often exceed them.

Changing Japanese Approaches to Environmental Protection: the 1990s

The emergence of global environmental problems, such as stratospheric ozone depletion, forest loss, desertification and climate change, on the international policy agenda in the late 1980s and early 1990s has forced the Japanese government to make numerous changes to its environmental governance strategies and its environmental policy tool kit. These changes are in some ways bringing Japan a step closer to northern European models of environmental protection. The bureaucracy-centered model of environmental policy formation at the national level that had dominated since the 1970s has begun to be challenged as pressures to increase the role of NGOs in decision making emerged from both inside and outside of Japan.

Starting in the late 1980s and continuing in the 1990s, the character of Japan's environmental movement began to change. Several national environmental groups focusing on international environmental problems began to form, many with the help of international environmental groups and networks. These include groups such as Japan Tropical Action Network, the Sarawak Campaign, Greenpeace Japan and environmental NGO networks like Kiko Forum (Climate Forum) (Reimann 2001).

NGOs have also become more vocal and innovative in their methods of challenging construction and development projects which they consider environmentally unsound. In 1999, grassroots' initiatives (both led by university professors) helped to stop the construction of projects that would have destroyed environmentally important wetlands. The first was a garbage dump planned for Fujimae in Nagoya and the second the Chitose River

Diversion Channel in Hokkaido. International pressure and Japanese NGO protests led to the decision by Mitsubishi to give up on plans for the construction of a desalinization plant in a pristine marine environment off the coast of Mexico.[10]

Other groups in society also are becoming more concerned about a development path that places so much emphasis on construction and large-scale project development. Perhaps one of the most astounding signs of change relates to reformist Nagano Governor Yasuo Tanaka who when first elected governor announced his 'no more dams' policy. He terminated work on seven prefectural dams and plans for two others. This led to a no-confidence motion by the prefectural assembly, but Tanaka quit and decided to bring the issue to the voters. They reelected him in a landslide victory; he won 64 per cent of the votes in the September 2002 election.[11]

As a result of domestic pressure and the influence of international norms, government and corporate attitudes in Japan towards NGOs have begun to change as well. Government and industry slowly have started to accept NGOs as legitimate actors in the policy-making process and to recognize the role they can play in society in bringing attention to issues and helping to implement policy solutions. The passage of the NPO Law in 1998 was a major step towards making it easier for groups to obtain non-profit status. The establishment of the Keidanren Nature Conservation Fund is an example of a gradual shift in thinking by industry towards NGOs. The fund was set up by the peak industrial organization, Keidanren, in 1992 to support Japanese and foreign NGO activities for nature conservation in developing countries.[12] Another trend is the establishment of environmental think tanks, like the Institute for Global Environmental Strategies (IGES) set up in 1998.

While in terms of environmental governance, Japan has moved a step closer to the situation of many European countries or the USA with a more active and diverse environmental NGO community that is more accepted by traditional political elites, there are still more substantial institutional barriers that the community in Japan faces than is the case in western Europe or North America. One of the largest hurdles for NGOs is bringing in donations and increasing membership due to both institutional and cultural constraints. Lacking sufficient funding, still few environmental NGOs can afford to hire professional staff. Thus, most are run by volunteers, many of whom have full-time day jobs. Thus, while there are important signs of change, environmental NGOs in Japan remain too small and poorly financed to match their Western counterparts in terms of the size or scale of their campaigns or their ability to critique government plans and proposals or to make substantive policy recommendations.

Policy Instruments

Along with changes to inter-actor relations, Japan is embracing new approaches to environmental protection that resemble changes occurring in the range of policy instruments employed in Europe and the USA. Several new approaches to environmental management, some based on old approaches and others that are rather new experiments, are being tried. These include the use of voluntary agreements between government and industry to reduce greenhouse gas emissions (similar to the agreements that voluntary agreements that were established in Germany), experimentation with various flexible mechanisms, especially joint implementation and the clean development mechanism, eco-labeling, and to some degree, eco-taxation. Japan's interest in these new policy instruments (or new applications of existing instruments) is in part due to cross-societal learning. It is also, however, very much a reaction to Japan's difficult situation in relation to its Kyoto Protocol pledge to reduce its greenhouse gas emissions.

Japan found itself in a difficult situation when the George W. Bush administration announced it was withdrawing from the Kyoto Protocol. Although a strong ally of the USA, there was sufficient public pressure that Prime Minister Koizumi opted to side with the EU in pursuing the agreement even without participation by the USA (Schreurs 2002).

When Japan ratified the Kyoto Protocol in 2002, it committed itself to reducing its greenhouse gas emissions by 6 per cent of 1990 levels by 2008-12. In fiscal 2002, however, carbon dioxide emissions were 7.6 per cent higher than in 1990, meaning that Japan is close to 14 per cent above where it needs to be to meet its Kyoto Protocol commitments.[13]

Voluntary agreements for climate change
Voluntary agreements have been a popular approach to implement emissions reductions at the local level in Japan. They are also becoming widespread at the national level and resemble such agreements in the Netherlands, Germany, and to some extent, the UK. The Federation of Japanese Industry (Keidanren, which merged with another industry union to form Nippon Keidanren in 2002) in 1997 established guidelines for Japanese industry in the development of voluntary action plans to reduce greenhouse gas emissions and material consumption. There are now many voluntary action plans that have been established by entire industries and major corporations. A 2002 survey conducted to assess the effectiveness of these voluntary action plans found that combined 34 industries in the energy and industrial sectors had, through the use of voluntary action plans, reduced their combined carbon dioxide emissions by 3.2 per cent in fiscal 2001.[14]

In addition, there is now much interest among Japanese industry in obtaining the International Standard Organization (ISO) 14001 environmental management series certification. Japanese corporations lead the world in terms of certifications. At the end of 2002, 10,620 Japanese corporations has obtained certificates, far more than the USA (2,620) and more than the combined total for Germany (3,700), the UK (2,917) and France (1,467).[15] Of course, it should be noted that European corporations may instead apply for the EU's Eco-management and Audit Scheme and this may explain the lower interest in ISO 14001 there. Japan's voluntary initiatives are certainly interesting and appear to be having some impact, but they do not appear to be sufficient on their own to alter industrial behavior sufficiently to achieve Japan's Kyoto Protocol target.

Flexible mechanisms: joint implementation and clean development mechanism

At the seventh Conference of the Parties to the Framework Convention on Climate Change where the rules for implementing the Kyoto Protocol were hammered out, Japan fought hard to allow maximum flexibility in how nation's could achieve their goals. Japan was largely successful in these efforts and is now actively pursuing joint implementation and clean development mechanism projects that it can pursue in developing countries, and obtain credit for, towards its emission reduction requirements. In 2003 feasibility studies were conducted for 20 projects, ranging from a wind-power generation project in Hungary, to a sugar industry waste-to-energy project in São Paulo, Brazil, to the planting of a rubber tree plantation in Cambodia's Mondul Kiri highlands.[16]

Carbon taxes

The EU's plans to launch a carbon emissions' trading system beginning in January 2005 are being watched with much interest in Japan. Japan too has begun to explore the possibility of initiating a carbon emissions' trading system domestically.[17] The Ministry of the Environment also is eager to establish a climate change (carbon) tax, but this has met with opposition from other ministries.[18] Compared with the EU where numerous countries have introduced some form of carbon tax and the world's first international carbon emissions' trading system is about to begin, Japan is still just beginning to look more seriously at taxation and emissions' trading to reduce emissions.

Regional Agreements

The East Asian region has few international programs or agreements governing economic and other behavior that might impact the environment because of the strained relations among states that characterized the region for most of the twentieth century. With the substantial improvements in regional relations (with the important exception of North Korea) since the end of the Cold War, Japan has initiated numerous programs for enhancing ties among nations in the region related to the environment. While it could be argued that this is being done to spare Japan from downwind pollution, to improve Japan's own environmental technology export possibilities, or to counter Japan's still blemished image in the region, the developments are noteworthy.

In 1993 Japan initiated the East Asia Acid Deposition Monitoring Network (EANET), which has as its goal the development of monitoring capacities throughout the region and the sharing of data. The EANET brings together scientific experts from Japan, Mongolia, the Philippines, Korea, Cambodia, Indonesia, Laos, Malaysia, Russia, Thailand and Vietnam. The network moved beyond study and planning to implementation of programs in 2002.[19] While still a long way removed from the European Long Range Transboundary Air Pollution agreement in its achievements, Japan also participates in the Long Range Transboundary Air Pollutants in Northeast Asia research effort.

Japan has been an active participant in the more or less annual, Tri-partite Environment Ministers Meeting (TEMM), which since 1999 have brought together the Environment Ministers of Japan, China and Korea to discuss programs and provide the political momentum necessary to move forward on joint programs. In Johannesburg, South Africa, during the 2002 World Summit on Sustainable Development, Prime Minister Jun'ichiro Koizumi announced a program entitled, IDEA or Initiative for Development in East Asia. The program is to focus on environmental education, renewable energies, safe drinking water and addressing climate change, biodiversity loss and forest loss.[20]

In the long run, moving beyond national approaches to environmental protection to broader regional and international environmental programs will be important for the region. Japan has made considerable efforts in this direction in the past decade although it must still cope with lingering anti-Japanese sentiment in the region.

Japan's Environmental Performance in International Comparison

There are several comparative data sets that one can use to try to get a handle on how Japan performs relative to other industrialized states. The picture is mixed. An international team commissioned by the OECD to assess Japan's environmental policy performance, found that 'Overall the mix of instruments used to implement environmental policy is highly effective. Regulations are strict, well enforced and based on strong monitoring capacities. Significant progress has been made in tackling non-conventional air pollutants (e.g. dioxin, benzene) and waste management can be expected to improve further with the relevant overhaul of the relevant legislative framework.' The report further notes that strict standard setting has had a technology-forcing effect and pushed Japanese industries to reduce their ecological footprint. Japan can, however, further expand its range of policy instruments, including greater use of market mechanisms (Organization for Economic Cooperation and Development 2000).

Redefining Progress and Earthday Network have developed an international database comparing national ecological footprints, a measure of the amount of productive land area that is required to support a nation's consumption of energy, food, natural resources and waste disposal. According to this database, Japan does quite well when compared to North America or Australia and is on a par with major European countries. On average the US life style requires 9.7 hectares per person, the Canadian 8.8 and the Australian 7.6. In comparison, the Japanese life style requires an average of 4.8 ha per person roughly on a par with the average German's 4.7, and somewhat more than the average Korean's 3.3. In comparison, the ecological footprint per person in developing countries is far lower: for China 1.5, Indonesia 1.1 and the Philippines 1.2.[21] Japan's land mass, however, is not sufficient to meet its national consumption levels given the size of the Japanese population. Japan has a large deficit of 4.1 ha per person comparing the size of the country to the amount of land required to meet the Japanese life style. This suggests that much of what Japan consumes is done at the expense of the environment in other countries.

Japan performs less well in the international Environmental Sustainability Index (ESI) ranking that was prepared by the World Economic Forum in collaboration with the Yale Center for Environmental Law and Policy and CIESIN.[22] This index measures a nation's global sustainability performance in five core areas: the quality of a nation's environmental systems, its progress towards reducing stresses on those systems, its progress towards reducing human vulnerability and its contribution to global stewardship. The 2002 index was built using a total of 68 variables that measure such factors as air and water quality, biodiversity levels, protected land, reduction in waste and consumption, reduction in population growth, longevity, infant mortality rates and the nation's social and institutional capacity for achieving sustainable development. This includes such factors as the capacity for debate, science and technology achievements and extent of subsidies provided for energy development or commercial fishing.

Based on this index, which it should be noted is still at an early stage of development, Japan ranks 78th out of 142 countries. Its ESI totaled 48.6 out of a possible 100. In comparison, Finland ranked first internationally with an ESI of 73.9; Canada came in fourth with an ESI of 70.6; the USA was 45th with a ranking of 53.2 and Germany 50th with a ranking of 52.5. Japan's comparatively lower ranking can be attributed to a considerable extent on its high population density and the extreme land and pollution pressures that result from this. Japan may also be penalized in this dataset since most of its most dramatic environmental improvements occurred in the 1970s and 1980s and the database only measures improvements over the 1990s. Where Japan performed relatively well in relation to its peers in this index was on variables measuring social and institutional capacity, reduction of human vulnerabilities and global stewardship. It was weaker in terms of reducing greenhouse gas emissions, water stress, waste consumption, and biodiversity and land pressures. It will be important to see if Japan's rankings improve in the coming years as a result of the numerous legislative changes of recent years.

CONCLUSION

The experiences of Japan, the USA and European countries with balancing economic development with environmental protection suggest that they have had much learning to do. Their histories are replete with stories of pollution-related tragedies and environmental destruction. Currently, they still cast long ecological shadows on the planet. Yet, their histories also suggest that there has been much learning about ways to protect the environment and human health while promoting economic growth and technological advancement.

A comparison of these three regions shows that cross-societal learning has been an important element of environmental management (Social Learning Group 2001). This learning can include the borrowing or adaptation of environmental policy instruments, institutional arrangements and even norms and values. On their own, these states would not have made as much progress in environmental management had they not had each other's examples to learn from. In all three regions, there has been a broadening of definitions of the environment. Initially, pollution was categorized by type: air, water, land, waste, noise, etc. Nature conservation was basically a matter of setting aside land for protection and restricting its use. This meant that at times, policies that were introduced to deal with one pollution problem actually exacerbated other pollution problems. The first generation of environmental laws did not take a comprehensive view of the relationship between human activities and the natural environment. While none of the countries has yet achieved a sustainable system from an environmental perspective, there have been efforts to make environmental protection a more integrated component of government planning. The emergence of new kinds of environmental problems suggests that environmental learning is not a finite process. It is an ongoing process that continues to challenge the advanced industrialized states.

There has also been a learning process in how governments go about making environmental decisions. It is recognized that environmental policy making requires inputs from all actors who have a stake in the matter. Initially, pollution control was a highly contentious policy area. This is still true to some extent. Yet, today environmental groups are accepted as a necessary and important element of societal efforts to promote environmental protection. More and more, corporations, governments and NGOs are finding it necessary to talk with each other about how to best promote environmental goals. Consultative decision making is gaining ground.

There are many similarities in the experiences of the advanced industrialized states in addressing pollution and environmental protection. Yet, there are also important differences among them. These differences stem from differences in geographical constraints and natural resource endowments. They are also strongly influenced by governmental structures and institutions and political culture.

Japan, Europe and the USA have strengths and weaknesses in different environmental management areas. The USA has dominated scientific research and influenced strongly philosophical debates on the environment. It has also been a leading proponent of nature conservation. In the 1970s, the rest of the world watched the USA because of its innovative environmental policy and institutional developments. Increasingly, however, opponents of environmental regulations have succeeded in blocking new environmental initiatives and relaxing some environmental laws. These domestic trends have carried over into the international realm. As a result, the USA is not a party to several important international environmental agreements, including the Kyoto Protocol and the Convention on Biological Diversity. The USA has lost some of its ability to claim environmental leadership internationally even though the USA remains an important country to watch because of the new environmental management philosophies (and especially the emphasis on market approaches to environmental protection) that are gaining ground there.

Europe, since the rise of the green parties, has become increasingly influential in promoting new ideas about environmental management, including collective decision making and comprehensive environmental planning. Some of the most innovative programmatic ideas related to environmental protection are now emerging in Europe. The EU is leading the world with its establishment of an international carbon trading system. Yet, Europe too faces many challenges. The complexity of decision making within the EU can make reaching agreement on environmental policy goals difficult and expansion of the EU is likely to make this an even larger challenge (Carmin and VanDeveer 2004).

Japan too has become an important source of environmental policy innovation. Japan's strengths lie primarily with enforcement of pollution control on stationary sources of air and water pollution and in technological innovations for energy efficiency. Government and industry have worked closely together in making it possible for industry to meet pollution control goals with some flexibility. Past successes with air pollution control and energy efficiency improvements are now being extended to broader environmental challenges such as sustainable development. How successful Japan can be in doing this remains to be seen. Japan has been weakest in terms of involving citizens in environmental decision-making processes. This is something that is slowly starting to change as environmental NGOs gain greater societal acceptance. Meanwhile, Japan is becoming one of the dominant players influencing environmental policy developments elsewhere in Asia. Thus, the model that Japan employs domestically is likely to be exported in part to other regions of Asia.

Environmental learning must continue. Ecological degradation continues within the advanced industrialized states and internationally as a result of their economic activities. The advanced industrialized states must consider how their policy examples influence the policy decisions of developing states in the world. Developing countries, which face serious pollution problems that are threatening human health and long-term sustainability, must consider how they will tackle these problems. The experiences of the advanced industrialized societies provide many ideas for consideration.

NOTES

[1] www.eia.doe.gov/emeu/env/japan.html.
[2] Department of Transport, UK, www.statistics.gov.uk/cci/nugget.asp?id=24.
[3] Department of Transport, UK, 'Car Use in Great Britain, Personal Travel Factsheet,' 2003, www.dft.gov.uk/stellent/groups/dft_transstats/documents/page/dft_transstats_508295.pdf.
[4] Ministry of Land, Infrastructure and Transport, Japan www.mlit.go.jp/road/road_e/index.e.html.
[5] The survey was conducted in October 2000 by Japan Guide. Most respondents were between the ages of 18-30. The survey results are posted at www.japan-guide.com/topic/0011.html, 30 June 2004.
[6] sedac.ciesin.columbia.edu/entri/index.jsp.
[7] Discussion with Michio Hashimoto in 1991.
[8] See www.env.go.jp/en/jeg/nps/pamph/.
[9] See the Greens Network, nvc.halsnet.com/jhattori/green.net.
[10] I am grateful to Richard Forrest for suggesting these examples.
[11] See Japan Foreign Press Center, 'Nagano Governor Tanaka Loses Job and Then Announces Candidacy in Next Gubernatorial Election,' 26 July 2002, www.fpcj/e/shiryo/jb/0225.html and Japan Foreign Press Center, 'Tanaka Wins Landslide Reelections as Nagano Prefecture Governor,' 12 September 2002, www.fpcj/e/shiryo/jb/0232.html.
[12] See www.keidanren.or.jp/kncf/eng_index.html.
[13] Eriko Arita, 'Japan Struggles to Cut Emissions as Levels Increase: Kyoto Protocol Promise Difficult to Keep as Lifestyle Changes Drive Up Carbon Dioxide,' Japan Times, 17 June 2004, www.japantimes.co.jp/cgi-bin/getarticle.pl5?nn20040617f1.htm.
[14] Nippon Keidanren, 'Results of the 5th Follow-up to the Keidanren Voluntary Action Plan on the Environment, Section on Global Warming Measures,' 17 October 2002,

www.keidanren.or.jp/ english/policy/2002/064/report.html.

[15] International Standard Organization, 'The ISO Survey of ISO 9000 and ISO 14001 Certificates, Twelfth Cycle: Up to and Including 31 December 2002,' pp. 29-31, www.iso.org/iso/en/iso9000-14000/pdf/survey12thcycle.pdf.

[16] Ministry of the Environment 'Feasibility Studies on Climate Change Mitigation Projects for Clean Development Mechanism and Joint Implementation in 2003,' www.env.go.jp/en/topic/cc/030828.pdf.

[17] Takyua Ogushi and Seiki Kure, 'Carbon Dioxide Emissions Trading Test Project in Japan,' OECD Global Forum on Sustainable Development: Emissions Trading, Concerted Action on Tradable Emissions Permits Country Forum, OECD Headquarters, Paris 17-18 March, 2003, CCNM/GF/ENV(2003)13/FINAL, www.oecd.org/dataoecd/11/30/2957719.pdf.

[18] Expert Committee on Tax Systems to Combat Climate Change Joint Committee on General Policy Planning and Global Environment, Central Environment Council, 'Draft of Climate Change Tax: Proposal for a National Dialogue,' www.env.g.jp/en/topic/cc/040209.html.

[19] See www.rrcap.unep.org/projects/acidDNM.cfm.

[20] See www.mofa.go.jp/policy/environment/wssd/2002/kinitiative.html.

[21] See www.earthday.net/goals/footprintnations.stm. Data is for 1999.

[22] See www.ciesin.columbia.edu/indicators/ESI/rank.html.

14. Evaluating Japan's Environmental Policy Performance

Hidefumi Imura

INTRODUCTION

Japan's environmental policy was influenced by developments in the USA and some European countries. Yet, it developed distinct characteristics as a result of Japan's need to confront some of the worst environmental problems experienced by any industrialized country in the world, a consequence of rapid economic growth and the failure of government and industry to appreciate the need for pollution control. Japan's pollution tragedy should neither be forgotten, nor repeated.

Lessons were learned, however, and beginning in the 1970s, Japan initiated an ambitious nationwide project to clean up its pollution problems. One of the most outstanding achievements of these efforts was the development of stringent framework environmental legislation that did much to stem and cleanup pollution problems without inhibiting economic growth, and some would argue even helped it. In many countries, environmental regulations are established, but problems emerge in the implementation stage. Motivated by its past experiences with economic and health problems from pollution, Japan has done relatively well with cleaning up pollution, especially industrial pollution.

There may be lessons in this experience for developing countries. A strength of the Japanese approach has been that once environmental targets are set, government and industry cooperate in sometimes unique ways, and in many cases (albeit not all) meet those targets. This was done with both local and national policy instruments that resulted in relatively effective policy implementation. This book has examined some of the approaches that have developed in Japan, including strategies for the development of pollution control technologies, financial mechanisms for promoting pollution control technology research and development and voluntary pollution control agreements. It also has assessed environmental institutions that have emerged and the changes that have occurred in the relationships among government, industry and non-governmental organizations (NGOs) from one of contention to one of greater inter-actor cooperation.

Japan is still learning about pollution control, environmental protection and sustainable development and new policy approaches are developing. In the twenty-first century, Japan will have to rely more on market forces and initiatives of businesses and citizens, moving away from its interventionist government style. The role of government in environmental policy will shift increasingly from that of a regulator to that of a planner that encourages voluntary environmental protection efforts by stakeholders. Japan, for example, is now experimenting with creating a socio-economic structure based on what the Ministry of Environment has termed, a 'sound material cycle.' This goal requires the participation of all societal actors and the promotion of new environmental industry, which in turn could facilitate an industrial transformation towards sustainable development. It is the hope of the authors of this book, that others have also learned lessons about approaches to avoid, and some which may be useful for finding a balance between economic development and protection of the environment from reading about Japan's approaches to environmental management.

Japan's model of environmental policy was adapted from US and European models and modified to the unique conditions of Japan. Japan itself devoted great efforts to the development of its own environmental policy systems and advanced control measures. This chapter summarizes some of the unique characteristics of Japan's environmental management style as it has developed over the course of the past 30 to 40 years.

Japan's desire to catch up with the West economically led the country to focus all of its efforts on industrial development. It did this with little and, one could even argue, no attention to the environment. The country's success with this effort is nothing short of astounding: Japan lay ruined at the end of World War II; it was the second largest economy in the free world by the end of the 1960s. This is a success story that many developing countries wish to emulate. But, the authors of this book stress that this growth came at a tremendous cost to the environment and human health, and one for which Japan had to pay a heavy price for decades to follow. Not only did this focus on development first; pollution control later resulted in loss of much natural and scenic beauty, it turned the country into a pollution nightmare that threatened human survival.

This approach to development, moreover, proved politically destabilizing and led to nationwide protests against government and industry. It resulted in legal battles in a country that typically shies away from litigation. It resulted in strong international criticism of Japan's failure to protect humans from pollution, which resulted in sicknesses and death. It is a model that has scarred Japan. Japan is still healing from these wounds.

While Japan's pollution history is sobering, it also gave birth to a new national interest in pollution control beginning in the late 1960s and early

1970s. Japan proved that in a decade's time a country could go from being among the most polluted in the world to being a leading world producer of pollution control technologies. As a result of strong citizen protest, the Japanese government formed institutions for pollution control and implemented stringent environmental pollution control regulations. In addition to environmental regulations, a variety of unique policy instruments were developed that helped Japan to implement regulations with a level of success found in few other countries. This was particularly true in regards to energy efficiency improvements and air pollution reduction (Committee on Japan's Experience in the Battle against Air Pollution 1997, pp. 113-30). This project has assessed some of the factors that contributed to this pollution turnaround.

There have been many improvements in Japan's approach to environmental protection, although problems remain. The Japanese government and industry were criticized for not giving citizens a greater voice in the policy-making process, for ignoring damage to natural areas in an effort to promote a 'resort society' and neglecting the environmental degradation that Japan was contributing to overseas. Partly in reaction to this criticism and partly in an effort to play a larger global role, since the 1990s, Japan's environmental policy has entered a new phase in terms of its scope and objectives. Japanese policy makers and society are addressing new challenges, such as the risks posed by chemicals, climate change and biodiversity loss. During this time, not only has Japan become one of the world's top donors of official development assistance, it has done much to 'green' its aid, which in the past was often criticized as being too 'brown,' that is, focused too much on infrastructural development at the cost of the environment. Steps are also being taken to enhance the role of citizens in environmental decision making and adopting elements of the European approach to inter-actor cooperation or stakeholder participation in decision making. In response to changing economic and social conditions domestically, there is also growing recognition of a need to find more cost-effective ways to approach pollution control, and as a result Japan is experimenting with many new policy instruments.

Several questions have been posed implicitly or explicitly in the chapters in this book and are taken up again in this chapter. What positive and negative lessons can we draw from Japanese experiences and practices? Japan did not react to its pollution problems until acute and severe damage to health had occurred. How could such damage have been avoided? It is often assumed that developing countries have little choice but to focus on development first and pollution control later. Yet, this assumption fails to consider what the short and long-term costs of pollution may be to a society. What was the economic impact of pollution on Japanese society in the short and long term? It is often assumed that pollution control is a luxury that is only available to rich countries. How much did it cost to introduce pollution control measures in Japan? On balance, what has the economic impact of the introduction of stringent environmental policies been? While not all pollution and environmental problems can be solved with 'technological fixes,' technology certainly plays an important role in pollution mitigation. What was the role of pollution control technology in Japan, and how was it possible to develop an advanced pollution control industry? How does Japan perform in environmental pollution control relative to other countries? In what areas is Japan a good country from which to learn lessons? In what areas may other countries be better examples? What ideas can developing countries take from Japan's experiences with pollution and environmental protection? Finally, what must Japan do to improve its approach to the protection of the global environment and in helping developing countries protect their environments?

This chapter considers the factors that made it possible for Japan to clean up the worst of its pollution problems and forge a role as a leader in various pollution control measures. It focuses on the key policy instruments and governance mechanisms that have evolved in Japan. It examines the importance of environmental regulations and their enforcement and recognizes that effective implementation requires the existence of 'social capital.' The chapter summarizes briefly the roles played by local initiatives, the greening of industry and business and voluntarism. The chapter then turns to the question of the compatibility of economic growth and environmental protection. The Japanese experience suggests that economic growth and environmental protection can be compatible when environmental protection if taken seriously by government, industry and society.

In the next section, the chapter turns to the equally important lessons that can be learned from what Japan did wrong. It argues that pollution damages were severe and came at an unacceptably high price and that this was caused by government and industry failure. Development plans were inadequate in their failure to consider the environmental consequences of uncontrolled growth. Lack of coordination among ministries exacerbated problems and the political parties failed to champion environmental causes. The chapter then considers and critiques the strengths and weaknesses of factors that could be considered characteristic of Japan's approach to environmental management. These include the establishment of action plans, public works projects, the limited use of economic instruments and financing mechanisms for environmental protection. Finally, the chapter concludes with an overview of new challenges facing Japan and the reform of Japan's environmental policies. Slowly efforts are emerging to take Japan in the direction of a more sustainable form of development. Japan is now playing a larger role in addressing global environmental issues and in providing international cooperation for environmental protection.

CHARACTERISTICS OF JAPAN'S ENVIRONMENTAL MANAGEMENT APPROACH

Strict Enforcement of Environmental Regulations

One notable achievement of Japan has been its success in enforcing strict environmental regulations. The USA is known for the leadership role it played in initiating the modern environmental policy movement in the 1960s. Various northern European countries are known for the new ideas they have developed regarding environmental protection, such as ecological modernization or Green Plans. Japan's real success story is in its enforcement of environmental policies.

The Organization for Economic Cooperation and Development (OECD) conducted a review of environmental policies in Japan three times; first in 1976-77, second in 1993-94 and most recently in 2001-2. As noted in the introductory chapter, the first OECD report (1977) concluded that Japan had won many pollution abatement battles although it had not yet won the war for environmental quality. It identified the Japanese approach to environmental protection as being based on a combination of regulations and sophisticated technologies, but pointed out the need for Japan to develop a broader-based approach to environmental protection that dealt not only with pollution control but also with the preservation of natural and cultural heritage and with the promotion of well-being in general. This report, perhaps because of the importance of *gaiatsu* (foreign pressure) to Japanese policy formation, had a major impact on Japan. It helped Japan to develop pride in its achievements, but also pushed the country to expand the scope of its environmental programs and became an incentive for people to get involved in new policy areas, such as urban environmental amenities. A quarter of a century later, the third OECD environmental report (2002) concluded that while there was still room for improvement, especially in terms of opening up decision-making processes to greater NGO participation and using more economic instruments (like environmental taxes) for policy enforcement, on the whole, the mix of instruments used to implement environmental policy is already highly effective. Japan was characterized as having strict environmental regulations that are well enforced and based on strong monitoring capacities.

Role of Action Plans

An important policy instrument of the Japanese central and local governments is the use of action plans. There are various national and local plans for economic development, energy supply and demand, construction of infrastructures and environmental management. This is a legacy of the control the government had over all economic and social activities in the country especially when Japan was seeking to become a rich and strong nation economically and militarily in the first half of the twentieth century. Japan is now a country of capitalism and has a free market system, but it still has a large public sector. Major industries, such as the electric utilities, iron and steel, chemical and construction industries, were under the control and guidance of government. Government plans were utilized for government and industries to establish consensus about national economic policies and take concerted actions. This planning system in Japan is somewhat similar to the plans used in socialistic countries, such as China, and differs substantially from the more *laissez-faire* approach of the USA.

Implementation of Japan's national and local environmental policies is also based on environmental plans. The national Basic Environmental Plan, which was drawn up in 1994 in accordance with the Basic Environmental Law of 1993, is being used to set environmental goals and targets for actors to achieve.

The successful implementation of such plans, however, depends upon the power of government to influence positively the behavior of businesses and citizens and the willingness of businesses and citizens to act.

Social Capital

What were the preconditions that enabled the successful implementation of environmental regulation in Japan? One important factor lies in Japanese society, which showed a will to enforce control measures. This will emerged, no doubt, because society saw for itself how serious environmental risks can be and an implicit agreement emerged within society regarding basic environmental goals that needed to be achieved. One key factor in explaining Japanese success in controlling pollution might be 'social capital' or 'informal institutions' that govern Japanese society. According to Sanjaya Lall (2002), groups or countries with strong social capital are able to function better: Members interact more closely with each other, spend less effort on formal methods of enforcing contracts, reach greater consensus on common aims and are able to implement joint actions more efficiently. According to the World Development Report 2002, 'informal institutions' comprise social norms or networks that supplement or supplant formal laws and institutions; where they work well, they can lower the costs and risks of economic transactions, thereby improving information flows and spreading risks (World Bank 2002, pp. 171-9; World Bank 2003, pp. 37-58).

Japanese society has been characterized by social anthropologists and sociologists as being oriented towards group decision making, mass culture and cultural homogeneity. These traits helped Japan to eventually confront its past mistakes and deal with the devastating environmental pollution problems that the country's thirst for economic development had created. Pushed by the demands coming from below, the pressures coming abroad and the activism of local governments and the courts, networks of political leaders and government and industry elites came to agreement on the need to introduce tough environmental regulations with leading standards internationally. They also agreed on the need for large-scale investment in pollution control technologies. Initially, these actions were delayed because industries argued that the economic costs would be too high and would make Japan uncompetitive internationally. Industry and government also initially argued there was not sufficient scientific evidence that economic activities were posing environmental risks. But the environmental impacts of industrial growth had surpassed the breaking point. Political, social and economic stability were threatened. The government and industry had no choice but to alter course. In the so-called Pollution Control Session of the National Assembly in 1970, 14 environmental laws and amendments to existing laws were passed putting Japan in the ranks of the countries with the most advanced environmental regulations in the world. In addition, local governments and factories concluded thousands of pollution control agreements (PCAs) that often went beyond the requirements of these new national laws; the PCAs were based on mutual trust rather than any kind of formal laws, not unlike the 'covenants' among government, industry and NGOs that have become quite well known in the Netherlands.

Once introduced, regulation and standards were strictly implemented thanks to the effectiveness of local environmental administration and the emergence of a culture requiring firms to be 'socially responsible' (a practice that has been influenced by Western notions of philanthropy and the watchful eye of the Japanese press, citizens groups and NGOs, domestically and overseas). Also important is that relative to many other transition economies, Japan was fortunate to have relatively clean government, and thus, although there are certainly exceptions, corruption and bribes were not systematically used to circumvent standards. Relatively clean government has lowered the transaction costs.

As will be discussed more below, there was also another very important factor in turning industry a shade greener. The good will of industry alone would not have sufficed. Government assistance was necessary to encourage enterprises to make investments in pollution control measures as was close dialogue between government and industry. Another factor was the important role played by local initiatives.

Local Initiatives Backed by the Voice of the People

Local governments played a significant role in improving environmental conditions in Japan. Although it was the central government that instituted national environmental laws and regulations and extended financial assistance to help industries come into compliance, local governments played a leading role in environmental protection at the local level. Numerous prefectures and municipalities pioneered environmental regulations backed by the support of local residents. They enforced stricter regulations than the national government, and established sophisticated environmental monitoring and inspection systems to achieve their goals. These developments occurred in the context of a society where because freedom of speech and political discussion are guaranteed, media campaigns and local protest movements were able to point out government and industrial failures. Such anti-pollution public opinion forced the government and industry to take effective control measures or risk losing legitimacy in the eyes of the public.

This decentralized approach to environmental administration not only helped significantly in the implementation of regulations and standards, it saved major costs in terms of monitoring and inspection. A relatively small number of officials in the center and environmental departments of local governments were able to oversee the implementation of environmental policy. They were aided by advanced monitoring and measurement techniques, such as automatic sampling and measurement and telemeters, which reduced their administrative costs.

Greening of Industries and Business Voluntarism

Japan's environmental policy management has relied to a considerable extent on the 'voluntary' initiatives of businesses. Local governments made extensive use of pollution PCAs that were established with industries and required high environmental performance standards. There were several background conditions that have made PCAs relatively effective in this task. These include a relatively high degree of local government autonomy in the realm of pollution control with support from the national government. Also very important was the rapid development of local government capacity to know about pollution problems and to negotiate with local businesses on a scientific basis. Resident support for PCAs could be turned into a positive incentive for industries to establish and comply with PCAs, as they could help businesses obtain local acceptance despite considerable local skepticism towards industry in a country where geographical factors force industry and residential areas to lie adjacent to each other. Because of the pioneering role played by local governments in initiating pollution measures, an atmosphere of acceptance of local initiatives persisted and this resulted in national acceptance of the legal legitimacy of PCAs. The PCA approach also worked thanks to a somewhat unique Japanese business culture of espousing corporate obedience and bureaucratic ethics. In the 1990s, Japanese industries have started to look towards other voluntary initiatives, including voluntary action plans, acquiring ISO 14000 accreditation and publishing environmental statement reports. Whether this latest shift towards a new form of voluntarism will work as effectively as the PCAs have remains to be seen. Questions can be raised about whether businesses actions can be motivated by pure ethical motives or if they require the push provided by the kind of 'quasi-voluntary' regime that retains outside regulatory oversight as a form of 'encouragement' to industry as has been the case with PCAs.

Compatibility of Economy and Environment

Macroeconomic impact
Multiple economic lessons can be drawn from Japan's experiences. The most important is that there can be compatibility between environmental regulation and economic development.

Although no overall cost benefit analysis of Japan's environmental regulations has ever been conducted (nor may such an analysis really be possible), it is noteworthy that throughout the 1970s and 1980s when Japanese industries were investing heavily in pollution control technologies, the Japanese economy continued to grow rapidly. The extra cost burden imposed by fluctuating oil prices on the economy often proved to be much greater than the added costs of pollution control measures. Most pollution control costs were offset by growth effects. At the micro-level, environmental regulations undoubtedly posed hardships for certain weak industrial sectors, but the macroscopic impacts were far less significant than many industries argued before they began introducing pollution control technologies and improving production methods. It could even be argued that strict enforcement of pollution control enhanced economic growth in Japan as energy efficiency improvements and changes in production reduced costs, reduced the need for energy and raw material inputs, improved industrial relations with society and led to the development of new export industries.

The prime objectives of environmental policy are to prevent ecological disasters, protect human health and preserve the natural environment. Japan's case shows that environmental policies can also have other unintended positive impacts upon the national economy. First, coupled with increased oil prices, environmental policies accelerated energy saving, especially by energy consumptive manufacturing industries. Second, they stimulated the development and diffusion of various control technologies. A market for such technologies was created, which now assumes a significant position in the national economy. Many firms seek the label of an 'environmental industry' or 'eco-industry.' Third, and most importantly, environmental and health damages were avoided with a relatively small investment cost. If the air pollution of the late 1960s Japan had continued through today, there would have been countless health victims. The compensation payments that the government and industry would have been required to make to them would have been tremendous, much exceeding the cost actually spent for control measures. This was the lesson of such infamous cases as the Yokkaichi pollution case.

Technological solutions
Japan's success in controlling pollution heavily relied upon sophisticated technologies. With its poor natural resource base for industrial production, Japan's postwar economic development policy emphasized science education and research and development of industrial technologies. Japan's environmental policies were implemented on the shop floor by engineers and technical experts who were in charge of operating machines and equipment. The system that Japan developed of certifying pollution engineers throughout most industries proved highly effective and is something that could relatively easily be implemented in other countries. China has studied this system in order to introduce pilot projects in some provinces and municipalities.

Japanese firms must operate under extremely severe environmental, resource and space conditions, a condition found in many other developing countries as well. Japan's conspicuously high concentration of economic and social activities in a limited land area (in terms of habitable land area) compared with other industrialized countries has placed a heavy burden on the environment, especially in some industrial regions. Under these conditions, the role of industrial innovation and the development of technology have been of extreme importance to the survival of Japanese firms in competitive domestic and international markets and to their ability at the same time to conform to stringent environmental requirements. Counter-intuitively, these harsh business conditions have helped to ensure an innovative response by Japanese firms to environmental regulations.

The costs of achieving environmental standards proved to be considerably smaller than was initially expected. This was largely due to the efforts made in industrial innovation and technological development. Environmental policy did not undermine Japan's economic growth, but rather growth was sustained by environmental policy. Japan has taken advantage of new industrial processes, which are not only economically and financially justified in themselves, but have resulted in environmental improvements. Pollution control and energy-saving technologies rapidly progressed mainly because there was aggressive investment in new plants and equipment during the 1970s, a period of continued high growth. This investment was spurred on by tightened anti-pollution regulations and increased energy prices. Thus, the Japanese experience suggests that in the early stages of environmental measures, end-of-pipe (EP) technology, such as the retrofitting of pollution control equipment to existing production facilities, can be quite effective. Japan is now in a different stage of economic development and EP solutions no longer prove sufficient or are entirely cost effective. As a result, Japan is now moving in the direction of replacing facilities and equipment with cleaner production (CP).

Dynamic efficiency: favorable impact on technology development

The efficiency of Japan's technology-based approach should be examined from the viewpoint of dynamic efficiency, and its important ancillary effects. Not only does this approach eliminate pollution, it also strengthens technological capacity and competitiveness. An example of this is that after the oil crisis in 1973, Japanese industries developed energy-saving and CP technologies, achieving a win-win solution of environmental control and cost reduction.

Strictly mandated government pollution standards helped foster company technological breakthroughs in pollution control technology. The resulting pollution control technology can produce positive effects for the national economy. It can create new products to meet the new, mandated demand and employ new workers to make the products. On the macro economic level, these positive effects can offset any negative economic effects resulting from enforced company investment in pollution control. In order to induce compliance by polluting industries, the Japanese government provided extensive financial support for industries to install expensive pollution control equipment. In effect, this support spreads out the micro economic costs of pollution control, reducing the burden on any given factory or firm, hence lowering the barriers to individual change.

In sum, it can be argued that environmental control measures were promoted in no small way by public pressure, environmental regulations, local initiatives, the nurturing of environmental industries and the role played by consultants and engineers specializing in environmental management. Yet, Japan's tale also suggests avenues that should be avoided. Below, some of the lessons that can be learned from Japanese failures are considered.

FAILURES AND LESSONS

Lack of Information Caused Delayed Response

The most serious negative lesson of Japan's economic growth is that it resulted in severe damage to health and even death from pollution. Japan bears the misfortune of being known world-wide for Minamata disease and Yokkaichi asthma. Government, business, academia and civil society as a whole failed to recognize the nature and severity of the damage that was occurring around them until it reached crisis proportions. The incidences of health damage, the human suffering and the loss of ecosystems could have been largely prevented if the problems had been recognized and measures had been taken with the foresight that the global community now has as a result of the painful experiences of countries like Japan. One reason for Japan's delayed response to its pollution problems was lack of adequate knowledge and information necessary to accurately comprehend the situation. This suggests the importance of taking a 'precautionary' approach to pollution and acting to mitigate its effects or avoid it altogether when the potential for health or ecological damage is substantial. Another major reason for the delayed response was an attitude among government and industry that the country could not survive if industry were hampered by the need to act against pollution. Instead, the failure to act proved costly to industry, which had to pay compensation to victims of pollution, retrofit technologies and repair its image.

Severity of Damage Once it Occurs

Questions can be raised regarding the efficiency of the Japanese approach of growth first, control pollution afterwards. First, remedial actions were very costly. Industries had to spend large sums to compensate victims for the health damages they suffered. Considering the huge total costs of these compensation payments, one cannot help but think that preventive measures would have been more cost efficient. There is data regarding the scale of environmental and health damages in Japan. It is not easy to translate the damage to human health and the environment into monetary terms. The case of Minamata, however, teaches us that willful neglect of pollution by a company can result in thousands of health victims. In the Minamata case, the Chisso Corporation was put on the verge of bankruptcy because it had to pay compensation to these victims and cover the living allowances of the Minamata patients throughout the remainder of their lives. And the town and the company must now live with the realization that this compensation can never pay for the pain and suffering brought to families of victims.

Governments should not wait for pollution to reach a crisis point before they act. The resulting compensation and treatment costs could well exceed greatly the costs of controlling the pollution early on and threaten corporate survival and government legitimacy.

To prevent similar problems from occurring, the Japanese government empowered society by introducing a nationwide pollution monitoring system and enhanced pollution control and prevention research capacities. Information is a powerful tool that can aid greatly in controlling pollution. Freedom of speech within society, freedom of information and freedom of the media must be established to ensure that society can help government to address pollution and other environmental problems before they become crises or can no longer be solved. Japan has been under pressure to open decision-making processes more to NGOs so that they can provide greater input into the policy making process as well.

Inadequate Development Policies, Plans and Projects

By and large, experiences in many countries show that economic and environmental objectives can be compatible when viewed in the long term. In contrast, shortsighted development policies often cause damage to human health or result in ecological destruction. Unfortunately, environmental tragedies are being repeated in many places around the world because short-term economic objectives are still given preference over long-term ecological values.

In Japan, there have been a number of controversial government-supported development projects or 'public works' projects that were pushed ahead by government and industry against the strong opposition of residents, NGOs and academicians. This has resulted in the building of dams on almost all of Japan's rivers, the filling in of marine estuaries that are rich in biological diversity, the construction of highways in ecologically sensitive regions and the building of golf courses and leisure hotels in areas where no one travels.

These development projects are examples of failures of politics and government decision making. Until recently, there was no effective method to stop such government projects. An EIA Law was not enacted in Japan until 1997 due to the opposition of development ministries although an environmental impact ordinance with no real teeth was in place earlier than this. Japan was the last country among the OECD countries to adopt an EIA Law. Moreover, the EIA Law in Japan is not still strong enough to stop questionable projects when they are backed by alliances of pro-development powers. Nor can it correct planning decisions that were approved in the past despite the environmental consequences those decisions might have.

Japan's environmental policy in the 1960s and 1970s was developed primarily to control industrial pollution (as opposed to other forms of or causes of pollution). Japan was relatively successful in controlling air and water pollution without seriously hampering the nation's economic growth although a number of problems, such as traffic air pollution in large cities and eutrophication of lakes and semi-closed water bodies, persist. It was less effective in dealing with the negative environmental consequences of development (such as the loss of a once beautiful coastline) or in dealing with the overseas consequences of its high resource dependency (e.g. as a major consumer of fish and hardwoods).

Thus, today some of the biggest tasks facing Japan are dealing with the environmental problems associated with consumption and public works. In this new battlefield, government control has proved neither practical nor effective. In fact, in terms of public work projects, it was the central and local governments themselves that pushed ahead environmentally disruptive projects against the opposition of local residents.

Lack of Coordination among Government Ministries

In some areas, Japan's bureaucracy has developed considerable technical capacity and can be commended for the role it has played in recent decades in helping to create and enforce environmental regulations. Yet government ministries and the structure of the ministries more generally, can also be criticized for their failure to deal more effectively with environmental policy development. There is not only a big gap in terms of coordination among ministries, meaning that there is considerable redundancy of efforts and at times counter-productivity in their efforts (such as when the efforts of one ministry to solve a problem cause another ministry a new headache in the form of an additional environmental problem to have to address), at times the ministries are pitted against each other in fierce disputes. These essentially political struggles are occurring without open public debate and, because they are often won by the stronger ministries, may result in policy outcomes that are not environmentally sound or desired by the public.

Weak Role of Political Parties

The social acceptability of environmental policy has been generally high in Japan. There has been strong and continuous public support for environmental policy in Japan since at least the 1970s. In the 1990s, people's environmental consciousness was directed into new areas by international discussions on global environmental issues, and this has promoted new environmental thoughts concerning the relationship between economy and the environment.

In spite of this, however, the environment has not been a matter of serious policy debate in national politics. Electoral votes have sometimes played a crucial role in local decision making on projects which might affect the local environment and there are instances where environmental issues have resulted in debate at the national level. Still, on the whole it can be said that there is no real debate among political parties on environmental issues. While there are several political parties in Japan, they have failed to develop distinctive environmental positions. Moreover, there is no Green Party in Japan at the national level as is found in many European countries. As a result, environmental policy has a rather 'technology-focused' flavor as compared to the more comprehensive approaches followed in countries where Green Parties are quite strong and policy debate is often restricted to the backrooms of bureaucratic halls.

The lack of an environmental party in Japan may also be a factor in Japan's rather passive attitude towards international agreements. International decisions are generally taken only after an external force (*gaiatsu*) against which Japan cannot resist pushes Japan to do so. International environmental agreements have not stimulated major debate among the political parties.

THE NEED FOR NEW POLICY DIRECTIONS

Economic Instruments

The Japanese have shown a preference for government intervention to market forces in environmental control. The third OECD review of Japan's environmental policy, however, concluded that important gains in cost-effectiveness could be achieved through wider use of economic instruments. Japan has to a large extent been indifferent to the use of economic instruments such as taxes and charges in environmental policy although it did use economic incentives in the form of government subsidies and tax reductions to promote environmental investment by companies in control technologies.

More recently, however, because of concerns about combating global warming, discussions have started on the possible benefits of introducing environmental taxes on fossil fuels. The relatively high oil prices throughout the 1980s encouraged Japanese industries to save energy but the improvements made in energy efficiency over the previous decades stopped in the 1990s as oil prices dropped and consumers made use of more and more electric appliances. The success of Japan's laws in promoting 'rational' use of energy over the 1970s and 1980s were primarily limited to the industrial sector. In the future, reductions must be achieved in the transport and domestic sectors where energy use is growing. Consumer behavior can most easily be changed through market-based incentives such as environmental taxes. Whether or not Japanese society will accept such taxes, however, remains to be seen.

Financing Mechanisms

The Japanese government introduced various financing mechanisms to aid industry make the transition to production processes that were less polluting. This is despite the fact that the OECD Council Recommendation of 1974 urged governments to pursue the polluter pays principle (PPP). The PPP was to prevent the use of government subsidies to private enterprises for environmental measures so that such public assistance would not cause distortion in the allocation of resources and set up trade barriers. In Japan, however, PPP was adopted as a legal rather than an economic principle to ensure fairness, commanding enterprises to bear the cost necessary for installing pollution control technologies, undertake clean-up projects and pay compensation for the damages they caused.

Thus, for the purposes of providing support to industries in making the transition towards cleaner production, government created a policy-based financing system that was operated by public corporations, such as the Pollution Control Service Corporation (antecedent of the JEC), and public banks, such as the Japan Development Bank. Japan's unique Fiscal Investment and Loan System supported these organizations' work. For 30 years, they provided low-interest loans to private companies, which essentially are government subsidies. This policy-based financing system is now under critical review because the country is trying to reduce the government role while enhancing the role of market forces.

Policy Reforms

Despite Japan's general success in addressing classic pollution issues and improving energy efficiency, many new challenges have arisen that are pushing Japan in new policy directions and altering policy-making styles towards more participatory structures. The dominant focus of environmental policy in Japan through the 1980s was domestic. Since the 1990s, the orientation has rapidly shifted towards a more globally oriented perspective and looking more holistically at the relationships among economic, societal and environmental linkages.

In the 1990s, Japan began a process of major environmental policy reform in order to cope with new global environmental challenges and respond to changes in domestic and international socio-economic conditions. This has included the formation of a new Basic Environmental Law, the EIA law, a Global Warming Law and a Sound Material-cycle Society Law. Together these laws suggest a shift in environmental norms in Japan from a focus on preventing pollution in order to protect human lives to a greater appreciation of the impacts of Japanese economic activities on the global ecological system as well as a sense that Japan has an ability, and even a responsibility, to assist developing countries meet their own environmental challenges. It is significant that the Environment Agency born in 1971 was upgraded to the Ministry of the Environment in January 2001.

Basic Environmental Law

A number of new environmental laws were enacted in the 1990s, reorienting the direction of national environmental policies. The most important among them was the enactment of the Basic Environmental Law in 1993. Under this new framework legislation, the scope of environmental policies was expanded to include not only the control of pollution but also to deal with broader issues related to 'sustainable development.'

Japan's environmental policies under the Basic Environmental Law can be characterized as following a programmatic approach. Long-term environmental targets and national action plans can be found in the Basic Environmental Plan that was created in 1994 to help realize the Basic Environmental Law's goals. The objective and method of environmental policy making has shifted from individual control to holistic planning and from government regulation to voluntary, participatory and cooperative initiatives among various stakeholders. In many ways, however, the policy targets of the Environment Basic Plan are harder to achieve than were the environmental targets of earlier regulations precisely because the promotion of sustainable development requires deep changes throughout society. It is no longer just industries that are being asked to clean up their pollution, but consumers who are being asked to change their behavior.

Establishment of a Sound Material-cycle Society

The idea of a sound material cycle society, also sometimes referred to as a 'resource-cycling society', is an example of a new policy concept of the 1990s that has received strong public support but that remains difficult to fully implement. In June 2000, the government enacted the Basic Law for the Formation of a Sound Material-cycle Society in order to encourage industry, local government and citizens to take actions towards this goal. A series of laws have been enacted to promote recycling of different categories of wastes, including containers packaging, home electric appliances, construction waste and food. The principle of extended producer responsibility has been adopted as a guide for these new laws. Industries are trying to find new business chances for environmental technologies.

The mere promotion of resource recycling or EP-type recycling is not, however, sufficient to realize a sound material-cycle society. Indeed, recycling can even be counter-productive if it encourages recycling for the sake of recycling but does not prevent the abuse of resources. What is required is the entire restructuring of today's economic and social systems so that economic, regulatory and ethical incentives to minimize the environmental impacts associated with the use of resources are embedded there. This is a true challenge for Japan as a leading state in the advanced industrial community, but one to which it is slowly moving.

THE ROLE OF JAPAN IN INTERNATIONAL ENVIRONMENTAL COOPERATION

Finally, in conclusion, it should be noted that the Japanese government has recognized its past pollution mistakes to at least some extent and has urged developing countries not to walk in its footsteps in terms of allowing pollution to be ignored until it is no longer possible to ignore it any more. Instead, the Japanese government and society are hopeful that they can play a small role in persuading countries that are now developing to pursue a different path, one that incorporates environmental protection into industrial development plans.

As a result, the Japanese government in the last decade has come to attach special importance to environmental protection in its development assistance programs. Japan was the largest donor of official development assistance in the 1990s and much of this aid was used for environmental protection in East and Southeast Asia.

But it is not only in the area of official development assistance that a transfer of environmental know-how and experiences can occur. This book, which grew out of a World Bank project on 'Japan's Environmental Policy, Lessons for Developing Countries,' has attempted a critical analysis of Japan's experiences with industrial growth, pollution, environmental clean-up and policy development in an effort to provide a more systematic analysis of what Japan did wrong, where it has itself learned lessons, how Japan eventually coped with many of its own worst pollution problems and where Japan is still learning and changing.

Japan's environmental authorities and experts must pay greater attention to the transferability of these approaches to other countries, as well as their limitations, and to reconsider the mode of Japan's environmental cooperation with a view to improving environmental development assistance.

References

Abe, Takao (2001), *Korekara no Nippon, Korekara no Chiho Jichi (Future of Japan and Local Autonomy)*, Tokyo, Japan: Fukoku Shuppan.

Abe, Yasutaka (1995), '*Kankyo Hozen no Shuho* (Method of Environment Preservation)', in Yasutaka Abe and Takehisa Awaji (eds), *Kankyo Ho (Environmental Laws)*, Tokyo, Japan: Yuhikaku, pp. 45-58.

Ajia Shakai Mondai Kenkyusho (1991), *Ajia Chiiki no Hatten to Kankyo Hogo ni Kansuru Chosa Kenkyu (Research and Study on Development and Environment Preservation in Asia)*, Tokyo, Japan: Sangyo Kenkyusho.

Amano, Akihiro (1994), 'Integrating Economy and the Environment', *Environmental Research Quarterly*, 93, Tokyo, Japan: Environmental Research Center, pp. 39-47.

Aminzade, Ronald (1992), 'Historical Sociology and Time', *Sociological Methods and Research*, 20 (4), pp. 456-80.

Asano, Naohito (1994), 'Development of Japanese Environmental Laws and the Basic Environmental Law' ('Nihon no Kankyo Ho no Tenkai to Kankyo Kihonho'), *Environmental Research Quarterly*, 93, Tokyo, Japan: Environmental Research Center, pp. 26-38.

Asano, Naohito and Akemi Ori (1999), 'Issues and Challenges of the Present Laws Concerning Solid Waste Disposal and Recycling' ('Haikibutsu Recycle ni Kansuru Genko Hoseido no Mondaiten to Taisaku'), in Society of Environmental Law and Policy (ed.), *Toward the Recycle-Oriented Society (Recycle Shakai o Mezashite)*, Tokyo, Japan: Shoji Homu Kenkyukai, pp. 1-11.

Ashworth, Graham (1992), *The Role of Local Government in Environmental Protection*, Harlow, UK: Longman Group Ltd.

Awaji, Takehisa (1989), 'Pollution Litigation: Development in Environmental Jurisdiction', in Shigeto Tsuru and Helmut Weidner (eds), *Environmental Policy in Japan*, Berlin, Germany: Edition Sigma Rainer Bohn Verlag, pp. 123-38.

Barrett, Brendan and Riki Therivel (1991), *Environmental Policy and Impact Assessment in Japan*, London, UK: Routledge.

Barrett, Brendan (1997), 'Environmentalism in Periods of Rapid Societal Transformation: Legacy of the Industrial Revolution in the United Kingdom and the Meiji Restoration in Japan', United Nations University/Institute of Advanced Studies Working Paper No. 31.

Barrett, Brendan F.D. (ed.) (2005), *Ecological Modernisation and Japan*, London, UK: Routledge/Curzon.

Begley, Sharon and Hideo Takayama (1989), 'The World's Eco-Outlaw', *Newsweek*, 1 May.

Bellah, Robert (1985), *Tokugawa Religion: The Cultural Roots of Modern Japan*, 2nd Edition, New York, NY, US: The Free Press.

Bevis, William W. (1995), *Borneo Log: The Struggle for Sarawak's Forests*, Seattle, WA, US: University of Washington Press.

Bomberg, Elizabeth E. (1998), *Green Parties and Politics in the European Union*, London, UK: Routledge.

Broadbent, Jeffrey (1988), 'State as Process: The Effect of Party and Class on Citizen Participation in Japanese Local Government', *Social Problems*, 35 (2), pp. 131-42.

Broadbent, Jeffrey (1989a), 'Environmental Politics in Japan: An Integrated Structural Analysis', *Sociological Forum*, 4 (2), pp. 179-202.

Broadbent, Jeffrey (1989b), 'The Technopolis Strategy vs. Deindustrialization: High-Tech Development Sites in Japan', in Michael P. Smith (ed.), *Pacific Rim Cities in the World Economy*, New Brunswick, NJ, US: Transaction Publishers, pp. 231-53.

Broadbent, Jeffrey (1998), *Environmental Politics in Japan: Networks of Power and Protest*, Cambridge, UK: Cambridge University Press.

Broadbent, Jeffrey (2000), *The Japanese Network State in US Comparison: Does Embeddedness Yield Resources and Influence?* Occasional Paper, Stanford University, Stanford, CA, US: Asia/Pacific Research Center, www.soc.umn.edu/research/broadnet.pdf.

Broadbent, Jeffrey (2001), 'Social Capital and Labor Politics in Japan: Cooperation or Cooptation?' in John D. Montgomery (ed.) with Alex Inkeles, *Social Capital as a Policy Resource in Asia and the Pacific Basin*, Boston, MA, US: Kluwer Academic Publishers, pp. 81-95.

Broadbent, Jeffrey (2002), 'Japan's Environmental Regime: The Political Dynamics of Change', in Uday Desai (ed.), *Environmental Politics and Policies in the Industrialized Countries*, Cambridge, MA, US: The MIT Press, pp. 295-355.

Broadbent, Jeffrey and Yoshito Ishio (1998), 'The Embedded Broker State', in Mark Fruin (ed.), *Networks, Markets, and the Pacific Rim: Studies in Strategies*, New York, US: Oxford University Press, pp. 79-108.

Brown, Philip (2000), 'Popular Epidemiology and Toxic Waste Contamination: Lay and Professional Ways of Knowing', in Richard Scott Frey (ed.), *The Environment and Society Reader*, New York, NY, US: Pearson, Allyn and Bacon, pp. 301-19.

Brown, Valerie, D.I. Smith, R. Weissman and J. Handmer (1995), *Risks and Opportunities: Managing Environmental Conflict and Change*, London, UK: Earthscan Publications Ltd.

Bryner, Gary (1995), *Blue Skies, Green Politics: The Clean Air Act of 1990 and Its Implementation*, Washington, DC, US: Congressional Quarterly Press.

Cabinet Office (Naikaku fu Seisaku Tokatsu kan) (2001), Summary of the Basic Survey on Citizens Activity Groups 2000, in People's Life Bureau, Cabinet Office (ed.), *The Final Report of the Comprehensive Planning Department of the People's Life Committee (Kokumin Seikatsu Shingikai, Sogo Kikaku Bukai)*, Tokyo, Japan: People's Life Bureau, Cabinet Office (Naikakufu Kokumin Seikatsu kyoku), pp. 1-6.

Cabinet Office (Naikaku fu Seisaku Tokatsu kan) (2002), *Social Capital of Japan*, Tokyo, Japan: Zaimusho Insatsu kyoku.

Calder, Kent E. (1988), Crisis and Compensation: Public Policy and Political Stability in Japan, 1949-1986, Princeton, NJ, US: Princeton University Press.

Calomiris, Charles W. and Charles P. Himmelberg (1994), *Government Credit Policy and Industrial Performance: Japanese Machine Tool Producers, 1963-1991*, Washington, DC, US: World Bank, Financial Sector Development Department.

Carmin, Joann and Stacy VanDeveer (eds) (2004), EU Enlargement and the Environment: Institutional Change and Environmental Policy in Central and Eastern Europe, London, UK: Frank Cass Publishers.

Carraro, Carlo and François Lévêque (eds) (1999), *Voluntary Approaches in Environmental Policy*, Boston, MA, US: Kluwer.

Cavender-Bares, Jeannine and Jill Jäger with Renate Ell (2001), 'Developing a Precautionary Approach: Global Environmental Risk Management in Germany', in Social Learning Group (William C. Clark, Jill Jäger, Josee van Eijndhoven and Nancy Dickson (eds)), *Learning to Manage Global Environmental Risks, Vol. 1: A Comparative History of Social Responses to Climate Change, Ozone Depletion, and Acid Rain*, Cambridge, MA, US: The MIT Press, pp. 61-92.

Chiba Prefecture (1994), *Chiba ken no Kogai Boshi Kyotei no Ayumi (The Progress of Pollution Control Agreement of Chiba Prefecture)*, Chiba, Japan: Chiba Prefecture.

Chiba Prefecture (2000a), *Kogai no Boshi ni Kansuru Kyoteisho (Agreement on Pollution Control Measures)*, Format of Pollution Control Agreement of Chiba Prefecture, Chiba, Japan: Chiba Prefecture.

Chiba Prefecture (2000b), *Kogai no Boshi ni Kansuru Saimoku Kyotei (Specification Agreement on Pollution Control Measures)*, Format of Specification Agreement Attached to Main Agreement, Chiba, Japan: Chiba Prefecture.

Chikyu Kankyo Keizai Kenkyukai (Study Group on the Global Environmental Economics) (1991), *Nihon no Kogai Keiken (Japanese Pollution Experience)*, Tokyo, Japan: Godo Shuppan.

Choy, Jon (1989), 'MITI To Revise Energy Demand Outlook', *JEI Report*, 19B, 12 May, pp. 5-6.

Chuman, Norichika (1992), 'Groundwater Contamination with Chlorinated Solvents in the Southern Fukushima Basin, Northern Japan', *The Annual Report of Synthetic Study of Fukushima University, Nature and Humanization*, Fukushima, Japan: Fukushima University, pp. 19-30.

Clayton, Andrew (1996), *Governance, Democracy and Conditionality: What Roles for NGOs?* Oxford, UK: An Intrac Publication.

Committee on Japan's Experience in the Battle against Air Pollution (1997), *Japan's Experience in the Battle against Air Pollution*, Tokyo, Japan: The Pollution-related Health Damage Compensation and Prevention Association.

Committee on Transportation Policy (Unyu Seisaku Shingikai) (1999), '*Report on the Measures to Promote Low-fuel Economy Cars*', 20 May 1999, Tokyo, Japan: Ministry of Transport.

Committee on Transportation Technology (Unyu Gijutsu Shingikai) (1998), *Interim Report on the Tightening of Automobile Fuel Economy Standards* (17 December 1998), Tokyo, Japan: Ministry of Transport.

Committee on Transportation Technology (Unyu Gijutsu Shingikai) (1999), *Report on the Future Transportation Policy Considering Safety and Environment*, 14 June 1999, Tokyo, Japan: Ministry of Transport.

Comprehensive Research Committee on the EIA System (Kankyo Eikyo Hyoukka Seido Sogo Kenkyuukai) (1996), 'Present Situation and Issues of the EIA System', *Study Report of the Environment Agency (June 1996)*, Tokyo, Japan: Environment Agency.

Comprehensive Study Group on Strategic Environmental Assessment (Senryakuteki Kankyo Eikyo Hyoka Sogo Kenkyukai) (2000), *Report of the Comprehensive Study Group on Strategic Environmental Assessment*, Tokyo, Japan: Ministry of the Environment.

Council for Decentralization Reform (1996), 'Idea and Objective of Decentralization Reform', in Office of the Prime Minister (ed.), *Final Report of the Council for Decentralization Reform – Creation of a Decentralized Society: The Roadmap,*

Tokyo, Japan: Office of the Prime Minister, pp. 1-10.

Cruz, Wilfrido, Kazuhiko Takemoto and Jeremy Warford (1998), *Economic and Industrial Management of the World Bank, Urban and Industrial Management in Developing Countries*, Washington, DC, US: World Bank.

Cruz, Wilfrido, Koichi Fukui and Jeremy Warford (eds) (2002), 'Protecting the Global Environment Initiatives by Japanese Business', *World Bank Institute Learning Resources Series*, Washington, DC, US: World Bank.

Daly, Herman (1996), *Beyond Growth: The Economics of Sustainable Development*, Boston, MA, US: Beacon Press.

Dauvergne, Peter (1997), *Shadows in the Forest: Japan and the Politics of Timber in Southeast Asia*, Cambridge, MA, US: The MIT Press.

Dauvergne, Peter (2001), *Loggers and Degradation in the Asia-Pacific: Corporations and Environmental Management*, Cambridge, UK: Cambridge University Press.

della Porta, Donatella and Mario Diani (1999), *Social Movements: An Introduction*, Oxford, UK: Blackwell.

Denki Sangyo Shimbunsha (1973), *Kogai Boshi Kyotei sho Soran Denryoku hen* (Collection of Pollution Control Agreements: Electric Power Industry), Tokyo: Denki Sangyo Shimbunsha.

Desai, Uday (2002), 'Institutional Profiles and Policy Performance: Summary and Conclusions', in Uday Desai (ed.), *Environmental Politics and Policies in the Industrialized Countries*, Cambridge, MA, US: The MIT Press, pp. 357-81.

Development Bank of Japan (2002), *Annual Report of DJB 2002*, Tokyo, Japan: Development Bank of Japan.

Doi, Naomi (1994), *Landscape Policy and Environmental Administration: Environmental Administration of Local Government (Toshi Jichitai no Kankyo Gyosei)*, Tokyo, Japan: The Tokyo Institute for Municipal Research, pp. 98-118.

Dryzek, John S. (1997), *The Politics of the Earth: Environmental Discourse*, Oxford, UK: Oxford University Press.

Dunlap, Riley and William R. Catton, Jr. (1994), 'Toward an Ecological Sociology: The Development, Current Status and Probable Future of Environmental Sociology', in William D'Antonio, Masamichi Sasaki and Yoshio Yonebayashi (eds), *Ecology, Society and the Quality of Social Life*, New Brunswick, NJ, US: Transaction Publishers, pp. 11-31.

Dunlap, Riley, George Gallup, Jr. and Alec Gallup (1992), *The Health of the Planet Survey*, Princeton, NJ, US: The George H. Gallup International Institute.

Economic Planning Agency (Keizai Kikaku Cho Kokumin Seikatsu Kyoku) (1999), *Establishing Environment Friendly Lifestyles based on Partnerships*, Tokyo, Japan: Okurasho Insatsukyoku.

Economic Planning Agency (2000), 'Chapter 5: Promotion of Voluntary Activities and the Role of NPOs', in Economic Planning Agency (ed.), *Kokumin Seikatsu Hakusho (White Paper on the People's Life)*, Tokyo, Japan: Economic Planning Agency.

Economy, Elizabeth (2004), *The River Runs Black: The Environmental Challenge to China's Future*, Ithaca, NY, US: Cornell University Press.

Edelman, Murray (1977), *Politics as Symbolic Action: Mass Arousal and Quiescence*, New York, NY, US: Academic Press.

Energy Data and Modeling Center (EDMC) (2002), *Handbook of Energy and Economic Statistics*, Tokyo, Japan: Energy Conservation Center.

Environment Agency of Japan (1971-2000), *Kankyo Hakusho (White Paper on Environment)*, Tokyo, Japan: Okurasho Insatsukyoku (Tokyo, Japan: Gyosei for 2000 edition).

Environment Agency of Japan (1976), *Environmental Policies in Japan: References for OECD Review*, Tokyo, Japan: Environment Agency of Japan, pp. 142-48.

Environment Agency of Japan (1977a), 'Economic Impact of Pollution Control Cost', in *Kankyo Hakusho (Quality of the Environment in Japan) 1977*, Tokyo, Japan: Okurasho Insatsukyoku, pp. 49-58

Environment Agency of Japan (1977b), *Kankyo Hozen Choki Keikaku (Long-term Plan for Environmental Preservation)*, Tokyo, Japan: Environment Agency of Japan.

Environment Agency of Japan (1980), 'Development of Environmental Policy', in *Kankyo Hakusho (Quality of the Environment in Japan) 1980*, Tokyo, Japan: Okurasho Insatsukyoku, pp. 106-12.

Environment Agency of Japan (1981), 'Promotion of Efficient Use of Resources and Energy', in *Kankyo Hakusho (Quality of the Environment in Japan) 1981*, Tokyo, Japan: Okurasho Insatsukyoku, pp. 84-90.

Environment Agency of Japan (1982), *Kankyo Hakusho (Quality of the Environment in Japan) 1982*, Tokyo, Japan: Okurasho Insatsukyoku.

Environment Agency of Japan (1983a), *Kankyo Hakusho (Quality of the Environment in Japan) 1983*, Tokyo, Japan: Okurasho Insatsukyoku.

Environment Agency of Japan (1983b), 'Premier Tanaka Vows Efforts to Fight Pollution in Speech', *Japan Environment Summary 1973-1982*, Tokyo, Japan: Environment Agency of Japan, p. 43.

Environment Agency of Japan (1987), *Kankyo Hozen Choki Koso (Long-term Vision for Environmental Preservation)*, Tokyo, Japan: Okurasho Insatsukyoku.

Environment Agency of Japan (1990), *Gyoshubetsu Kogaiboshi Kyotei Jireishu (Pollution Control Agreement Collection of Different Industries)*, Tokyo, Japan: Gyosei.

Environment Agency of Japan (1991), *Kankyocho 20 Nenshi (Twenty-year History of the Environment Agency)*, Tokyo, Japan: Environment Agency of Japan.

Environment Agency of Japan (1992), 'Bitter Experience of Japan which Sacrificed Sustainability', in Environment Agency of Japan (ed.), *Kankyo Hakusho (Quality of the Environment in Japan) 1992*, Tokyo, Japan: Okurasho Insatsukyoku, pp. 111-34.

Environment Agency of Japan (1997a), 'Are Japanese Environment Measures Making a Progress?' ('Nihon no Kankyo Taisaku wa Sussunde Iruka'), I, II, III, Tokyo, Japan: Printing Bureau of the Ministry of Finance.

Environment Agency of Japan (1997b), *Kankyo Hakusho (Quality of the Environment in Japan) 1997*, Part II, Tokyo, Japan: Okurasho Insatsukyoku.

Environment Agency of Japan (1998), *Kankyo Hakusho (Quality of the Environment in Japan) 1998*, Part II, Tokyo, Japan: Okurasho Insatsukyoku.

Environment Agency Research Group (Kankyocho Kokenhou Kenkyukai) (1988), *Kaisei Kokenho Handoboku (Handbook of the Revised Pollution-related Health Damage Compensation Law (Kaisei Kokenho Handbook)*, Tokyo, Japan: Energy Journalsha.

Evans, Peter (1995), *Embedded Autonomy: States and Industrial Transformation*, Princeton, US: Princeton University Press.

Ex Corporation (1996), 'Japan's Experience in Urban Environmental Management, Vol. 1', World Bank Departmental Working Paper, No. 17942.

Expert Panel on Eco-Business (1990), 'Environment-friendly Industry: Eco-Business', *Environmental Research Quarterly* (Kikan Kankyo Kenkyu), 78, Tokyo Environmental Research Center, pp. 6-52.

Feinerman, James and Koichiro Fujikura (1998), 'Japan: Consensus-based Compliance', in Edith Brown Weiss and Harold Jacobson (eds), *Engaging*

Countries: Strengthening Compliance with International Environmental Accords, Cambridge, MA, US: The MIT Press, pp. 253-90.

Flavin, Christopher and John Young (1993), 'Shaping the Next Industrial Revolution', in Lester Brown (ed.), *State of the World*, New York, NY, US: W. W. Norton & Co., pp. 180-99.

Foreign Press Center of Japan (1999), 'Changing Japanese Politics', *About Japan Series* (24), Tokyo, Japan: Foreign Press Center, pp. 11-26.

Foreign Press Center of Japan (2000), 'Government', in Foreign Press Center (ed.), *Facts and Figures of Japan*', Tokyo, Japan: Foreign Press Center, pp. 14-20.

Fujii, Toshio (2001), 'Expectation for the Ministry of the Environment Toward Sustainable Society: From the Viewpoint of Local Government', *Environmental Research Quarterly (Kikan Kankyo Kenkyu)*, 120, Tokyo, Japan: Environmental Research Center, pp. 11-18.

Fujikura, Ryo (1998), 'Kogai Taisaku no Shakai Keizaiteki Yoin Bunseki' ('An Analysis of Socio-economic Factors of Pollution Control Measures'), in Kitakyushushi Sangyoshi Kogai Taisakushi Dobokushi Henshu Iinkai, Kogai Taisakushi Bukai (The Section of Pollution Control Measure History in the Editorial Committee of Histories of Industries, Pollution Control Measures and Engineering Works of Kitakyushu City) (ed.), *Kitakyushushi Kogai Taisakushi: Kaisekihen (The History of Pollution Control Measures of Kitakyushu City: Analyses)*, Kitakyushu, Japan: Kitakyushushi, pp. 183-247.

Fujikura, Ryo (1999), 'Trial Estimation on Industrial Investment in Pollution Control', *Proceedings of Countermeasures to Environment and Resources*, Tokyo, Japan: Japan International Cooperation Agency, p. 53.

Fujikura, Ryo, Tora Matsumoto and Hidefumi Imura (1996), 'Review Environmental Investment in Asian Countries from Japanese Experience', *Proceedings of the Workshop on Global Environmental Issues, the Society of Civil Engineering*, p. 241.

Fukuda, Shin-ichi., J. Chong, M. Okui, and K. Okuda (2000), 'Long Term Loans and Investment in Japan: An Empirical Analysis Based on Panel Data of Japanese Firms', CIRJE F-80.

Fukui, Haruhiro (1992), 'The Japanese State and Economic Development: A Profile of a Nationalist-Paternalist Capitalist State', in Richard Appelbaum and Jeffrey Henderson (eds), *States and Development in the Asian Pacific Rim*, Newbury Park: Sage Publications, pp. 199-225.

Funabashi, Harutoshi (1995), 'Kankyo Mondai he no Shakaigakuteki Shiza Shakaiteki Jirema Ron to Shakaiteki Shisutemu Ron' ('Sociological Perspectives on Environmental Problems: The Theory of Social Dilemmas and the Theory of Social Control Systems'), *Kankyo Shakaigaku Kenkyu*, 1, pp. 5-20.

Funabashi, Harutoshi (1986), 'Sociological Aspect of Shinkansen Superexpress Railway Traffic Pollution', *Environmental Research Quarterly (Kikan Kankyo Kenkyu)*, 57, Tokyo, Japan: Kankyo Chosa Center, pp. 73-81.

Funabashi, Harutoshi, Koichi Hasegawa and Nobuko Iijima (eds) (1998), *Kyodai Chiiki Kaihatsu, Keikaku to Kiketsu (Gigantic Regional Development: Its Plan and Results)*, Tokyo, Japan: Tokyo University Press.

Funabashi, Harutoshi, Kouichi Hasegawa, Soichi Hatanaka and Harumi Katsuta (1985), *Shinkansen Kogai (Shinkansen Pollution)*, Tokyo, Japan: Yuhikaku.

Gamson, William (1992), *Talking Politics*, New York, NY, US: Cambridge University Press.

George, Timothy S. (2001), *Minamata: Pollution and the Struggle for Democracy in Postwar Japan*, Cambridge, MA, US: Harvard University Asia Center,

Distributed by Harvard University Press.

Gibney, Frank (1998), *Japan: The Fragile Super Power*, 3rd edition, Tokyo, Japan: Charles E. Tuttle.

Glasbergen, Pieter (1998), 'Partnerships as a Learning Process: Environmental Covenants in the Netherlands', in Pieter Glasbergen (ed.), *Co-operative Environmental Governance: Public-Private Agreements as a Policy Strategy*, Dordrecht: Kluwer Academic Publishers, pp. 133-56.

Global Environmental Committee of the Council of Industrial Structure (1997), 'Report of Global Environmental Committee of the Council of Industrial Structure of 12 March 1997', www.meti.go.jp/press/past/h70421rf.html, 21 June 2004.

Global Environmental Department (Kankyocho Chikyukankyobu) (1992a), *Chikyu Ondanka Taisaku Handobuku (Handbook of Countermeasures Against Global Warming)*, Transportation Sector, Tokyo, Japan: Daiichi Hoki.

Global Environmental Department (Kankyocho Chikyukankyobu) (1992b), *Chikyu Ondanka Taisaku Handobuku (Handbook of Countermeasures Against Global Warming)*, Energy Sector, Tokyo, Japan: Daiichi Hoki.

Global Environmental Forum (1992), *Environmental Data (Kankyo Yoran) 1992*, Tokyo, Japan: Kokin Shoin.

Global Environmental Forum (2001), *Environmental Data (Kankyo Yoran) 2001*, Tokyo, Japan: Kokin Shoin.

Global Environmental Forum (2003), *Environmental Data (Kankyo Yoran) 2003*, Tokyo, Japan: Kokin Shoin.

Golub, Jonathan (1998), *New Instruments for Environmental Policy in the EU*, London, UK: Routledge.

Green Korea United (1998), 'Green Korea Reports', 5 (2), Seoul, Korea: Green Korea United.

Gresser, Julian, Koichiro Fujikura and Akio Morishima (1981), *Environmental Law in Japan*, Cambridge, MA, US: The MIT Press.

Hadano City (1993), *General View of Environment Countermeasures*, Hadano, Japan: Hadano City.

Hadano City (1996), *Cleanup of Geo-pollution by Simple Cleanup System*, Hadano, Japan: Hadano City.

Haley, Arthur (1991), *Authority without Power: Law and the Japanese Paradox*, Oxford, UK: Oxford University Press.

Hamada, Koichi (1977), *Economic Analysis of Casualty Compensation*, Tokyo, Japan: Tokyo University Press.

Hamamoto, Mitsutsugu (1998), *Environmental Regulations and Corporate Behavior: Essays on Environmental Policy Choice and Dynamic Adjustments of Firms in Japan*, Ph.D. Dissertation, Kyoto University, Japan.

Hamamoto, Mitsutsugu and Kazuhiro Ueta (1996), 'Public Policies Promoting Technological Innovation for Sustainable Development', in Flavio Casprini (ed.), *The Development of Science for the Improvement of Human Life*, Third Kyoto Siena Symposium, Section: Economics, Siena: Siena University Press, pp. 73-89.

Hanashima, Masataka, Hiroshi Takatsuki and Osami Nakasugi (1996), 'A Case Study of Environmental Contamination Caused by Illegal Dumping of Hazardous Waste', *Waste Management Research*, 7 (3), p. 4.

Hanayama, Yuzuru (1978), *Kankyo Seisaku o Kangaeru (Thoughts on Environmental Policy)*, Tokyo, Japan: Iwanami Shinsho.

Hanayama, Yuzuru (1989), 'Land Use Planning and Industrial Siting Policy', in Shigeto Tsuru and Helmut Weidner (eds), *Environmental Policy in Japan*,

Berlin, Germany: Edition Sigma Rainer Bohn Verlag, pp. 415-36.

Hannigan, John A. (1995), *Environmental Sociology: A Social Constructivist Perspective*, New York, NY, US: Routledge.

Harada, Naohiko (1994), *Kankyo Ho, Hosei ban (Environmental Laws, revised version)*, Tokyo, Japan: Kobundo.

Harashima, Yohei and Tsuneyuki Morita (1998), 'A Comparative Study on Environmental Policy Development Processes in the Three East Asian Countries: Japan, Korea, and China', *Environmental Economics and Policy Studies*, 1 (1), pp. 39-67.

Harashina, Sachihiko (1996), 'Improvement of Environmental Impact Assessment System in Japan', *Environmental Information Science*, 25, Tokyo, Japan: Center for Environmental Information Science, pp. 34-40.

Hashimoto, Michio (1987a), 'Development of Environmental Policy and Its Institutional Mechanisms of Administration and Finance', in United Nations Centre for Regional Development and United Nations Environmental Programme (eds), *Management for Local and Regional Development: The Japanese Experience*, Nagoya, Japan: United Nations Centre for Regional Development and United Nations Environmental Programme, pp. 57-105.

Hashimoto, Michio (1987b), 'Thought on the Twenty Years Anniversary of the Basic Law for Pollution Control' ('Kogai Taisaku Kihonho 20 Shunen ni Omou'), *Environmental Research Quarterly (Kikan Kankyo Kenkyu)*, 67, Tokyo, Japan: Kankyo Chosa Center, pp. 81-7.

Hashimoto, Michio (1988), *Shishi Kankyo Gyosei (My Personal History with Environmental Administration)*, Tokyo, Japan: *Asahi Shimbun*.

Hashimoto, Michio (1989), 'Administrative Guidance in Environmental Policy: Some Important Cases', in Shigeto Tsuru and Helmut Weidner (eds), *Environmental Policy in Japan*, Berlin, Germany: Edition Sigma Rainer Bohn Verlag, pp. 252-9.

Hashimoto, Michio (1999), *Kankyo Seisaku (Environmental Policy)*, Tokyo, Japan: Gyosei.

Hashimoto, Ryutaro (1994), 'Fulfilling the Role of Japan in the International Community through Sharing Our Experiences as Common Asset', *Environmental Research Quarterly* (93), Tokyo, Japan: Environmental Research Center, pp. 82-7.

Hata, Naoyuki (1998), *Overview of Japan's Fiscal Policy and its Effect on Global Warming*, Tokyo, Japan: Peoples' Forum 2001.

Hatch, Michael T. (1995), *Environmental Policymaking: Assessing the Use of Alternative Policy Instruments*, (Albany, NY, USA: State University of New York).

Hayashi, Kentaro (2000), 'Unexpected Partners Move into Power', in Masuzoe Yoichi (ed.), *Years of Trial: Japan in the 1990s*, Tokyo, Japan: Japan Echo, Inc. pp. 29-39.

Himi, Koji (2000a), 'Establishment of Flue-gas Desulfurization Technology', in Japan Association of Air Pollution (ed.), *Nippon no Taiki Osen no Rekishi (The History of Air Pollution in Japan)*, II, Tokyo, Japan: Koken Kyokai, pp. 465-76.

Himi, Koji (2000b), 'Establishment of Automobile Exhaust Gas Control Technology', in Japan Society of Atmospheric Environment (JSAE), *Nippon no Taiki Osen no Rekishi (The History of Air Pollution in Japan)*, II, Tokyo, Japan: Koken Kyokai, pp. 659-68.

Hirota, Masao (1994), *Countermeasures against NO_x Automobile Emission in Metropolitan Areas, Environmental Administration of Local Government (Toshi Jichitai no Kankyo Gyosei)*, Tokyo, Japan: The Tokyo Institute for Municipal

Research, pp. 75-94.

Hobo, Takehiko (1996), *Naihatsuteki Hattenron to Nippon no Nousanson (Theory of Endogenous Development and Japanese Agricultural and Mountainous Areas)*, Tokyo, Japan: Iwanami Shoten.

Honma, Yoshito (1991), *Kokudo Kaihatsu Keikakuno Shiso (Idea of Consolidated National Plan)*, Tokyo, Japan: Nippon Keizai Hyoron, p. 7.

Horiuchi, Akiyoshi, and Qing-Yuan Sui (1993), 'Influence of the Japan Development Loans on Corporate Investment Behavior', *Journal of the Japanese and International Economies*, 7, pp. 441-65.

Hu, Angang (1991), *China Towards the 21st Century*, Beijing, China: Chinese Environmental Science Press.

Huddle, Norie and Michael Reich with Nahum Stiskin (1975), *Island of Dreams: Environmental Crisis in Japan*, New York, NY, US: Autumn Press.

Huisingh, Donald (1989), 'Cleaner Technologies through Process Modifications, Material Substitutions and Ecologically Based Ethical Values', *Industry and Environment*, 12, pp. 4-8.

Hukkinen, Janne (1999), *Institutions of Environmental Management: Constructing Mental Models and Sustainability*, London, UK and New York, NY, US: Routledge.

Hyogo Prefecture (1995), *White Paper of Environment*, Kobe: Hyogo Prefecture.

Ichimura, Masakazu (1992), 'Transferring Low-pollution Production Technologies and Methods to Developing Nations: Activities of UNEP's Industry and Environment Programme Active Centre (IE/PAC)', *Measures for Conservation of Resources (Shigen Kankyo Taisaku)*, 28, pp. 729-33.

Iijima, Nobuko (ed.) (1979), *Pollution Japan: Historical Chronology*, Tokyo, Japan: Asahi Evening News Press.

Iijima, Nobuko (1998), 'Environmental Deterioration and the Interrelationship Between Global and Local Inequalities: Perspectives from Asia and Australia', *Presented at the World Congress of Sociology*, 26 July – 1 August, Montreal, Canada.

Ikuta, Tadahide (1995), *Kanryo: Japan's Hidden Government*, New York, Tokyo, Osaka and London: ICG Muse, Inc.

Imaizumi, Mineko (2001), *Freiburg Kankyo Report*, Tokyo, Japan: Chuo Hoki.

Imamura, Tsunao (1989), 'Environmental Responsibilities at the National Level: The Environment Agency', in Shigeto Tsuru and Helmut Weidner (eds), *Environmental Policy in Japan*, Berlin, Germany: Edition Sigma Rainer Bohn Verlag, pp. 43-53.

Imura, Hidefumi (1983), 'Trend of Environmental Expenditures in Japan', *Environmental Research Quarterly (Kikan Kankyo Kenkyu)*, 42, Tokyo, Japan: Environmental Research Center (Kankyo Chosa Center), pp. 86-99.

Imura, Hidefumi (1989), 'Administration of Pollution Control at Local Level', in Shigeto Tsuru and Helmut Weidner (eds), *Environmental Policy in Japan*, Berlin, Germany: Edition Sigma Rainer Bohn Verlag, pp. 54 -96.

Imura, Hidefumi (1992a), 'Kaisetsu: Chikyu Kankyo to Shijo Keizai' ('Global Environment and Market Economy'), in Hidefumi Imura (ed.) *Chikyu Kankyo no tame no Shijo Keizai Kakumei (Revolution of Market Economy for the Global Environment)*, Tokyo, Japan: Diamondsha, pp. 311-12.

Imura, Hidefumi (1992b), 'History and Future of Japanese Environmental Policy in Response to Energy Growth', in Helmar Krupp (ed.), *Energy Politics and Schumpeter Dynamics: Japan's Policy between Short-term Wealth and Long-term Global Welfare*, New York, NY, US: Springer-Verlag, pp. 138-53.

Imura, Hidefumi (1993), 'Incentive Effect of Pollutant-load Levy System', *Kankyo*

18 (9), Tokyo, Japan: Gyosei, pp. 12-15.

Imura, Hidefumi (1994a), 'Air Pollution Control Polices and the Changing Attitudes of the Public and Industry: Paradigmatic Changes in Environmental Management in Japan', in *Air Pollution Control in Japan*, Tokyo, Japan: The United Nations University, pp. 55-85.

Imura, Hidefumi (1994b), 'Japan's Environmental Balancing Act: Accommodating Sustained Development', *Asian Survey*, 34 (4), pp. 355-8.

Imura, Hidefumi (1995), 'The Present State and Challenges of Japan – China Environmental Cooperation', in H. Imura and K. Katsuhara (eds), *Chugoku no Kankyo Mondai (Environmental Problems in China)*, Tokyo, Japan: Toyo Keizai Shinposha, pp. 223-39.

Imura, Hidefumi and Yuichi Moriguchi (1995) 'Economic Interdependence and Eco-Balance: Accounting for the Flow of Environmental Loads Associated with Trade', in S. Murai (ed.), *Toward Global Planning of Sustainable Use of the Earth*, Amsterdam, London, New York, Tokyo: Elsevier, pp. 189-208.

Imura, Hidefumi (1997), 'Kigyo no Kankyo Kanri System' ('Environmental Management Systems of Enterprises'), *Keizai Seminar*, 515, Tokyo, Japan: Nihon Hyoronsha, pp. 34-43.

Imura, Hidefumi (1998a), 'The Use of Unilateral Agreements in Japan: Voluntary Action Plans of Industries against Global Warming', *Report prepared for the OECD Environment Directorate*, Paris, France: OECD, ENV/EPOC/GEEE, 98 (26/Final).

Imura, Hidefumi (1998b), 'Environmental Regulatory Reform in Japan', in Sangwhan Lho (ed.), *Environmental Regulatory Reform in OECD Countries*, Seoul, Korea: Korean Environment Institute, pp. 231-67.

Imura, Hidefumi (1999), *The Use of Voluntary Approaches in Japan: An Initial Survey*, Paris, France: OECD, ENV/EPOC/GEEI (98) 28/FINAL.

Imura, Hidefumi (2002), 'Environmental Problems in Asia', in Ken'ichi Miyamoto (ed.), *Environment and Development: Kankyo to Kaihatsu*, Tokyo, Japan: Iwanami Shoten, pp. 91-120.

Imura, Hidefumi and Ken Katsuhara (1996), 'Industrialization and Environmental Policy in East Asia: A Comparative Study of Japan, Korea, and China', *East Asian Economic Perspectives*, 2, Kitakyushu, Japan: ICSEAD, pp. 39-49.

Imura, Hidefumi and Ken Katsuhara (1999), 'Industrialization and Environmental Policy in East Asia: A Comparative Study of Japan, Korea, and China', in F. Gerard Adams and William E. James (eds), *Public Policies in East Asian Development*, Westport, CT, US: Praeger Publishers, pp. 65-80.

Imura, Hidefumi and Rie Sugiyama (2002), *Voluntary Approaches: Two Japanese Cases – Pollution Control Agreements in Yokohama City and Kitakyushu City*, Paris, France: OECD, Environment Directorate, ENV/EPOC/WPNEP.

Inoguchi, Takashi and Tomoaki Iwai (1987), *'Zoku Giin' no Kenkyu: Jiminto Seiken o Gyujiru Shuyakutachi (Studies in Policy Tribes: The Actors who Control the LDP)*, Tokyo, Japan: Nihon Keizai Shimbunsha.

Inose, Naoki (2003), *Doro no Kenryoku (The Power Structure of Roads)*, Tokyo, Japan: Bungei Shunzyu.

Institute for Global Environmental Strategies (IGES) (1999, 2000), *Country Reports on Environmental Governance in Asian Countries*, Kanagawa, Japan: Institute for Global Environmental Strategies.

Intergovernmental Panel on Climate Change (IPCC) (2002), *Climate Change 2001: Mitigation, Contribution of Working Group III to the Third Assessment Report of the Intergovernmental Panel on Climate Change*, Cambridge, UK: Cambridge University Press.

International Development Center (1998), *Basic Study for Plan Making of Economic Cooperation: Environmental Model Cities in China*, Tokyo, Japan: International Development Center.

International Energy Agency and Organization for Economic Cooperation and Development (2004), *Oil Crises and Climate Challenges: 30 Years of Energy Use in IEA Countries*, Paris, France: OECD.

International Panel on Climatic Change (IPCC (2001), *Climate Change 2001: 'Mitigation', Contribution of Working Group III to the Third Assessment Report of the Intergovernmental Panel on Climate Change*, Cambridge, UK: Cambridge University Press.

International Trade Administration (1993), *Environmental Technologies Exports: Strategic Framework for US Leadership (Export Trade Information Report Number PB-94-154044/XAB)*, Washington, DC, US: ITA Office of Environment Technologies Export.

Ishikawa, Eisuke (1994), *Oedo Risaikuru Jijo (Waste Recycling in Edo)*, Tokyo, Japan: Kodansha, pp. 242-73.

Ishino, Koya (1989), 'Waste Management', in Shigeto Tsuru and Helmut Weidner (eds), *Environmental Policy in Japan*, Berlin, Germany: Edition Sigma Rainer Bohn Verlag, pp. 320-31.

Ishino, Koya (1994), 'Legislative History and Outline of the Basic Environmental Law', *Environmental Research Quarterly* (93), Tokyo, Japan: Environmental Research Center, pp. 96-112.

Ishizaka, Masami (2000), *Environmental Policy (Kankyo Seisaku Gaku)*, Tokyo, Japan: Chuo Hoki, pp. 88-106.

ISO World (1993), 'ISO14000', www.ecology.or.jp/isoworld/.

Jan Bojo, Karl-Goran Maler and Lena Unemo (1992), *Environment and Development: An Economic Approach*, Dordrecht, Boston, MA, US and London, UK: Kluwer Academic Publishers.

Jänicke, Martin and Helmut Weidner (eds) (1995), *Successful Environmental Policy: A Critical Evaluation of 24 Cases*, Berlin, Germany: Edition Sigma Rainer Bohn Verlag.

Jänicke, Martin and Helmut Weidner (eds) (1997), *National Environmental Policies: A Comparative Study of Capacity-building*, Berlin and Heidelberg, Germany and New York, NY, US: Springer-Verlag.

Jänicke, Martin and Helge Jörgens, (1998), 'National Environmental Policy Planning in OECD Countries: Preliminary Lessons from Cross-National Comparisons', *Environmental Politics*, 7 (2), Summer 1998, pp. 27-54.

Jänicke, Martin and Helmut Weidner (eds) with Helge Jörgens (1997), *National Environmental Policies: A Comparative Study of Capacity-Building*, Berlin, Heidelberg and New York, NY, US: Springer-Verlag.

Jansen, Marius B. (1995), *The Emergence of Meiji Japan*, Cambridge, UK: Cambridge University Press.

Japan Automobile Manufacturers Association (1999), *Automobile Production Report*, Tokyo, Japan: Japan Automobile Manufacturers Association.

Japan Bank for International Cooperation (JBIC) (2002a), 'Japan Bank for International Cooperation Environment Report 2002', www.jbic.org.br/.

Japan Bank for International Cooperation (JBIC) (2002b), 'Japan Bank for International Cooperation Guidelines for Confirmation of Environmental and Social Considerations, April 2002', www.jbic.org.br/.

Japan Development Bank (1976), *Japan Development Bank History of 25 years, (Nihon Kaihatsu Ginko 25 nen shi)*, Tokyo, Japan: Japan Development Bank.

Japan Development Bank (1994), 'Policy-based Finance: The Experience of Postwar Japan', *World Bank Discussion Paper No. 221*, Tokyo, Japan: Japan Development Bank.

Japan Development Bank, Annual Business Report (various years), Tokyo, Japan: Japan Development Bank.

Japan Environmental Association (2001), *Kankyo NGO Soran (Environmental NGO Database)*, Tokyo, Japan: Nihon Kankyo Kyokai, www.eic.or.jp/jfge/NGO/.

Japan Environmental Council (1997, 1998), *Asian Environmental White Book*, Tokyo, Japan: Toyo Economic Press.

Japan Environmental Council (2000), *The State of the Environment in Asia, 1999/2000*, Singapore: Institute of Southeast Asian Studies, Tokyo, Japan and New York, NY, US: Springer-Verlag.

Japan Environmental Sanitation Center (Nihon Kankyo Eisei Center) (1986), *Kogai Boshi Keikaku Kaiseki Kento Chosa (Report on the Analysis and Survey of Pollution Control Programs)*, Tokyo, Japan: Japan Environmental Sanitation Center.

Japan Environmental Management Association for Industry (JEMAI) (2002), *Environmental Handbook*, Tokyo, Japan: Sangyo Kankyo Kanri Kyokai.

Japan Industrial Machinery Association (Nihon Sangyo Kikai Kogyokai) (1999-2001), 'Production of Environmental Equipment' ('Kankyo Sochi Seisan Jisseki'), Tokyo, Japan: Nihon Sangyo Kikai Kogyokai.

Japan International Cooperation Agency (JICA) (2001), *Second Report of the Study Group on Development Assistance in Environmental Sectors*, Tokyo, Japan: Japan International Cooperation Agency.

Japan International Cooperation Agency (JICA) (2003), *Guide to JICA*, Tokyo, Japan: JICA.

Japan Iron and Steel Federation (2004), *Tekko Jukyu no Ugoki (Steel Demand and Supply Trend), 20 May 2004*, Tokyo, Japan: Japan Iron and Steel Federation

Japan's Official Development Assistance Charter, *Ministry of Foreign Affairs*, www.mofa.go.jp/.

Japan: Profile of a Nation (1995), Tokyo, Japan: Kodansha International.

Japan Sewage Association (*Nihon Gesuido Kyokai*) (2005), *Gesuido Arekore (Information on Sewage Systems)*, www.alpha-web.ne.jp/jswa/.

Japan Society of Atmospheric Environment (2000), *Nihon no Taiki Osen no Rekishi (The History of Air Pollution in Japan) Vols I, II and III*, Tokyo, Japan: Koken Kyokai.

Japan Society for International Development (JASID), Evaluation Committee on Environmental ODA (2003), *Evaluation Report on Environmental Center Approach*, Tokyo, Japan: Japan International Cooperation Agency.

Japan Water Pollution Research Association (Nihon Suishitsu Odaku Kenkyu Kyokai (1986), *Chikasuishitsu Hozen Taisaku Chosa Jirei Chosa (Groundwater Contamination Measures Research Case Study)*, Tokyo, Japan: Nihon Suishitsu Odaku Kenkyu Kyokai.

Jichiro (All Japan Prefectural and Municipal Workers' Union) (1993), *Kankyo Jichitai Zukuri no Tenkai (Development of Environmental Actions by Local Governments)*, Tokyo, Japan: Jichiro.

Johnson, Chalmers (1982), *MITI and the Japanese Miracle*, Stanford, CA, US: Stanford University Press.

Jones, Charles O. (1975), *Clean Air: The Policies and Politics of Pollution Control*, Pittsburgh, PA, US: Pittsburgh University Press.

Kagaku Kogyo Nipposha (1991), *Chikyu Kankyo Taisaku (Global Environmental Measures)*, Tokyo, Japan: Kagaku Kogyo Nipposha

Karan, Pradyumna P. (2005), *Japan in the Twenty-first Century: Environment, Economy, and Society*, Lexington, KY, USA: University of Kentucky Press.

Kashima, Shigeru (2000), 'Discussion on Policies and Measures to Reduce CO_2 from Road Traffic', *Environmental Research Quarterly*, 117, Tokyo, Japan: Environmental Research Center (Kankyo Chosa Center), pp. 33-7.

Katagiri, Yoshinori (1996), 'Improvement of Environmental Impact Assessment Procedure in Kanagawa Prefecture', *Environmental Information Science* (25) 4, Tokyo, Japan: Center for Environmental Information Science, pp. 29-33.

Katayama, T. (1970a), 'Chihokokyodantai no Kogaiboshi Taisaku ni tsuite (2)' ('On Pollution Control Measures of Local Autonomies (2)'), *Chiho Zaimu (Local Finance)* (198), pp. 4-14.

Katayama, T. (1970b), 'Chihokokyodantai no Kogaiboshi Taisaku ni tsuite (3)' ('On Pollution Control Measures of Local Autonomies (3)'), *Chiho Zaimu (Local Finance)* (199), pp. 1-9.

Kato, Kazu (2002), *The Web of Power: Japan and German Development Cooperation Policy*, Lexington, MA, US: Lexington Books.

Kato, Saburo (1989), 'Air Pollution', in Shigeto Tsuru and Helmut Weidner (eds), *Environmental Policy in Japan*, Berlin, Germany: Edition Sigma Rainer Bohn Verlag, pp. 263-99.

Kawana, Hideyuki (1988), *Dokyumento: Nihon No Kogai (Documents: Japan's Pollution)*, Tokyo, Germany: Ryokufu Shuppan.

Kawana, Hideyuki (1996), 'Circumstances of Environmental Impact Assessment in Japan', *Environmental Information Science*, 25, Tokyo, Germany: Center for Environmental Information Science, pp. 18-23.

Keck, Margaret and Katherine Sikkink (1998), *Activists Beyond Borders: Advocacy Networks in International Politics*, Ithaca, NY, US: Cornell University Press.

Keidanren (Federation of Economic Associations) (1991a), 'Keidanren Global Environmental Charter', 23 April 1991, Tokyo, Japan: Keidanren.

Keidanren (Federation of Economic Associations) (1991b), 'Ten Points: Environmental Guidelines for the Japanese Enterprises Operating Abroad', in *Keidanren Global Environment Charter*, 23 April 1991, Tokyo, Japan: Keidanren, www.keidanren.or.jp/english/speech/spe001/s01001/s01b.html.

Keidanren (Federation of Economic Associations) (1997), 'Keidanren Voluntary Action Plan on the Environment,' 17 June 1997, Tokyo,' Japan: Keidanren.

Keidanren (Federation of Economic Associations) (2003), 'Results of Fiscal 2003 Follow-up to the Keidanren Voluntary Action Plan on the Environment: Section on Global Warming Measures', 21 November 2003, Tokyo, Japan: Keidanren.

Keizai Doyukai (1999), 'Chikyu Ondanka ni Muketa Wareware no Ketsui', 2 February 1999, www.doyukai.or.jp.

Kern, Kristine (2000), *Die Diffusion von Politikinnovationen: Umweltpolitische Innovationen im Mehrebenensystem der USA*, Opladen, Germany: Leske and Budrich.

Kerr, Alex (2002), *Dogs and Demons: Tales from the Dark Side of Modern Japan*, New York, NY, US: Hill and Wang.

Kimitsu City Department of Environment (1993), *The First Report of Clean-up Measures of Geopollution*, Kimitsu, Japan: Kimitsu City.

Kissinger, Henry (1979), *White House Years*, Boston: Little, Brown & Company.

Kitakyushu City (1998), *Kitakyushushi Kogai Taisakushi (The History of Pollution Control Measures in Kitakyushu City)*, Kitakyushu, Japan: Kitakyushushi.

Kitakyushu City (1999), *Pollution Control Countermeasures of the City of Kitakyushu*, Kitakyushu, Japan: Kitakyushushi.

Kitamura, Yoshinobu (1997), *Jichitai Kankyo Gyosei Ho (Local Environmental Administrative Laws)*, Tokyo, Japan: Ryosho Fukyukai.

Kitamura, Yoshinobu (1998), 'Recent Development of EIA Systems in Local Governments', *Sangyo to Kankyo*, 7, Tokyo, Japan: Oto Rebyusha, pp. 28-36.

Kitamura, Yoshinobu (2003), *Jichitai Kankyo Gyosei Ho (Local Environmental Law and Policy)* 3rd edition, Tokyo, Japan: Daiichi hoki.

Kitschelt, Herbert P. (1986), 'Political Opportunity Structures and Political Protest: Anti-nuclear Movements in Four Democracies', *British Journal of Political Science*, 16 (1), pp. 57-85.

Kobayashi, Osamu, Yoshio Kanazawa, Naohiko Harada, Yoshihiro Nomura, Akira Wakasugi and Kiyotaka Kodama (1970), 'Kigyo Ritchi to Kogai Boshi Kyotei – Tokyo Denryoku ni Kiku' ('Location of Business and Pollution Control Agreement – Listening to the Tokyo Electric Power Company'), *Kogyo Ritchi (Industrial Location)*, 9 (3), 21-32.

Kondo, Hiroshi (1983), 'Change in Financial Conditions and Environmental Organizations of Local Governments' ('Chiho Zaisei Sosiki no Doko'), *Environmental Research Quarterly*, 42, pp. 63-73.

Kondo, Jiro (2001), 'Reform of the National Institute of Environmental Studies to a Self-supporting Administrative Agency', *Environmental Research Quarterly*, 120, Tokyo, Japan: Kankyo Chosa Center, pp. 4-10.

Kriesi, Hanspeter, Ruud Koopmans, Jan Willem Duyvendak and Marco Guigni (1995), *New Social Movements in Western Europe*, Minneapolis, MN, US: University of Minnesota Press.

Kurasaka, Hidefumi (2004), *Kankyo Seisaku Ron (Environmental Policies)*, Tokyo, Japan: Shinzansha.

Lafferty, William M. and James Meadowcroft (eds) (2000), *Implementing Sustainable Development: Strategies and Initiatives in High Consumption Societies*, Oxford, UK and New York, NY, US: Oxford University Press.

Lafferty, William, M. and Frans Coenen (2000), 'The Diffusion of Local Agenda 21 in Twelve European Countries', *Paper presented at the international workshop 'Diffusion of environmental policy innovations'*, Berlin, Germany, 8-9 December 2000.

Lall, Sanjaya (2002), 'Social Capital and Industrial Transformation', in Sakiko Fukuda, Parr Carlos Lopes and Khalid Malik (eds), *Capacity for Development*, London, UK: Earthscan, pp. 101-19.

Lam, Peng Er (1999), *Green Politics in Japan*, London, UK: Routledge.

Lee, Soo Choel (1999), 'Public Finance and Environmental Subsidies in Japan, The Research and Study', *Economic Review*, Special Issue, 18, 30-48.

Lesbirel, Hayden (1998), *NIMBY Politics in Japan: Energy Siting and the Management of Environmental Conflict*, Ithaca, NY, US and London, UK: Cornell University Press.

Li, Zhidong (1999), *Chugoku no Kankyo Kanri System (Chinese Environmental Protection System)*, Tokyo, Japan: Toyo Economic Press.

Loehman, Edna Tusak and D. Marc Kilgour (1998), *Designing Institutions for Environmental and Resource Management*, Cheltenham, UK and Northampton, MA, USA: Edward Elgar.

Lovins, Amory B., Ernst von Weizsaecker and L. Hunter Lovins (1997), *Factor Four*, London, UK: Earthscan.

Lu, Xianxang (1996), *West Neo-institutional Economics*, Beijing, China: China Development Publishing House (in Chinese).

Makino, Noboru, Shinzaburo Oishi and Yutaka Yoshida (1991), 'Nippon Gata Kankyohozen no Genryu' ('The Origin of the Japanese Model of

Environmental Protection'), *Gendai Nogyo* (September), Tokyo, Japan: Nobunkyo, pp. 6-127.

Masuhara, Yoshitake (1994), *Zu de Miru Kankyo Kihonho (Basic Environmental Law by Charts)*, Tokyo, Japan: Chuo Hoki.

Masumi, Junnosuke, L. Carlile (trans.) (1995), *Contemporary Politics in Japan*, Berkeley, CA, US: University of California.

Matsubara, Haruo (1971), *Kogai to Chiiki Shakai (Pollution and Regional Society)*, Tokyo, Japan: Nihon Keizai Shimbunsha.

Matsuno, Yu (1996), 'Kogai Kenko Higai Hosho Seido Seiritsu Katei no Seiji Keizai Bunseki' ('Political Economic Analysis of the Process of Establishment of the Japanese Compensation System of Pollution-Related Health Damage'), *Keizai Ronso (The Economic Review)* 157 (5, 6), pp. 51-70.

Matsuno, Yu (1997), 'Tekkogyo ni Okeru Iou Sankabutsu Haishutsu Sakugen he no Kakushu Kankyo Seisaku Shudan no Kiyo (1) (2)' ('How Effective Were Policy Instruments in Reducing Sulfur Oxide Emissions from Steel Mills in Japan (1) (2))', *Keizai Ronso (The Economic Review)* 159 (5, 6), pp. 100-20; 160 (3), pp. 19-38.

Matsuno, Yu (2000), 'Kuni no Kogaiboshi Kyotei ni taisuru Taido' ('The Attitude of the National Government towards Pollution Control Agreements'), *Keiei Ronshu (Meiji Business Review)*, 47 (4), pp. 75-87.

Matsuno, Yu (2001), 'Pollution Control Agreements in Japan: Conditions for Their Success', Presented at European Consortium for Political Research (Workshop 1. The Politics of New Environmental Policy Instruments), *Institute of Political Studies*, Grenoble, France, 6-11 April 2001 www.essex.ac.uk/ECPR/events/jointsessions/paperarchive/grenoble.asp?section=1.

Matsuno, Yu (2002), 'Kogaiboshi Kyotei no Jittai to Sono Kon'nichiteki Sonzai Riyu no Chosa to Kenkyu' ('Pollution Control Agreements in Japan, Current State and Reasons of Persistence'), *Meiji Daigaku Shakai Kagaku Kenkyusho Kiyo (The Institute of Social Sciences, Meiji University)*, 40 (2), pp. 45-56.

Matsuno, Yu and Kazuhiro Ueta (2000), 'A Socio-economic Evaluation of the SO_x Charge in Japan', in Mikael Skou Andersen and Rolf-Ulrich Sprenger (eds), *Market-based Instruments in Environmental Management*, Cheltenham, UK and Northampton, MA, USA: Edward Elgar, pp. 194-214.

Matsuno, Yu and Kazuhiro Ueta (2001), 'Chiho Kokyo Dantai ni Okeru Kogai Kankyo Seisaku ni Kansuru Anketo Chosa', in Hokokusho Kogai Boshi Kyotei o Chushin ni ('Environmental Policies of Local Governments in Japan Focusing on Pollution Control Agreements: Report of Questionnaire Survey,' Keizai Ronso Bessatsu Chosa to Kenkyu (Research and Study), special issue of *The Economic Review*, 23, pp. 1-155.

Matsuoka, Nobuo (1989), 'Energy Policy and the Environment', in Shigeto Tsuru and Helmut Weidner (eds), *Environmental Policy in Japan*, Berlin, Germany: Edition Sigma Rainer Bohn Verlag, pp. 437-50.

Matsuoka, Shunji, Reishi Matsumoto and Ikuho Kochi (1998), 'Economic Growth and Environmental Issues in Developing Countries: Does the Environmental Kuznets Curve Exist?' *Journal of Environmental Science*, 11 (4), pp. 349-62.

McKean, Margaret (1977), 'Pollution and Policymaking', in T.J. Pempel (ed.), *Policy Making in Contemporary Japan*, Ithaca, NY, US: Cornell University Press, pp. 201-38.

McKean, Margaret (1981), *Environmental Protest and Citizen Politics in Japan*, Berkeley, CA, US: University of California Press.

McSpadden, Lettie (1997), 'Environmental Policy in the Courts', in Norman J. Vig and Michael E. Kraft (eds), *Environmental Policy in the 1990s*, 3rd edition,

Washington, DC, US: Congressional Quarterly Press, pp. 168-86.

Metropolitan Environmental Improvement Program (1990), *Japan's Experience in Urban Environmental Management*, Washington, DC, US: World Bank, Asia Technical Department, Environment & Natural Resource Department.

Milieu Defensie (1992), 'Action Plan: Towards a Sustainable Society', May 1992, Amsterdam, The Netherlands: Milieu Defensie.

Miller, Alan and Curtis Moore (1990), 'Japan and the Global Environment: Problem Solver or Problem Maker?' www.gwjapan.org/ftp/pub/policy/jec/jec5-5.txt, 5 June 1998.

Ministry of the Environment (2000), *Kankyo Hakusho (Quality of the Environment in Japan) 2000*, Tokyo, Japan: Gyosei.

Ministry of the Environment (2001a), *Kankyo Hakusho (Quality of the Environment in Japan) 2001*, Tokyo, Japan: Gyosei.

Ministry of the Environment (2001b), *Junkan-gata Shakai Hakusho (The Annual Report on the Sound Material Cycle Society) 2001*, Tokyo, Japan: Gyosei.

Ministry of the Environment (2001c), *Basic Environmental Plan (Kankyo Kihon Keikaku)*, Tokyo, Japan: Gyosei.

Ministry of the Environment (2001d), *Water Environment Management in Japan (June 2001)*, Tokyo, Japan: Planning Division, Water Environment Department, Environmental Management Bureau, Ministry of the Environment.

Ministry of the Environment (2002a), *Kankyo Hakusho (Quality of the Environment in Japan) 2002*, Tokyo, Japan: Gyosei.

Ministry of the Environment (2002b), 'Basic Plan for the Policy Performance Review of Ministry of the Environment' ('Kankyosho Seisaku Hyouka Kihon Keikaku'), www.env.go.jp/guide/seisaku/index.html.

Ministry of the Environment (2003a), *Kankyo Hakusho (Quality of the Environment in Japan) 2003*, Tokyo, Japan: Gyosei.

Ministry of the Environment (2003b), *Junkan-gata Shakai Hakusho (Annual Report on the Sound Material-cycle Society) 2003*, Tokyo, Japan: Gyosei,.

Ministry of the Environment (2003c), *Tei Kogaisha Guidebook (Guidebook of Cleaner Cars) 2002*, Tokyo, Japan: Kankyosho Kankyo kanri kyoku.

Ministry of the Environment (2004a), *Kankyo Hakusho (Quality of the Environment in Japan) 2004*, Tokyo, Japan: Gyosei.

Ministry of the Environment (2004b), *Chemical Substance and Environment*, Press Release, 1 March 2004, Tokyo, Japan: Ministry of the Environment.

Ministry of Environment, Republic of Korea (1997), *Environmental Protection in Korea*, Gyeonggi do, Ministry of Environment, Republic of Korea.

Ministry of Finance, Financial Bureau (1999), *Fiscal Investment and Loan Program 99*, Tokyo, Japan: Publication Office of the Ministry of Finance.

Ministry of Finance (2003), *Statistical Data for Foreign and Domestic Direct Investment*, www.mof.go.jp/fdi/.

Ministry of Foreign Affairs (1997), *ODA Annual Report 1997*, Tokyo, Japan: Ministry of Foreign Affairs.

Ministry of Foreign Affairs (1998), *ODA White Paper 1997*, Tokyo, Japan: Ministry of Foreign Affairs.

Ministry of Foreign Affairs (1999), 'Japan's ODA in China', Chapter 3 in *Japan's ODA Annual Report 1999 (Wagakuni no Seifu Kaihatsu Enjo Hakusho, 1999)*, www.mofa.go.jp/policy/oda.

Ministry of Foreign Affairs (2002a), 'Environmental Conservation Initiative for Sustainable Development (Eco ISD)', August 2002, ww.mofa.go.jp/policy/environment/wssd/2002/kinitiative3-2.html.

Ministry of Foreign Affairs (2002b), *Japan's ODA Annual Report 2002*, Tokyo, Japan: Ministry of Foreign Affairs.

Ministry of Foreign Affairs (2002c), *Japan's Official Development Assistance Charter*, Tokyo, Japan: Ministry of Foreign Affairs, www.mofa.go.jp/policy/ oda.

Ministry of Foreign Affairs (2003), *Revision of Japan's Official Development Assistance Charter*, www.mofa.go.jp/policy/oda/reform/charter.html.

Ministry of Home Affairs (1970), 'Kogai Taisaku Yoko: Kogai Boshi Taisaku no Sekkyokuteki na Tenkai' ('Outline of Pollution Control Measure: Active Development of Pollution Control Measures'), *Chiho Zaimu (Local Finance)*, 195, pp. 109-11.

Ministry of Home Affairs and Environment Agency (eds) (1971), *Kogai Boshi Jorei Kyotei Shu (Collection of Pollution Control Ordinances and Agreements)*, Tokyo, Japan: Daiichi Hoki.

Ministry of International Trade and Industry (1988), *Japan's Energy Conservation Policy*, Tokyo, Japan: Ministry of International Trade and Industry.

Ministry of International Trade and Industry (1998), *Business Investment Plans of Major Japanese Industries (Shuyou Sangyo no Setsubi Toshi Keikaku)*, Tokyo, Japan: Publication office of Ministry of Finance.

Ministry of International Trade and Industry (1988-90), *Business Investment Plants of Maior Jananese Industries, (Shuyou Sangyo no Setsubi Toshi Keikaku)*, Tokyo, Japan: Publication office of Ministry of Finance.

Ministry of Public Management, Home Affairs, Posts and Telecommunications (2004), Seisaku Hyoka no Sogo Madoguchi (Policy Evaluation), www.soumu.go.jp/, 28 January 2004.

Minowa, Yasuhiro (2004), 'Laws related to the Prevention of Global Warming', in *Kankyo Seisaku to Kankyo Ho Taikei (Environmental Policy and Law Systems)* Tokyo, Japan: Japan Environment Management Association for Industry, pp. 81-2.

Mitsubishi Research Institute (2002), *Chugoku Joho Handbook (China Data Handbook) 2001*, Tokyo, Japan: Sososha.

Mitsuhashi, Norihiro (1999), 'Expectations to Pro-environment Business Leaders' ('Kankyo wa Keizaijin eno Kitai'), in *The Global Environment and Japanese Economy (Chikyu Kankyo to Nihon Keizai)*, Tokyo, Japan: Iwanami Shoten, pp. 1-17.

Mitsuhashi, Tadahiro (ed.) (2000), *Japan's Green Comeback: Future Visions of the Men Who Made Japan*, Subang Jaya: Malaysia Pelanduk Publications.

Mitsuo, Eiichi, Yoshio Kanazawa, Naohiko Harada, Yoshihiro Nomura, Akira Wakasugi, Nobutoki Inoue and Shizuo Kaji (1970), 'Kigyo Ritchi to Kogai Boshi Kyotei: Tokyoto ni Kiku' ('Location of Business and Pollution Control Agreement: Listening to the Tokyo Prefectural Government'), *Kogyo Ritchi (Industrial Location)*, 9 (4), pp. 4-16.

Miyamoto, Ken'ichi (1973), *Chiiki Kaihatsu wa Korede Yoinoka (A Critic to Regional Development)*, Tokyo, Japan: Iwanami Shoten.

Miyamoto, Ken'ichi (1981), 'Environmental Policies of the Past Twenty Years: A Balance Sheet', in Haruo Nagamine (ed.), *Nation-Building and Regional Development: The Japanese Experience*, Tokyo, Japan: Maruzen Asia, pp. 235-68.

Miyamoto, Ken'ichi (1989), *Environmental Economics*, Tokyo, Japan: Iwanami Shoten.

Miyaoka, Isao (1998), 'More than One Way to Save an Elephant: Foreign Pressure and the Japanese Policy Process', *Japan Forum*, 10 (2), pp. 167-79.

Miyaoka, Isao (2004), *Legitimacy in International Society: Japan's Reaction to Global Wildlife Preservation*, New York, NY, US: Palgrave Macmillan.

Miyata, Hideaki (1999), *Dioxin*, Tokyo, Japan: Iwanami Shoten.

Mol, Arthur and David Sonnenfeld (eds) (2000), *Ecological Modernization Around the World: Perspectives and Critical Debates*, London, UK: Frank Cass.

Moore, Curtis and Alan Miller (1994), *Green Gold: Japan, Germany, the United States, and the Race for Environmental Technology*, Boston, MA, US: Beacon Press.

Mori, Akihisa (2002), 'Environmental Soft Loan Programme for Industrial Pollution Control in Developing Countries: A Case Study of OECF's Indonesia AJDF Category B/Small Enterprise and Pollution Abatement Equipment (PAE) Programme', *Proceedings of the 3rd Special Study Meeting, The Japan Society for International Development*, Nagoya, Japan: Japan Society for International Development, pp. 236-41.

Morishima, Akira (2004), 'Japanese Experience in Small and Medium Enterprises', in Financial Mechanisms Task Force, CCECED (ed.), *Financial Mechanisms for Enviornmental Protection in China*, Beijing, China: Secretariat of China Council for International Cooperation on Environment and Development, pp. 324-58.

Motani, Kosuke (1999), 'Chiiki Sangyo Seisaku no Kako, Genzai, Mirai o Tenbo suru' ('Looking at the Past, Today and Future of Regional Industrial Policy'), Chiho Zaimu, 546, Tokyo, Japan: Gyosei, pp. 123-47.

Murai, Yoshitaka (1988), *Shrimp and the Japanese*, Tokyo, Japan: Iwanami Shoten.

Muramatsu, Michio (1997), *Local Power in the Japanese State*, Berkeley, CA, US: University of California Press.

Muto, Hiromi (2003), *Nyusatsu Kaikaku: Dango Shakai o Kaeru' ('Reform of Bidding System: Change the Society of Collusion')*, Tokyo, Japan: Iwanami Shoten.

Nagoya City (2001), *Annual Report of the Waste Collection and Disposal Work (Nagoyashi Haikibutsu Jigyo Gaiyo) 2001*, Nagoya, Japan: Environmental Bureau of Nagoya City, pp. 80-1.

Nakajima, Fuminori (2000), 'Establishment of Flue-gas Denitrification Technology', in Japan Association of Air Pollution (ed.), *Nihon no Taiki Osen no Rekishi (The History of Air Pollution In Japan)*, II, Tokyo, Japan: Koken Kyokai, pp. 493-520.

Nakane, Chie (1970), *Japanese Society*, Berkeley, CA, US: University of California Press.

National Environmental Protection Agency of China (1996, 1997), *Environmental Statistics*, Beijing: Chinese Environmental Science Press.

National Environmental Protection Agency of China (1997), *The Collections of Environmental Laws and Regulations of China*, (in Chinese), Beijing, China: Chemical Industrial Press.

National Environmental Protection Agency of China (1994), *Two Decades of Chinese Environmental Administration*, Chinese Press of Environmental Science.

National Geographic Society (1992), *National Parks of the United States*, Washington, DC, US: National Geographic Society.

National Institute of Environmental Research, Korea (2004), *Tripartite Environment Ministers Meeting*, www.temm.org/.

National Land Agency (1999), *The Grand Design of National Land in the 21st Century*, Tokyo, Japan: Jiji Tsushin, pp. 237-8.

Nihon Bengoshi Rengokai, Kogai Taisaku Kankyo Hozen Iinkai (1995), *Nihon No Kogai Yushutsu to Kankyo Hakai: Tonan Ajiya ni Okeru Kigyo Yushutsu to ODA (Japan's Export of Pollution and Environmental Destruction: Industrial*

Location and ODA in South East Asia), Tokyo, Japan: Nihon Hyoronsha.

Nihon Gesuido Kyokai (2002), Gesuido Tokei Yoran (Statistics of Sewage System) Tokyo, Japan: Nippon Gesuido Kyokai.

Nihon Gesuido Kyokai (Japan Sewage Works Association), www.alpha-web.ne.jp/jswa/ accessed 21 June, 2004.

Nippon Steel Human Resources Development Co. Ltd. (1999), Nippon: The Land and Its People, Tokyo, Japan: Gakuseisha.

Nishimura, Hajime (ed.), (1989), How to Conquer Air Pollution: A Japanese Experience, Amsterdam, The Netherlands: Elsevier Publishing Co.

Nishimura, Yukio (2002), 'Renovation of Urban Space and Amenities', in Fumikazu Yoshida and Ken'ichi Miyamoto (eds), Environment and Development (Kankyo to Kaihatsu), Tokyo, Japan: Iwanami Shoten, pp. 121-50.

Nixon, Richard (1970), 'Special Message to the Congress on Environmental Quality, February 10' in Richard Nixon (1974), Public Papers of the Presidents of the United States, Richard Nixon: Containing the Public Messages, Speeches, and Statements of the President, Washington DC, US: United States Government Printing Office.

Numao, Fumihiko (1994), 'Environmental Management Plan, Environmental Administration of Local Government' ('Toshi Jichitai no Kankyo Gyousei'), Tokyo, Japan: The Tokyo Institute for Municipal Research, pp. 36-51.

Oberthür, Sebastian and Hermann E. Ott (1999), The Kyoto Protocol: International Climate Policy for the 21st Century, New York, NY, US: Springer-Verlag.

Ochiai, Ryoji (1986), 'IC Industry and Environmental Issues', Environmental Research Quarterly (62), Tokyo, Japan: Environmental Research Center, pp. 110-9.

O'Conner, David (1994), Managing the Environment with Rapid Industrialization: Lessons from the East Asian Experience, Paris, France: OECD.

O'Connor, James (1996), 'The Second Contradiction of Capitalism', in Ted Benton (ed.), The Greening of Marxism, New York, NY, US: Guilford.

Ohta, Hajime (2000), 'Industry's Effort in Promoting Voluntary Action: Regarding Results of the 2nd Follow-up to the Keidanren Voluntary Action Plan on the Environment', Environmental Research Quarterly, 117, Tokyo, Japan: Environmental Research Center (Kankyo Chosa Center), pp. 42-54.

Ohta, Susumu (2000), 'Climate Protection Policies on Automobiles', Environmental Research Quarterly, 117, Tokyo, Japan: Environmental Research Center (Kankyo Chosa Center), pp. 27-32.

Okimoto, Daniel (1989), Between MITI and the Market: Japanese Industrial Policy for High Technology, Stanford, CA, US: Stanford University Press.

Oku, Mami (1994), Cooperation with Private Enterprises: Measures of Local Government in Environmental Administration, Environmental Administration of Local Government (Toshi Jichitai no Kankyo Gyousei), Tokyo, Japan: The Tokyo Institute for Municipal Research, pp. 53-74.

O'Neill, Kate (2000), Waste Trading Among Rich Nations: Building a New Theory of Environmental Regulation, Cambridge, UK: The MIT Press.

O'Neill, Michael (1997), Green Parties and Political Change in Contemporary Europe: New Politics, Old Predicaments, Aldershot, UK: Ashgate.

Ootsuka, Katsuo (1998), 'Value of Agriculture and Rural Districts and the Living Economics', Environmental Information Science (Kankyo Joho Kagaku), 27 (1), pp. 6-9.

Organization for Economic Cooperation and Development (1977a), Environmental Policies in Japan, Paris, France: OECD.

Organization for Economic Cooperation and Development (1977b), *Polluter Pays Principle*, Paris, France: OECD.

Organization for Economic Cooperation and Development (1984), *International Conference on Environment and Economics, Background Papers*, II, Paris, France: OECD, pp. 105-34.

Organization for Economic Cooperation and Development (1991), 'Guidelines for the Application of Economic Instruments in Environmental Policy', *Environment Committee Meeting at Ministerial Level, Background Chapter* No. 1, January 30-31, Paris, France: OECD.

Organization for Economic Cooperation and Development (1994a), *Environmental Performance Reviews: Japan*, Paris, France: OECD.

Organization for Economic Cooperation and Development (1994b), *Regulatory Cooperation for an Interdependent World*, Paris, France: OECD.

Organization for Economic Cooperation and Development (1997), *Environmental Performance Reviews: Korea*, Paris, France: OECD.

Organization for Economic Cooperation and Development (1999), *Voluntary Approaches for Environmental Policy*, Paris, France: OECD.

Organization for Economic Cooperation and Development, Working Party on Economic and Environmental Policy Integration (1999), 'The Use of Unilateral Agreements in Japan: Voluntary Action Plans of Industries against Global Warming', EVN/EPOC/GEEI (98) 26/Final, Paris, France: OECD.

Organization for Economic Cooperation and Development (2000), *Environmental Performance Review: Japan*, Paris, France: OECD.

Organization for Economic Cooperation and Development (2001), *Extended Producer Responsibility*, Paris, France: OECD.

Organization for Economic Cooperation and Development (2002), *Environmental Performance Review: Japan*, Paris, France: OECD.

O'Riordan, Tim and Jill Jäger (1996), *Politics of Climate Change: A European Perspective*, New York, NY, US: Routledge.

Osaka Prefecture (1980), *Kogai hakusho (White Paper on Pollution)*, Osaka, Japan: Osaka Prefecture.

Ostrom, Elinor (1997), *Governing the Commons: The Evolution of Institutions for Collective Action*, Cambridge, UK and New York, NY, US: Cambridge University Press.

Overseas Environmental Cooperation Center (2001), *Study Report on the Definition and Classification Guidelines of Environmental ODA* (in Japanese), Tokyo, Japan: OECF, pp. 157-9.

Overseas Environmental Cooperation Center (OECF) (2004), *Report of the Information Exchange Project on Japan – China Environmental Cooperation* (in Japanese), Tokyo, Japan: OECF.

People's Republic of China (2002), *National Report on Sustainable Development*, Beijing, China: China Environmental Science Press.

Pearce, David and Jeremy Warford (1993), *World without End: Economics, Environment and Sustainable Development*, Oxford, UK: Oxford University Press.

Pekkanen, Robert (2000), 'Japan's New Politics: The Case of the NPO Law', *Journal of Japanese Studies*, 26 (1), pp. 111-48.

Pempel, T.J. (1982), *Policy and Politics in Japan: Creative Conservatism*, Philadelphia, PA, US: Temple University Press.

Poole, P. (1988), 'China Threatened by Japan's Old Pollution Strategies', *Far Eastern Economic Review*, 140 (25), 23 June 1988, pp. 78-9.

Porter, Michael (1990), *The Competitive Advantage of Nations*, London, UK: Macmillan.

Porter, Michael and Claas van der Linde (1995), 'Toward a New Conception of the Environment – Competitiveness Relationship', *Journal of Economic Perspectives*, 6 (4), 119-32.

Potter, David (1996), *Japan's Foreign Aid to Thailand and the Philippines*, New York, NY, US: St. Martin's Press.

Prendiville, Brendan (1994), *Environmental Politics in France*, Boulder, CO, US: Westview Press.

Pressman, Jeffrey and Aaron Wildavsky (1973), *Implementation*, Berkeley, CA, US: University of California Press.

Prime Minister's Office (ed.) (1971), *Kogai Hakusho (White Paper on Pollution)*, Tokyo, Japan: Printing Bureau, Ministry of Finance.

Prime Minister's Office and Ministry of Health and Welfare (1970), 'History of Pollution Control Administration' ('Kogai Gyosei no Rekishi'), in Environment Agency of Japan (ed.), *Kogai Hakusho (Quality of the Environment in Japan) 1970*, Tokyo, Japan: Okurasho Insatsukyoku, pp. 5-10.

Princen, Thomas, Michael Maniates and Ken Conca (eds) (2003), *Confronting Consumption*, Cambridge, MA, US: The MIT Press.

Pyle, Kenneth B. (1996), *The Making of Modern Japan*, 2nd edition, New York, NY, US: Houghton Mifflin.

Reimann, Kim (2001), 'Building Networks from the Outside In: International Movements, Japanese NGOs and the Kyoto Climate Change Conference', *Mobilization*, 6 (1), pp. 69-82

Reischauer, Edwin, O. (1964), *Japan: Past and Present*, North Clarendon, US and Tokyo, Japan: Tuttle.

Reischauer, Edwin, O. (1977), *The Japanese Today: Change and Continuity*, Tokyo, Japan: Tuttle.

Ren, Yong (2000), 'Japanese Approaches to Environmental Management: Structural and Institutional Features', *International Review for Environmental Strategies*, 1 (1), pp. 79-96.

Ren, Yong (2000), *Japanese Environmental Management and Experience in Industrial Pollution Control*, Beijing, China: Chinese Environmental Science Press (in Chinese).

Ren, Yong, M. Chang, and Hidefumi Imura (2000), *Urban Environmental Governance of East Asia, Research Report*, Kanagawa, Japan: Institute for Global Environmental Strategies.

Reschovsky, Clara (2004), 'Journey to Work', U.S. Census Bureau, C2KBR, March 2004, www.census.gov/prod/2004pubs/c2kbr-33.pdf.

Resources and Energy Agency (1997), *Energy Conservation Handbook (Sho Energi Binran 1997)*, Tokyo, Japan: Energy Conservation Center.

Resources and Energy Agency (1999), *Energy Conservation Law (Sho Energi Ho)*, Tokyo, Japan: Energy Conservation Center.

Resources and Energy Agency (2000), *Energy Conservation Handbook (Sho Energi Binran)*, Tokyo, Japan: Energy Conservation Center.

Rock, Michael T (2002), *Pollution Control in East Asia: Lessons from Newly Industrializing Economies*, Singapore: ISEAS; Washington, DC, US: Resources for the Future.

Sabatier, Paul (1975), 'Social Movements and Regulatory Agencies: Toward a More Adequate – and Less Pessimistic – Theory of "Clientele Capture"', *Policy Sciences*, 6, pp. 301-42.

Sadler, Barry and Rob Verheem (1996), *Strategic Environmental Assessment*, The

Hague, The Netherlands: Ministry of Housing, Spatial Planning and the Environment.

Sakai, Shin'ichi (1999), *Waste After Twenty Years*, Tokyo, Japan: Catalogue House.

Sakaiya, Taichi (1993), *What is Japan?*, New York, NY, US: Kodansha America.

Sakaiya, Taichi (2000), 'The 1993 Watershed and the Agenda for Reform', in Masuzoe, Yoichi (ed.) *Years of Trial: Japan in the 1990s*, Tokyo, Japan: Japan Echo Inc., pp. 116-32.

Samsung Electronics (1999), *Green Management Report*, Samsung Electronics, samsung.com/AboutSAMSUNG/SocialCommitment/EHSReport/GreenManag ementReport/downloads/greport_1999.pdf.

Samuels, Richard (1987), *The Business of the Japanese State: Energy Markets in Comparative and Historical Perspective*, Ithaca, NY, US: Cornell University Press.

Sangyo Kenkyusyo (1991), *Ajia Chiiki no Hatten to Kankyo Hogo ni Kansuru Chosa Kenkyu (Study on Development and Environment Preservation in Asia)*, Tokyo, Japan: Sangyo kenkyusho.

Saruta, Katsumi (1971), 'Chiho Jichitai no Kogai Taisaku' ('Pollution Control Measure of Local Government'), in Yoshiharu Shimizu, Katsumi Saruta and Kazuo Toyama (eds), *Keihin Kogyo Chitai (Tokyo–Yokohama Industrial Area)*, Tokyo, Japan: Shinhyoron, pp. 95-163.

Saruta, Katsumi (1981), 'Kogai Boshi Kyotei no Enkaku to Yokohama Hoshiki ni Tsuite' ('On the History of Pollution Control Agreements and the Yokohama Method'), in Ningen Kankyo Mondai Kenkyukai (The Society for the Research on Human-environmental Problems) (ed.), *Kogai Kankyo ni Kakaru Kyotei to no Hogakuteki Kenkyu (Legal Study on Pollution Control Agreements and the Like)*, Tokyo, Japan: Yuhikaku, pp. 241-72.

Saruta, Katsumi (1999), Interview by Yu Matsuno and Kazuhiro Ueta on Pollution Control Agreements, memo.

Saruta, Katsumi (2000), 'Negishi wan Kaihatsu to Kogai Boshi Kyotei' ('The Negishi Bay Development and Pollution Control Agreement'), in Japan Society of Atmospheric Environment (ed.), *Nihon no Taiki Osen no Rekishi (The History of Air Pollution in Japan)* III (Taiki Kankyo Gakkai), Tokyo, Japan: Koken Kyokai, pp. 689-73.

Sasaki, Komei (1999), 'Environment and Folklore: Japanese View for Environment', *Environmental Information Science (Kankyo Joho Kagaku)*, 28 (1), p. 1.

Sato, Makoto (1990), *Resort Retto (Resort Island)*, Tokyo, Japan: Iwanami Shoten.

Schmidt-Bleek, Friedlich (1994), *Wieviel Umwelt braucht der Mensch? Das Mass fuer oekologisches Wirtschaften*, Berlin, Germany; Basel, Switzerland and Boston, MA, US: Birkhauser Verlag.

Schnaiberg, Allan and Kenneth Alan Gould (1994), *Environment and Society: The Enduring Conflict*, New York, NY, US: St. Martin's Press.

Schreurs, Miranda A. (1994) 'Policy Laggard or Policy Leader? Global Environmental Policy-making Under the Liberal Democratic Party', *The Journal of Pacific Asia*, 2, pp. 3-33.

Schreurs, Miranda A. (1997), 'Domestic Institutions and International Environmental Agendas in Japan and Germany', in Miranda A. Schreurs and Elizabeth Economy (eds), *The Internationalization of Environmental Protection*, Cambridge, MA, US: Cambridge University Press, pp. 134-61.

Schreurs, Miranda A. (2000), 'Japan: Law, Technology and Aid', in William M. Lafferty and James R. Meadowcroft (eds), *Implementing Sustainable Development: Strategies and Initiatives in High Consumption Societies*, New York, NY, US: Oxford University Press, pp. 112-41.

Schreurs, Miranda A. (2002), *Environmental Politics in Japan, Germany, and the United States*, Cambridge, UK: Cambridge University Press.

Schreurs, Miranda A. and Dennis Pirages (eds) (1997), *Ecological Security in Northeast Asia*, Seoul, Korea: Yonsei University Press.

Scott, James (1998), *Seeing Like a State: How Certain Schemes to Improve the Human Condition Have Failed*, New Haven, CT, US: Yale University Press.

Seko, Kazuho (1999), 'NPO's Role to Create a Sustainable Society' (Kankyo Joho Kagaku), 28-4, Tokyo, Japan: Environmental Information Science Center, pp. 23-7.

Sen, Amartya (1999), *Development as Freedom*, NY, US: Alfred A. Knopf.

Seoul City Government (2000), *Seoul Green Vision 21*, Seoul, Korea: Seoul City Government.

Shibata, Tokue (1989), 'The Influence of Big Industries on Environmental Policies: The Case of Car Exhaust Standards', in Shigeto Tsuru and Helmut Weidner (eds), *Environmental Policy in Japan*, Berlin, Germany: Edition Sigma Rainer Bohn Verlag, pp. 99-108.

Shima, Nobuhiko (2000), *New Central Government Ministries and Agencies*, Tokyo, Japan: Chukei Shuppan.

Shimada, Haruo (2000), 'Asset Inflation and the Strained Social Fabric', in Yoichi Masuzoe (ed.), *Years of Trial – Japan in the 1990s*, Tokyo, Japan: Japan Echo Inc., pp. 133-45.

Snow, David A. and Robert D. Benford (1992), 'Master Frames and Cycles of Protest', in A. D. Morris and C. McClurg Mueller (eds), *Frontiers in Social Movement Theory*, New Haven, CT, US: Yale University Press, pp. 133-55.

Social Learning Group (William C. Clark, Jill Jäger, Josee van Eijndhoven and Nancy Dickson (eds)) (2001), *Learning to Manage Global Environmental Risks*, Cambridge, MA, US: The MIT Press.

State Environmental Protection Administration of China (1998), *The Ninth Program and Long-term Prospect for the National Environmental Protection*, Beijing, China: State Environmental Protection Administration.

State Environmental Protection Administration of China (2001), *China's Environmental Statistics*, Beijing, China: Chinese Press of Environmental Science.

Statistics Bureau (2002), *Statistics of Japan*, Tokyo, Japan: Japan Statistical Association, Tokyo, Japan: Nippon Tokei Kyokai.

Statistics Bureau of Management and Coordination Agency (2002), *Statistical Handbook of Japan 2002*, Tokyo, Japan: Japan Statistical Association.

Sterner, Thomas (2002), *Policy Instruments for Environmental and Natural Resource Management*, Washington, DC, US: Resources for the Future.

Study Group on the Global Environmental Economics (Chikyu Kankyo Keizai Kenkyukai, (1991), *Japan's Pollution Experiences (Nippon no Kogai Keiken)*, Tokyo, Japan: Godo Shuppan.

Study Group on Environmental Measures in Asia and Other Developing Regions (1997), *Study Report*, Tokyo, Japan: Economic Cooperation Division, the Ministry of International Trade and Industry, Japan.

Suda, Shunkai and Masako Nakamura (1995), 'The Future of Public Participation in Law Making Process based on the Experience of New Law on Containers and Packaging', *Recycle Bunka* (50), Tokyo, Japan: Recycle Bunkasha, pp. 15-22.

Sugiyama, Rie and Hidefumi Imura (1999), 'Voluntary Approaches in Japan: Proven Record of Pollution Control Agreements and New Industrial Initiatives for the Protection of the Global Environment', *Eco-Management and Auditing*, 6, pp. 28-34.

Sugiyama, T. (1998), *SO$_x$ Emissions of East Asia: A Historical Comparative Analysis of SO$_x$ Emissions of East Asian Countries and its Implication on Chinese Emission Outlook, Research Report*, Tokyo, Japan: Central Electric Power Research Institute of Japan.

Suido Sangyo Shimbunsha 2001, *Annals of Sewage Work (Gesuido Nenkan)* 2000, Tokyo, Japan: Suido Sangyo Shimbunsha.

Sutherland, Mary and Dorothy Britton (1995), *National Parks of Japan*, Tokyo, Japan: Kodansha International.

Suwa, Yuzo (1997), *Nippon wa Kankyo ni Yasashiinoka (Is Japan Friendly to the Environment?)*, Tokyo, Japan: Shin Hyoron, pp. 203-28.

Suwa, Yuzo (2001), 'Ministry of the Environment Should Use More PI Measures', *Environmental Research Quarterly*, 120, Tokyo, Japan: Kankyo Chosa Center, pp. 25-32.

Suzuki, Motoyuki (2000), *Realization of a Sustainable Society – Zero Emissions Approaches*, Tokyo, Japan: United Nations University Press, www.unu.edu/zef/publications.html.

Tachibana, Hiroshi (1994), 'Activities of Japanese Industry toward Sustainable Development', *Environmental Research Quarterly*, 93, Tokyo, Japan: Environmental Research Center, pp. 74-81.

Takagi, Koichi (1994), *Trends of Environmental Problems in Local Government, Environmental Administration of Local Government (Toshi Jichitai no Kankyo Gyousei)*, Tokyo, Japan: The Tokyo Institute for Municipal Research, pp. 19-35.

Takasugi, Singo (1999), *Kitakyushu Eco-Town o Mi ni Iku (Going to See Kitakyushu Eco-Town)*, Tokyo, Japan: Diamondsha.

Tanaka, Kakuei (1972), *Nippon Retto Kaizo Ron (Building a New Japan: A Plan for Remodeling the Japanese Archipelago)*, Tokyo, Japan: Japan: Nikkan Kogyo Shinbunsha.

Tanaka, Kazuaki (2004), *Itsuwari no Mineika (False Privatization)*, Tokyo, Japan: Wack.

Tanakura, Tadayuki (1994), *The Status Quo and Main Issues of Environmental Administration in Local Government, Environmental Administration of Local Government (Toshi Jichitai no Kankyo Gyousei)*, Tokyo, Japan: The Tokyo Institute for Municipal Research.

Taniyama, Tetsuro (1990), 'Terrible Pollution of Golf Courses: Resort Area Development and Agricultural Chemical Disasters Destroying Ecosystems (Osorubeki Gorufujo Osen: Seitaikei o Hakai suru Rizotokaihatsu to Noyakuka)', in *Resort Area Development and Agricultural Chemical Disasters Destroying Ecosystems*, Tokyo, Japan: Godo Shuppan.

Teranishi, Shunichi and Kenichi Oshima (1997), 'Compressed Industrialization and Population Explosion' ('Asshuku Kogyouka to Jinko Bakuhatsu'), in Azia Kankyo Hakusho (ed.), *Asian Environment White Paper (Nihon Kankyo Kaigi)*, Tokyo, Japan: Toyo Keizai Shinposha, pp. 7-16.

Terao, Tadayoshi (1994), 'Nihon no Sangyo Seisaku to Sangyo Kogai' in Reiitsu Kojima and Shigeaki Fujisaki (eds), *Kaihatsu to Kankyo – Ajia 'Shin Seicho ken' no Kadai (Development and the Environment – The Issues of the Asian 'New Growing Sphere')*, Tokyo, Japan: Ajia Keizai Kenkyusho, pp. 265-348.

The Asahi Shimbun (2002), *Japan Almanac 2002*, Tokyo, Japan: The Asahi Shimbun.

Tochigi Prefecture (1994), *White Paper of Environment*: Utsunomiya, p. 208.

Totman, Conrad (1989), *The Green Archipelago: Forestry in Pre-Industrial Japan*, Berkeley, CA, US: University of California.

Tsuru, Shigeto (1989), 'History of Pollution Control Policy', in Shigeto Tsuru and Helmut Weidner (eds), *Environmental Policy in Japan*, Berlin, Germany:

Edition Sigma Rainer Bohn Verlag, pp. 15-42.

Tsuru, Shigeru (1999), *The Political Economy of the Environment: The Case of Japan*, London, UK: Athlone Press.

Tsuru, Shigeto and Helmut Weidner (1989), *Environmental Policy in Japan*, Berlin, Germany: Edition Sigma Rainer Bohn Verlag.

Uekusa, Kazuhide (2000), 'The Making and Breaking of a Bubble Economy', in Yoichi Masuzoe (ed.), *Years of Trial – Japan in the 1990s*, Tokyo, Japan: Japan Echo Inc., pp. 146-62.

Ueta, Kazuhiro (1992), *Economics of Solid Waste Management for Recycling*, Tokyo, Japan: Yuhikaku.

Ueta, Kazuhiro (1993), 'The Lessons of Japan's Environmental Policy: An Economist's Viewpoint', *Japan Review of International Affairs*, 7 (1), pp. 30-49.

Ueta, Kazuhiro (1994), 'The Role of Local Government in Urban Environmental Management', *Regional Development Dialogue*, 15 (2), pp. 146-64.

Ueta, Kazuhiro (1995), 'Environment and Economy: Lessons of Japan's Environmental Problems and Policies', in Reeitsu Kojima et al. (eds), *Development and the Environment: The Experiences of Japan and Industrializing Asia*, Tokyo, Japan: Institute of Developing Economies, pp. 55-67.

Ueta, Kazuhiro (1996), *Kankyo Keizaigaku (Environmental Economics)*, Tokyo, Japan: Iwanami Shoten.

Ueta, Kazuhiro, T. Oka and H. Niizawa (eds) (1997), *Economics of Environmental Policy: Theory and Practice*, Tokyo, Japan: Nihon Hyoronsha.

Ui, Jun (1989), 'Lessons for Developing Countries,' in Shigeto Tsuru and Helmut Weidner (eds), *Environmental Policy in Japan*, Berlin, Germany: Edition Sigma Rainer Bohn Verlag, pp. 553-70.

Ui, Jun (2002), 'Japanese Pollution Experiences,' in Fumikazu Yoshida and Ken'ichi Miyamoto (eds), *Environment and Development (Kankyo to Kaihatsu)*, Tokyo, Japan: Iwanami Shoten, pp. 61-89.

United Nations (1992), 'Local Authorities' Initiatives in Support of Agenda 21' in *Agenda 21*, New York, NY, US: United Nations Publications.

United Nations Economic and Social Commission for Asia and the Pacific (ESCAP) and Asian Development Bank (ADB) (2000), *State of the Environment in Asia and the Pacific*, New York, NY, US: United Nations, pp. 127-28.

United Nations Economic and Social Commission for Asia and the Pacific (ESCAP) (2000), *Ministerial Declaration, Regional Action Programme 2001-2005, and Kitakyushu Initiative for a Clean Environment*, New York, NY, US: United Nations.

United Nations Environment Program/Industry and Environment Programme Active Centre (1993), 'Cleaner Production Worldwide', New York, NY, US: United Nations.

Upham, Frank K. (1987), *Law and Social Change in Postwar Japan*, Cambridge, MA, US: Harvard University Press.

Vernon, Raymond (1995), 'The Triad as Policymakers', in Henry Lee (ed.), *Shaping National Responses to Climate Change*, Washington, DC, US: Island Press, pp. 147-75.

Vogel, David (1986), *National Styles of Regulation: Environmental Policy in Great Britain and the United States*, Ithaca, NY, US: Cornell University Press.

Vogel, Ezra F. (1979), *Japan as Number One: Lessons for America*, New York, NY, US: Harvard University Press, pp. 27-52.

Vogel, Ezra F. (2000), *Is Japan Still Number One?* Pelanduk, Malaysia: Selangor Darul Ehsan.

Von Weiszacker, Ernst, Amory Lovins and Hunter Lovins (1997), *Factor Four: Doubling Wealth, Halving Resource Use*, London: Earthscan.

Wakaizumi, Kei (1994), *Tasaku Nakarishi o Shinzemu to Hossu (I Would Like to Believe We Had no Choice)*, Tokyo, Japan: Bungei-Shunju.

Walden, Bello W. and Stephanie S. Rosenfield (1990), *Dragons in Distress, Asia's Miracle Economies in Crisis*, San Francisco, CA, US: Institute for Food and Development Policy.

Wallace, David (1995), *Environmental Policy and Industrial Innovation: Strategies in Europe, the US and Japan*, London, UK: Earthscan Publications, Ltd.

Watanuki, Reiko (1979), *Seimeikei No Kiki (Crisis in the Life System)*, Tokyo, Japan: Anvil.

Weidner, Helmut (1989a), 'An Administrative Compensation System for Pollution-Related Health Damage', in Shigeto Tsuru and Helmut Weidner (eds), *Environmental Policy in Japan*, Berlin, Germany: Edition Sigma Rainer Bohn Verlag, pp. 139-65.

Weidner, Helmut (1989b), 'Environmental Monitoring and Reporting by Local Government', in Shigeto Tsuru and Helmut Weidner (eds), *Environmental Policy in Japan*, Berlin, Germany: Edition Sigma Rainer Bohn Verlag, pp. 461-76.

Weidner, Helmut (1989c), 'Japanese Environmental Policy in an International Perspective: Lessons for a Preventive Approach', in Shigeto Tsuru and Helmut Weidner (eds), *Environmental Policy in Japan*, Berlin, Germany: Edition Sigma Rainer Bohn Verlag, pp. 479-552.

Weidner, Helmut (1996), *Basiselemente einer erfolgreichen Umweltpolitik: Eine Analyse und Evaluation der Instrumente der japanischen Umweltpolitik*, Berlin, Germany: Sigma Rainer Bohn Verlag.

Wey, Klaus-Georg (1982), *Umweltpolitik in Deutschland: Kurze Geschichte des Umweltschutzes in Deutschland seit 1900*, Opladen: Westdeutscher Verlag.

Wilkening, Kenneth (2004), *Acid Rain Science and Politics in Japan: A History of Knowledge and Action Towards Sustainability*, Cambridge, UK: The MIT Press.

Woodall, Brian (1996), *Japan Under Construction*, Berkeley, CA, US: University of California Press.

World Bank (1994), *Japan's Experience in Urban Environmental Management*, Washington, DC, US: World Bank.

World Bank (2000), 'New Directions in Development Thinking', in *World Development Report 1999-2000*, Oxford, UK and New York, NY, US: Oxford University Press, pp. 21-4.

World Bank (2002), 'Norms and Networks' in World Bank (ed.), *World Development Report 2002*, Washington, DC, US: World Bank, pp. 171-9.

World Bank (2003), 'Institutions for Sustainable Development' in World Bank, (ed.), *World Development Report 2003*, Washington, DC, US: World Bank, pp. 37-58.

World Commission on Sustainable Development (1987), *Our Common Future*, Oxford: Oxford University Press.

World Health Organization and United Nations Environment Program (1992), *Urban Air Pollution in Megacities of the World*, Oxford, UK: Blackwell Reference.

World Meteorological Organization and United Nations Environment Program (2001), *Climate Change 2001: Synthesis Report*, Cambridge, UK: Cambridge University Press.

World Meteorological Organization and United Nations Environment Program (2001), *Climate Change: Mitigation*, Cambridge, UK: Cambridge University Press.

Wuppertal Institut für Klima, Umwelt, Energie (1998), *Zukunftsfähiges Deutschland: Ein Beitrag zu einer global nachhaltigen Entwicklung*, Basel, Switzerland: Birkhäuser Verlag.

Yagishita, Masaharu (1986), 'New Development of Local Environmental Administration', *Environmental Research Quarterly*, 62, Tokyo, Japan: Environmental Research Center, pp. 36-51.

Yamagata, Yoshiki (2000), Carbon Sink under the Kyoto Protocol: Discussion of the IPCC Special Report, *Environmental Research Quarterly*, 117, pp. 65-70, Tokyo, Japan: Kankyo Chosa Center.

Yamaguchi, Mitsutsune (2000), *The Global Environment and Enterprises (Chikyu Kankyo to Kigyo)*, Tokyo, Japan: Iwanami Shoten.

Yamagata Prefecture (1995), *White Paper of Environment*, Yamagata Prefecture.

Yamamoto, Yoshimasa (1987), 'Pollution Diet and the Start of Environment Agency', ('Kogai Kokkai to Kankyocho no Hossoku'), *Environmental Research Quarterly (Kikan Kankyo Kenkyu)*, 67, Tokyo, Japan: Kankyo Chosa Center, pp. 28-30.

Yamanouchi, Kazuo and Otsubo Kiyohara (1989), 'Agreements on Pollution Prevention: Overview and One Example', in Shigeto Tsuru and Helmut Weidner (eds), *Environmental Policy in Japan*, Berlin, Germany: Edition Sigma Rainer Bohn Verlag, pp. 221-45.

Yamauchi, Hirotaka (1999), *Japanese PFI (Nippon no PFI)*, Tokyo, Japan: Chi'iki Kagaku Kenkyu kai.

Yanagi, Kenichiro (2004), 'Green Purchasing Law', in 'Laws Related to the Prevention of Global Warming', in *Kankyo Seisaku to Kankyo Ho Taikei (Environmental Policy and Law Systems)*, Tokyo, Japan: Japan Environment Management Association for Industry, pp. 112-13.

Yano Tsuneta Kinenkai (1998), *Sekai Kokusei Zue (World Data Book) 1997/98*, Tokyo, Japan: Kokuseisha.

Yano Tsuneta Kinenkai (2001), *Nihon Kokusei Zue (Data Book of Japan) 2000-2001*, Tokyo, Japan: Kokuseisha.

Yano Tsuneta Kinenkai (2003), *Nihon Kokusei Zue (Data Book of Japan) 2002-2003*, Tokyo, Japan: Kokuseisha.

Yokoyama, Akira (1994), 'Energy Tax and Environmental Tax', in Hiromitsu Ishi (ed.), *Environmental Tax (Kankyozei)*, Tokyo, Japan: Toyo Keizai Shinposha, pp. 47-62.

Yokohama City (1976), *Kogai to no Tatakai: Showa 50 Nen Ban (Battle against Pollution: 1970 FY edition)*, Yokohama, Japan: Yokohama City.

Yokohama City (1997), *Yokohama Kankyo Hakusho (Yokohama White Paper on Environment)*, Yokohama, Japan: Yokohama City.

Yoneyama, Toshinao (1998), 'Agricultural Climate and Japanese View for Environment', Environmental Information, *Science*, 27, pp. 2-5, Tokyo, Japan: Kankyo Joho Kagaku Center.

Yoshida, Fumikazu, Akio Hata and Haruo Tonegawa (1999), 'Itai-Itai Disease and the Countermeasures against Cadmium Pollution by the Kamioka Mine', *Environmental Economics and Policy Studies*, 2 (3), pp. 215-29.

Yoshida, Fumikazu (1998), *Haikibutsu to Osen no Seijikeizaigaku (The Political Economy of Waste and Pollution)*, Tokyo, Japan: Iwanami Shoten, Chapter 1

Yoshida, Fumikazu (2004), *Jyunkangata Shakai, (3R society)* Tokyo, Japan: Chuo Koron Shinsha, Chapter 2.

Yoshida, Hitoshi (2001), *Chiho Jichitai no Kokusai Kyoryoku (International Cooperation of Local Governments)*, Tokyo, Japan: Nihon Hyoronsha.

Yoshida, Katsumi (2000), 'The Development of Petro-Industry Complex and Air Pollution in Yokkaichi' ('Yokkaichi Sekiyu Kombinato no Kaihatsu to Taiki Osen'), in Japan Society of Atmospheric Environment (ed.), *The History of Air Pollution in Japan (Nihon no Taiki Osen no Rekishi)*, III, Taiki Kankyo Gakkai, Tokyo, Japan: Koken Kyokai, pp. 726-39.

Yuhikaku Dictionary of Economic Terms (1998), Tokyo, Japan: Yuhikaku.

Zhang, Xingsheng (1989), *Research Concerning Occupational and Pollution Related Diseases Resulting from Lead Reprocessing Activities*, Taipei, Taiwan: National Taiwan University Institute of Public Health (in Chinese).

NEWSPAPERS CITED

Asahi Shimbun, Osaka morning edition, 21 February 2000, p. 4.

Asahi Shimbun, Tokyo morning edition, 15 August 1968, p. 15; 7 September 1968, p. 15; 11 September 1968, pp. 1 and 5; 10 October 1968, p. 14; 19 November 1968, p. 7; 2 May 1969, p. 4; 15 May 1969, p. 5; 12 July 1990, p. 30.

Zhonggou Shibao, 26 February 1990

Index

Printed and bound by CPI Group (UK) Ltd, Croydon, CR0 4YY

12/03/2023

03200833-0001